Editing: Alison Romer, Lancaster, UK
Typesetting: Ulrike Weingärtner, Gründau, Germany – info@textakzente.de

Contents

Acknowledgements

I am very grateful for meeting such extraordinary people during my PhD research. I would like to express my sincere thanks to them for supporting me and for contributing to this project in different ways.

Above all, I would like to thank my two supervisors, Ursula Apitzsch und Lena Inowlocki. You both followed my project and enriched it with profound insights, critical questions and helpful comments. Thank you for your openness, trust and great support in all respects. I would like to express my deepest gratitude for the opportunity several times of discussing my research project during a colloquium, which you led with humour and a profound understanding of different spheres of social reality.

I am grateful for the chance of taking part in a number of seminars, workshops and interpretation groups at the Goethe University in Frankfurt and elsewhere, as part of which I was able to discuss my research and the underlying interviews and discover new dimensions hidden in the narratives. Heartfelt thanks to Anil Al-Rebholz, Janine Cunea, Stefica Fiolic, Ayumi Takeda, Elise Pape and many others with whom I discussed parts of my interviews. I also want to thank Minna-Kristiina Ruokonen-Engler and Irini Siouti for lending an open ear, giving valuable advice and for showing me new and exciting spheres of sociological inquiry.

This PhD project would not have been possible without the generous backing by the DAAD, which financially supported the project for three years. Thanks to Anne Kuckartz for providing me with the MAXQDA program for qualitative analysis, which proved to be an excellent tool for organising empirical data. I would also like to thank Sarah Mandl for her patient and professional editing and proof-reading of the draft thesis.

My deepest appreciation goes out to the remarkable people around me. Thank you, Patrick, for your immense support, understanding and encouragement throughout the years. I am thankful to my children Jonas and Lena for encouraging me to slow down and to see the world through their inquisitive eyes. Many thanks to Dáša and Tomáš and to Moni and Klaus, who travelled long distances in order to look after them so that I could work on my thesis, as well as to Louisa and Philipp for their kind support. Last but not least, I am immeasurably grateful to all of the interviewees who shared their unique stories, perceptions, and dreams with me, which became the basis of this thesis.

Preface: Pathways to the research questions

From the end of the 1990s onwards, borders seemed to be breaking down. Distance changed its meaning and suddenly everything became closer and more easily reachable. It was at this time that some of my friends started to discover life beyond the border of the Czech Republic, and so did I. We visited one another not only in Prague, but increasingly in Cork, Dublin, Galway or London where we lived and worked – in hotels, restaurants, pubs, or as cleaners and child minders. Some of us only stayed for a few months, others for many years or even until the present day. These early experiences turned the world as I knew it upside down. They opened up new possibilities for me, new tastes, sounds and colors – the blue-grey sky over Dublin can be found nowhere else. These experiences followed me through my own future migration projects and also shaped my scientific interest in researching migration. Hence, it was this very biographical moment which led me to want to research new migratory spaces in Europe, which I watched being created and reshaped all around me, and which were so closely linked to the changing meaning of borders in this region of Europe in the last decades.

At the time I decided to write a thesis on the migration of highly skilled individuals from the Czech Republic to Germany, it had just started to become a very relevant and emotional topic discussed across the political scene and the media. Debates centered on the "need for qualified labour" on the one hand, and the threat of a "brain drain" and "loss of intelligentsia", i.e. an "exodus of physicians" (see e.g. Vítková 2010; Králová 2010), on the other hand. My aim was to approach this phenomenon from a different perspective than was usually the case by drawing on the narratives of those who had actually moved country. However, when crossing the border myself and listening to migrants in their homes, places of work, or cafés, the focus of my interest shifted. Their stories turned my attention increasingly to the complex and sometimes ambivalent processes of de-valuation and re-valuation of skills, qualifications, knowledge and resources in the course of migration, which were so central to the narratives. Moreover, they invited me to rework the notion of "highly skilled migrants", which discursive notions usually associated with highly mobile professionals moving in the upper spheres of social strata. Hence, their life stories made me think, and subsequently write about the realities faced by highly skilled migrants, which go far beyond the "brain drain" and "brain gain" debates, and which are an increasingly important yet surprisingly under-researched topic in today's Europe.

1 Introduction

In public and scientific discourses, highly skilled migrants were often pictured as those well educated professionals who jet around the globe with their business suitcases, who cross borders in order to work in research laboratories, IT companies, or hospitals, or who move internationally within multinational corporations and institutions. They were all seen as being those people who profit from the liberalization of migration policies oriented increasingly towards skilled workers, which were implemented by a number of economically prosperous countries in the last decades. Diverse programs and quota systems were introduced for the selection of migrants with certain sought-after qualifications, skills and professional experience, as well as multilateral agreements which facilitated the obstacles connected to migration for some groups of people (Lavenex 2008). This shift in migration policies, which was linked to the developments in global and local economies, caused some authors to increasingly speak of a polarization of migration flows in terms of skills and level of education – represented by highly skilled professionals on the one side and low skilled workers on the other side of social stratum (Sassen 2007, p. 70). The migration of the former group has over the last decades been discussed in detail and remains a controversial topic across scientific disciplines. While the focus of researchers has diversified, debates have been dominated by the perspective of states and global and local economies – expressed by terms such as "brain drain", "brain gain" or "brain circulation", highlighting the outflow of intelligentsia from particular countries to others, and to the impact on the societies linked by migration flows (Freitas et al. 2012, p. 3).

This image of highly skilled migrants profiting from their high level of education when crossing the border is not, however, complete. It overlooks those highly educated people who move country for reasons other than work – be it in order to escape political or economic oppression, to follow or join their spouses or other family members, or those who move just for the sake of trying to live in another country. It also fails to take into account those highly educated people who do not fit into the selective schemes of migration programs and policies because they were educated in fields other than those listed in the tables issued by foreign offices, or because they did not fulfill other conditions such as age or a certain level of salary (Guth 2007; Kofman 2009b). Hence, these migrants are obliged to search for other migration pathways, often resulting in a de-valuation of their skills and leading them through the informal economy. Furthermore, the predominant discourse does not cover those who have already experienced a devaluation of their qualifications and skills prior to migration and who would therefore not be included within the "brain drain" or "brain gain" categories (Nowicka 2014). Finally, it also overlooks those highly educated migrants who already live in the targeted country and are looking for ways to make use of their initial or newly acquired qualifications, skills and knowledge (Kontos, Voswinkel 2010).

The narratives of these "other" highly skilled migrants have already found their way into a number of newspaper articles, literature and movies some time ago[1] – describing different facets of migration and social pathways and pinpointing the processes of de-evaluation or re-evaluation of the individuals' own qualifications in moving places. However, they have only recently become the subject of scientific study. Michael P. Smith and Adrian Favell (2008) were among the first to question the binary division of migration flows into highly skilled "elites" and low skilled "proles". They invited one to rethink the category of highly skilled migrants, highlighting the social construction of skills which is not a static and given category but construed in terms of the demands of the global economy and in terms of who possesses the skills. They showed those highly skilled people who were moving country to be a much more diverse group than presented by current scientific research. Other authors expanded this approach by the gender dimension, emphasising gendered migration pathways and gendered policies which have a different impact on highly skilled women and men (see e.g. Kofman, Raghuram 2005; Riaño 2012). Moreover, recent studies have focused on the processes of de-valuation or re-valuation of one's own skills, qualifications, and knowledge[2] in the course of migration. They highlighted diverse migration pathways and the processes of social mobility of migrants, often balancing on the fine line between a "regular" (legal) and "irregular status" and between "low skilled" and "highly skilled" professions (see e.g. Erel 2004, 2010; Liversage 2009b; Trevena 2011). The present thesis is embedded within this scarce but growing body of research which includes those highly skilled migrants who have moved outside the typical migration corridors of professionals in specific sectors of economy.

---

1   See for example the novel "Nebe pod Berlínem" ("The sky below Berlin") written by Jaroslav Rudiš, or the novel by Alexander Kalashnikoff "Allergic to magic mushrooms". The former novel narrates the story of a man who initially works as a teacher in Prague and who decides to move to Berlin in the course of the 1990s in order to escape the stereotypical everyday life and in order to discover new places and possibilities. The fact that he started to play the music in a punk rock band in Berlin – or more precisely below Berlin in tube stations – was not planned, but initiated an important turn in his life. The latter book tells the story of a lawyer who was forced to leave Russia for economic reasons and moved to Ireland where he worked on a mushroom farm in Ireland for several years.

2   I understand "skills" in the wider sense as "what one can do", "knowledge" as "what one knows", and "qualifications" as formal educational achievements.

12

The migration of highly skilled people[3] has become an increasingly important topic over the last decades. In one decade alone, between 2000 and 2010, the number of tertiary educated migrants living in OECD[4] countries increased by 70 percent (OECD 2013, p. 1) and this trend is expected to continue. On average, tertiary educated people compose about 30 percent of all migrants living in OECD countries (ibid.). This rising proportion of highly educated people within migration flows has been linked to a number of developments, such as the restructuring of global and local economies, the turn towards knowledge economies in some parts of the world, the need for qualified labour and the associated implementation of selective migration policies in some countries, as well as the accessibility of university studies for wider groups of people in diverse locations (Freitas et al. 2012, p. 7). Nevertheless, while those highly educated who decided to move to another country during the course of their life appear in the statistics – according to the respective points of view – as a "brain drain" or "brain gain", their experience of the opportunity structures and de-valuation and re-valuation of their qualifications both in the country of origin and in the country of migration often go far beyond these terms (see e.g. Muhirwa 2012).

1.1 The context of EU enlargement

The gradually enlarging European Union is an arena par excellence for researching the migration processes of highly skilled people. It is a space which has experienced intensive changes in border regimes, power relations, migration policies and opportunity structures in the last decades. The fall of the Iron Curtain in 1989 and the ensuing processes reshaped borders within Europe and initiated large societal, political and economic transition processes in post-communist countries. The partial opening up of the borders led to the establishment of altered migration patterns, such as cross-border commuting, circular, short term or "suitcase" migration on an East-West axis (see e.g. Morokvasic 1994; Iglicka 1998). Movements across the border to countries in the European Union became for many migrants a possibility of overcoming the economic impact of transition processes which exacerbated the structural inequalities among and within post-communist countries. The eastward enlargement of the EU in 2004 and 2007 again changed migration patterns in

---

3   I understand "highly skilled migration" as the migration of tertiary educated people (OECD 2008, p. 69). Hence, I use the terms "highly skilled migrants" and "highly educated migrants" as synonyms. For a discussion on the use of this terminology, see e.g. Csedő 2008.

4   The OECD is the abbreviation of "Organisation for Economic Co-operation and Development" which was founded in 1961 and is made up of 34 world countries who cooperate on various political and economic topics.

this region of Europe. The new EU citizens gained the right of free movement within the EU, although not all countries opened their labour markets until 2011. These policies shaped the migration flows within Europe and influenced the possibilities of entering the formal labour market in the countries which applied the transitory restrictions, such as Germany and Austria.

However, the enlarged European Union is not only an arena of changing border regimes and migration policies, but also an arena of remaining inequalities (Amelina, Vasilache 2014). They have been particularly visible concerning the migration of highly educated people moving East to West and back, which has become a hotly debated topic. The different facets of and perspectives on this phenomenon have revealed certain controversies and revealed structural inequalities across Europe concerning wage differences, working conditions and possibilities of professional and personal development. Highly skilled migration on an East-West axis, which has often been motivated by underpayment and unstable working conditions in the country of origin (Trevena 2011), has become a very diversified field, including those moving within academia and transnational institutions (see e.g. Guth, Gill 2008), those moving to European "global cities" as professionals (see e.g. Csedő 2008), as well as the large group of migrants who have exchanged their relatively stable positions in their country of origin for insecure, low skilled positions in the country of migration (see e.g. Trevena 2013; Nowicka 2014). These developments indicate that despite the establishment of a free migratory space within the EU, the inequalities concerning the positioning of migrants both in the country of origin and the country of migration seem to prevail.

My work focuses on the migration of highly educated people moving from the Czech Republic to Germany after 1989 and is therefore to be seen in this context. The Czech-German migratory space is an arena which has experienced immense shifts in border regimes and migration policies over the last two decades. While these two neighbouring countries were once divided by the Iron Curtain, they are now united within the EU and within the Schengen Area, which has considerably changed the ways in which borders can be crossed between these countries. Hence, these structural changes can be seen as a precondition for the establishment of diverse transnational processes, having an impact both on policies and economies as well as on the everyday lives of people living in this changing region of Europe. In the present study I will focus on transnational links "from below" (Smith, Guarnizo 1999), as they are established, reworked and given meaning by the migrants themselves.

14

1.2 Outline of my research questions

At the core of my research are three main questions. First: how is the decision to move linked to biographical and societal processes? I am interested in the way in which migration pathways develop and which biographical meanings they have, as well as in the way in which migration is related to the societal changes in the Czech Republic in particular and in Europe in general in the last decades. Secondly: how do social and spatial pathways interact? Or more specifically: how are migration processes linked to shifts in social position over the course of time? In order to answer this question, it is necessary to understand how migrants perceive the opportunity structures both in the Czech Republic and in Germany, how they evaluate the migration policies and how they position themselves in both societies. Moreover, it is necessary to understand how they use, re-valuate and create knowledge, skills and qualifications in the course of migration. And lastly: do migrants establish transnational social and cultural links and practices, and if so how do they do this and what do these links mean to them?

The answers to these questions can be elaborated on the basis of the life stories of highly educated migrant women and men who moved to Germany at some point in time after 1989. They represent both the "transition generation" (Williams, Baláž 2005, p. 463), since they experienced the extensive transformations in Czech society in their adolescence or early adulthood, and the "new migration flows" (Lutz, Koser 1998, p. 1) on an East-West axis, which were initiated by the societal and political shifts in Europe in the early 1990s. Hence, their biographies have become part of the "new map of European migration" (King 2002), at the heart of which, so Russell King, lie the new European geopolitics after the Cold War, the new time-space flexibilities, shifted international labour divisions as well as changed perceptions and possibilities of self-realisation (King 2002, pp. 90, 100).

1.3 Studying migration and social pathways by means of life stories

The biographical approach presents the main theoretical and methodological background for this study. It offers both theoretical and methodological tools which allow one to grasp the individual and social processes and their mutual embeddedness through biographical narrations. Biographical narratives, which are the main focus of the biographical narrative interview – an interview method for generating life stories or biographical renderings on particular events or phases of life (Schütze 1983) – allow one to access past experiences, events, actions, meanings, as well as past and present explanations and view-points from an agent-centered perspective. Moreover, they make it possible to reconstruct "from below" both the individual action and the experiences of limiting social structures within which individuals are embedded (Apitzsch, Inowlocki 2000, p. 61). At the same time, the biographies are not understood as a mirror of past sequences of events, but as a shape which is construed and re-construed in ongoing processes (Breckner 2007, p. 117). They are the means of communicating "who we are", "how we became who we are" and "how we make sense of past experiences" (ibid.).

The biographical approach has been shown to be useful for approaching migration and transnational processes (see e.g. Apitzsch 2003c; Apitzsch, Siouti 2007), as well as the processes of social positioning and social mobility (see e.g. Bertaux, Thompson 1997b). It allows one to follow the perspectives of the migrants, the decision making processes and the meanings ascribed to migration, as well as the shifts in orientation and patterns of action in the course of migration (Breckner 2007, p. 118). It makes it possible for the researcher to access the different social contexts within which migrants are embedded over time and across space. Moreover, it allows one to grasp the social, cultural and political links and processes that go beyond the borders of one nation state, and which have been overlooked by classical migration research (Glick Schiller et al. 1992b). Since the life stories contain indications as to the social frameworks, relationships and opportunity structures, they become a means of studying the processes of social positioning across diverse locations as well as their shifts (Anthias 2008; Ruokonen-Engler 2012). As Daniel Bertaux and Paul Thompsen (1997a, p. 7) stated:

"life stories show the centrality of subjective perceptions and evaluations in shaping the life choices. They are redolent with descriptions of feeling and experience of relationships with significant others, with interpretations of turning-points, with influences which were rejected rather than followed, with dreams of lives that might have been. They also reveal the crucial importance of local contexts, local structures of opportunities, and local games of competition."

Hence, life stories – containing the experiences of migrants over the course of time and across space, giving explanations for their action, and outlining their possibility spaces, dreams and positioning – will be the starting point and subject matter of the present study.

1.4 Structure of this thesis

In the second chapter I will situate my study within the historical context of changing migration patterns in Europe. In order to outline their development,

I will go back in history and describe the moves within and out of the continent against the backdrop of shifting geopolitical powers. I will pay particular attention to East-West migration patterns and their changes after the fall of the Iron Curtain 1989 and after the enlargement of the European Union eastwards from 2004 on, since these events had a particularly significant influence on the migration paths of people from the Czech Republic and other new EU countries. While taking into account the wider societal processes, I will outline the history of the Czech-German border and its crossings, as well as the changes in the Czech society, which are crucial for understanding the life stories of migrants.

Subsequently, in chapter three I will turn my attention to contemporary research on highly skilled migration in Europe. First I will position the discussion on highly skilled migration within the wider social, economic and political context, depicting the processes towards the liberalisation of skilled migration flows by migration policies and the implementation of diverse multilateral agreements. Afterwards I will discuss recent scientific approaches to highly skilled migration and outline the research agenda calling for gender sensible approaches and for the opening up of the discussion to include other highly skilled migrants who have hitherto been overlooked by research, be it due to the non-recognition of their qualifications or their positioning within other – often low skilled – spheres of the economy. After outlining the research agenda, I will introduce recent studies which correspond to it and focus on migration and social pathways of highly educated people to and within Europe. I shall start with studies which have approached this theme from a macro perspective – giving statistical evidence on the usability of university education after migration and studying the impact of policy and the mechanisms of labour market inclusion and exclusion. Subsequently, I will introduce recent studies which have focused on the migration and social pathways of highly skilled people from an agent-centred perspective. Since downward social mobility after migration was described as a frequent phenomenon experienced by university graduates after migration, I will pay particular attention in the next section to migrants' experiences and strategies for coping with deskilling and "contradictory class mobility" (Parreñas 2001). Finally, before discussing the state of the art and outlining the research desideratum – calling for a biographical and transnational perspective in researching spatial and social mobility in transnational spaces –, the role of the family and social networks in studies on highly skilled migration will be highlighted.

In the fourth chapter I will elaborate on the research desiderata in more detail and outline the theoretical framework of the present study, building on the biographical approach, migration studies, and transnational approach as well as theorizing on social mobility and social positioning in transnational spaces. As a first step I will introduce biographical research and biographical approaches. I will outline the history of biographical research and subsequently discuss the crucial concepts of biographical research, such as biography, agency and structure, biographical process structures and biographical experience and knowledge, which became central for the present study. Next I will narrow down the focus of biographical approaches to migration. I will outline the first biographically oriented migration studies against the background of wider theoretical and methodological discussions concerning migration. I will then introduce the transnational approach and draw a link between the biographical and transnational approaches. Lastly, I will add the notions of social positioning and social mobility in transnational spaces to the theoretical framework.

The research process will be described in chapter five. At first, I will discuss the theoretical background of the biographical narrative interview – the method I used for generating the life stories. Afterwards I will explain the logic behind the reflexive research process and describe how I proceeded when conducting the research: from the construction of the sample, through reflections on the setting and the course of the interviews, taking ethnographic notes, and transcription to the main analytical steps. In addition, I will give a brief summary of the interviews and the reflections on the research process and the role of language in it, as well as contemplating my own positioning in the field.

Only afterwards, in chapter six, will the four central biographies be presented and discussed. The biographies of Martin, Lenka, Barbora and Arnošt will be used to represent four different types of spatial and social mobility on an East-West axis. Their biographies reveal multiple movements across the border, the establishment of transnational links and their different meanings, the role of the recognition and diverse ways of positioning oneself in transnational spaces.

After presenting the central biographies, the seventh chapter will include the voices of other interviewees and systematically present the core findings resulting from cross-case comparisons. I will at first pay attention to biographical reflections on the history, borders and border crossings – both geographical and mental – which was the central theme throughout the life stories. Subsequently I will turn my attention to the role of migration within the biographies. I will point out the role of structural inequalities within the Czech Republic and draw a link to and between internal and international migration. I will show how the initial border crossings shaped later migrations and how the decisions to move within the newly established transnational spaces were negotiated. In addition, I will pay attention to transnational links and to the meaning given to them by the biographers. Moreover, I will take a closer look at the links between spatial and social mobility. I will reveal the structural settings shaping the possibilities and, subsequently, the ways in which migrants negotiated their skills, knowledge and qualifications within these frameworks. Finally, I will reflect on the question of the "translatability" of social positions across borders and the role of recognition in transnational settings.

The conclusion will provide a brief summary of the core findings, position them within the wider theoretical discussion and outline potential future research goals which are still to be carried out in this complex and fascinating field of research.

2 Context: Czech-German border crossings against the backdrop of the shifting landscape of European migration

The migratory space between the Czech Republic and Germany is in many aspects unique. It is an area shaped by close economic, social and cultural encounters resulting from the close geographical proximity of these two countries and from the long history of their mutual interconnections. However, it is also an area which has been shaped by shifts in power relations, migration regimes, constructions of belonging, and turbulent changes in migration patterns over time. Not only have the borders in this region of Europe been rewritten many times depending on the division of powers at that particular time, but their significance has also often changed. In order to understand migration processes in this region of Europe nowadays, it is necessary to view them in the historical context of border lines that have shifted, as well as the various power relations and changing migration patterns. Furthermore, since these processes go beyond national dimensions and national states, it is necessary to embed them within the larger context of changing migration patterns in Europe.

In this chapter I shall outline the history of the Czech-German border and border crossings within the structural and societal changes and shifting landscape of European migration. I shall start this chapter by outlining the first encounters and migration processes in this region. Research on migration in the past evidences the migration and settlement of people across the areas which are today known as Germany and the Czech Republic since the 10th century, which is seen as the beginning of the Czech state. People from what is today known as Germany played an important role in the development of medieval towns and mining areas in the Czech lands. Later on they migrated to developing industrial areas in West and North Bohemia, as did workers from Czech lands, finding jobs in agriculture and industry on the other side of the border. The events of World War I, the disintegration of the Austro-Hungarian Monarchy, and the establishment of independent national states in 1918 rewrote the borders and changed the migration map of Europe again. It was at this time that the significance of said borders changed: they were increasingly becoming political instruments and the subject of control. I shall follow these changes and describe how the borders were radicalised by the events of World War II and the subsequent polar division of the World on the "East" and "West". The end of the bipolar world order signified the relaxation of border controls and the establishment of new migration patterns. I shall first outline the transformation processes in Central and Eastern Europe and link them to (re-)emerging patterns of migration within and outside of this region, paying particular attention to changes in the Czech society and to the establishment of new migratory spaces. The enlargement of the EU eastwards in 2004 and 2007 gave a new legal framework to migration processes in this region of Europe, and coupled with events connected to the European financial crisis significantly changed cross border movements.

2.1 Historical interconnections over the past millennium

The notion of German speaking inhabitants in Czech lands[5] dates back to the 10th century, which is the date perceived to be the beginning of the Czech state. Merchants as well as members of the clergy who arrived from what is today known as Germany in the course of Christianisation were the first parties to settle in Prague and other establishing towns in the Czech lands (Rogall 2001, p. 35). In the 12th century peasants from Bavaria and Austria, and later from Saxony, Franconia, Thuringia and Silesia, found uncultivated fertile land in Bohemia and Moravia (Rogall 2001, p. 37). They were recruited by rulers and enjoyed privileged rights. In the 13th century, silver mines were discovered in Ostrava and Kutná Hora which attracted miners from the Harz Mountains and from Tyrol (Rogall 2001, p. 39). These places grew into influential cities and centres of commerce. Migrants from what nowadays constitutes Germany were moving to Czech lands in larger numbers until well into the 19th century. They shared neither a common sense of belonging nor the same language (Rogall 2001, p. 39). Those coming from more distant areas, such as Tyrol and Saxony, often did not even understand one another because of their differing accents. Newcomers often maintained political, social and language connections to the places they had moved from. At the same time, Slavic family names in some regions, such as Brandenburg or Leipzig, indicate that migration processes and mutual influence took place in the opposite direction too (Seibt 1993, p. 62).

Besides seasonal labour migration across the border from Bohemia to the neighbouring states of Bavaria, Franconia and Saxony for the purpose of helping with agricultural harvesting, there was also extensive migration based on religious or political views. In the course of the Thirty Years' War in the 17th century, thousands of Protestants emigrated from Bohemia to abroad. The cruelties of the war as well as the efforts of the Habsburg monarchy to

---

5   I use the term "Czech lands" in relation to the historical territories of Bohemia, Moravia and Czech Silesia, which compose what is today known as the Czech Republic.

re-catholicise the Bohemian lands, which were until then characterised by a heterogeneous protestant culture (Seibt 1993, p. 165), forced many people to move. It is estimated that more than 100,000 people left the country and settled in Saxony (Schunka 2006, p. 37). The Bohemian community which lived in Saxony for centuries, retaining its language and religious practices, never gained the attention of public discourse or collective memory (ibid.). However, exile biographies were often politicized during the "Czech national revival" in the 18th and 19th century. The events of the Thirty Years' War have retrospectively been reinterpreted as "national" conflicts, establishing and sharpening the dividing line between the "Czechs" and "Germans". The time of the Habsburg rule has been seen as the time of "temno", the "darkness", because it was then that the Czech lands fell under Austrian rule (Bahlcke 2001, p. 57). These discourses of "national suffering", supported by political rhetoric and art, have shaped collective national memory until nowadays.

2.2 The 19th and 20th century

Expanding industrialisation as well as political shifts in the 19th and at the beginning of the 20th century led many people to move places, mostly into growing cities and emerging industrial areas (Fassmann, Münz 1994, p. 520). The mines and factories in France, Germany and the United Kingdom attracted hundreds of thousands of workers predominantly from Poland and Ukraine (Fassmann, Münz 1994, p. 520). Large numbers of migrants also moved from Italy to France, Austria-Hungary, and Switzerland, and from the Czech lands to cities and industrial areas mostly in Germany or into economic and agricultural centres in Austria-Hungary (Zeitlhofer 2008, p. 49). During this time, seasonal and temporary transnational migration was a common social practice in diverse regions of Europe and a means of overcoming poverty and bettering ones situation (Zeitlhofer 2008).

While migration from the Czech lands to Austria and the German Reich was until then mostly temporary and connected with agricultural labour, emerging factories and mines, construction works and the development of new technologies called for thousands of workers, both male and female. However, people were not attracted only by booming towns and industrial areas. Lutz Vogel, for example, has shown that there was intensive migration from some parts of Bohemia to saxonian rural areas in the 19th century (Vogel 2014). Those who moved were young people and families from the same regions who settled together. Despite the relaxed border crossing between the Austrian Reich, of which the Czech lands were part, and the German Reich at this time, settling abroad was coupled with diverse restrictions. For example, those who wanted to settle in the German Reich had to submit passports or certificates in order to legitimise their nationality and prevent any social costs being incurred by the state. Social costs were supposed to be borne by the country of origin (Vogel 2014, p. 79). The newcomers worked mostly as weavers and in agriculture. Despite the assumption that migrants were mostly men, Vogel points out that half of all migrants were women, who migrated not only as spouses of workers but also in large numbers as workers in their own right (Vogel 2014, p. 84).

Besides migration to nearby regions, there was also large scale migration from Czech lands to some less inhabited areas in the Balkan regions and Russia (Nešpor 2002a, pp. 35–37) and to overseas areas. Migrants from Czech lands were among around 42 million Europeans who left in the period between the second half of the 19th century and the outbreak of World War I to seek their fortunes in the USA, Australia or South America (Mau, Büttner 2010, p. 546). Migration took diverse forms, from long-term to return and circular migration, which was eased by cheaper and faster transportation possibilities towards the end of the 19th century (Bade 2000, p. 141).

It is estimated that at the beginning of the 20th century there were around 330,000 people from Bohemia living in other European countries outside the Austro-Hungarian Empire. The majority of them had moved to the German Reich (Zeitlhofer 2008, p. 50). Besides long-term settlements, there was also an extensive rate of seasonal and short-term migration, especially between certain regions. One of the regions in Bohemia with a large population on the move was Šumava, the Bohemian Forest, the mountainous area bordering Bavaria to the west side and Austria on the south. Historical migration research portrays diverse forms of migration processes during this time – spanning from seasonal workers in agriculture, mobile workers offering various handicrafts, everyday commuters or those who settled over many years – as being the common phenomenon influencing the everyday life of people (see Zeitlhofer 2008; Vogel 2014).

The shift in power relations and the political structures in Europe after World War I has considerably influenced the European migration landscape. The newly drawn frontiers of the just-emerging national states in Central, Eastern and Southern Europe gave rise to new minorities and initiated a wave of new migrations (Kaya et al. 2002, p. 15). In some cases, traditional internal seasonal migration turned into transnational border crossings and vice versa (Bade 2000, p. 245).

Migration from newly established Czechoslovakia to Austria and Germany is an example par excellence of such shifted migration patterns. After the disintegration of the Austro-Hungarian monarchy and the establishment of Czechoslovakia in 1918, previously internal migration from Bohemia and Moravia to Austria changed to more restricted and controlled external migration. The borderlands between recently established Czechoslovakia and Germany also changed: the mountainous border area across which produce from mines and factories, including musical instruments, as well as people had traveled every day in both directions without the necessity for passports became more restricted and possible only at certain places (Murdock 2010; Řezník 2013, p. 13). Additionally, from 1918 onwards the borders increasingly became political instruments, thereby radicalizing the regions in a new way. Nationalist politics on both sides of the border changed the definition of ethnic minorities, thus affecting Czech-German relations. The national discourse of supposed radical division of "Czechs" and "Germans" has also shaped the way in which history has been interpreted by historians, politicians and social scientists during the 20th century. Nonetheless, there is evidence of informal exchanges, border crossings and encounters even in times of violent border protection policies during the Cold War (Murdock 2010).

It is estimated that in the inter-war period more than 9 million people moved country from "East" to "West" for labour purposes, in search of political exile or because of ethnic displacement (Fassmann, Münz 1995, p. 45). Migrants from Czechoslovakia headed mostly to other European countries: Germany, Austria, France, the Netherlands and the United Kingdom. The turn away from overseas emigration to remaining in Europe was partly caused by the increasingly restrictive migration politics of the USA (Nešpor 2002a, p. 36). Nearby Germany became the most frequent destination of choice. Czechoslovaks were, besides Poles, the most numerous migrant group in German cities such as Dresden, Berlin, Leipzig, Hamburg or Bremen, during this time (Brouček 2003). Nevertheless, many migrants from Czechoslovakia and other countries who worked in the mines, industrial areas and booming cities returned in the course of the world economic crisis in the 1930s (Kaya et al. 2002, p. 17). A few years later, the events of World War II initiated a massive wave of forced migration, expulsions and deportations across Europe of up to 60 million people in total (Bade 2000, p. 285).

Nationalist politics in Central Europe reached its peak during World War II, which rewrote the borders again. At the very beginning of the war, the Czechoslovak border regions – the Sudeten lands – were attached to the German Reich and the rest of Bohemia and Moravia became a German protectorate. The war caused 100,000 people who until then had resided in Czechoslovakia to move. At first, many fled the Nazi regime from occupied border regions to the midlands and later on westwards and overseas. Until emigration was banned in 1941, around 27,000 Jews managed to emigrate from Czechoslovakia (Holocaust Education and Archive Research Team 2013). Another 100,000 people were deported from the Protectorate to working and concentration camps. Around 263,000 Jews who resided in Czechoslovakia in 1938 were killed during the war (ibid.). The Czech population was drafted in to work in the war industry: in mines, the iron industry and production which was about to support the armed forces. It is estimated that around 400,000 people from Czechoslovakia were recruited and forced to move to Germany during the war in order to work under discriminatory conditions both in private and public industrial companies and organizations (Jelínek 2003, p. 29).

This large scale population movement did not come to an end with the end of the war. The new political order after World War II gave rise to new means of forced mass migration on the grounds of ethnic origin, religion or political orientation. Mass population movement affected not only Poles, Czechs, Hungarians and other ethnic groups living in various regions of Europe but also around 12 million ethnic Germans who were forced to leave their places of residence in Poland, Czechoslovakia, Ukraine and other countries (Fassmann, Münz 1994, pp. 521–523). In Czechoslovakia, the Beneš decrees, the set of laws elaborated during the war in exile by the Czechoslovak president Edvard Beneš and which came into force in 1946, legally supported the confiscation of property and the loss of Czechoslovak citizenship for people of German or Hungarian origin. Moreover, it initiated the forced resettlement of more than 3 million ethnic Germans who until then had lived in the territory of former Czechoslovakia (Sládek 2002, p. 151). After the organized resettlement had been completed, only around 192,000 German nationals remained in Czechoslovakia – only 6 per cent in comparison with numbers prior to 1939 (ibid.). The depopulated houses and fields were offered to Czechs coming from the midlands, as well as to Slovaks and Bulgarians, or Greeks arriving as political refugees after fleeing the civil war in Greece at the end of the 1950s (Uherek 2003, p. 198). Moreover, some of the Czech "compatriot" communities were offered the chance to return and settle in the border regions of Czechoslovakia (Nešpor 2002a, pp. 39–41). The resettlement of people with German nationality also continued in subsequent years, yet to a lesser degree (Titzl 2006, p. 48).[6]

2.3 Border crossings during the Cold War

The altered global order and the division of Europe into "East" and "West" again encouraged new migration flows within Europe. Hundreds of thousands of people made use of transnational links in order to migrate overseas (Bade 2000, p. 301). At the same time, however, some regions of Europe were slowly becoming places of immense immigration. The economic boom in Germany, France and the United Kingdom led to new migration flows

---

6   For example, in 1950 and 1951 up to 10,000 disabled people, elderly and patients, among them also children, of German origin were relocated to Germany since, according to the government, they could not contribute to the labour system (Titzl 2006, p. 48).

within and from outside of Europe. Migration between some European countries and their former colonies intensified, such as between France and Algeria, Morocco and Tunisia, the Netherlands and Indonesia, or the United Kingdom and India (Currle 2004). In addition, starting in the 1950s, the economically booming countries began recruiting labour migrants, so called "guest workers", mostly from the Mediterranean region (Bade 2000, p. 304). Despite the halt to recruitment in the 1970s, the transnational interconnections among these countries have stayed alive until the present and have led to ongoing migrations of new generations and family members in both directions (see e.g. Apitzsch, Siouti 2013). The recruitment of industrial labour from abroad was also a political goal on the other side of the Iron Curtain. Bilateral agreements on the exchange of workers led to migration flows from Vietnam, Mongolia, Cuba and other countries to the countries of the "Eastern bloc" (see e.g. Zwengel 2011), establishing dense transnational networks shaping the migration processes within these countries until nowadays (Schmiz 2011).

During the Cold War, migration also proceeded on the axis from East to West, even though on a much lower scale than before. The reason for the decrease in migration flows were the very restrictive migration politics applied by the Soviet Union and other communist countries, along with their intense surveillance of the border. The empty buildings at border checkpoints as well as ruins of high wires and watch towers in some border regions in Central and Eastern Europe still remind us of the existence and the relevance of these borders, which divided Europe into "East" and "West". The protection of borders made forms of cross border mobility, such as seasonal and temporary labour migration, which had until then been common social practice for many people, impossible. According to official statistics, around 14 million people from the "Eastern bloc" left to west between 1950 and 1992. However, the actual number of migrants is estimated to be much higher, as irregular migration was only partly documented (Fassmann, Münz 1994, p. 523). Most of the migrants crossed the east to west border as "ethnic or religious minorities", such as about 3 million native Germans moving to Germany, or about 1.5 million people migrating from the Soviet Union to Israel or the USA (Fassmann, Münz 1994, p. 526). Another considerable group of migrants consisted of political refugees and labour migrants (Fassmann, Münz 1994, p. 527).[7] The latter were mostly from Yugoslavia, as it was the only "Eastern bloc" country that allowed its citizens to cross borders.

---

7   The classification of migrants as political refugees and labour migrants which appears in numerous historical documents is problematic, as the boundaries between these categories are often blurred. Contrary to the time after 1989, during the Cold War the majority of migrants crossing the "East-West" border were perceived as political refugees and would find asylum despite their actual migration motives (see e.g, Fassmann, Münz 1994; Morokvasic, Rudolph 1994a).

At the time of the economic boom, about half a million Yugoslavs were recruited by Germany and Austria and were subsequently followed by their families (ibid.).

In Czechoslovakia, the pattern of border crossings has not been replicated in the same quality and to the same extent as before World War II. The government claimed that travelling over the border posed a threat to the economic and political interests of Czechoslovakia, thereby using restrictive politics to justify the lack of foreign exchange permits. Travelling abroad for private or professional reasons became very difficult for the citizens of Czechoslovakia (Rychlík 2012, pp. 10–11). From 1948 onwards, when the communists took over government, migration politics became even more restricted. Restrictive politics and intensified border control was to great extent the answer for the mass migration flows out of the country at that time, accounting for around 60,000 people between 1948 and 1951 according to certain estimates (Nešpor 2002a, p. 42).[8] After 1951, the issue of passports became even more difficult, with the result that leaving the country for private purposes became nearly impossible. Moreover, crossing the border without the relevant documents was a criminal act under a new law issued in 1951, punishable with up to five years of prison (Mašková, Morbacher 2014, p. 1). In order to more effectively control the border, special border guards were positioned along the border. Villages situated on the frontiers were removed and partly demolished. Some parts of the border were reinforced with barbed wire and minefields. Such strict border controls and the altered legal framework, which in effect labeled those who tried to cross the border as enemies of the regime, limited but did not stop migration and dangerous border crossings for diverse purposes (Mašková, Morbacher 2014, pp. 3–10).

During the 1960s, Czechoslovakia experienced a "release" after the political persecutions, nationalization and economic transformations endured in the 1950s. The issue of visas and passports became more accessible for Czechoslovak citizens. Many made use of the opportunity of migration with the help of invitations, business trips and holidays abroad (Trapl 2000, p. 40). Processes aimed at the democratization of society, and the ensuing period of potential improvement in the economic situation in Czechoslovakia – the so-called "Prague Spring" – were interrupted by the invasion by Warsaw Pact troops in 1968 and consequent "normalization". Censorship and party cleansing were re-established. Diverse social and political organisations were abolished and many people experienced massive dismissals from work because of their political views. The events of 1968 resulted in around 160,000 leaving the country (Fassmann, Münz 1994, p. 527). Over the coming decades, mi-

---

8   Estimates of the number of migrants vary. While official statistics only mention a few thousand, Libuše Paukertová for example estimates that the wave of migration may have comprised up to 260,000 people (Paukertová 2000, p. 27).

gration from Czechoslovakia decreased somewhat as a reaction to stricter migration policies (Mašková, Morbacher 2014, p. 11).

According to Libuše Paukertová, those who emigrated were mostly young people moving alone or with families. They came predominantly from Prague and other big cities in Czechoslovakia and were largely university educated (Paukertová 2000, p. 28). Besides economic motives, people also migrated as a result of their disagreement with the communist government, discrimination, professional downgrading or fear of persecution (Trapl 2000, p. 39). Among those legally or illegally crossing the border were people of diverse professions, such as politicians, diplomats, scientists, clerics, students, businessmen or laborers (ibid.). The destinations of choice of migrants leaving Czechoslovakia have shifted over time. In the 1950s the majority wished to go to the United States, even though before getting there many had to spend several years in refugee camps in Germany or elsewhere. From the 1960s onwards, the main target of migrants was "Western Europe", although the majority found the asylum in Germany (Paukertová 2000, pp. 28–29).

Illegal border crossings became a strongly politicized topic and the subject of communist propaganda. "Emigrants"[9] were pictured by political rhetoric as "state enemies", "imperialists' flunkeys" and "betrayers", undermining the work ethics and economic system (Kostlán 2011, pp. 25–26). The image of foreign countries that was presented to the nation was also shaped by public rhetoric and limited access to information. "The Western countries" were presented as rich yet inhuman countries that oppressed and exploited laborers (Mücke 2009). Political rhetoric was also supported by popular art productions, which were to a great extent controlled by the state. Official literature, TV series and popular movies in Czechoslovakia pictured "emigrants" and those who crossed the border as criminals and potential political agents, threatening the communist regime and Czechoslovak citizens (for literature see e.g. Ulč 2000, pp. 62–63). Public discourse about "emigrants" and "the West", created by the state authorities and at the same time de-construed and challenged by dissidents' activities and everyday interactions of those having contacts abroad, influenced the self-positioning of migrants themselves

---

9 Migration from Czechoslovakia during the Cold War is usually explained using the terms "exile" and "emigration". Both terms describe the character of migration processes, which were seen as permanent moves, since the possibility of returning and keeping links to the country of origin was restricted. "Emigrants" are mostly understood as those who left the country and settled long-term in another country without the perspective of come back. They moved for economic and political reasons. Those in "exile", on the other hand, left Czechoslovakia for political reasons, actively worked towards social change in the country from abroad and aimed to return (Trapl 2000, p. 36). Nevertheless, as qualitative works based on the narrator's experiences reveal, these two categories are often blurred because the motives and experiences of migration processes have shifted and overlapped over time (see e.g. Kleinova 2013, p. 13). Furthermore, these two expressions do not include those who crossed the border temporarily because of trade or labour, nor other forms of migration. For these reasons I prefer the term "migrant", which is more general and less politicised.

(Mücke 2009; Kostlán 2011, pp. 25–26). Discourses about "emigrants" had impacted on the perception of migrants returning to Czechoslovakia after the revolution in 1989 (Nešpor 2002a, p. 46).

2.4 The fall of the Iron Curtain in 1989 and the establishment of new migratory spaces

J: Yes, it was such strong moment, yeah. Because (1) suddenly (-) there was something in the air. Such tension or such: rm: (she smacks) (1) All people were suddenly somehow connected together. [I: Hmm] They fight for the same thing, right. [I: Hmm] And: I felt it everywhere. Because for example (breathing in) erm: (1) I went by subway somewhere and: suddenly I hear how they announce from that erm: the stations so suddenly they did not say I don't know Kosmonautů10, but they said some other name. Spontaneously! The drivers of the subway. (1) And: all people glanced at each other and they smiled. It was such, well, yeah [I: Hmm] erm: (1) yes. It was in such things very strong. [I: Hmm] (1) (clearing her throat) All communists' names were immediately changed for some (1) erm: (1) more normal ones (laughing) (Jana, p.15-16, l. 477-488)

The end of the Cold War and the disintegration of the Soviet Block after 1989 changed the face of Europe significantly and marked the beginning of a new historical era. Revolutions in countries all over Central and Eastern Europe that had been communist until then called for the restructuring of their political, economic and social systems, for the revision of international relations and for a new positioning within Europe. "Returning to Europe" became the political program during and after the revolutions (Domnitz 2011, p. 39). In Czechoslovakia, the revolutionary events and consequent changes were perceived as a reorientation from Soviet dominance and from the "backwardness" discursively connected with being part of "Eastern Europe", and as a step towards achieving a "Western type of society" with its democratic principles (Kürti 1997). Catchphrases such as "belonging to Europe" and to "Western civilisation" had already been used by dissidents during the 1980s, and became dominant discourse during the political shift (Domnitz 2011). At the same time, the shift in 1989 was also seen as the return to sovereignty of the states and to newly acquired national consciousness, as shown by rhetoric and the use of national symbols during the revolutions (Holý 1996).

The processes of economic transformation affected many people living in post-communist countries. Economic and societal shifts changed the structure of power relations, which in turn had an impact on deepening social inequalities among the inhabitants and the regions within the respective countries (see e.g. Gorzelak 1996; Kundera, Kundera 2011). In the Czech Republic, the

10   "Kosmonantů" can be freely translated as "Cosmonauts' station".

number of private companies grew 18 fold to more than 1 million officially registered companies within just four years after the turn (Machonin 1994, p. 6). The number of employees in the private sector reached 1,5 million towards the end of 1992 (ibid.). Nevertheless, since the legal framework was not yet fully elaborated and in fact contained many unclear provisions, the change from state-owned enterprises to private ownership was often followed by illegal practices, which led to a quick enrichment of certain individuals and social groups (Machonin 1994, p. 9). At the same time, the processes of privatization cost many people their jobs, especially in particular regions. In the Czech Republic, some regions, such as Eastern Bohemia, Northern Bohemia and Northern Moravia were particularly affected by structural changes and suffered from rising unemployment which was caused by the restructuring of the heavy and textile industry sectors and the lack of other job opportunities in the regions (Drbohlav, Rákoczyová 2012, p. 8). In Northern Bohemia, for example, the average wage was not even 2/3 of the average wage in Prague, the capital of the Czech Republic (Jeřábek 1999, p. 169). Work opportunities and life standards decreased in these regions, bringing along high rates of unemployment and increased migration of young people out of the affected regions (Zich 2002, p. 329; Jeřábek 1999, p. 169). Other regions experienced an economic boom, such as Mladá Boleslav, the centre of the automobile industry, the Pilsen region or big cities which became the centres of a rapidly developing service sector.

Despite these structural changes, spatial mobility within the Czech Republic remained relatively low in comparison with other European countries (Drbohlav, Rákoczyová 2012, p. 8). Low spatial mobility during the 1980s decreased even more in the course of the 1990s (ibid.). Some authors explained that low mobility was the heritage of the politics of full employment and of the aims of the government to control the passage to and within the labour market. During the communist regime it was usual for workers to stay in the same position for decades without the necessity to move places because of better job opportunities (Musil 2006, p. 10). Furthermore, mobility was also hindered by housing politics: state housing construction was stopped and the majority of inhabitants could not afford the new housing (Drbohlav, Rákoczyová 2012, p. 8). In the last decades, the structure of internal movers shifted. Those who moved across the borders of regions were increasingly young and tertiary educated people, while people with solely a basic education moved mostly within the regions (ČSÚ 2005, p. 11). Tertiary educated people moved mostly to the metropolitan areas around Prague and Brno, the two biggest cities in the Czech Republic. In contrast, the smaller cities and villages have been losing their tertiary educated people. The migration of tertiary educated people into metropolitan areas thus had as a consequence further social differentiation and growing inequalities among the regions

(Drbohlav, Rákoczyová 2012, p. 9; Ouředníček et al. 2011, p. 99; Novák et al. 2011, p. 99).

After the "Velvet Revolution", the possibility of choice in many fields of social life brought together new forms of social action (Machonin 1994, pp. 17–18). The former communist government with its centralized politics had influenced both the private and public spheres of life. The state had to a great extent regulated ones choice of education and position within the labour market (Musil 2006, p. 5). This centralised regulation of all spheres of life as well as limited possibilities for self-development had as a consequence that life patterns became "standardized". Societal changes, among them the possibility to choose what and where to study and move the borders, led to new options of developing ones biography (Pařízková 2011b, p. 47).

The fall of the Iron Curtain in 1989 changed the physical appearance and the symbolic meaning of borders. The highly protected borders, which had divided not only two geographical regions but also two social and cultural spheres (Langer 1996, p. 63), were opened. Although border inspectors were still present at the border checkpoints over the next decades, controls became rare and altered in character, increasingly being moved from border lines to locations situated many kilometres in front of or behind the actual border. New options for crossing the border appeared from the beginning of the 1990s onwards, enabling the reestablishment of transnational social networks, cross-border cultural activities, and trade cooperation (see Langer 1996; Iglicka 1998; Wallace, Stola 2001) which had in the past been strongly restricted and regulated by governments.

The changes in society and border regimes after the revolution hence prompted new movements of people across the national borders. In Czechoslovakia or the Czech Republic, as the case may be, around 120,000 soldiers who had been part of the Warsaw treaty troops, along with their families, moved out of the region and left behind empty military quarters and residential areas (Sígl 2014). Some of these residences were offered to Czech nationals moving from Ukraine, Belarus or Rumania to Czechoslovakia. These migration flows were partly organised and supported by the government (Nešpor 2002a, pp. 54–55). Besides "return migration" from the East, there was also a considerable number of people who had migrated west during the Cold War and in the first years of transformation returned back to Czechoslovakia with their families. As some authors suggest, the majority of those who actually moved to Czechoslovakia from "Western countries" were Czech nationals returning to the country (Nešpor 2002b, p. 790). After their return, some of them managed to start businesses and privatize property which, after their initial migration, had been confiscated by the communist government. Others went back to work in one of the subsidiary companies or factories established by foreign companies in Czechoslovakia, or made use of their language skills (Nešpor 2002b, p. 803). Zdeněk Nešpor reveals that returning migrants re-established family ties and close friendships in spite of experiencing a negative atmosphere at work and in relation to the majority of society. In many cases, they were not able to use the experience they had acquired abroad, either because of a lack of interest from the majority of the public or due to prejudices aimed at returning migrants (ibid.).

At the same time as Czechoslovakia became a target for other migrants from post-communist countries and the countries of the West, thereby shifting from a country of emigration to a country of immigration (see e.g. Wallace 2002, p. 604), there was also migration out of Czechoslovakia or the Czech Republic, as the case may be. In the early 1990s the Czech state eased restrictions on travelling abroad. The requirement for visas to certain other European countries was removed and Czech citizens were allowed to stay abroad for up to three months on a tourist permit. In addition, a number of bilateral agreements were established between Czechoslovakia or the Czech Republic, as the case may be, and other European states with regard to short term seasonal labour and student exchanges. Looking at Czech-German relations, in 1991 an agreement came into force enabling the entry of Czech seasonal labourers on special contracts which were limited for a period of three months a year (Meduna 2004, p. 80). Work permits were mostly issued for work in agriculture, forestry, catering, or construction. Furthermore, bilateral agreements concerning the mutual employment of Czech and German citizens were introduced. They were limited for a period of one year with the possibility of a 6-month extension. Their aim was to support language and vocational proficiency and provide an opportunity for gaining new experiences from living abroad (Meduna 2004, p. 79). Work permits were mostly issued in the fields of catering and nursing. Both programs were limited to a few hundred applicants a year (ibid.). The other option for entering the German labour market was via a "Green card", which was introduced between 2000 and 2004. The "Green card" was aimed at attracting IT specialists to the country by easing the process of application and access to the German labour market. Nevertheless, only 983 applicants from the Czech Republic and Slovakia made use of this opportunity (Kolb 2005). Besides these bilateral agreements on seasonal and short term labour, there were some other possibilities for entering and residing in the country: as ethnic Germans, as family members, on the basis of au pair contracts or for time limited periods of study placement. Another option was to start a job with a work permit. However, obtaining a work permit was difficult, since nationals and other EU citizens had the priority right to any such job position. Furthermore, the issue of work permits was connected to various administrative obstacles and costs for the employee and the employer. For these reasons, many people simply continued working in the private sector or without a work permit.[11] In some border

---

11 See for example the case of Lenka presented in one of the following chapters.

regions, also commuting to work to nearby Bavaria or Saxony became a common social practice. Despite the lack of statistics, some authors have estimated that there were up to 50,000 people from the Czech Republic, especially from the regions in Western and Southern Bohemia, commuting to Germany for work every day (Jeřábek 1999, p. 170).

Unemployment, low wages, limited future perspectives and the overall insecure economic situation in the regions of origin were important motives for considering migration (see e.g. Okólski 2000, p. 158; Morokvasic 1994). Nevertheless, the economic situation was not the only reason for migration. Education, love, family reunion or simply the wish to discover countries behind the borders to live there for a while also played an important role for those who considering moving.[12] During the 1990s, the prime European country of destination for migrants from Central and Eastern Europe was Germany, followed by Austria and Italy (Hárs et al. 2001, p. 262; Okólski 2000, p. 147; Drbohlav 2000, p. 167). The reasons for extensive migration flows especially to these countries were geographical proximity, cultural, historical and transnational interconnections and, of course, the prospering economic situation offering higher wages than the regions of origin. At the same time, migration overseas also increased (Engbersen et al. 2010, p. 9).

All in all, it is estimated that between 1989 and 2004 more than 3 million people migrated from Central and Eastern European countries that joined the EU in 2004 and 2007 (Engbersen et al. 2010, pp. 9–10). If one were to add migrants moving on a circular or temporary basis to this calculation, as well as migrants and asylum seekers leaving other regions of the former "Eastern bloc", then numbers would be much higher.

Be that as it may, looking back, actual migration numbers are nowhere near as high as the extensive migration flows expected after the break-down of the communist regimes. Some politicians and scientists had predicted mass migrations consisting of 25 or even 48 million migrants from East to West (Bade 2000, pp. 386–387). The misrepresented and exaggerated picture of millions of unemployed and derived migrants walking westwards made migration one of the central topics of national politics of some EU countries. Effectively controlling migration became one of the main political goals. Thus, paradoxically, at the time the borders of post-communist countries were opening, the countries of the West were seeking ways of restricting and regulating them again. More restrictive asylum policies were the answer in relation to increased migration of asylum seekers during the 1980s and

---

12 For example, Jaroslav Rudiš, the Czech writer, describes in his novel "Nebe pod Berlínem" ("The sky under Berlin") the decision of one young Czech man to leave for Berlin shortly after the revolution in order to start a new life there as a musician. It pictures the biographical metamorphosis connected to migration and the way the desire to live in different social, cultural and lingual milieus behind the Iron Curtain shapes one's perceptions and future perspectives.

1990s. During this time, cooperation among the EC/EU states and also with the states bordering the EU intensified (Nygård, Stacher 2001). After the fall of the Iron Curtain, citizens of some Central and Eastern European countries gained the right to enter EC/EU countries without a visa for periods shorter than three months. At the same time, accessibility to the labour market continued to be restricted for citizens of certain other countries until the enlargement of the EU in 2004 and 2007 and, in some cases, for even longer. Besides these regulations, agreements were established in respect of student exchanges, vocational training, short term and seasonal labour (Münz 2000). Programs like these were increasingly labelled "exchanges" in order to underline their temporary character and to prevent permanent migration (Morokvasic, Rudolph 1994a, p. 17). During the 1990s some authors warned that increasingly restrictive politics and the protection of the EU borders might lead to the establishment of a "Gold Curtain", replacing the Iron Curtain, which would in fact affect Central and Eastern European countries and support the people-trafficking business (Okólski 1994, p. 140).

Shifted migration and border regimes of the EC/EU countries shaped migration patterns on the East-West axis considerably. Permanent immigration, which had dominated during the Cold War, decreased. This was due to the change in the structure of border crossings and the nature of migration. The heavily guarded border between the East and the West, as well as the perception of migration as illegal and a criminal act as disseminated by the former communist governments, had prevented many from returning to their countries of origin. Thus, it was the possibility of return which gained importance after the political shift. New options for crossing the border after 1989 also enabled the establishment of diverse forms of migration. Permanent migration was to a large extent replaced by circular, short term and repeated migrations and diverse forms of commuting (Morokvasic 1994; Okólski 1994, 2001; Tarrius 1994). Cross border activities, including petty trade (Iglicka 1998; Morokvasic 1994), a circular system of migration of women into the care sector (Morokvasic 1994; Lutz 2008c; Apitzsch 2010b; Satola 2010; Karakayali 2010b), au pair contracts (Hess 2009), work on construction sites, seasonal work in the agricultural sector, or work in the service sector, became means of bettering or maintaining one's situation in the country of origin.

The discrepancy between wages during the nineties throughout European countries and the impossibility of getting by in ones country of origin led many people to take a low qualified job abroad despite their actual qualifications or social status in their country of origin. Work in the care sector, agriculture or cross border trade was often carried out as a means of earning extra income in addition to the professions of teachers, academics, or engineers performed back home (Morokvasic 1994). For many, downward mobility in one place meant maintaining or bettering social mobility in another place (Morokvasic, Rudolph 1994a, p. 22). Social downgrading in the country of migration, and the discrepancy between the status, qualification and experience of migrants and their actual position in their country of origin, became one of the features of migration flows along the East-West axis (Morokvasic 1994, p. 185; Tinguy 1994; Karakayali 2010b). As Mirjana Morokvasic puts it, for many people migration became a strategy enabling them "to stay at home" (Morokvasic 1994, p. 185).

Migration patterns after 1989 are not absolutely new. In many cases migration continued the processes which had begun during the Cold War or even earlier (Morokvasic, Rudolph 1994b; Quack 1994; Black et al. 2010). However, what is new is the intensity and scale of these migration flows, in some cases affecting the everyday life of whole villages, towns and regions in diverse parts of Europe (see e.g. Kempf 2013; Palenga-Möllenbeck 2014). Furthermore, as for example Morokvasic argues, migration processes were increasingly the result of people's own initiative leading to the establishment of migration paths along transnational networks and new forms of solidarity within the ethnic community, rather than being due to state recruitment policies as was the case in the fifties and sixties (Morokvasic, Rudolph 1994a, p. 22; Morokvasic 1994). Since "official" migration corridors stayed closed to the majority of them, migrants resorted to using any other available means of action in order to realise their goals.

2.5 The enlargement of the EU in 2004 and 2007 and the financial crisis

The enlargement of the EU in 2004 and 2007 once again had a significant impact on shaping the migration map of Europe. Migrants from Poland, the Czech Republic, Slovakia, Hungary, Slovenia, the Baltic states, and later on from Romania and Bulgaria were now no longer migrants from outside of the EU but instead "internal movers" who enjoyed new rights and privileges. The eastward enlargement of the EU meant that the right of free movement was extended to citizens of the new member states. Citizens of new EU states could now enter the country solely with a passport or ID card, since all visa requirements had already been removed before accession. Furthermore, a residence permit was no longer required in the majority of cases. All migrants needed to do was register with the relevant local authority. As Adrian Favell puts it, these rounds of enlargement completed a geo-political shift that had started in 1989 (Favell 2008, p. 701) and dramatically changed the context of migration (Favell 2008, p. 711). The process of EU enlargement emphasised the differences between those coming from new EU countries and those coming from outside of the Union. While the EU made the next step towards achieving an "area of freedom, security and justice, in which the free movement of persons is assured" (European Union 1997, p. 5), it increasingly subjected migrants from non-EU countries to more restrictive migration politics with limited rights to enter the country, reside and work there (Pécoud, Guchteneire 2006, p. 73; Campani 2008).[13]

However, not all barriers for citizens of the new member states were removed, as for example full access to the labour markets of some older member states of the EU. These states, notably Germany, Austria, France, and Italy, perceived the influx of people from the new member states as a threat to their own populations, welfare systems and labour markets, and this was thoroughly supported by populist rhetoric (Favell 2008, p. 703; Campani 2008, p. 48). With the exception of the UK, Ireland and Sweden, all EU countries required work permits for new EU citizens for varying periods of time, the maximum being up to seven years after accession. Furthermore, they protected their labour market by means of regulations which gave their own nationals and other EU citizens priority over citizens of new EU countries and over those coming from outside the EU. Thus, some "new Europeans" already living in the "old European countries" gained official residence permits, but at the same time lots of them continued to perform their occupations illegally (see e.g. Favell, Nebe 2009). The transitional restrictions lasted up to May 2011. Bulgarians and Romanians had to wait a further three years until January 2014 for unrestricted movement within the EU. Germany and Austria were the only countries to make use of the maximum period of transitional restrictions permitted by the EU commission, not removing barriers for the citizens of countries which joined the EU in 2004 until seven years after accession. For Bulgarians and Romanians nearly all of the doors into the European labour market stayed shut until the very last moment. In 2013 Croatia also joined the EU. Fourteen EU member states allowed Croatian citizens to enter their labour market without any further requirements. However, the remaining member states, among them France, Germany and the UK, retained the restrictions.

The lack of restrictive politics of the UK, Ireland and Sweden supported increased migration flows of new EU citizens to these countries (CSO 2014; Wadensjo 2007; Vargas-Silva 2014). During the 1990s and early 2000s these countries became a destination for migrants from Central and East European countries. Ireland, which experienced a great economic boom at the beginning of the 21st century, turned from a country of emigration to a country of immigration in only one decade. Besides Irish nationals returning from the UK and overseas, increasing numbers of non-EU migrants, among them Poles, Czechs and Slovaks, arrived in the country. They found jobs easily in

---

13 The notion of "fortress Europe", protecting its borders no matter how many people die every day while trying to reach it, or how many undergo the risks of being trafficked into Europe (Pécoud, Guchteneire 2006, p. 73; Campani 2007, 2008), is a fitting description of this pattern.

the booming labour market, the majority of them as employees in construction, manufacturing, in hospitality and the expanding service sector (CSO 2008). The majority of newcomers only stayed temporarily or returned repeatedly for seasonal work. The opening up of the labour market in 2004 helped many migrants to legalise their status, since obtaining a work permit was until then costly, time-consuming and difficult. In 2004 and 2005, the number of applicants for so-called PPS numbers[14] increased twofold from 54,000 to 110,000 and rose constantly in subsequent years, whereby half of applicants were Polish nationals (Ugba 2007, p. 172). According to the Central Statistics Office of Ireland, the majority of all migrants were from new EU countries: they accounted for a little less than 50,000 people in 2006 and around 73,000 in 2007 (CSO 2012, p. 5). The economic crisis which began in 2008 again affected migration flows in and out of the country. It is estimated that between 2009 and 2012 about 60,000 people originating from new EU countries left Ireland and returned to their countries of origin or migrated elsewhere (CSO 2014).

The UK and Sweden experienced similar dynamics in connection with EU enlargement. In the UK, the number of people moving from new EU countries doubled to 1.3 million in 2004 (Duvell 2007, p. 350). The majority were from Poland, Lithuania, Slovakia and the Czech Republic, most of whom only stayed for a short period of time (ibid.). Alena Pařízková, who studied labour migration from the Czech Republic to the United Kingdom, gives a number of insights into Czech migrants in the United Kingdom. According to her research, which is based on qualitative narrative interviews, migrants were active in diverse fields within the labour market, although the majority worked in occupations characterised by lower wages. Females often found work in the care sector as au pairs and nannies, in hotel services, catering and administrative positions, while men worked as construction workers, gardeners or hotel and restaurant staff (Pařízková 2011a, pp. 93, 97). Pařízková also shows that despite the low positioning of migrant men and women within the local labour market at the beginning of their careers, the interviewees developed strategies on how to overcome the inequalities and attain better positions over time (Pařízková 2011a, p. 110). Furthermore, the majority of migrants interviewed would consider returning to the Czech Republic (Pařízková 2011a, p. 155). As some researchers have suggested, migration from the Czech Republic to abroad has a circular or short term character rather than being aimed at permanent residency (Drbohlav, Rákoczyová 2012, p. 7).

Concurrently with migration flows from the new EU member states to Northern Europe, migration also intensified towards Southern European

---

14 PPS number (Personal Public Service) is a document which is required for every communication with public bodies. Because of the lack of statistics, the number of migrants is estimated on the base of the assigned PPS numbers (Ugba 2007, p. 172).

countries. Italy, for example, became the destination of choice for Romanians and Poles, as well as Ukrainians (Kosic, Triandafyllidou 2007, p. 189). Interestingly, migration flows from Ukraine and Poland consisted predominantly of women. According to statistics, they accounted for about 85 per cent of migration flows from these regions (ibid.). These women were predominantly employed in households, caring for children, the elderly and doing housekeeping (ibid.). During the 1990s and early 2000s, transnational links between particular regions in Romania and Italy were established and kept alive (see e.g. Kempf 2013).

In the late 2000s, the financial crisis affected a number of European countries. In the Czech Republic, the economic crisis in 2009 affected the production in some fields of industry which had as a consequence the reduction of job positions and rising unemployment. During the crisis, it was not only the elderly who suffered from dismissals and unemployment, but increasingly also young people. The level of education had an impact on the possible threat of unemployment. As for example EUROSTAT data from 2010 reveals, young people between the ages of 20 and 34 who completed secondary or basic school suffered much more from unemployment then those of the same age who successfully finished tertiary education: while the unemployment of university graduates ages 20 to 34 reached less than 5 per cent in 2010, it was about 8 per cent of secondary school graduates and more than 30 per cent of those who possessed solely a basic education (Koucký, Zelenka 2011, p. 5). Women with only a basic or secondary education were particularly affected by the crises (Křížková, Formánková 2011). However, crises affected also university graduates. More than before, graduates in certain fields, such as mechanical engineering which was particularly affected by the crisis, had to take jobs which did not correspond to their actual qualifications and knowledge (Koucký, Zelenka 2011, p. 16). The level of willingness to take a job which did not correspond to the individual's actual qualifications differed according to time and the field of study (ibid.). Taking up a job in a field which does not closely correspond to the acquired qualifications was not the exception in the Czech Republic. In fact, in 2010 only 20 per cent of graduates worked in a position which was an exact match to their field of study. The rest worked either in a less strongly related or completely different field than that of their actual qualification (Koucký, Zelenka 2011, p. 13). In addition, university educated women, who were particularly affected by the gender pay gap[15], often took a job for which they were overqualified in order to overcome the threat of poverty and unemployment (Křížková, Formánková 2011).

The unstable situation all over the Europe had an effect not only on migration processes but also on those who were dependant on remittances. The

---

15 University educated women were paid 31 per cent less on average than university educated men (APERIO 2011, p. 5).

countries with high inflows of migrants in the first half of the 2000s, such as the UK, Ireland, Spain and Italy, experienced a significant outflow of EU citizens. However, it is unclear how many returned to their countries of origin or how many moved elsewhere. Those who stayed and lost their job in the course of the crisis looked for other possibilities. As in the case of Italy or the Czech Republic, the level of self-employment of migrants grew significantly (Koehler et al. 2010, p. 5), as did participation in the "informal economy" (ibid.). Interestingly, the financial crisis had a different effect on migrant men and migrant women: while the men – employed to great extent in the construction and manufacturing sectors and therefore more affected by job shortages – were more exposed to job losses and wage shortages, women who on the other hand were more highly represented in the (informal) care sector were less affected by the crisis (Koehler et al. 2010, p. 4). These new power relations within migrant families, where women became the main bread winner and gained more responsibilities, had an impact on a shifted gender order (see e.g. Bernat, Viruela 2011, p. 58).

The various EU countries responded differently to the crisis. Some of them restricted admissions and adapted new legislation to control irregular migration (Koehler et al. 2010, p. 6). In some cases, such as in the Czech Republic or Spain, "voluntary return migration" was encouraged (ibid.). Migration programs based on quotas and occupational status, which nearly all European countries had applied in recent decades in order to attract professionals from particular professions to their labour markets, such as health care, IT and engineering, were heightened but nonetheless continued during the crisis, since the lack of professionals in these sectors still prevailed (ibid.) At the same time, many of those who possessed the relevant qualifications and already lived in the respective country did not get access to qualified positions because of a lack of recognition of certificates and work experience over the border, bureaucratic burdens and gender bias (Kogan 2011; Kofman 2009b). These inequalities and contradictions were slowly starting to be recognised by European governments. Germany, for example, adopted the "Concept of Securing a Skilled Labour Base" in 2011, aimed at easing the recognition of foreign qualifications and diplomas and assisting migrants already living in the country in the labour market (OECD 2012b, p. 323).

Germany was one of the countries which did not experience a decrease in migration into the country at the end of 2000s and beginning of 2010s. Looking at Czech-German relations, the number of Czech citizens residing in Germany continually grew from 20,000 in 1998 to 36,000 in 2008 up to 44,000 in 2013 (Eurostat 2014a). Because of a lack of reliable statistics on migration from the Czech Republic to Germany, it is difficult to provide an estimate of the actual number of migrants. Estimates are also difficult because of temporal, return and short term migration connected in some cases with irregular employment, for which there are no reliable statistics. On the

Czech side of things, statistics on migration out of the Czech Republic to abroad are practically non-existent with the exception of estimates put forward by the Czech Ministry of Foreign Affairs. These state that there are currently approximately 50,000 Czech citizens living in Germany (Ministry of Foreign Affairs of the Czech Republic 2014). More detailed estimates are provided by the German Central Register of Foreigners (Ausländerzentralregister). According to these statistics, the number of registered Czech migrants has risen constantly since 1994: in 1994 there were about 15,000 Czech migrants, in 2004 30,000 and 35,000 in 2012 (Statistisches Bundesamt 2014d). Women make up 66 per cent of these migration flows (Statistisches Bundesamt 2014a). Another source of information is the Census in 2011 and the Micro Census in 2012, both carried out by the German Statistical Office. According to the Micro Census, there were about 121,000 people of Czech origin residing in Germany in 2012. However, these numbers include not only those who actually migrated but also the descendants of migrants moving to Germany over the last decades. A large part of them has gained German citizenship or migrated as ethnic Germans. Of 121,000 people who have stated that they are of Czech origin, about 94,000 have experienced migration themselves. Around 38,000 German residents possess exclusively Czech citizenship and are therefore labelled by the Statistical Office as "foreigners" (Statistisches Bundesamt 2014b). The Micro Census in 2012 also gives an insight into the structure of this migrant group. The majority is between the age of 25 and 45. About 24 per cent of Czech migrants have a university degree. Interestingly, according to the Micro Census, about 74 per cent of migrants are women (ibid.).

Migration flows to Germany from other new EU countries which joined the EU in 2004 and 2007 also intensified. In 2012 in comparison with previous years around 60 per cent more migrants arrived from Slovenia, around 30 per cent more from Hungary and 23 per cent more from Romania. The number of people crossing the German-Polish borders also increased (Statistisches Bundesamt 2013). Migrants from Poland were the most numerous group arriving in Germany in 2012, followed by Romanians and Hungarians (Statistisches Bundesamt 2014c, p. 98). The increase in the number of people crossing the border was caused by the opening up of the German labour market in 2011 as well as the effects of the crisis in Central and Eastern European countries. Moreover, in 2012, the number of people arriving from Spain, Portugal, Italy and Greece – those countries affected by economic instability and unemployment that in some cases reached up to 50 per cent – rose by about 45 per cent in comparison to the previous year (Statistisches Bundesamt 2013). Many of those who came to Germany and other countries in the course of the financial crisis were able to use transnational links that had been established either by their own prior migration experiences or by the migration of their relatives and acquaintances, going back deep into the history of complex migration processes in Europe.

3 Research on highly skilled migration in Europe: state of the art

Highly skilled migration is a topic which has shaped political and economic discussions over the past decades. The way it has been perceived has shifted over time depending on the context. While for some countries that recognised the need for skilled professionals from abroad and tried to attract them by means of special policies it has often been perceived as a "gain", for the state the workers have left behind it has been discussed in the terms of a loss of intelligentsia, or "brain drain". The diversity of viewpoints on highly skilled migration – supported by the variety of studies reaching from ethnographical case studies to macro-economic and political models analysing the impact of skilled migration on economic growth and development – had an impact on the establishment of different, sometimes controversial, theories and policy implementations. However, despite the different approaches to highly skilled migration, most authors would argue that highly skilled migration plays an increasingly important part within global migration processes. Moreover, with the rising impact of education and skills on the global economy, the differences between highly skilled migration at one end of the migration spectrum and low skilled migration at the other end have been increasing (King 2002, p. 98; Lutz, Koser 1998, p. 2). In the following chapter I will discuss these new divisions of migration flows according to education and skills and their impact on conceptualising highly skilled migration. Subsequently I will discuss the different definitions of "highly skilled migrants" and propose a new way of analysing and studying this phenomenon.

In the following section, recent studies on highly skilled migration pathways in and to Europe will be presented and discussed. I shall then summarise the main results, position my research within the existing body of literature and outline the research agenda.

3.1 Changing contexts of highly skilled migration: working towards the liberalisation of skilled migration flows

"Globalisation essentially means flows across borders - flows of capital, commodities, ideas and people. Nation-states welcome the first two types, but remain suspicious of the last two. Differentiated migration regimes have been set up which encourage elites and the highly skilled to be mobile, while low-skilled workers and people fleeing persecution are excluded." (Castles 2007, p. 360).

Despite the assumption of some globalisation theorists that the nation-state would lose its power in the processes of ongoing global interconnections, Stephen Castles pointed out the persisting role of the state in controlling and selecting migration flows. He suggested that the criteria according to which migrants have been selected is, besides their ethnic and cultural background, also education and skills, since they have been seen as crucial for maintaining growth and development.

At the core of this new dividing line lies the restructuring of local and global labour markets in recent decades. Demographic changes, globalisation of the production of goods and services as well as technological development had an impact on the changing structure of the economy. From the 1980s onwards, the importance of the service sector began to grow in some European countries. Services became the most important source of GDP, accounting for about 71 per cent in EU countries (European Commission 2014b, p. 1). The shift towards the service sector in the global economy also had an impact on the creation, destruction and transformation of job opportunities. While the number of jobs in agriculture and industry were declining, newly created jobs in the service sector grew rapidly: from the early 1980s to mid-1990s, about 18 million jobs were created in the service sector and it is predicted that from the beginning of the twenty-first century to the early 2020s, an additional 20 million jobs will be created in the service sector in the EU (Lavenex 2008, p. 32; European Commission 2008, p. 7). In 2011, employment in the service sector made up 67 per cent of employed people in the EU (European Commission 2014b, p. 6). Despite the inequalities within EU countries, most countries have experienced increasing growth in business services, information and communication technologies, as well as the health and social sectors. Most recently, the knowledge-intensive service sector has developed rapidly and accounted for more than 50 per cent of employment within the service sector as a whole in 2013 (European Commission 2014a, pp. 65–69). The shift towards the service sector and a knowledge-based economy also impacted on the rising importance of education and skills. As the long-term demographic statistics on EU population show, there has been an ongoing increase in tertiary graduates within EU countries. However, the proportion of university educated people has differed among the EU countries: in Belgium, Finland and France, for example, university graduates make up about 45 per cent of the population, while in the Czech Republic and Romania they make up about 20 per cent. At the same time, the proportion of people with a primary education has been constantly declining (OECD 2012a, p. 243).

As indicated by Castles, the shift towards skills and education has also shaped the migratory regimes of national states. In recent decades, some states have introduced special migration policies with the aim of easing the migration of qualified people in certain special fields. Germany introduced its green card in 2000 in order to attract ICT specialists. Other European countries, such as the UK, France and Ireland, applied preference schemes for particular professions according to job vacancies on the local labour market. Norway, for example, introduced programs which allowed highly skilled professionals to enter the country and to seek a job for a limited period of time (Sopemi 2005, pp. 132–135). The UK, Sweden, Belgium and Austria introduced special fiscal incentives for highly skilled migrants (Sopemi 2005, p. 134). Selective politics have also been applied by the USA, New Zealand, Canada and Australia (Avato 2009, p. 12). In contrast to selected highly skilled migrants, irregular migrants and low skilled migrants have experienced tightening migration policies throughout most of the world, as exemplified by Europe and its rising surveillance of its borders (Pécoud, Guchteneire 2006).

Moreover, the regulation of skilled migration flows is no longer the issue of solely national politics. It is more and more shaped by global economic interests and processes which exceed national frameworks. Processes that are geared towards international and supranational cooperation concerning the facilitation of cross-national flows of highly skilled workers can be observed both within Europe and worldwide.

The large majority of international multilateral agreements include provisions for skilled labour. Within the EU (resp. the EEC then), the free movement of workers was introduced in 1968. It became one of the most important pillars of EU agreements concerning the open market, together with the free movement of goods, capital and services. The idea behind it was both economic and political: it should support economic development but also abolish discrimination based on nationality in the context of employment and economic activities. In 1992, the right of free movement was extended from workers to all EU citizens and their foreign relatives (Lavenex 2008, p. 37). In addition, agreements concerning the partial free movement of people were established between the EU and some other European countries, allowing the citizens of the contracting states to enter any EU member state for the purposes of business (Lavenex 2008, p. 38). Similar, though more restrictive contracts concerning the mobility of workers in some specific professions were also included in trade agreements established between the EU and some non-European countries, such as Mexico, Morocco and Tunisia (Lavenex 2008, p. 38). Similar tendencies are to be found in other regions of the world. Provisions concerning the facilitation or full mobility of skilled labour were also included in other regional economic agreements, such as the North American Free Trade Agreement (NAFTA), the Common Market of Eastern and South Africa (COMESA) and the Australia-New Zealand Closer Economic Relations Trade Agreement (ANZCERTA) (Lavenex 2008, pp. 38–42).

Important developments towards the facilitation of skilled migration occurred in the service sector. The General Agreement on Trade and Services (GATS), the treaty of the World Trade Organisation (WTO), which envisages the liberalisation of international trade, introduced provisions not only for cross-national services, but also for the cross border movement of service providers, such as teachers, doctors or telecommunication specialists. Nevertheless, member states still retain the right to make decisions on long-term residency, granting citizenship and access to the employment market (WTO 2014; Lavenex 2008, p. 47).

Besides the trend towards liberalising skilled migration among the national states and supranational organisations through multilateral agreements, skilled migration has also been liberalised within internal legal and labour frameworks, since the power to make decisions concerning the migration of skilled labour has increasingly been delegated from state authorities to private organisations. This concerns especially the movement of workers within multinational corporations. In many cases it is the company which decides not only about the placement of employees within the internal labour market, but also about the issue of work permits (Lavenex 2008, pp. 48–49).

Furthermore, the landscape of skilled migration has been shaped by the various processes leading towards the internalisation of professions (Iredale 2001). According to Robyn Iredale, the professions are no longer operated solely by national bodies but have increasingly been shaped within the transnational framework. An important role in these processes is played by the internalisation of education through higher institutional cross-national cooperation and exchanges and through the opening up of study programs for foreign students. Furthermore, the shift from national standards and procedures towards international regulations of the respective professions were encouraged by multilateral agreements, mutual recognition of education, the globalisation of entrepreneurs and companies and the global labour market in general (Iredale 2001).

As these developments show, the migration of skilled professionals has been the subject of ongoing liberalisation and multilateralism, in contrast with other types of migration which have predominantly remained under the control of national states (Lavenex 2008, p. 50). Saskia Sassen brought up the topic of increasing global inequalities concerning skills and education in her work analysing the relationship between the global economy and migration processes (Sassen 1988, 2000, 2001, 2008). According to Sassen,

"[t]he ascendance of information industries and the growth of a global economy, both inextricably linked, have contributed to a new geography of centrality and marginality. This new geography partly reproduces existing inequalities but also is the outcome of a dynamic specific to current forms of economic growth. It assumes many forms and operates in many arenas, from the distribution of telecommunications facilities to the structure of the economy and of employment. Global cities accumulate immense concentrations of economic power while cities that were once major manufacturing centers suffer inordinate declines; the downtowns of cities and business centers in metropolitan areas receive massive investments in real estate and telecommunications while low-income urban and metropolitan areas are starved for resources; highly educated workers in the corporate sector see their incomes rise to unusually high levels while low- or medium-skilled workers see theirs sink. Financial services produce superprofits while industrial services barely survive." (Sassen 2000, p. 82)

In order to retain their functionality, global cities on the one hand need highly skilled professionals who are responsible for the core tasks of the global cities, and on the other hand those who provide low-paid services both in the public and private sphere, mostly servicing the highly skilled and higher positioned (Sassen 2001). As Sassen puts it, "(m)ore generally we can capture these and other such dynamics in the strong trend for bimodal immigration in terms of education levels, with concentrations of low-wage, poorly educated workers and concentrations of highly educated workers." (Sassen 2007, p. 70).

The developments towards the liberalisation of skilled migration flows as well as empirical evidence have revealed the increasing role of education and skills on rising inequalities of migration flows as conceptualised by globalisation theorists. In many cases, migration based on the particular education and skills actually became the only possibility to legally cross the border and settle abroad (Scott 2006, p. 1107). Nevertheless, bimodal polarisation on the basis of education as outlined by Sassen also evokes many questions. Are all migrants who possess a university degree really among those who are privileged? What about highly qualified asylum seekers? Or highly educated women working as maids or au pairs in private households in Germany? What about recent graduates in non-technical fields, such as the humanities, theology or art, who just do not fit in with the preference schemes of the respective national migration policies? And many other highly educated people who do not a priori want to move for economic reasons but because of a partnership or education, because they are searching for exile or simply just for the sake of living in another country? All of these questions expose the problems associated with the assumption of highly educated migrants being per se more privileged then less educated migrants. They imply that skills and education do not suffice for understanding the migration regimes and migration processes of the highly skilled. Furthermore, they bring to mind that other dimensions, such as gender, nationality or class, have to be taken into account as well. Finally, they invite one to rethink the opposing concepts of "highly skilled professionals" and "low skilled migrants".

3.2 Rethinking the migration of highly skilled people: the research agenda

3.2.1 "Highly skilled migrants" as the subject of research

In the large body of literature on global migration, highly skilled migrants have been portrayed as "frontier free" elites who can overstep the borders of national states without any limitations. Since the 1960s, when research on highly skilled migration developed, researchers have concentrated mostly on "brains", "transferees" within multinational corporations, "economic elites", and "expatriates" (see e.g. Salt 1988; Findlay et al. 1996; Beaverstock 2002). For many, these groups embodied the image of globalisation: free to move and disconnected from local settings. The image of "expatriates" and "economic elites" in these early studies developed within the context of colonialism and post-colonialism. The term "expatriate" has been used mostly in connection with "white Western migrants" working overseas or in another country in order to make a distinction from other "migrants" and thus assure their privileged perception (Fechter, Walsh 2010, p. 1199). Despite the fact that this image of free movers disconnected from national policies and localities was challenged by some authors (Willis, Yeoh 2002; Beaverstock 2002), these early works influenced the way in which highly skilled migration was perceived within migration studies and in the public discourses.

The migration of highly qualified people is not a new phenomenon in European migration history. Evidence of migration for the purpose of studying or for qualified work abroad dates back to the antiquity and middle ages (see e.g. Holý 2013). Nevertheless, research on highly skilled migration only started to develop quite recently in the 1970s. Since then, the body of research on this topic has risen significantly (Koser, Salt 1997, p. 285). Research on highly skilled migration developed simultaneously across diverse disciplines. It is established in the fields of geography, economics and political sciences but has only recently become a subject of study for social scientists as well. As the migration of highly skilled workers was mostly observed from an economic and political point of view, it was mainly studied from the perspective of the sending and receiving states and their economies. Only recently have the experiences of migrants themselves been studied by scientists. They have emphasised agency, i.e. their capacity to act independently and make their own free choices, and their role in shaping the migration processes "from below" (see e.g. Favell et al. 2008).

At the beginning of the 1960s, the British Royal Society initiated the "brain drain" debate through its report on the emigration of British scientists to the USA (Koser, Salt 1997, p. 285; Balmer et al. 2009, p. 1). Soon afterwards, the "brain drain" debates which looked at the outsourcing of highly educated people from one country to another, predominantly moved to a different context, namely the study of the migration of highly qualified people from "developing countries" to "developed countries" (see e.g. Fortney 1970; Portes 1976). The main concern of these studies was the effects of migration on local economies and development. The migration of skilled people from developing countries was perceived as a threat for local economies on the one hand and a gain for the destination countries on the other hand. According to these debates, "brain drain" deepened the inequalities among the world's regions, since some countries were losing human capital while others were acquiring it.

From the 1990s onwards, some authors called for a different outlook on highly skilled migration, criticising the perception of skilled migration as a one way process. They argued that skilled migration is a complex phenomenon which in many cases encompasses repetitive movements between the countries of origin and the country of migration. They suggested that the term "brain drain" should be replaced by the term "brain circulation" and argued that the migration of skilled people might even contribute to the development of countries from which migrants moved forth (see e.g. Gaillard, Gaillard 1997). The benefits were seen in remittances, which supported local development, in the establishment of social links and businesses and in the application of new technologies and knowledge, which migrants learned abroad, in the region of origin. By coining the term "brain circulation", the clear lines between the country that profits from migrant mobility and the country that loses out in social and economic terms have become blurred.

The shift from "brain drain" to "brain circulation" in discussions went hand in hand with the shift within the social sciences from system theory and dependency theory, which underlined the structural inequalities of world regions, towards approaches that acknowledged the possibility of individuals to change the structures from below (Freitas et al. 2012, p. 3). However, the topic of skilled migration remained controversial. While some authors have argued in favour of its positive effects on the economy and development of countries left behind (see e.g. Docquier, Rapoport 2007), others have pointed towards deficiencies in technology, health, the public and social sphere which have been exacerbated by the outflow of professionals to other countries (see e.g. Muhirwa 2012).

Within the large body of studies on "brain drain", "brain gain" or "brain circulation", highly skilled migrants are seen as the carriers of knowledge and skills which have been outsourced from one country to another. These studies often overlooked the actual impact on migrants' biographical and career pathways, however. Jean-Marie Muhirwa (2012, p. 46), for example, pointed out that only a small number of those highly skilled migrants moving to Europe or North America actually managed to get jobs which correspond to their actual qualifications and skills. The majority of highly skilled migrants experienced deskilling, being underpaid or having to undergo a professional reorientation after migration, which in turn had an impact not only on the countries of origin from a macro-economic perspective, but also on the self-perception, sense of belonging and the career development of the migrants themselves. At the core of this finding lies the unclear definition of "highly skilled migrants", as well as "skills" and "qualifications".

3.2.2 The neglected gender dimension within studies on highly skilled migration

Within traditional migration research, highly skilled migrants have been assumed to be men. Since the beginnings of highly skilled migration research in the 1970s and 1980s, migrants were perceived as economic elites moving across the borders without any boundaries, or as professionals who were sent to another country because of their specific technical skills (Kofman et al. 2000b, p. 130; Salt 1988; Kofman 2009b). Women were excluded from these assumptions, since professional fields of work such as finance, information and communication technology or engineering, which have been the focus of the majority of research, were perceived as predominantly male domains. Only recently has the presence of women within highly skilled migration flows been recognised and included in the research agenda (see e.g. Kofman et al. 2000a; Kofman, Raghuram 2005; Kofman 2009b; Riaño 2012).

In the last decades, the way migration has been approached has changed somewhat. Throughout nearly all of the 20th century, the focus of migration researchers had been predominantly on migrant men (Zlotnik 2003). Women were rarely included in research. In those instances in which women were the subject of interest, they were usually ascribed the role of dependent followers of other family members (for the critique see Apitzsch 1994, p. 240; Villares-Varela 2014). This selective and "gender blind" approach is connected to the illusory perception of a gendered role division in relation to migration: while men have been seen as pioneers of migration and the "breadwinners" for their families, women have been imagined to be passive companions (Pessar, Mahner 2003, p. 814; Ruokonen-Engler 2012, p. 29). Nevertheless, despite missing statistics on migrating men and women in certain periods of time, historical migration research has revealed that women were always part of the migration flows. They moved not only as spouses and family members but also as independent migrant workers (Apitzsch 1994, p. 240; Zlotnik 2003; Sinke 2006). From the 1980s onwards, feminist scholars began to criticise the invisibility of women within migration studies (see e.g. Morokvasic 1984). They gave many examples showing that women were not passive players, but in many cases active pioneers of migration processes and "breadwinners" for their families. Furthermore, they pointed out the slowly rising numbers of women within global migration flows, which in some world regions even exceeded the number of migrant men (Zlotnik 2003). While some authors have described the changes as a "feminisation of migration" – a term which describes the rising impact of women within migration flows, as well as shifted gendered patterns, since more women have been migrating on their own (INSTRAW 2007, p. 1) – others have instead spoken of the "feminisation of the scientific interest in the issue of gender and migration", pointing towards the booming interest in feminised forms of migration within migration studies (Villares-Varela 2014).

These pioneer studies initiated an extensive body of research focussing on migrant women and acknowledging their presence within diverse migration flows and social locations. However, the focus on women has been criticised by later works. Recent feminist scholars have called for a shift in approach from "women" to "gender" (Pessar, Mahner 2003; Donato et al. 2006). They argued that the "addition" of migrant women to migration studies does not grasp the gendered structures, processes and hierarchical power relations in which migrant men and women are embedded and within which they develop their actions. Gender – understood as a process and "work", since the gender divisions and hierarchies are socially (re-)produced and therefore changeable – has been recognised as one of the principle dimensions to shape migration pathways, biographical decisions, as well as constraints and possibilities of action and self-development in the social locations in which the relevant individuals have been involved (see also Anthias 2001; Ruokonen-Engler 2012).

Despite the acknowledgment of the role of gender within migration studies, and despite the growing number of studies carried out in this field, research on highly skilled migration continued to ignore highly skilled migrant women and the gender perspective for more than two decades. The debate on gender within highly skilled migration started in early 2000 (see e.g. Kofman et al. 2000b; Kofman 2000). The focus of feminist researches had until that time concentrated predominantly on migrant women in precarious work relations, overlooking, beside some exceptions, other forms of migration such as the mobility of skilled migrant women (Kofman et al. 2000a, p. 131).

The small amount of attention paid to skilled migrant women and to the gender aspects within the body of research on highly skilled migration has been in contradiction to the rising number of highly educated women within migration flows (Dumont et al. 2007). Jean-Christophe Dumont (2007, p. 10), for example, pointed out that the proportion of highly skilled migrant men and women was almost equal in OECD countries. Furthermore, in some European countries the number of skilled migrant women even exceeded the number of skilled migrant men (ibid.). In some European countries the proportion of highly educated migrants comprised up to 45 per cent of all migrants, thereby in some cases exceeding the proportion of highly educated people within the respective countries (Dumont, Monso 2007, p. 133). The rising number of skilled migrant women in migration flows is connected to the growing participation of women in higher education across the European countries and worldwide. Within most European countries, the number of women enrolling for studies at university has significantly risen over the last decades and in most cases the number of women attaining tertiary education has exceeded the number of men (European Commission 2013). At the same time, there have been gendered patterns which shape the choices of field of studies by women and men: while women have dominated in the fields of social sciences, business and law, humanities and art, as well as health and welfare, men have outnumbered women in the fields of engineering, manufacturing and construction, science, mathematics and computing (Eurostat 2014b). These divisions along the professional fields have, among other factors, impacted on further work opportunities after migration. Despite the fact that after migration both migrant men and women often worked in positions which did not correspond to their qualifications and skills, women experienced unemployment and deskilling to a greater extent than migrant men (Dumont, Monso 2007, p. 138). Their settling in fields which are often connected with low qualified positions, such as the care sector, led them to disappear from the radar of most pieces of research on highly skilled migration.

The reason for the late recognition of gender within the studies on skilled migration can also be explained by the way in which highly skilled migration has been approached. While migration studies which focused on other less privileged forms of migration soon established themselves in social sciences and across disciplines (Apitzsch 1994, p. 240; Brettell 2008), studies on highly skilled migration were until recently almost exclusively the domain of geography, economics and politics (Favell et al. 2008, p. 4). This division along the relevant scientific discipline also influenced the choice of methodological tools: in contrast with the rising recognition of qualitatively oriented migration studies within the social sciences, highly skilled migration had been approached through quantitative macro-economic and macro-political lenses. Because of its focus and different research interests, focusing predominantly on the economic and political perspective of the country of origin and the country of migration, such designed studies left only little space for actual experiences of skilled migrant men and skilled migrant women. The agent-centred perspectives on migration processes of the highly skilled have only been encouraged recently, calling for a "human face" of skilled migration (Favell et al. 2008).

The perception of skilled migrants as economic and political actors led to the assumption that highly skilled migrants move solely within transnational corporations and other labour corridors. It had as a consequence that other forms of migration, such as family reunification, student mobility or migration because of asylum, all of which also involve skilled migrant men and women, have not received much scientific attention. Skilled women who have moved country not only through the known labour corridors but also for example as dependent family members, have thus stayed invisible in academic discussions (Kofman 2012, pp. 64–65; Riaño 2012, p. 25).

Eleonore Kofman and Parvati Raghuram (2005, pp. 150–151), who were among the first to initiate discussions on the gender dimension of highly skilled migration, explained the invisibility of skilled migrant women within migration studies by the socially construed definition of skills, inter alia. According to them, the definition of skills according to which the migrants have been divided into unskilled, low skilled, (semi-) skilled or highly skilled has been problematic. While some professions, such as engineering or consultancy, have been considered as highly skilled, others requiring a similar education level, such as teaching, have often been considered as semi-skilled or skilled. As Kofman and others pointed out, these divisions are not arbitrary, but shaped by the logic of the global economy, demands of local labour markets and national politics (Kofman, Raghuram 2005, pp. 150–151; Freitas et al. 2012, p. 2). Furthermore, there is also a gender logic behind the definitions of skills (Anthias 2001; Kofman, Raghuram 2005; Kofman 2012). Feminist scholars argued that the professions which have been commonly considered as highly skilled have been occupied predominantly by men. The individuals working within these professions can to a great extent profit from the liberalisation of these flows by selective migration politics. Other profession, such as social work, teaching or care and healthcare, which have been often categorised as semi-skilled despite the level of education required and acquired, have been dominated by women. Furthermore, these professions have often been regulated by more restrictive national welfare systems (Kofman 2012, p. 64). In line with the definition of skills and the demands of local and global labour markets, migration studies on highly skilled people concentrated predominantly on particular professions within the field of ICT, finance, health, science and technology. Professionals in the fields of art, humanities and social sciences were, with few exceptions, largely overlooked (Freitas et al. 2012, p. 2).

As some authors further argued, there is a gender logic behind migration politics and the processes of selection of highly skilled migrants (see e.g. Iredale 2005; Kofman, Raghuram 2005; Kofman 2009b, 2012; Jungwirth 2011). In these processes, the socially construed and gendered definition of skills is crucial. In most European countries, gaps in the labour market have been sought to be filled by selecting migrants trained in certain required occupations, such as ICT, engineering and science. Such bias led to heavily masculinised migration flows, as men have heavily dominated these occupations. While the recruitment of workers in such professions already began two or three decades ago, the shortages of labour in the health and care sector and in education were only recognised relatively recently, leading to the establishment of new migration flows (Kofman, Raghuram 2005; Kofman 2009a). However, skilled migrant men and women who did not succeed at getting through the selective filter based on particular skills had to search for different ways to migrate, very often following the low skilled or informal migration channels. For educated women from Central and Eastern Europe this has, for example, been the au pair visa, which for a long time was the only possibility to get residence and work permits in Germany for instance (Hess 2009). Similar trends can be seen in the participation of tertiary educated women in domestic labour (see e.g. Lutz 2008d; Williams, Gavanas 2008) or prostitution (Kofman et al. 2000a; Campani 2007).

If we take a closer look at the selective policies of some states, we uncover gender inequalities imposed on skilled migrants. Some countries, such as Germany and the UK, require a certain level of earnings for skilled professionals prior to their entry into the country. This affects not only younger people, who commonly have lower wages (Guth 2007), but women as well, whose earnings are in general lower than those of men[16] and who are concentrated in more regulated and less paid sectors, such as nursing, teaching and social work (Kofman 2009b, p. 5). A further important role is played by the regime on the recognition of education degrees and skills acquired in the country of origin (Rubin et al. 2008, p. 10).

Over the past years, there have been number of scientific works which recognised the necessity to include gender dimension within studies on highly skilled migration. Important work has been done on questioning gendered migration regimes of highly skilled migrants in diverse countries (see e.g. Iredale 2005; Kofman 2012; Kofman 2014). The body of research focused on the feminised forms of migration into some specific fields, such as healthcare (see e.g. Raghuram, Montiel 2003; Kingma 2006; Wismar et al. 2011), social work (see e.g. Bartley et al. 2012), science (see e.g. Guth 2007; Ackers, Gill 2008), or to the male dominated sectors, such as ICT or technology (see e.g. Raghuram 2008). Besides the studies that have concentrated on the migration of professionals into specific sectors, there is a slowly growing body of research on the migration of male and female university graduates and their upwards and downwards social mobility in the course of migration (see e.g. Trevena 2011, 2013; Liapi, Vouyioukas 2013). Moreover, authors such as Riaňo (2012) initiated the discussion on the role of family dynamics within highly skilled migration processes and on the strategies of migrant women, who move as spouses and family members, to develop their biographical and career pathways after migration. All of these studies raise important questions on the way in which highly skilled migrants have been perceived and represented within migration studies, and give important indications for redefining highly skilled migration and migration studies in general.

---

16   As Kofman (2009b, p. 5) notes, gender differences in wages vary on average by about 16 per cent.

3.2.3 Going beyond the dichotomy of "low skilled migration" and "highly skilled migration"

Within the traditional body of migration research, diverse models were introduced in order to explain complex migration processes. A large part of these conceptualisations were based on binary categories, such as legal versus illegal migration, forced and voluntary migration, internal and international, economic and non-economic migration, short term and long term migration, immigration and emigration, low-skilled and high-skilled migration (for details see e.g. King 2002; King, Skeldon 2010). These conceptualisations shaped the way migration was studied and perceived. Over the past decades, migration patterns changed and new migration pathways were established. These were the answer to geo-political changes, such as the collapse of the bipolar world order or the enlargement of the European Union eastwards, and tightening or releasing migration regimes accordingly for certain groups of people. In line with the various forms of migration, the motivation of migrants to move country and our knowledge about migration have been increasingly diversifying, Russell King argued that up-to-date "theorizing" about European and global migration has to be rethought. He called for multidisciplinary and comparative approaches in research, which would correspond to increasingly complex social processes in a globalising world (King 2002, 2012). King argued that the distinctions between the binary categories which lie at the core of the conceptualisation of migration are becoming increasingly blurred. For example, there is a fine line between "legal migration" and "illegal migration", since migrants can experience a shift from one category to the other in the course of their life as a consequence of changing migration policies, or they can experience the impact of both categories at the same time according to the social locations in which they participate (King 2002, pp. 93–94). Similarly, internal and international migration is interconnected. The divisions between these two categories are not fixed but they change over time. For example, geopolitical shifts at the beginning of the 1990s redrew the borders in many regions in Europe and overnight changed internal migration into international migration and vice versa. The enlargement of the European Union was also in many cases connected to shifted legal frameworks for migrants and their possibilities to move back and forth (King 2002, p. 92).

The conceptualisation of migration within Europe and world-wide in the binary categories of "highly skilled elites" and "unskilled migrants" has been criticised by some researchers (see e.g. Scott 2006; Weiß 2006; Verwiebe 2006; Favell et al. 2008; Favell, Recchi 2011; Freitas et al. 2012). They argued that the economic scope of the migration of highly skilled people often overlooks other migration movements which are not a priori motivated by economic factors. They showed that highly skilled migrants move for a variety of reasons in diverse migration corridors, which do not have to be connected to the global labour market.

Furthermore, Kofman and Raghuram argued that seeing migration as a bipolar stream of highly skilled and low skilled migration reinforces the perception of women as unskilled labourers, imprisoned in the household and care sectors in which migrant women can be found in large numbers. This perception has been reinforced by academic discussions which focused predominantly on migrant women in these sectors and overlooked migrant women in other fields and social locations (Kofman 2000, p. 54; Kofman, Raghuram 2005, p. 151). Kofman and Raghuram revealed that there is indeed a discrepancy between "highly skilled migration" and "highly skilled migrants", where the former is a category of migration path while the latter reflects the attributes attached to the individuals. These two categories do not necessarily overlap, as many skilled migrants join low skilled or other migration corridors in order to enter a host country and its labour market (ibid.).

Indeed, we need to rethink the gap between highly skilled migration and low skilled migration to clarify the concept of highly skilled migration and to deconstruct a picture of highly skilled migrants traditionally being perceived as elites, disconnected from local communities and moving freely above national borders and policies. In their book "The Human Face of Global Mobility", Thomas Smith and Adrian Favell showed that the flows of educated and highly skilled people inevitably contain students, nurses, the middle classes, clerical employees, adventurous youths, pensioners etc. (Favell et al. 2008, pp. 1–2; Smith, Favell 2008). Many of those cannot be declared as privileged or elites, as they very often face different kinds of obstacles, not being released from the complex structures of social hierarchies specific to particular social and local contexts which are firmly embedded in national frameworks (Favell 2003).

Moreover, the authors argued that the binary division of migration processes based on education and skills is not sufficient for understanding the contemporary migration pathways in Europe, which differ in many aspects from other world regions – mainly because of the legal and institutional frameworks (Scott 2006; Verwiebe 2008a; Favell, Recchi 2011). Roland Verwiebe argued that migration within the European Union consists increasingly of people from a range of social classes possessing a wide variety of education levels and skills (Verwiebe 2008a, p. 6). Moreover, he stated that European migration is increasingly a middle-class phenomenon. According to him, European global cities attract not only those who at the top and bottom of the social ladder, but also many people who are in the middle of the social stratum and who have a university degree. However, they may often experience downward social mobility as a result of social and structural constraints imposed on them in the country of migration (ibid.).

In order to explain the experiences of people who do not necessarily belong to the categories of "highly skilled elites" and "low skilled migrants", David Conradson and Alan Latham introduced the term "middling transnationals" (Conradson, Latham 2005, p. 229). They argued that despite the growing number of studies on transnational migration processes, the migration of well-educated, predominantly middle class individuals has been the subject of only few research papers. This, so the authors, is in contradiction to the growing importance of these migration flows in contemporary Europe and world-wide.

3.2.4 Redefining "highly skilled migrants" and "highly skilled migration"

According to an OECD study, "highly skilled refers to persons possessing tertiary-level qualifications" (OECD 2008, p. 69). However, some authors prefer to include not only the level of education, but also skills and occupation in the definition. According to Khalid Koser and John Salt (Koser, Salt 1997, p. 287), "[b]eing a graduate is not in itself sufficient to be regarded as highly skilled in labour market terms, since many graduates are not employed in jobs requiring high-level expertise. Conversely, many people whose work is deemed to be highly skilled are not graduates. Skills can be acquired through experience rather than by education or training, and there is a strong case for distinguishing between skills-based and qualifications-based procedures for recognising a migrant's professional expertise." Salt identified twelve occupational groups of highly skilled migrants: corporate transferees; technicians; professionals; project specialists; consultant specialists; private career development and training movers; the clergy and missionaries; entertainers, sportspeople and artists; business people and the independently wealthy; academics, including researchers and students; military personnel; and lastly spouses and children (Salt 1997; quoted in Koser, Salt 1997, p. 288). Besides education, skills and occupation, other authors have grouped highly skilled migration according to a time and spatial dimension. William T.S. Gould, for example, distinguished between circulatory and permanent migration and between moves between and within the world regions (Gould 1988, p. 381). The definition of highly skilled migrants differs across different fields of studies and is shaped by the perspective on migration processes in general. It is to a great extent also influenced by the definition of skills, which is gendered and socially construed (Freitas et al. 2012, p. 2).

The definition of highly skilled migrants based on occupation as outlined by Salt provides a possibility of comparing professionals in diverse occupational fields. Moreover, it includes spouses and children, who for a long time have been neglected within studies on highly skilled migration (Riaño 2012).

Nevertheless, it overlooks other professions which are increasingly becoming part of migration flows, such as health personnel, teachers or workers in social spheres. The definition of "highly skilled migrants" as outlined above does not make it possible to analyse the different migration pathways and the location of highly skilled migrants in less expected occupations. It does not give any leeway to analyse diverse biographical and career paths, or the strategies of highly educated people to use their own resources in overcoming structural barriers in the course of migration.

For these reasons, I prefer to define "highly skilled migrants" in this study as people who have completed tertiary level education prior to migration. This definition enables one to focus on highly skilled migrants in diverse educational and career fields. Furthermore, it also encompasses those who are either continuing their studies in another country or working within fields which are generally assumed to be "less qualified" and mismatched to the actual qualifications of migrant women and men. Moreover, such a wide definition enables one to include in the analysis people who initially did not move country for work reasons, but because of family, partnership, asylum or adventure. At the same time I am aware that the focus on tertiary educated people disregards migrants who do not possess a university degree or who acquired their diplomas in other countries. An analysis of their biographies would surely deliver important insights into the various biographical and career trajectories after migration, which in many instances might be quite different to tertiary educated individuals. These other forms of migration, notwithstanding that they would surely deserve the attention of researchers, shall with only few exceptions nevertheless remain outside the scope of this study.

The definition of "highly skilled migrants" according to their level of education puts the up-to-date theorising of highly skilled migration into question. Perceiving highly skilled migrants not only as those moving in upper-class transnational spaces but also as those belonging to different classes, questions the division on "low skilled migration" and "highly skilled migration" which in scholarly discussions has often been construed according to the distinctive migration corridors and professions after migration. A perception of "highly skilled migration" which is not based on socially construed definitions of skills and classifications of migration corridors but on the migrants' individual attributes, enables a comparison to be made of different paths of skilled migrants through diverse social locations spanning across the borders of national states, "balancing" on the thin line between upward and downward social mobility. My approach therefore builds on the relatively scarce number of studies which focus on highly educated migration within Europe, a field which is increasingly important within the sphere of migration flows, but at the same time surprisingly under researched.

3.3 An overview of recent studies on highly skilled migration pathways to and within Europe

Michael P. Smith and Adrian Favell (2008) were among the first to initiate discussions on the various different facets of highly skilled migration from an agent-centred perspective. They outlined a research agenda which went beyond the dichotomy of low skilled and highly skilled migration and which dealt with other less known but increasingly important migration processes and experiences. In the following section I will give an overview of the recent studies connected with this research agenda which concerned, from different perspectives, the pathways of highly educated people to and within Europe. Smith and Favell pointed out diverse factors which shape these pathways, including migration policies, labour market conditions and agency.

First I will examine studies which focused on the pathways of highly skilled migrants from a macro perspective, studying the impact of policy and the mechanisms of labour market inclusion and exclusion. I shall start with the statistical evidence concerning the usability of a university education after migration and continue by introducing studies which analysed the legal and institutional frameworks affecting migrants' possible pathways. The studies discussed here revealed that highly educated migrant men and women were particularly affected by deskilling, i.e. working in a job position which was below their actual qualifications and professional skills. In order to explain the unequal social pathways of migrants, these studies highlighted the impact of gendered migration policies, the recognition of qualifications, the inclusion and exclusion mechanisms prevalent in the labour market as well as the role of social discourse in respect of gender and ethnicity. Subsequently, I will turn my attention to studies which focused on migration and the various passages to the professional life from an agent-centred perspective and I will discuss the typologies of these pathways as detailed by authors. Since downward social mobility after migration has been described as a frequent phenomenon experienced by university graduates after migration, I will pay particular attention in the next section to the migrants' experiences and strategies for coping with deskilling and contradictory class mobility. Finally, before outlining the research desideratum, the role of family and social networks in studies on highly skilled migration will be highlighted.

The studies included in this overview differ by national frameworks and sampling strategies. They concerned not only migration to Germany, which is the main focus of this empirical study, but also migration to other European countries, such as Great Britain, Denmark, Italy and Switzerland. Despite the different migration policies in respective countries which had an impact on migrant men and women, they all had in common the "release" of migration movements within and from the EU and ongoing tightening policies concerning non-EU migrants. The interviewees whose stories were collected for the respective studies had a different legal status, education, gender, migration history and class background, which in turn enabled comparisons of different migration pathways to be made. At the same time, the different sampling strategies influenced the results of the studies. Therefore, a description of the sample and methodology will also be provided when presenting the studies and their results. Furthermore, the overview will also mention studies which did not explicitly examine highly skilled migrants but which were nevertheless part of the sample and whose experiences were therefore taken into account.

3.3.1 Education – the ticket to work? Statistical evidence.

The migration of tertiary educated people within and to Europe only became the subject of quantitative analysis in last decade. Until recently, information on the person's level of education and gender was missing from most statistics on migration. Besides investigating the role of the person's educational level in migration processes, some studies focused on how the educational level of migrants matched their labour market positioning.

The link between the level of education of migrants and the relevant passage through the labour market was investigated by the OECD study "Matching Educational Background and Employment: A Challenge for Immigrants in Host Countries" (Dumont, Monso 2007). The study, which was based on a large body of statistical data collected by national and international surveys in OECD countries, revealed that migrants tend to be overrepresented at the lowest and at the highest levels of education, compared with the native populations of particular countries. In 16 out of 21 European countries examined, the proportion of tertiary educated migrants exceeded the proportion of native people with the same level of education. In some countries, such as Ireland, the United Kingdom, Norway and Denmark, the proportion of highly educated people in the migrant population was more than 34 per cent. However, the employment rate, with the exception of certain southern European countries, Hungary and Luxembourg, was much lower for the migrant population and, according to the authors of the study, this gap between native workers and immigrants was still increasing in nearly all EU countries (Dumont, Monso 2007, p. 134). Furthermore, the study showed that migrants were much more likely to be overqualified for the occupation they performed in the country of destination, taking into account their skills and education. This was particularly true for migrant women. A closer look at the data uncovered great discrepancies concerning female employment in some European countries: for example, 27 per cent of migrant women in Italy were working in jobs they were overqualified for, in comparison to 20 per cent of migrant men and 7 per cent of native women. Similar trends occurred in many other countries as well, although the values differed somewhat (Dumont, Monso 2007, p. 139).The authors argued that there was a "racial" and ethnic context that went along with gender. Foreign women born outside of the OECD countries experienced greater de-skilling and de-qualification than foreign women migrating within the OECD countries (see also Kofman 2009a, p. 6). Thus, nationality, ethnicity and skin colour also had their share in determining which occupations migrant women and men had access to or not (see also Kofman 2009a, p. 1).

In Germany, data from the 2007 micro census revealed that migrants who had finished their university education abroad suffered from unemployment twice as much as those who had acquired their university degree in Germany (Kontos, Voswinkel 2010, p. 212). Moreover, more than half of all highly skilled migrants with foreign university degrees residing in Germany worked in less qualified positions in relation to their qualifications and skills (Bundesministerium für Arbeit und Soziales 2009, p. 3, quoted by Kontos, Voswinkel 2010, p. 212). Similar findings were reported in other European countries (for Denmark and Italy see e.g. Nielsen 2011; Brandi 2001).

The authors explained the over-qualification of migrants by a combination of a variety of factors, such as restrictive migration policies, limited access to the labour market, insufficient recognition of educational degrees acquired abroad and, lastly, discrimination in the labour market. In the next chapter I will introduce studies which analyse the legal and institutional frameworks in more detail and examine the mechanisms which affect men and women in different ways, as well as looking at different class and ethnic background as influencing factors.

3.3.2 Legal and institutional frameworks affecting highly skilled migrants: studying the interplay of class, gender and ethnicity

There has been a growing body of research focussing on migration policies which affect migrant men and women in different ways (Kofman 2000, 2009a, 2014; Iredale 2005). Eleonore Kofman (2014), for instance, argued that selective migration politics shape the possibilities of migrants to enter the country and to position themselves within the local labour market. She showed that the mechanisms of migration policies according to which migrants are selected were increasingly directed towards people educated in particular professions which satisfy the country's particular economic need at that time. These were, so the author, predominantly the professions centred on the so-called knowledge economy. Professionals educated in other spheres were made to migrate in different, less privileged ways.

Yvonne Riaño showed the effect of migration policies from the perspective of migrants themselves. She studied the migration processes and professional positioning of highly skilled migrant women in Switzerland (Riaño 2012). Her investigation was based on biographical narrative interviews with 57 tertiary educated women who came from non-EU countries and moved to Switzerland as "marriage migrants" or asylum seekers. The author found that about half of the women were at the time of the interview either unemployed or working below the level of their skills and qualifications. Although the other half of the women worked in positions which corresponded to their education and skill level, they nonetheless experienced their work as insecure and irregular, since they worked on a part-time basis or in unstable conditions as self-employed persons. Thus, only about 12 per cent worked in more secure skilled positions on the labour market (Riaño 2012, p. 32). Riaño found that the main difference between women with regard to their professional positioning was not their level of education and range of professional skills acquired elsewhere, but rather the education and practical work experience gained in Switzerland. Women who completed their university degrees in Switzerland were less disadvantaged than women who had studied and worked abroad. These results pointed out the difficulties women experienced when trying to transfer their knowledge and experiences across the border. They revealed the situational character of "cultural capital" – bound in many cases to the country in which it was acquired (Riaño 2012, p. 32). As Riaño argued, the positioning of women on Swiss labour market was shaped by an interplay of diverse factors, including official policies, social practices, as well as prevailing ideas about gender and ethnicity (Riaño 2012, p. 36). In many regards the Swiss migration policies disadvantaged highly skilled migrants, especially those from non-EU countries. In practice, the only option of legally moving to Switzerland was by means of a highly skilled migration permit, family reunion or asylum. Whereas EU citizens could apply for permanent residency after five years in Switzerland, non-EU nationals had to wait ten years for it. This fact had an impact on labour market participation, since most employers preferred workers with a permanent residency status. People who come as "marriage migrants" were also confronted with this problem, since they had to obtain an annual permit which was dependent on their spouse. In addition, Swiss and EU nationals enjoyed priority rights to labour market positions over non-EU citizens. Their qualifications were also more easily recognised due to existing contracts concerning the mutual recognition of diplomas within EU countries (Riaño 2012, p. 36). Moreover, the women were confronted with biased perceptions of employers and representatives of institutions in relation to gender and ethnicity. Migrant women often experienced a devaluation of their skills and qualifications, since they were imagined by employers to be less capable then people from Switzerland or EU countries.

Robyn Iredale (2005) focused on processes concerning the selection of highly skilled migrants in different countries and on the recognition of university degrees acquired abroad. She argued that migration policies as well as difficult mechanisms of evaluating and recognising diplomas from abroad prevented many migrant men and women from using their qualifications and continuing their profession in the country of migration. Iredale showed that the country of origin of migrants was crucial for the successful or unsuccessful recognition of educational and professional certificates. While the mutual recognition had been embedded in the EU Directive on the recognition of professional qualifications, thus facilitating the move by EU nationals to other EU countries[17], the recognition of the university degrees of migrants from outside the EU was regulated by the respective country (Iredale 2005, p. 160). There were different methods of diploma recognition, each country applying a different strategy: methods ranged from recognition by the national authority based on mutual recognition agreements, recognition by the relevant occupational group, a probationary or trial period of supervised work, or competency tests and assessments. Each of these procedures, according to Iredale (2005, pp. 162–163), may to a greater or lesser extent be "contaminated" by gender and/or ethnicity bias and affect the passage to the labour market of migrant women and men in different ways.

The situation involving highly skilled migrants living in Germany – characterised by a high unemployment rate and over-qualification – was the starting point for research conducted by Maria Kontos and Stephan Voswinkel (2010). Taking a different research approach, the authors studied the factors which lead to the exclusion and experiences of de-qualification of highly skilled migrant men and women on the German labour market. Kontos and Voswinkel turned their attention to mechanisms of labour market inclusion and exclusion from an institutional point of view. They conducted interviews with members of educational and non-profit organisations, as well as with recruitment personnel in diverse companies. Their aim was to reveal the process by which the highly skilled workers were recruited and which possi-

---

17 The agreement on the mutual recognition of professional skills and university degrees among EU countries came into force in 2005 and was amended in 2013 (Directive 2005/36/EC 2005; Directive 2013/55/EU). The aim was to facilitate the process of recognition and make it accessible for a wider migrant population living in the EU. The procedures and the decision concerning partial or full recognition of university degrees and further qualifications have, however, been regulated differently in respective countries. Improving the recognition of skills also became an important political agenda in some European countries. The background to policy making on facilitating the recognition procedures was the argument that in order to retain development and prosperity, countries need highly qualified workers. In Germany, for example, one of the arguments for eased legislation concerning the recognition of foreign university degrees was the integration of highly qualified migrants into the labour market who already live in the country but who perform low qualified jobs (Bundesministerium für Arbeit und Soziales 2009, p. 2).

ble manifest or latent exclusion mechanisms highly skilled migrants experienced. Kontos and Voswinkel argued that even though a university degree presented an important resource for highly skilled migrants, it did not necessarily guarantee them access to a position on the labour market which would correspond to their educational level (Kontos, Voswinkel 2010, p. 213). The analysis of interviews revealed that highly skilled migrants were often disadvantaged in the process of recruitment, whereby the disadvantages occurred rather latently and unintentionally. The authors saw the reason for the exclusion of highly skilled migrants in the process of recruitment in the stereotypical ideas concerning the different cultural and social backgrounds, as well as in the great impact of the linear and clearly structured professional careers of applicants, which did not evidence any ruptures, discontinuities or atypical developments. The authors pointed out that these expectations for professional careers had an impact on highly skilled migrants, who often experienced discrepancies in their biographies due to phases of de-qualification or unemployment. As Kontos and Voswinkel concluded, the recognition of foreign university degrees played an important role in the inclusion of highly skilled migrants on the labour market. Nevertheless, it would not entirely solve the problem of the de-qualification of migrants.

Studies on the role of education of highly skilled migrants in joining the labour market revealed a shaky transfer of knowledge and skills across the border. They showed that a high level of education could be an important resource in many cases, but the qualification per se was not sufficient when entering the local labour market or moving from one position to another. Eased procedures concerning the recognition of university diplomas certainly opened up new possibilities for migrants to position themselves within society and on the labour market after migration. Nevertheless, the studies also showed that despite full recognition and valuation of foreign university degrees, there were ongoing institutional and structural inequalities concerning gender, the country of origin, ethnicity or skin colour, which continued to shape the experiences of migrants.

3.3.3   An agent-centred approach to pathways to the labour market

Besides studies which have focused on the evaluation of migration policies and labour market exclusion and inclusion mechanisms, there have been other studies which analysed the pathways of highly educated migrants to the labour market from an agent-centred perspective. In this chapter I will introduce two works which are of particular interest for the purposes of this paper. The first study was conducted by Anika Liversage and focused on the pathways taken by highly qualified migrants when joining the Danish labour market. The second one, which was set up by the research group of the "cultural capital during migration" project, focused on highly skilled migrants joining the German labour market. I will at first introduce both studies and then discuss their results.

Anika Liversage studied the pathways to the professional life of highly qualified women and men moving to Denmark (Liversage 2009b, 2009a). Her sample included people who were "Eastern European" university educated in diverse fields of study who migrated to Denmark for reasons other than a priori work. Nevertheless, to find a job in their profession after migration was the initial goal of all of these migrants. In order to reveal the possibilities of and strategies for entering working life in Denmark, Liversage conducted 19 biographical narrative interviews with migrants. Most of them came as spouses of Danish citizens or as asylum seekers. More than half of all interviewees were working in highly skilled positions, while the others were either unemployed or working in lower qualified areas. Liversage used the concept of "vital conjunctures" as an analytical framework as elaborated by Jennifer Johnson-Hanks (2002; Liversage 2009b). According to Johnson-Hanks (2002, p. 871), "[t]he analytic concept of the vital conjuncture refers to a socially structured zone of possibility that emerges around specific periods of potential transformation in a life or lives. It is a temporary configuration of possible change, a duration of uncertainty and potential." Migration and the challenge of using one's education and skills acquired in another country, could so Liversage (2002, p. 120) be seen as a vital conjuncture – as a critical life phase in which different future perspectives and identities are challenged. Furthermore, she made use of the concepts of "life time" and "historical time" (Liversage 2009a). Liversage investigated the intersections of these two dimensions of temporality, where the former concerned the course of one's life and the latter involved global and local events and shifts of social structures and institutions over a longer period of time.

On the basis of biographical narrations Liversage coined a typology of possible ways of entering the professional life. She labelled them "path of re-entry", "path of ascent", "path of re-education", "path of re-migration", and finally "path of marginalisation" (Liversage 2009a, p. 209). The first method of joining the labour market – the "path of re-entry" – included those migrants who after a period of time were able to re-enter with the profession they had carried out prior to migration and use their initial qualifications. Liversage observed that those who succeeded in making the connection after migration were educated in fields which were easily transferable across borders and in demand in Denmark, namely natural and life sciences. Therefore, doctors, dentists, ICT specialists and engineers in the sample were able to profit from the labour market situation and start to practise their profession at some point in time after migration (Liversage 2009b, p. 127). They experienced fewer obstacles in entering the labour market and getting their qualifications and skills recognised. The others, however, were trapped in vital conjuncture – the period of uncertainty – for a longer time before finding the connection to their profession. As Liversage showed, migrants often experienced difficulties in entering the workforce in Denmark, which in turn would serve as starting point for their further career development. To find the first job was demanding, since employers expected them to provide evidence of local work experience in Denmark, which they did not have (Liversage 2009b, p. 128). The lacking local work experience coupled in some cases with a lack of recognition of their qualifications led to professional closure and (temporary) unemployment. Female stories revealed the difficulties experienced in respect of unemployment and "being just a housewife" (Liversage 2009b, p. 131). They felt that their qualifications and newly acquired skills, such as language proficiency, would lose its worth when not practised (ibid.). In order to challenge the future perspectives of unemployment, some people made efforts to rework initial plans to enter one's field of qualification, to change future perspectives and to re-orientate themselves. As the author summarises: „[i]n some cases this reorientation enabled them to integrate as skilled people employed in good and meaningful work in the higher parts of the labour market. They did so in three different ways: through making use of the immigrant identity that they acquired during the immigration process; through acquiring a new professional identity by re-educating themselves either in their old field or in new ones; or through returning to their home country and thus returning to their old, pre-migratory identities." (Liversage 2009b, pp. 131–132).

One possibility of reorientation was to enter a low skilled position and work one's way up. Liversage labelled this type of entry to the labour market as the "path of ascent" (Liversage 2009a, pp. 212–214). Some interviewees made use of their migration experiences and started to work as teachers or counsellors, nevertheless often in less qualified positions than their initial qualifications (Liversage 2009b, p. 132). In some cases, however, were able to reach highly skilled positions while following this path. Liversage gave an example of a Czech linguist who re-qualified as an "immigrant teacher" and was shortly afterwards employed in a school, first as an unskilled assistant and later on as a teacher and manager. Liversage argued that this path was unpredictable and unplanned but nevertheless led to a highly qualified position.

Another possibility of gaining access to a qualified position was additional education in the country of destination. Liversage called this method the "path of re-education". This was the case with a Croatian lawyer who had to complete her studies in Denmark again since her initial university degree from Croatia was not recognised. She experienced her new studies as a way of overcoming professional closure and reaching her goal of working in her field of expertise (Liversage 2009b, p. 133). The author argued that the age of interviewees was crucial for considering the risks and opportunities of undertaking a renewed course of studies. Moreover, family constellations and their financial situation were also important (Liversage 2009a, p. 216).

The next strategy of reorientation is the "path of re-migration" - the return to the country of origin and continuing the career commenced there prior migration. This strategy was used by migrants who did not succeed at making a connection to the Danish labour market, felt that they were losing their resources over time and fell into a personal crisis as a result of their limited opportunities for development. Besides starting a qualified job again and fulfilling their goals, the return also meant new family arrangements, especially when the family members were located in and had moved to different countries (Liversage 2009b, pp. 133–134).

Nevertheless, reorientation was not an option for all migrants, since starting new studies, or returning to the country of origin was demanding or unimaginable for some people who found themselves in different life situations. After an extended period of searching for a job in a qualified position which would correspond to their professional experience and qualifications, the only option and future prospect was taking on low skilled work (Liversage 2009b, pp. 134–135). Liversage called this "the path of marginalisation" (Liversage 2009a, pp. 219–221). As she concluded, the possibility of using one's own resources while entering the professional life depended on changing social structures in which the women were embedded, as well as on the type of university degree and its transferability to other nation-states. Furthermore, her study revealed the role of gender and family arrangements in negotiating access to the labour market.

The next study that concentrated on the pathways taken by highly qualified migrants in accessing the labour market was the international research project "Cultural Capital during Migration. On the Importance of Educational Qualifications and Status Passages into the Labor Market" (Nohl et al. 2006; Nohl et al. 2010b; Nohl et al. 2014). The research focused diverse groups of people. They differed by educational level, their field of studies, migration status, and the place in which their studies had been achieved. The authors compared not only the experiences of those who had studied abroad and moved to another country after finishing their studies, but also the narratives of people belonging to the so-called second generation – the children of migrants who live in the country to which at some point in their life their parents moved to and settled in. The study was based on the analysis of biographical interviews, expert interviews and on the analysis of statistics and legal frameworks. The research was conducted in four countries – Germany, Canada, Turkey, and the United Kingdom – in order to enable cross-national comparisons.

Of particular interest for the purposes of this paper was the analysis of status passages of highly qualified migrants into the German labour market (Nohl et al. 2010a; Thomsen 2009). The researchers based their study on biographical interviews with highly qualified migrants who moved to Germany at some time after graduation. At the core of the analysis was the concept of "cultural capital" – a term introduced by Bourdieu which refers to the interplay of individuals' abilities, knowledge, language, preferences as well as diplomas and certificates acquired – and the possibilities of and barriers to recognition in the course of the migration (Nohl et al. 2006, p. 6; Thomsen 2009, p. 12). The focus of the research was thus not only on the recognition of diplomas, but also on the possibilities and strategies of migrant men and women to utilize their knowledge and the resources acquired prior to migration in the country to which they moved. The analysis of biographical interviews revealed that people's biographical orientation and the context of migration had an impact on labour market inclusion. The empirical evidence showed that highly skilled migrants move country not only because of better chances on the labour market but for diverse reasons, including partnership, socio-economic amelioration, qualifications, asylum seeking or exploration (Nohl et al. 2010a, p. 71). The research revealed that the utilization of cultural capital, such as the recognition and valuation of university degrees, was important but in many cases not the main goal of migrants. Researchers explained this finding by different migration motives and the varying biographical orientation of interviewees (Nohl et al. 2010a, pp. 81–82).

In their study of labour market inclusion, the authors made use of the concept of multidimensional status passages (Schittenhelm 2005). This concept enabled one to study the interplay of individuals' decisions and actions on the one hand and structural conditions on the other hand. In addition, the perception of the passage from one social position to another as being a linear and "prescribed" process from education to relevant profession was questioned. The concept of multidimensional status passages also enabled the authors to study ruptures, discontinuities and unintended developments (Nohl et al. 2014, p. 51). The acknowledgement of multidimensional status passages – i.e. the intertwinement of status passages in different areas of life, such as gaining a work permit after marriage – enabled the researches to include other dimensions into their analysis of status passages to the labour market as well, such as family status, intergenerational transmission, family background and wider social networks, as well as the role of gender and ethnicity (Nohl et al. 2006). Three main dimensions of status passage were elaborated and analysed: the dimension of migration; the professional career dimension; and thirdly the dimension of social relationships. The dimension of migration contained both individual motives and decisions, along with legal and institutional contexts. The professional career dimension encompassed the person's educational and professional pathway, as well as structural conditions for labour market inclusion and exclusion. Lastly, the dimension of social relationships contained family and partnership relations and further social networks (Thomsen 2009, pp. 103–104). These three dimensions and their interplay were crucial for the identification of five typical phases of status passage into the labour market: the pre-migration phase; transition phase; initial phase; phase of establishment; and lastly the phase of reorientation (Thomsen 2009, p. 104; see also Nohl et al. 2014, p. 69; Nohl et al. 2010a, pp. 71–73). The pre-migration phase was the phase in which the ideas and decisions to migrate developed. The transition phase described the move from the country of origin to the county of destination. It encompassed departure, travel, arrival into the country of destination as well as the time in which the initial legal barriers were being overcome. The length of this phase depended on biographical orientation and migration status (Thomsen 2009, p. 114). After the initial phase – the period of time during which the migrants actively started to establish their position and possibly entered the labour market – followed the phase of establishment, in which the motives for staying or returning developed. The last possible phase was the phase of reorientation, in which the individual's professional and biographical options were re-evaluated.

Besides the typical phases of status passage, the authors introduced typical schemes of migrant experiences of joining the labour market. They paid particular attention to the way in which cultural capital was utilized or devalued in the migration process. The authors identified six types of passage in which the dimensions of experience, biographical orientation and phase of status passage were intertwined. The first type encompasses migrants who were unable to use their university degrees and qualifications because of their unclear legal status on their passage to the labour market. Instead, the "ascribed" attributes, such as gender or country of origin, became their main asset for entering the professional life. Migrants often found employment in the gendered and ethnicised spheres of the labour market, such as the care or cleaning sectors. Some of them managed to use their language skills and knowledge of the country of origin as translators and advisers. The second type concerns migrants who in contradiction to the first type enjoyed legal rights but were not successful in utilizing the cultural capital acquired prior to migration. Not until they had re-qualified and acquired new skills and knowledge, often in non-academic fields, did they succeed in Germany. In these instances the authors highlighted the interplay of family and social networks in developing the migrants' motives for staying in Germany, resulting in them taking jobs which were beneath the level of their initial qualifications. The third type, which the authors refer to as "precarious balances between biographical orientations and utilization of cultural capital restricted to the country of origin", involves a specific way of using cultural capital, which was connected to the country or region of origin. The migrants included in this group moved to Germany for family or partnership reasons. In order to overcome initial legal barriers and counteract their exclusion from the labour market due to their foreign university degrees, they searched for opportunities in fields connected to their qualifications and country of origin, be it offering consulting services to companies expanding abroad or providing fiscal law expertise for the particular country or region. Starting from these positions, they later extended their possibilities by obtaining further qualifications or specialisations. Types 4 and 5 describe the passages of migrants who, due largely to their family status, enjoyed full access to the labour market, yet in order to use their university degrees they had to go through the "transition phase" – an institutionalised process based on professional law – which signified an initial downgrading to a lower position and subsequent full recognition of their profession. These two types encompass in particular migrants trained in the health sector. The last type involves those cases in which the utilization of university degrees, further qualification and skills acquired abroad did not present any barriers on the German labour market. The authors called this transnational cultural capital, i.e. a form of capital which can be translated and further developed in other national and social contexts (Nohl et al. 2007, pp. 184–190, 2010a).

The two typologies presented here as put forward by Anika Liversage and the "cultural capital in migration" research group differ in terms of sampling strategy and theoretical background by means of which the passages of migrants to the labour market were approached. In contradiction to Liversage who was concerned with "Eastern European migrants" coming as "marriage migrants" or asylum seekers, the study of "cultural capital in migration" focused on migrants from all around the world coming to Germany through different migration corridors. The other difference was the field of studies of interviewees included in the sample. While the former study included a wide variety of university degrees, the latter study focused predominantly on migrants in the fields of economy, engineering, technology and health services – i.e. the professions in demand in Germany. These differences in sampling – especially taking into account the fields of study and different legal frameworks of respective migrant groups – could explain why unemployment and re-orientation was such a central biographical topic for interviewees in Liversage's sample but only a marginal phase in the other project. Liversage's study revealed that the pathways of highly skilled migrants to the professional life were more often than not indirect, followed by repeated periods of unemployment or work in a low skilled sector. She showed that entry to the labour market did not necessarily result in the migrants feeling established, but instead gave rise to a phase of uncertainty, which Liversage called "vital conjunctures", which would possibly continue until professional goals, such as working in a qualified position again after a period of unemployment or work in the low skilled sector, were fulfilled. Despite the differences between these two projects, there were also features which appeared in both studies. Firstly, both studies showed that the way in which cultural capital could be utilized or not after migration was shaped by migrants' biographical orientation, legal status, and mechanisms of inclusion in or exclusion from the labour market, as well as social networks and the gender dimension. Secondly, both studies pointed out the role of one's ethnic and national background, which both enlarged migrants' chances on the labour market when the language and knowledge connected to the country of origin could be used as resource, and acted as a restraint in terms of ethnic and national stereotypes.

Both studies focused on the labour market participation of migrant men and women after migration. The focus on this particular phase of migrants' life overshadowed other possibly important events and experiences which may have contributed to understanding the positioning of skilled migrants, such as the structure of options in the country of origin and the transnational dimension of migration processes.

3.3.4 Experiences and coping strategies for deskilling and contradictory class mobility

A further body of research focused on the experiences of highly skilled migrants with de-skilling – i.e. working in positions which were below the actual education and professional experience of migrants prior to migration. I will at first introduce a study by Paulina Trevena, who investigated the participation of university educated Polish migrants in London. Afterwards I will turn my attention to studies focusing on the experiences of migrant women in the care and domestic sector. A variety of studies point to the fact that the care and domestic sector became the most important working sphere for migrant women in most European countries (see e.g. Apitzsch 2010a; Kontos 2009a; Kofman et al. 2000b). University educated migrant women were not the exception – they were also present in these working spheres. Studies carried out by Maria Kontos (2009b), Juliane Karakayali (2010a), Yvonne Riaño (2012) and Francesca Vianello (2014), which are discussed in this section, focused on the experiences of migrant women with downward social mobility. Not all of the studies discussed here explicitly concern highly educated migrants. Nevertheless, university graduates were part of the samples and their experiences were voiced. The results of these studies give some indications as to the coping strategies of men and women in bettering their situation, changing their social position and enlarging their sphere of possibilities in the course of migration.

Paulina Trevena's research was directed towards the migration of highly educated Polish migrants living and working in London (Trevena 2011, 2013). She observed that a large part of highly educated young people moving to the United Kingdom worked in low-qualified positions. Her aim was to describe and explain the processes leading to such deskilling in the course of migration. She studied the impact of migrants' positioning in low-qualified jobs on their self-perception and values. Moreover, her aim was to reveal eventual changes of migrants' positioning within the labour market over time and the factors in charge. Trevena built her analysis on the basis of ethnographic observations and semi-structured in-depth interviews with Polish university graduates who were between 25 and 35 years old, single and without dependants. The research was conducted in two phases. The first round of interviews was conducted in 2004 with Polish migrants who arrived before the EU enlargement. The second round, which was conducted four years later, enabled Trevana not only to observe possible changes in migrants' positioning, but also to include into the analysis those who came after the enlargement. All migrants whom Trevena interviewed worked for at least one year in low-skilled jobs in catering, construction, or the domestic sector. Over the course of time some of them moved on to "white collar" jobs, but only a few of them worked in positions that matched their actual qualifications (Trevena 2013, pp. 170–171).

In order to explain the gravitation of university educated Polish migrants towards low-skilled jobs in Great Britain, Trevena argued that the intersection of complex processes on macro, meso and micro levels needed to be taken into consideration. The author showed that structural conditions in both the country of origin and in the country of destination have a crucial impact on migration and the decision to take up jobs which do not match migrants' qualifications and work experience. She explained that the motive to move was connected on the one hand to the processes of re-structuring in Poland in the course of political and economic changes, which were followed by high unemployment rates, the boom of the English language as a lingua franca and an overall increase in graduates at Polish universities since 1989. The difficulties in finding a job and establishing one's position in the course of the transformation of society also affected university graduates, for whom migration was a possibility of learning a language, earning some money or trying to live on their own in another country (Trevena 2013, pp. 172–174). On the other hand, Great Britain experienced economic boom and need of migrant labour. It was generally known among migrants, so Trevena, that finding work in London was relative easy. Before the accession of Poland to the EU in 2004, Polish migrants were exposed to a variety of institutional barriers, such as obtaining a work permit or getting their educational degrees and skills recognised, which in turn led most of the newcomers to the informal sector. Migrants who arrived after the accession experienced more possibilities for migrating and entering the labour market, since they did not need to legalise their status or obtain a work permit. Nevertheless, low skilled jobs were consistently the starting point for the majority of Polish university graduates coming to London. The gravitation of highly educated Polish migrants towards the low-skilled job sector even after accession can partly be explained by the lack of or only partial recognition of diplomas by employers, the labour market demands or competition with British graduates on the labour market (Trevena 2013, p. 176).

From a meso perspective, Trevena argued that the social capital of migrants determined both the decision to move and to enter the local labour market, since newcomers were often helped by those already living in London and working in low-skilled sectors. Moreover, the other highly educated migrants who had arrived earlier and now worked in low or semi-skilled jobs acted as a reference for newcomers and often as "gate keepers" to the low skilled sector (Trevena 2013, p. 179).

Besides the macro and meso levels, Trevena revealed that individual motives, perceptions and life plans had a decisive impact on the positioning of highly educated migrants within the low skilled job sector. She showed that the large majority of Polish migrants did not move a priori for career reasons, but for the sake of living in London, learning the language or earning money for diverse future projects, be it building a house or travelling (Trevena 2013, p. 182). The easy accessibility to low-skilled jobs, financial rewards as well as flexibility made these kinds of job attractive for newcomers. However, Trevena also showed that motives and goals changed over time. Shifting one's social positioning and making use of one's own qualifications became the goal of most migrants in the later stages of their migration process (Trevena 2013, pp. 184–185). As the author concluded, "it follows that low-skilled jobs are often simply entrance jobs for Polish graduates, providing they wish to achieve career advancement in the British labour market and work towards reaching this goal. However, for educated migrants who concentrate on other aspects than their professional career, such as self-development, travel and saving or who lack the drive or are indecisive about their career plans, the phase of carrying out menial work may become long-term." (Trevena 2013, p. 185).

Furthermore, Trevena studied the impact of working in low skilled sector on the self-perception and class belonging of highly educated migrants (Trevena 2011). The author argued that despite university graduates, who were expected to use their cultural capital in order to enter qualified and socially recognised positions in Poland, taking on low skilled jobs in London, the term downward social mobility was inappropriate. Trevena instead put forward the term "contradictory social mobility" – introduced earlier by Rhacel Salazar Parreñas (2001), since despite working in low skilled positions, migrants in many cases improved their life situation and opened up new possibilities of self-development which were limited in their home country.

Trevena's study is important since it challenged the assumption of classic migration theories on highly skilled migration, which stated that migrants were rational social actors moving a priori for economic reasons. Her case study of young Polish graduates working in low skilled jobs in London showed different motives for migration, spanning from structural conditions to very personal reasons, and different meanings of work. The difficulties of migrants to position themselves within the socially construed categories of social class both within the country of origin and country of destination high-lighted the ever complex process of positioning in transnational and multicultural spaces. Moreover, the stories of migrants revealed that taking up a job in the low-skilled sector might be experienced not as a status quo but as a (planned or unintended) transition or moratorium phase before moving elsewhere.

The EU project "Integration of Female Immigrants into the Labour Market and Society. Policy Assessment and Policy Recommendations" concerned, among other topics, the different experiences of deskilling of migrant women in European countries and the strategies of coping with it (Kontos 2009b). The project was aimed at policy evaluation and was based on the combination of diverse methods, ranging from statistical analysis, analysis of documents, and expert interviews to biographical narrative interviews conducted with migrant women in selected European countries. The authors pointed out the vulnerable position of migrant women in European countries. According to them, migrant women arriving after the 1990s experienced more difficulties in accessing and positioning themselves within the labour market then the previous generation of migrants. Due to their legal status and the exclusion mechanisms related to local labour markets, a large proportion of migrant women entered the informal sector, taking on jobs in the care and domestic sphere, sex industries, tourism or agriculture (Kontos 2009a, p. 5).

One of the important findings of the research project was that the majority of women included in the sample were employed in positions which did not match their qualifications. The majority of migrant women who were interviewed for the study were either working in the care and domestic sector or had worked there in the past before entering other sectors of the labour market, despite their qualifications and skills (Liapi, Vouyioukas 2009a, p. 29). The presence of women within these sectors corresponds, so the authors, to the increasing demand for female labour in these fields caused partly by the restructuring of welfare systems across Europe, the migration policies disadvantaging migrant women as well as insufficient social and legal support which would ease the passage to other areas of the labour market, and to the validation of initial qualifications, skills and professional experience (Kontos 2009a). The biographical interviews revealed that despite the improving infrastructure relating to the recognition of educational certificates and professional skills within the EU, migrant women did not have access to suitable information or they were discouraged by difficult and time consuming procedures. A large proportion of them thus stayed trapped in uncertain conditions in the low-paid market sectors (ibid.).

As Maria Liapi and Anna Vouyioukas, co-researchers on the project, pointed out, "[f]or most migrant women deskilling is experienced and even accepted as an integral component of migration or as an obvious fact, i.e. migrants have fewer opportunities and have to work harder than others. What is more, for some migrant women deskilling and downwards social mobility is a process which has started in their countries of origin, before migration, and may have been the very reason for migrating. In these cases migration is an attempt to regain the lost social status." (Liapi, Vouyioukas 2009b, p. 165).

However, the study also revealed that despite the uncertain positions in which migrant women were often entrenched due to their legal status, irregular occupation and family responsibilities, they developed diverse strategies of overcoming language barriers and difficulties in finding work, and building social networks in the country of residence (Liapi, Vouyioukas 2009a, p. 30; Kontos 2009a, p. 13). As Maria Kontos writes in the executive summary to the research project, "[o]ur interviewees employed a range of strategies to access labour markets – frequently through informal work – and to legalize their status, frequently by marrying an EU citizen or a migrant with residence rights. When they could legalize their status, they searched to find access to formal sectors of the economy. Thus, *irregular residence paradoxically functions as a pre-phase to legal residence and social integration.*" (Kontos 2009a, pp. 12–13, italics in original). Legal status was the precondition for bettering one's position on the labour market, Kontos further argues. It enabled migrant women to use their educational capital and professional experience more effectively, since their qualifications and skills could then be recognised by official authorities in order to overcome possible deskilling. Moreover, attaining official legal status opened up for them the possibility of using the state and institutional support, such as requalification or language courses (ibid.).

Liapi and Vouyioukas described the processes of deskilling and reskilling in greater detail using the example of migrant women in Greece and other European countries (Liapi, Vouyioukas 2009a, 2009b, 2013). They argued that the possibilities of reskilling and social mobility depended, besides legal and institutional constraints, on a number of other factors, such as the course of migration and biographical obstacles before and after migration (Liapi, Vouyioukas 2009b, p. 166). According to the researchers, aspirations to reskill were influenced by migration plans and motives. Moving to another country in order to pursue new life plans might, so the authors, have a different impact on reskilling then temporary migration with the plan of returning (ibid.). Legal status, as already mentioned, influenced access to state supported courses, language courses or qualification and skills recognition processes to an exaggerated extent. Furthermore, official legal status was necessary for access to rights and public services, such as child care and social support (ibid.). Another important factor in the process of reskilling was, so the authors, the level of education and professional background: the authors suggested that more qualified women tended to have better access to requalification courses and other opportunities, since they could mobilise their skills and knowledge in order to orientate themselves within the institutional and legal structures (ibid.). The authors also identified age and women's positioning on the labour market as important factors influencing the willingness to shift social position. Finally, the authors also looked at the biographical dimension, such as life plans, the possibility to use biographical and professional resources, the awareness of risks and opportunities, and the possibility of migrants mobilising social networks in order to achieve their goals (ibid.).

The research based on the EU-project "Integration of Female Immigrants into the Labour Market and Society" revealed different strategies employed by migrants for reskilling and acquiring further qualifications and skills in order to better off their situation in society and improve their social and legal rights (Liapi, Vouyioukas 2009a, pp. 31–32). According to the researchers, women made efforts to professionally re-orientate, to repeat or continue their studies in the country of migration, to attend diverse training programs or to establish a new professional career through work as volunteers (Liapi, Vouyioukas 2009a, p. 31). In order to achieve their goals, migrant women took part in diverse support programs, such as language courses organised by NGO's or state requalification courses in their field of work. Women took also part in courses at their workplace. Self-employment was also one of the strategies for overcoming legal constraints and discrimination. Being self-employed became a strategy for migrant women to use their own qualifications and skills, or to enter other areas of the economy (see also Apitzsch, Kontos 2008, 2003). Another reskilling strategy was the professionalization of care and domestic work (Liapi, Vouyioukas 2009a, p. 32).

Language became an important resource in establishing new professional paths and in coping with deskilling. According to the researchers, the native languages played an important role in coming in contact with other migrants and overcoming social isolation. Furthermore, migrant women often used the knowledge of native and other languages as a professional qualification in order to improve their chances on the labour market. Migrant women thus often found a job as teachers, translators, in tourism or the service sector (Liapi, Vouyioukas 2009a, p. 31). The researchers found that knowledge of the official language of the country to which migrant women migrated was crucial for establishing social networks with natives. Such social capital was often an important resource in the process of social mobility. Migrants whose native language was similar or identical to the official language of the country to which they had moved found it easier to access reskilling courses and could therefore start a new career in fields other than their original profession or previous education (ibid.). Liapi and Vouyioukas found that the majority of migrant women did not attend official language courses but instead learned on their own at work or in their leisure time. This method, however, often led to "context specific" knowledge of the language related to work and basic everyday activities, which disadvantaged them in participating in other areas outside these spheres, such as civil society or political rights (ibid.).

Yvonne Riaño based her research on 57 biographical narrative interviews with highly skilled migrant women who had moved from non-EU countries to Switzerland for reasons of family reunification or seeking asylum. She focused on the way migrant women were positioned on the labour market, on the role of family in negotiating their professional goals and on their strategies of dealing with possible hurdles. The majority of women included in the study were educated in the field of commercial and business administration, social sciences, law or fine arts. Before migrating to Switzerland they had worked in qualified positions and spoke two or more languages fluently (Riaño 2012, p. 31). In accordance with other studies presented here, the narratives of women revealed that they had initially left their home country for diverse reasons, such as education, travel, establishing a family, new job opportunities, reunification with their parents or because of political persecution (Riaño 2012, p. 29). An important motive when considering migration to Switzerland was "an opportunity to break with traditional gender roles and gain more independence as women" (Riaño 2012, p. 29). Since the majority of women in the sample moved to Switzerland as "marriage migrants", they were not considered by statistics and authorities as skilled migrants but as dependants without economic aspirations, which had an impact on their legal status and labour market participation (Riaño 2012, p. 31).

Besides their experiences of deskilling – more than half of the women were either unemployed or worked in jobs that were below their qualifications (Riaño 2012, p. 32) – women faced the problem of a loss of self-confidence and loss of autonomy, since in many instances they became economically dependent on their spouses or other family members. According to the author, the path leading to obtaining a qualified job position was a very difficult one for women working in the low skilled sector, because they did had not practised their profession for an extended period of time and had not established contacts which would help them to reach the desired position in their professional field (ibid.).

Riaño showed that despite the structural and institutional constraints with which women were confronted in entering the professional life, they developed different strategies to reach their goals and to change their positioning. The author remarked that while some women developed a clear strategy on how to better their situation, for some the change came unexpectedly. Furthermore, plans and strategies were dynamic and changed over time, since new decisions were shaped by new experiences and knowledge (Riaño 2012, p. 39). Riaño presented five different types of coping strategy employed by migrant women with regard to labour market participation: First, after learning the German language women tried to access the labour market. When they failed to obtain a job position which matched their level of qualification, they then tried to take any accessible job, often in the low skilled sector. The other response to overcoming labour market barriers was self-employment. Interestingly, women often utilised their ethnic and national background as a resource to enter new areas of the economy. Secondly, some women responded to difficulties in entering the professional life either by withdrawing from the labour market and concentrating on family and household duties, or by doing other unpaid work. They became active in diverse voluntary organisations. As Riaño showed, the majority of women interviewed for the research project were active in migrants', intercultural, and home-country associations. The social network which they established through their volunteer activities was in some cases crucial for establishing contact to their future employers (Riaño 2012, p. 40). Thirdly, a different option of dealing with unemployment and work in the low skilled sector was the act of re-skilling. Women passed German language courses, repeated their university studies, qualified in some new academic fields, or started post-graduate studies. According to the author, re-skilling and repeating one's studies in the country of destination was in most instances the key to obtaining a qualified position (ibid.). Fourthly, women made efforts to establish new social networks and actively contacted potential employers. And lastly, the fifth response to the unstable situation was adopting the role of the victim or migrating back to the country of origin.

Juliane Karakayali applied a different research approach. She studied the processes of contradictory class mobility of "Eastern European" women working in the domestic sector as care workers (Karakayali 2010b, 2010a). Her starting point was the observation that many women in the domestic sector, which had been connected to low social recognition and prestige, often had a high level of education, in some case university degrees, and professional experience in diverse areas of the economy. Her aim was to analyse how migrant women experienced and assessed the mismatch between education and professional experience and their position within the domestic care sector, and which strategies for self-positioning were developed. She conducted biographical interviews with "Eastern European" migrant women living and working as care workers in Germany. On the basis of biographical reconstructions she identified four different coping strategies and means of positioning (Karakayali 2010a, pp. 170–174). The first category covered women who experienced their positioning as an act of deskilling and de-qualification. Women suffered under the lack of recognition of their initial education and skills. They failed several times to change their social position – be it trying to legalise their status, to make their qualifications officially recognised or just to enter other sectors of the economy – and stayed trapped within the care sector. As Karakayali exemplified by means of an interview with a university educated woman from Hungary, returning to the country of origin was not an option for diverse personal and economic reasons. In contrast, the second category described the perception of domestic care work as a stepping stone to a further professional career. Karakayali showed on the example of a university educated women from Romania that temporary care work after graduation was a strategic decision to earn some money in order to buy a house in Romania. While working in a German household, she kept up professional and personal contacts with people back in Romania in order to keep the option of returning and starting a professional career back in Romania open. Her relationship with care work was a very pragmatic and goal oriented one. Karakayali called the third category "the condition for a successful new biographical start". This category stood for those experiences in which working in the domestic sector was seen as a possibility of starting a new life phase after a personal crisis. Care work was thus not perceived a priori as deskilling or stigmatisation but as a means of stabilising one's difficult life situation. The final category describes domestic care work in Germany as a strategy for overcoming a difficult financial situation in the migrant's country of origin. In order to exemplify this, Karakayali introduced the biography of a Lithuanian women who commuted to Germany for the purpose of making money for herself and her son who had got in to a difficult financial situation. According to the author, the three latter categories of migrant managed to give care work a personal meaning, which in turn helped them to challenge the difficult and often unstable working conditions.

The work of Karakayali showed that working in the domestic sector, which is often associated with social stigma and deskilling, does not per se have to be perceived by individuals as downward social mobility or a personal failure. It might even be experienced as a chance to better one's situation, earn money for future projects and acquire new skills, such as language competency. For many, it may be the passage to some other life or professional phase.

Strategies for coping with downward social mobility after migration were also the topic of research of Francesca Alice Vianello (2014). On the basis of biographical interviews she studied the positioning of Ukrainian women in the domestic sector in Italy, taking into account that the majority of women were highly educated and had varying professional backgrounds. She investigated how downward social mobility in Italy was subjectively experienced and coped with. The author showed that women actually experienced two-fold downward social mobility: firstly in the course of the transformation of society after the dissolution of the Soviet Union 1989 and in the aftermath due to economic and political changes. Migration was for many migrant women a means of facing a difficult financial situation and maintaining the social status and standard of living of their family. The second encounter with downward social mobility was in the course of migration, since their qualifications and skills were not recognised and women found themselves in the domestic sector. (Vianello 2014, p. 94). Vianello's study revealed that one strategy for coping with the "devaluation" experienced in the domestic sector was to see the work as "an interlude in their life and as a sacrifice that serves to improve their families' upward social mobility" in their country of origin (Vianello 2014, p. 85). Furthermore, migrant women developed strategies to diminish the hierarchies and to establish a respectful relationship with their employers. Vianello also showed that migrant women preferred to work for families of higher social status, since they could better justify their positioning within the workforce than when working for families positioned on lower social strata. Moreover, they tried to differentiate themselves from migrants from other countries in order to negotiate better working conditions. Finally, they searched for recognition and self-fulfilment outside their place of work, be it by doing voluntary intellectual work or being active in diverse associations (Vianello 2014, p. 94).

3.3.5 The role of the family and social networks

Some studies have recently recognised the important role of family and social networks in migration and the career pathway of (highly) skilled migrants (see e.g. Erel 2004; Pusch 2010; Thomsen 2010; Klein 2010; Riaño 2012; Baghdadi, Riaño 2014). As the authors argued, family and social networks were crucial for migration decisions and for labour market participation. In this last section I will introduce these studies which focused on the role of family and social networks in migration processes.

In her study on the migration and career pathway of qualified migrant women, Umut Erel showed inter alia the importance of family and broad social networks both for migration and for the career path of qualified migrants (Erel 2004). She carried out research on migration processes affecting qualified women moving from Turkey to Great Britain and Germany and conducted biographical narrative interviews for this purpose. She underlined the importance of transnational social networks in migration processes. Transnational networks did not consist solely of ethnic and family connections but were heterogeneous and structured along the lines of the women's belonging to social class, gender, political and social participations or multiple ethnic senses of belonging (Erel 2004, p. 126). Transnational social contacts were crucial when establishing contact with future employers, both in the informal and formal sector of the economy in the country of migration. Erel pointed out the negotiation strategies concerning family and work, and the role of class positioning and legal status in these processes. While some women were able to mobilize their transnational social and cultural capital in order to negotiate family and child-care arrangements and to pursue upwards social mobility, others stayed trapped in the low skilled sector for a longer period of time due to their irregular status and lack of resources.

Yvonne Riaño made efforts to incorporate the family aspect into her study on highly skilled migration (Riaño 2012). She argued that the lack of attention given to the role of the family within migration processes was caused by the focus of researchers on highly skilled migrant men moving a priori for economic reasons. This approach neglected the presence of skilled migrant women within migration flows. Moreover, it overlooked the large number of highly skilled migrants moving in other migration corridors, be it as family members or asylum seekers (Riaño 2012, pp. 25–26). Riaño, who studied the migration of highly skilled women to Switzerland, argued that the participation of migrant women in the labour market was affected besides structural and legal constraints by gender stereotypes and ideas about the gendered role division within the family, as well as by insufficient child-care facilities in the country of migration. The biographical narratives of women revealed that they were often confronted with images of "foreign wives" who were supposed to prioritize caring for their family and household over pro-fessional self-realisation. Since the positioning of migrant women on the labour market was often worse than that of their spouses, they were the ones who usually looked after their children and the household, thereby postpon-ing their professional goals. While the lack of child-care facilities affected all families with small children, migrant women were more vulnerable because they missed the family and social structure which would support them (Riaño 2012, p. 38). Furthermore, Riaño observed that women who reached qualified positions decided against having children or enjoyed child-care support by other family members (Riaño 2012, p. 40).

The role of the family in migration processes was also studied by Barba-ra Pusch (Pusch 2010). She based her analysis on 88 biographical narrative interviews conducted with highly educated migrant men and women in Ger-many, Turkey and Canada. The study was part of a larger international pro-ject "Cultural capital in migration" (Nohl et al. 2010b). Pusch's starting point was the observation that highly skilled migrants very often moved to another country because of a partner or family. Her question was how the family and professional orientations interacted and shape one other. In order to answer this question, Pusch construed a typology of possible forms of family and professional overlapping (Pusch 2010, p. 286). For the purposes of terminol-ogy, she distinguished between migrants who moved to another country be-cause of a partner or other family members and those who moved for other reasons, such as improving one's economic or political situation.

For the migrants in the first category, the partner became the central fig-ure concerning not only the decision to migrate but also with regard to the migrants' integration into the labour market. He or she often provided finan-cial support, social contacts and the knowledge necessary for finding one's own path in the country of destination. Moreover, the partners were often important figures in obtaining official legal status and supporting migrants in their communication with authorities. The marriage to a partner who had legal status in the country of destination usually signified the acquisition of legal rights which enlarged the horizon of possibilities beyond and within the labour market. It enabled the migrant to start new studies and re-skilling courses, to start to practise their profession or to become self-employed (Pusch 2010, pp. 288–290). Cases in which the partner played an important role in decision making in relation to migration but where the partner was not decisive in the process of the migrant professionally establishing him or herself in the country of destination, were ascribed to the second category. Migrants in this category often found employment by chance, with the help of their own social networks or before migration. They often profited from previous migration experience in the relevant country, and from their privileged legal status, for example enjoying EU citizen rights in Germany (Pusch 2010, pp. 290–292). The third category concerned those cases in which the migrant's partnership and family did not only have positive effects on their integration into the labour market. Pusch highlighted the situation of migrant women with children. Mothers often experienced ruptures in their professional career, discrimination on the basis of motherhood and difficulties in (re-)entering professional life (Pusch 2010, p. 263). She pointed out different child-care structures and expectations concerning gender roles in the countries she studied.

Besides these three categories of people who moved country in the first instance because of their partners, there were also other migrants who moved for other reasons initially. Pusch summarised these types under the heading "the amelioration perspectives: the desire for a better life" (Pusch 2010, p. 294). People included in these categories moved to other countries because of the improved economic, social and political situation. As Pusch showed, family played an important role not only for migrants who moved with their families, but also for those people who moved on their own. For those migrants who moved together with other family members, family signified both financial and emotional support and an additional burden, when for example other family members did not speak the language and migrants were expected to take on the role of translators in everyday situations, or when migrants could not take part in re-skilling courses because of child-care and other family duties (Pusch 2010, p. 296). The desire to better one's situation may be both connected to the country of origin and to the country of migration. People who left their home countries because of a difficult financial situation in their country of origin did not focus primarily on their professional development after migration, but on receiving a regular salary. Examples included highly qualified women working in the domestic sector in Germany and Turkey. Since their families were in need of migrants' remittances, they could not risk unemployment or changing job position. Their families thus shaped their professional orientation, despite living in the country of origin (Pusch 2010, pp. 294–295). As Pusch showed, improving one's professional situation was not the main goal for many migrants. Often they were simply looking for a way to balance family, their financial situation and their professional goals (Pusch 2010, pp. 297–298).

On the basis of biographical narrative interviews collected for the "Cultural capital during migration" project, Sarah Thomsen investigated the role of social networks in labour market inclusion (Thomsen 2010; Nohl et al. 2010b). Her paper showed that professional social networks in the country of migration were crucial for gaining access to job positions that matched the migrants' professional background. People who were looking for a job in their profession could mobilize the social network they had established prior to migration, although this was often limited to one country. Moreover, they could profit from links established during their previous studies and work abroad. Thomsen showed that migrants established important contacts while participating in diverse professional associations after migration. These were often connected to the country of origin. Furthermore, migrants often gained access to the relevant job positions through unpaid work and internships. The social contacts established there often helped them to change position within the organisation or arrange other job opportunities. Migrants also profited from contacts outside the professional sphere, such as family members, co-nationals, or acquaintances. Nevertheless, even though these contacts were crucial for arranging potential access to the professional life and for enlarging the migrant's scope of possibilities, they did not usually lead to a job position that matched the professional background of the highly skilled migrants. These networks were crucial for entering the low skilled and informal sector, when other options of entering the official business sphere failed. However, both professional networks and networks related to family members and acquaintances were not social capital per se – i.e. the usability of social networks in order to achieve own goals. They presented a potential resource which might be transformed into social capital in the specific context. While some migrants actively worked on establishing social networks in their country of origin, in the country of destination or elsewhere in order to mobilize the ensuing social capital when trying to obtain a new job position, others experienced the help offered by others as unplanned or happening by chance (Thomsen 2010).

The aforementioned studies show the role of the family and social networks in migration processes. They highlight the points of intersection between the welfare system and social discourse on gender and ethnicity in the migrants' negotiation of their role within the family and their positioning on the labour market.

3.4 Summary and research desiderata

In the previous chapter I introduced studies which focused on the pathways of highly skilled migrants to and across Europe. As I have shown, focusing on highly educated migrants in Europe is a relatively new phenomenon. In contradiction to the idea of highly skilled migrants moving predominantly in higher spheres of the social strata, the studies introduced above revealed that university educated people move within different migration corridors and within different social class pathways, experiencing both downward and upward social mobility.

Most of the studies on highly educated migrants concentrated on their passage to the local labour market after migration. They described the various pathways towards obtaining a job and highlighted the role of gendered legal and institutional frameworks, as well as social discourse on gender and ethnicity in these processes. Despite the fact that the aforementioned projects concerned different instances of highly skilled migration – in terms of both the legal frameworks and structural conditions of the country of origin and country of destination – the authors showed that women were particularly affected by deskilling and downward social mobility. Nevertheless, the authors also showed that migrants developed diverse strategies to cope with deskilling, be it requalification, efforts to legalise one's status, self-employment, finding opportunities for self-realisation outside the workplace, or renewed migration.

Furthermore, I introduced studies which dealt with the role of family and social networks in the migration of highly educated migrants. These studies drew attention to the role of the welfare system, including child-care facilities, in the ability of migrants to negotiate their position within the labour market and within the family. They also illustrated the role of partners and other family members in migration processes and in gaining access to the labour market. They revealed that family members could on the one hand be "gatekeepers" and support for migrants, whilst on the other hand acting as a constraint. Furthermore, they demonstrated the role of social networks in establishing connections to the labour market, with a particular emphasis on professional (transnational) networks.

Processes that went beyond integration to the local labour market were not, however, dealt with by most of the studies or if so then they were only dealt with in part. The following questions therefore remain: how was the migrants' positioning prior to moving country? How were their chances and the constraints in their home country experienced prior to migration? How were the decisions to move embedded in the biographies of migrants and within the changing structural contexts of both the country of origin and the country of migration? How were resources, education and skills able to be used after migration and when moving back and forth in other national contexts? All of these questions call for a biographical and transnational approach to migration processes and to the positioning of migrants in varied social and geographical spaces.

4 Biographical approaches to migration and social mobility

The theoretical framework for the present study builds on biographical research, migration studies, transnational approach and theoretical thinking on social stratification and social mobility. I will pay particularly attention to the moments at which these streams of thought intersect. At first I shall introduce my biographical research and biographical approaches. I will refer back to history and follow the development of the flow of biographical research within which my study is embedded. Subsequently, I will introduce the main concepts and theoretical framework of biographical research, such as the concept of biography, agency and structure, biographical process structures and biographical experiences and knowledge which were also crucial for the present study. Next I will restrict my focus to biographical perspectives on migration. I will outline the first biographically oriented migration studies on against the background of wider theoretical and methodological discussions concerning migration. I will then introduce the transnational approach which gained in importance within the social sciences from the 1990s onwards and I will use the example of recent migration studies to draw links between biographical and transnational approaches. Lastly, I will introduce the notions of social positioning and social mobility in transnational spaces to the theoretical framework.

4.1 Biographical approaches

The biographical method is not merely a methodological instrument for generating empirical material and conducting an analysis. Rather, it is a manner of approaching social phenomena in a way which is firmly rooted in theoretical and methodological tradition developed over a century. The aim of this chapter is to outline this development and position my work within this stream of thought on the relationship between the individual and society, as well as on the embeddedness of empirical work and "theorizing".

In the first part of this chapter I shall follow the development of the biographical method from its beginnings in Chicago during the 1920s and 1930s, when sociologists tried to explain extensive societal changes through biographical material and field work. Subsequently, I shall outline the onward development of the biographical approach in Europe and discuss its position within contemporary scientific inquiry. In the second part of this chapter I shall clarify certain concepts of biographical research which became central to my work. I discuss the concept of biography, the interplay of agency and structure and "possibility spaces" connected thereto, the biographical process structures as developed by Fritz Schütze and the concepts of biographical experience and knowledge. I shall position these concepts within the scientific discussion and outline their mutual interconnection.

The historical and theoretical background outlined here is by no means complete. The biographical method is neither limited to the social sciences, nor to the exchange between the American and Western European tradition (Apitzsch, Siouti 2007). Rather, it has a long tradition in different parts of Europe and beyond.[18] However, this shall not be detailed here. It appeared to me to be more important here to limit my focus to the history of carrying out biographical research, which is rooted in the tradition of the Chicago school and developed further in Europe, being the stream of thought my work builds on.

4.1.1 Historical and theoretical background of the biographical approach

The beginnings in Chicago

At the turn of the century, the city of Chicago was experiencing extensive transformation and growth. The on-going industrialisation went hand in hand with the numerous migration flows into the city, whereby the majority of migrants were arriving from European countries (Zaretsky 1996, p. x). These migration processes attracted the attention of William I. Thomas, a Chicago sociologist (Thomas, cited by Blumer 1979, p. 103): "When I became a member of the faculty at Chicago, I gave, among other courses, one on immigration and one on social attitudes, and eventually I decided to study an immigration group in Europe and America to determine as far as possible what relation their home mores and norms had to their adjustment and maladjustment in America." This research interest led him to the office of the Polish Emigrants' Protective Association in Warsaw, directed by Florian Znaniecki. This connection brought Thomas and Znaniecki closer together. On the eve of the First World War in 1914, Znaniecki accepted the invitation of Thomas and went to Chicago to translate and assist, and later collaborate

---

18 For biographical research in Central and Eastern Europe see e.g. "Biographical research in Eastern Europe" edited by Humphrey (2003). For an overview of the development of biographical research in France see e.g. Pape (2010). For the UK see e.g. Roberts (2010).

on their joint project "The Polish Peasant in Europe and America", which is perceived as the fundamental piece of work on biographical research.[19]

The basis for their study, which spanned five volumes and was first published in 1918-1920, consisted of a number of biographical documents.[20] Thomas and Znaniecki collected about fifteen thousand private letters written by immigrant family members to each other, from which they chose more than seven hundred for their inquiry (Kohli 1981, p. 278). The other sources were voluminous autobiographies, of which one, the extensive autobiographical portrait of Wladek, was presented and analysed in the piece of work. Besides these, they also used church and court records, as well as local newspaper correspondence. By analysing this wide range of empirical material, Thomas and Znaniecki sought to explain how migration processes influence family structures, neighbourhood and other institutional settings of the migrant community. Moreover, they were interested in how changes on a personal and societal level were connected to one other. Furthermore, they paid attention not only to the transformation of the migrant community and reorganisation of "self" and "social" in the USA, but compared it with the changes in society back in Poland (Breckner 2007, p. 114).

The rising diversity and growth of ethnic communities in Chicago in the first half of the twentieth century caused immigration to be perceived as a burning problem for American society, and was subsequently the subject of diverse government studies and surveys (Zaretsky 1996, p. xii), mostly quantitatively oriented. Instead of collecting quantitative data, Thomas and Znaniecki (1958, p. 1834) suggested that biographical material would be the most suitable source for investigating the causal processes and discovering social regularities: "And since concrete social life is concrete only when taken together with the individual life which underlies social happenings, since the personal element is a constitutive factor of every social occurrence, social science cannot remain on the surface of social becoming, where certain schools wish to have it float, but must reach the actual human experiences and attitudes which constitute the full, live and active social reality beneath the formal organization of social institutions, or behind the statistically tabulated mass-phenomena which taken in themselves are nothing but symptoms of unknown causal processes and can serve only as provisional ground for sociological hypotheses." To find out about the various social relations and

---

19 For further biographical information, see for example Zaretsky 1996 and Znaniecki Lopata 1965.

20 Thomas explains his interest in the biographical material as follows: "It was, I believe, in connection with The Polish Peasant that I became identified with the "life history" and the method of documentation. Here again I may be oversimplifying, but I trace the origin of my interest in the document to a long letter picked up on a rainy day in the alley behind my house, a letter from a girl who was taking a training course in a hospital, to her father concerning family relationships and discords. It occurred to me at the time that one would learn a great deal if one had a great many letters of this kind." (Baker 1973, p. 250)

processes, Thomas and Znaniecki proposed generating theories from the empirical data and not vice versa (Thomas, Znaniecki 1958, pp. 1933–1934). With their work, Thomas and Znaniecki thus prepared the ground for the interpretative sociological empirical tradition.

However, the methodology of Thomas and Znaniecki soon became the subject of criticism. In his review of "The Polish Peasant" for the Executive Committee of the Social Science Research Council in 1939[21], Herbert Blumer (1979, p. 109) pointed out the unclear relationship between the empirical data and the generation of theories. On the one hand, the theories presented in "The Polish Peasant" were not the result of a thorough interpretation of the biographical material. Rather, the biographical material was presented in the form of introductions and footnotes by diverse sources and theoretical thoughts acquired by Thomas and Znaniecki aside from the collected data. Thus, the aim of the authors to proceed in an inductive manner was not adequately implemented. On the other hand, the study did not solely use deduction as research logic either. Blumer (1979, p. 39) expressed this ambivalence as follows: "Generally, with respect to the authors' use of letters as human documents, it may be said that the letters considered by themselves are not very meaningful; it is also clear that the theoretical analyses, if left to stand by themselves, would be formal, abstract, and rather dogmatic. The merging of the two does yield a concreteness and appreciative understanding that cannot be stated either as a mere illustration of the theory, nor as an inductive grounding of that theory. There seems to be involved a new relation, perhaps more in the nature of a psychological relation, that so far has not been stated or made clear." The relationship between the empirical material and theory was not entirely solved at the Social Science Research Council (Blumer 1979), nor did it become clear how Thomas and Znaniecki proceeded with the selection of the letters, autobiographies and further empirical material for their analyses (Kohli 1981, p. 278).[22] However, despite the criticism of the methodology of "The Polish Peasant", Thomas and Znaniecki stirred up an intense debate on the relevance of biographical material in the scientific community and instigated the on-going debate on the relation between the empirical material and theory within social research in general and within interpretative social research in particular.

---

21 The Social Science Research Council was established in 1923 to support the social sciences and to critically discuss the most significant works of the discipline. "The Polish Peasant" was chosen for closer appraisal, which only goes to show its importance within the social sciences at that time (Kohli 1981, p. 281).

22 For further information on criticisms of the methodology of "The Polish Peasant", see for example Kohli (1981) or Lamnek (2010).

Poland

Florian Znaniecki, who moved back to Poland after World War I, utilised the work with biographical material which he had co-developed and acquired during his stay in Chicago for several other research projects. Important sources for collecting biographical material were the public competitions organised by various institutions (Kazmierska 2009, p. 55). Soon after he gained a professorship at the University of Poznan, Znaniecki organised the first competition with the aim of collecting the autobiographies of Polish workers (Kohli 1981, p. 285). Over the coming years, other competitions followed dealing with other topics, such as homelessness or emigration. The biographies became popular not only in the science community, but also among the people themselves who participated heavily in the announced competitions. In Poland the biographical method was thus soon established as a dominant empirical approach, even turning into a social movement which aroused the interest of people from diverse social milieus.

Before the beginning of World War II, Znaniecki moved to New York, where he stayed until his death in 1958, refusing to return to communist Poland. Nevertheless, the biographical method was soon frequently used in Poland by Znaniecki's followers (Kazmierska 2009, p. 55). Paradoxically, as the international sociological milieu turned towards the theory of structural functionalism and methodological positivism from the 1940s onwards, the biographical method continued to be used as a powerful tool of politics and sociological research in Poland (ibid.). Due both to language politics, as the majority of biographical works were written in Polish and only a few were translated into "Western languages" (Kohli 1981, p. 283), and the position outside of the "main roots" of knowledge transfer (Knapp 2009, p. 217), biographical research remained for some decades exclusively constrained within the borders of Poland. Nonetheless, as biographical research experienced a new wave of interest in diverse places around Europe from the 1970s onwards, the tradition cultivated in Poland became an important source for the further development of biographical research.

The Chicago School

Meanwhile in the USA, sociologists in Chicago began to build on the research approaches of William I. Thomas and Florian Znaniecki soon after "The Polish Peasant" was published. The growing and changing Chicago of the 1920s and 1930s fascinated many sociologists, who were trying to grasp the links between extensive migration, industrialisation and other social processes, such as homelessness, the establishment of ethnic communities and rising criminality. Hence the streets and neighbourhoods of Chicago became the arena and field of research for many investigations. Building on the research approaches of Thomas and Znaniecki, bringing biographical material into the analyses and highlighting the link between the "objective" and the "subjective" elements of social reality (Fuchs-Heinritz 2005, p. 93), the Chicago sociologists enlarged the scope of research inquiry by other research sources, such as ethnographical observations, diverse biographical documents, and, most importantly, qualitative interviews. These data collection tools were aimed at methodologically controlling the formation of research material (Lamnek 2010, p. 601).

The development of qualitative methods in the USA was influenced considerably by two Chicago sociologists, Robert E. Park and Ernest E. Burgess, inter alia. Park, who initially worked as a reporter for more than 10 years, gained his PhD in Germany and eventually joined the Chicago school following the invitation of Thomas. Park encouraged his students and research fellows to go out and "find 'the big sociological news' in the everyday world around them" (Collins, Makowsky 1998, p. 184). Following the tradition of pragmatism, he understood sociology as a discipline aimed at discovering social relations from the reality observed. Accordingly, theory should be extracted from the empirical material and not emerge, as was the case with many sociological theories at that time, separated from the facts observed (Rosenthal 2005, p. 36). In his approach Park mirrored the works of John Dewey, with whom he had studied at Michigan, the studies of William James and Josiah Royce at Harvard, or thoughts of Georg Simmel in Bonn, to name just a few, who influenced his theoretical and methodological ideas (Bulmer 1984, p. 91). Under Park's direction at Chicago University, a collection of diverse qualitatively oriented works emerged studying particular aspects of life in Chicago.

The theoretical framework for the development of qualitative methods in general and the biographical approach in particular was not only pragmatism, elaborated in Michigan by John Dewey. The Chicago sociologists also drew on the theoretical thoughts of symbolic interactionism and of interpretative sociology, which has its roots in Germany at the beginning of the twentieth century and formed the basis for the development of interpretative social research[23] later on.

---

23   The interpretative research tradition builds on the long theoretical tradition going back to sociological thinking on the relation between the individual and society. It draws on the theoretical thoughts of Georg Simmel (1967), Max Weber (1970), Alfred Schütz (1972), George Herbert Mead and others.

The biographical method in Europe

Despite the success of studies appearing around the Department of Sociology at Chicago University in the 1920s and 1930s, the amount of attention given to the biographical method and other qualitative approaches declined considerably over the next decades. This corresponded to the growing influence of structural functionalism in the international sociological milieu, moving its focus away from the social actors towards the social systems (Fuchs-Heinritz 2005, p. 106). The qualitative approaches became overshadowed by quickly developing quantitative methods testing the hypotheses and theories by statistical means (ibid.). The positivist approach thus became a dominant stream in sociology. Not until the end of 1960s, possibly influenced by the revolutionary events and the battle for social change in European countries and worldwide (Bertaux 1981, p. 29; Apitzsch, Inowlocki 2000, p. 55), did historians and sociologists from diverse countries call for more subject oriented approaches to social events, recognising that some phenomena and experiences of certain groups, which were excluded from formal surveys, could only be approached by means of qualitative methods (Chamberlayne et al. 2000, p. 3).

Daniel Bertaux (1981, p. 31, italics in original), a French sociologist, was among the first of his generation to make the point that "there is *another way* to practice sociology." He criticised French sociology, which was at that time strongly dominated by structuralism and empirical positivism oriented towards large quantitative surveys. Contrary to the mainstream, Bertaux based his work on collecting and analysing life stories. According to him, "collecting life stories means not only a new empirical praxis, but also a step-by-step redefinition of the *whole* approach of sociological praxis." (Bertaux 1981, p. 31, italics in original). As a reaction to the criticism of his life history approach voiced by defenders of positivism and structuralism, Bertaux showed that the biographical method did not only allow one to attain representativity of samples (though on a theoretical, not statistical level) and proof of the hypothesis and theories. Life stories also proved to be an appropriate means of getting "direct access to the level of *social relations* which constitute, after all, the very substance of sociological knowledge." (Bertaux 1981, p. 31, italics in original). The biographical approach was for him the means of gaining access through the subjective perspective of biographical accounts to the socio-structural relations and the logics of social praxis, which were at the centre of Bertaux's interest (Pape 2010, p. 43). Bertaux thus rebutted the thesis that biographical accounts were trapped in subjectivity, detached from the "objective" structure of social relations (Bourdieu 1998b, p. 62, 2000).

The biographical method was soon discussed throughout the international milieu. In 1978, Daniel Bertaux organised three sessions on the life history approach at the IX. World Congress of Sociology in Uppsala, which resulted in the book "Biography and Society", first published in 1981 (Bertaux 1981, p. 2). This book consisted of papers written by respected biographical researchers, such as Paul Thompson, the pioneer of oral history as a research method in the United Kingdom (Roberts 2010, p. 24), Józef Chałasiński, a sociologist and one of the founders of the biographical method in Poland (Kazmierska 2009, p. 54), and Martin Kohli, who a year after the Congress in Uppsala established the working group "Biographieforschung" in Gottingen, Germany, which became institutionalised as a research division of the German Sociological Association in 1986 (Apitzsch, Inowlocki 2000, p. 55). The Uppsala sessions were followed by the establishment of the international working group "Biography and society" of the International Sociological Association (ISA). In Germany, sociologists in Bielefeld established a working group at the beginning of the 1970s whose aim, inter alia, was to critically contribute to evaluating the problem of the relationship between empirical data and theory and its methodological controllability (Riemann 2006b, p. 120). Fritz Schütze, one of the main actors in the Bielefeld group, argued that standardised interviews deviated from the scheme of everyday communication and the statements generated by commonly used standardised questionnaires did not correspond to the real action of interviewees (Riemann 2003, p. 18). Moreover, Schütze claimed that the process leading from empirical observation to theory was blurred, and that sociological "theorizing" did not correspond to the reality observed (ibid.). Proceeding from the theoretical and methodological background of phenomenological sociology, symbolic interactionism, the Chicago school, conversational analysis and Grounded Theory (Apitzsch, Inowlocki 2000, p. 53), Schütze developed a specific method of data generation, the "narrative interview", which was based on an open off-the-cuff narrative and which soon became the pillar of numerous biographical investigations.

The biographical method, profiting itself from the interdisciplinary exchange since the beginning, did not stay bound to one particular field of study but soon spread into the diverse disciplines of social sciences and beyond (Apitzsch, Siouti 2007, pp. 5–6). Biographical research became established in migration studies (see e.g. Apitzsch 1990, 2000; Apitzsch, Kontos 2008; Lutz 2007; Breckner 2009; Ruokonen-Engler 2012; Siouti 2013), gender studies (see e.g. Dausien 1996; Apitzsch 2003b; Lutz, Davis 2009), adolescence research (see e.g. Inowlocki 2000; Köttig 2004), educational science (see e.g. Alheit, Dausien 2008), history (see e.g. Passerini 1992; Kaźmierska 2012), criminology (see e.g. Shaw 1966) and other disciplines. Although biographical research has been constantly developing until today and is now implemented in varied research fields across the disciplines, often triangulated with other research methods, it by no means constitutes the mainstream of sociological inquiry (Apitzsch, Inowlocki 2000, p. 53). However, biographical research, as a method of for approaching social phenomena which is firmly rooted in theoretical and methodological discussions that have constantly developed over the century, became strong enough to convincingly show that "there is *another way* to practice the sociology", taking again the words of Bertaux (1981, p. 31), and critically develop it further.

4.1.2 The central biographical concepts

Within the body of biographical research, the history of which I outlined above, central theoretical concepts are elaborated and discussed. First I introduce the concept of biography, which was one of the key concepts for the present piece of work. Afterwards I discuss other central concepts of biographical research, namely the concepts of agency and structure. Subsequently, the concept of process structures, which include both the agency of individuals and the power of structures within which the individuals can develop their lives, are introduced. Finally, I outline the theoretical discussions on biographical experiences and biographical knowledge, which are crucial in order to understand the migrants' action and positioning.

Biography: the interplay of individual and social

In modern times, the individual is exposed more than ever before to being able to make oneself the narrator of one's self (Delory-Momberger 2011, p. 29). The so-called "presentation of the self" – that is telling others who one is and how one developed into what one is – has not stayed confined to the private sphere, but has increasingly penetrated into the public sphere as the subject of interest for various institutions (in the form of curricula vitae, health reports or diverse application forms) and new forms of media (such as talk-shows, internet social networks, blogs etc.) In this context, some authors have spoken of the emergence of a "biographical society" (Astier, Duvoux 2006, p. 8; Astier 1995, p. 129) in order to describe the passage of private narratives into the public sphere and the consequences thereof for society and the individual. This development indicates that narratives of the self in diverse contexts have become an essential, and to some extent unquestioned part of everyday life for most people these days (Alheit, Dausien 2009; Hanses 2011, p. 338).

"Self-narration" gained in importance with the transformed social order in the course of enlightenment in the 19th century. The societal changes connected to modernity opened up an even wider range of options and possibilities of life style and life patterns, which called into question the perception of the self as being constructed according to belonging to a certain social position. Instead, individual life plans increasingly gained in importance for constructions of the self (Kohli 1988, p. 35). As Anthony

Giddens (1991, p. 14), one of the social theorists of modernisation, puts it: "Modernity is a post-traditional order, in which the question, ‚How shall I live?' has to be answered in day-to-day decisions about how to behave, what to wear and what to eat – and many other things – as well as interpreted within the temporal unfolding of self-identity." However, the release of power of traditional institutions in the course of individual-isation processes did not mean that the social structures would disperse. Rather, the form of sociability, so Martin Kohli (1988, p. 35), was substituted by another, which placed the individual in the forefront. In this regard, the biography – the narration of the self and one's own development during the course of one's life – is not a static or universal concept, but is connected to specific historical, social and spatial contexts.

Narratives of the self, either in the form of biographies – that is narrated or written life stories – or institutionalised curricula vitae, became important instruments not only for the individuals themselves but for institutions too. Although the concepts of biography and curriculum vitae are often confused in everyday language, it makes sense to draw a line between them (Miethe 2011, pp. 11–13). One's curriculum vitae, as well as other institutionalised "presentations of the self", such as health, unemployment or visa requirement reports, are made up of a sequence of relevant biographical events. The forms of presentation, as well as its contents, are to a great extent structured by the particular requirements of the receiving institutions. Unlike biographies, the events presented in curricula vitae are not constrained by certain meanings which these events have for the individuals. They are solely lists of events presented in a meaningful sequence and corresponding to the expectations of the person or institution who receives them. Biographies, on the other hand, incorporate both the sequence of relevant events for the individual and par-ticular meanings connected to these events. Biographical data do not possess a meaning per se. The relevant meaning is created according to the individual experiences in the course of the relevant person's life (Miethe 2011). Howev-er, the forms of presentation are not separate units of self-narrative. They are interconnected and influence each other. Experiences that are depicted se-quentially in the form of biographical self-presentation are the basis for the development of the manner of institutionalised presentation of the self. Insti-tutionalised presentation, a technique one acquires during one's lifetime, may on the other hand structure the way we perceive and present our biog-raphies.[24]

At the core of understanding the concept of biography lies the relation-ship between the individual and society. Since biographies are situated within

---

24   The mutual influence of different presentations of the self could be re-construed on the basis of the biographical narrations of my interviewees. The biographical presentation was in many cases structured and narrated along the lines of a professional curriculum vitae, since the interviewees had internalised this as the "correct" form of presenting themselves.

concrete historical and spatial contexts, they encompass not only a subjective view of the individuals' development but also the social and historical framework in which the individual life story is embedded (Alheit, Dausien 1990, p. 8). Biographies thus give access to both individual and social processes and their ongoing interplay.[25]

The way in which biography is construed and narrated is shaped by the positioning of the individual within the social structure (Dausien 2004, p. 30). Dimensions such as gender, social class, place of origin, age and so on, as well as other social practices, be it the family or cultural patterns of action, are crucial for biographical constructions. At the same time, biographies are also shaped by the context in which they have been narrated. They are produced in diverse situations and for diverse purposes, and are shaped by internalised and normative ideas on the way in which the biography should be narrated, which events and experiences should or should not be presented (Dausien 1996, p. 4). However, biographies are not only responses to social structures. They are both the product of social and individual processes, and their producer. As Peter Alheit puts it (1990, pp. 17–18, italics in original, own translation): "The biography as a place in which subjective experiences are made over time is a fascinating example of the dialectics of social life; on the one hand the expression stands for the respective individual and hence by no means accidental *structure* of implied knowledge; on the other hand it represents the *emergence* of a living experience at the present time, allowing the subject's biographical background to potentially be viewed in a new light and permitting the future to remain open."

Understanding biographies as a social construction produced by interaction processes between the specific contexts increasingly shifts the focus of biographical research from the question of life stories or "life records" – introduced to scientific discussion by Thomas and Znaniecki (1958) – to the question of how the relevant biography is construed by individuals in the specific context (Dausien 2004, p. 34).

The dialectic of agency and structure

The concepts of agency – the capacity of individuals to act independently – and structure – which is understood as being the "objective" social frameworks and contexts for biographical developments – are concepts that are central to biographical research. According to the biographical approach, these terms are not perceived as being contradictory to each other, but as processes which are in mutual interplay and part of social reality (see e.g. Alheit 1992). These terms, and especially the concept of horizons of possibil-

---

25 The interplay of social and individual processes has been the subject of scientific discussion. For the discussion and different positions, see for example: Apitzsch 1990; Alheit 1992; Apitzsch 2003a; Apitzsch et al. 2006; Bourdieu 2000; Bukow, Spindler 2006.

ity and "possibility spaces", were also central to my research. In the following chapter I shall outline the history behind these concepts and the way in which they have been used within the biographical research tradition which this paper is built on.

The definitions of action and agency as often used in biographical research go back to the ideas of Max Weber and Alfred Schütz. The individuals' action was for Weber (1970, p. 25) the starting point for his sociological analysis: "If I have become a sociologist...it is mainly in order to exorcise the spectre of collective conceptions which still lingers among us. In other words, sociology itself can only proceed from the actions of one or more separate individuals and must therefore adopt strictly individualistic methods." Weber introduced the expression "interpretative sociology" into sociology, claiming that sociological analyses should always include an interpretative understanding of human actions, motives and meanings (Collins, Makowsky 1998, p. 124). The task of sociology should, according to Weber (1978b, p. 7), be "to interpret the meaning of social action and thereby give a causal explanation of the way in which the action proceeds and the effects which it produces." Action means human behaviour to which agents attribute a subjective meaning. Social action then, so Max Weber (1978b, p. 7, italics in original), is "an action in which the meaning intended by the agent or agents involves a relation to *another* person's behaviour and in which that relation determines the way in which the action proceeds." It was Alfred Schütz, who took up Weber's theory of social action and his approach to sociology and developed it further.

In 1932 Alfred Schütz published his book "The phenomenology of the social world" (1972), in which he connected some aspects of Max Weber's approach to social action and philosophical phenomenology. Starting with Husserl's phenomenology, Schütz made an effort to clarify the processes surrounding the social constitution of meaning, which was missing from Weber's philosophy. According to him, experiences that an individual had lived through had no meaning in themselves. However, meaning could be given to them retrospectively in the process of reflection. While it was not possible to ascribe a meaning to experiences at the moment at which they occurred, it was possible, so Schütz, to ascribe a meaning to future experiences. Schütz defined action as behaviour which is oriented towards the future, which has some goal and purpose. Future projected goals have to contain some notion of the past, i.e. the relevant action in the future has to be able to be projected as completed. There is, so Schütz, a distinction between action which is in progress, and the completed act. Furthermore, he distinguished between "in-order-to motives" (Um-zu-Motiv) of action and "because-motives" (Weil-Motiv) of action. The former is situated in the future and is directed towards the individual's goals. It could also be understood as a biographical project. The latter lies in the past and may can give an explanation for further action (Schütz 1972, pp. xxiii–xxiv). According to Schütz, even if it is possible for the actions of others to be observed, for the observer the complete subjective meaning ascribed to the action by the actor is inaccessible. He outlined the distinction between one's own experiences and the experiences of others, between the meaning one ascribes to one's own actions and the meaning of other people's actions, between self-understanding and the understanding of others (Schütz 1972, p. 8).

Generally, the concept of structure is used in order to describe the arrangements which have an impact on human action, their limits and possibilities (Juhasz, Mey 2003, p. 91). It concerns social dimensions, such as gender, class, ethnicity or age, which are often perceived by individuals as given and unquestioned. Moreover, the concept of structure is used in order to describe the sphere of possibilities accessible to an individual in order to act. This understanding of possibility spaces can be linked to Bourdieu's term of "habitus", which refers to the set of social conditions, dispositions, values and expectations connected to the position of the individual within society (Bourdieu 1998b, p. 14; Alheit 1992, p. 27). These structures thus provide individuals with a limited framework for action and development of oneself.

Biographical researchers have pointed out that such structures can be both experienced as determining and changeable. Peter Alheit called this ability as "biographicity" (Alheit 2009, p. 125, quotation marks in original): "Biographicity means that we can redesign again and again, from scratch, the contours of our life within the specific contexts in which we (have to) spend it, and that we experience these contexts as shapeable and designable. In our biographies, we do not possess all conceivable opportunities, but within the framework of the limits we are structurally set, we still have considerable scope open to us." Alheit thus outlined the mutual interconnections of action and structure and described the space of possibility as both constraining and changeable through social praxis. The concept of biographicity is crucial for my study, since it shows that the structures not only shape human action, but that they can also be shaped by individuals. Thus, the structures are not seen as static given facts, but they are perceived as changeable by human action, without neglecting their power in shaping the biographies of individuals.

Biographical process structures

Fritz Schütze contributed to the debate concerning the interplay of agency and structure with his concept of process structures. He argued that the mutual relation between agency and structure – and more general between individual and social processes – can be determined empirically. One instrument for approaching and analyzing this relation is the concept of biographical process structures, which can be developed on the basis of biographical material (Schütze 1980, 1984, 2012b). Schütze showed that any narrative of one's life history is closely connected to the development of the individual's identity (Schütze 2012b, pp. 8–9). This idea is based on the assumption, so Schütze, that narration is the elementary activity of biographical work. The narration of one's own life story or some of its phases does not only consist of sequences of outer events experienced by the narrator. Moreover, it encompasses the development of the inner state of the narrator who goes through the events, experiences them, reacts to them, shapes them and sometimes even changes them. In the course of narrating his or her life experiences, the narrator introduces into the story a basic order and structure of the development of his or her identity, ranging from past experiences to the present time and also outlining events in the near future (ibid.).

Schütze (1984, p. 92) distinguished four types of biographical process structure: the biographical action scheme, the trajectory of suffering, the institutional expectation pattern and the process structure of metamorphosis. The *biographical process structure of action scheme* is characterized by an active relationship between the biographer and the social processes. The biographer is the active player, who is able to plan and reach her or his goals. He or she is able by his or her actions to shape the biographical and social processes. In contrast with this intentionally oriented structure, the *biographical process structure of trajectory of suffering* is characterized by the inability to plan or to act. In this process structure, the biographer might feel overwhelmed by the social processes to which he or she cannot actively respond but which the biographer has simply to accept. The consequence of this trajectory of suffering might be the alienation of one's own consciousness of oneself, since the level of active participation in and planning of one's own life is restrained (Schütze 2012a, p. 23). The third process structure is that of the *institutional expectation pattern*. In this category, the biographer does not actively plan his or her goals, but instead follows the pre-prepared institutional paths expected of him or her. The biographer thus accepts the structure on offer and develops his or her own biography within the framework of these pathways. The *process structure of metamorphosis*, on the other hand, is neither planned nor conditioned by outer social processes, nor predetermined by any institutional framework. Changes experienced by the biographer originate from the inner world of biographer. However, these changes are not a priori planned, but instead experienced as something surprising and unexpected. The biographer might have the feeling that new perspectives and possibilities of action suddenly open up for him or her.

With his concept of process structures, Schütze developed different facets of interplay between agency and structure, and between the individual and social processes. He made it clear that an event does not have a meaning "in itself", but instead is given meaning by the individuals during the course of their life. The process structures also show that the possibilities to act are perceived very differently and shaped not only by "outer" conditions but by past biographical experiences and biographical knowledge.

Biographical experiences and biographical knowledge

Biographical experiences and biographical knowledge are further crucial concepts for biographical research. These concepts, which have been systematically developed especially by Peter Alheit and Erika M. Hoerning (Alheit, Hoerning 1989; Hoerning 1989, 2000), challenge the perception of experiences and knowledge as universal tools which can be applied by individuals in diverse contexts after they have been acquired. Rather, they underline the biographical dimension and contextual character of experiences and knowledge.

As Erika M. Hoerning (1989, p. 148) pointed out, experiences and any associated knowledge create a link between the past and the future contained in the biography. On the one hand, the experiences one had in the past and which became meaningful for the individual shape the further development of the individual's biography. Furthermore, past experiences have a crucial impact on the way in which the biography is retrospectively evaluated and construed. On the other hand, experiences do not stay bound to the past: they are sources of biographical knowledge, which can serve as a resource for present and future decision making and the development of biographical plans (ibid.). However, the way in which past experiences and knowledge can be transformed into present and future resources is not a linear process of simply applying the patterns of action and solutions acquired in the past to new contexts. Rather, it is an ongoing process of reworking and re-construing experience and knowledge (Hoerning 1989, pp. 153–154). Hoerning (1989, p. 153; 2000, p. 4) highlighted that biographical resources do not have to emanate only from the individual's past experiences, but also from the intra- and intergenerational experiences of others. Knowledge which stems from experiences which were not necessarily had by the individuals themselves can thus also have an impact on patterns of action and the development of future biographical projects.

Hoerning (1989, pp. 154–155; 2000, p. 4) pointed out that biographical experiences which one had in past and from which one learned are bound to certain contexts. She argued that the belonging of people to certain categories, such as class, age or gender, structure the possibilities to use such biographical knowledge in different contexts. However, she also underlined that the way these experiences are used on the subject's future biographical path is dependent both on societal expectations and on the overall shape of the subject's biography – i.e. the capability to integrate the biographical experiences into the subject's life path and future biographical projects.

To summarise, biographical knowledge is not a static "stockpile" of all experiences which can be recalled as biographical resources in an unchangeable way in the future. Rather, past experiences and knowledge are in an ongoing process reworked or put into question by new experiences. Biographical knowledge is thus changeable and open for corrections. This capability of re-construction enables one to integrate new and old experiences and knowledge into the biographical scheme, re-shape one's biographical project and change the perception of one's self. At the same time, these transformation processes – or biographical work (see e.g. Inowlocki 1993; Schütze 2012b, pp. 6–7) – are not arbitrary, but always embedded within the horizon of possibilities shaped by the historical and social positioning of the individual in society. This capability of transformation enables, paradoxically, the construction of continuity and coherence of one's own biographical path and the perception of one's self, which is so central for individuals in modern times.

4.2 Biographical approaches to migration

Migration – both internal and international – is an experience of biographical importance par excellence. Moving places requires new orientation in the unknown surroundings and it challenges to a greater or lesser extent one's previous knowledge of the social organisation and everyday practices. Moreover, moving places may initiate the process of biographical reflections on oneself and one's own positioning in society, since the perception of the self and patterns of action acquired in one set of surroundings does not have to be necessarily transferable to the new places. Taking into account these thoughts, it is striking that biographical approaches to migration only gained the attention of scholars relatively late on. With the exception of "The Polish peasant in Europe and America" written by Znaniecki and Thomas in 1920s, it was not until the 1980s that migration really started to attract the attention of biographical researchers. The reason for the hitherto invisible nature of the biographical and agent-centred approach to migration processes was no doubt the way in which migration was approached by researchers, studying migration flows from the perspective of nation states and local labour markets. This methodological nationalism – a research perspective which takes the national framework for granted – was later on criticised by scholars who underlined the transnational links of migrants, institutions and social movements which span the borders of the relevant nation state and which became the reality for an ever rising number of people. In this chapter I outline the history of biographical approaches to migration and transmigration processes against the backdrop of scientific discussions concerning migration. After introducing the first approaches to migration from biographical perspectives, I draw a link between the biographical and transnational approaches as elaborated by recent scholars and position my work within these streams of thought.

4.2.1 First approaches to migration from a biographical perspective

The study "The Polish peasant in Europe and in America" not only became a foundational piece of work on the biographical approach but also a classical study of migration research. Thomas and Znaniecki, the authors of the book, opened up discussions on the use of biographical material in researching migration, on the interconnection of social change and individual processes, the interplay of family relations and migration processes as well as transcultural links. However, despite migration becoming a phenomenon that was heavily followed and studied over the 20th century, these themes were not fully continued by the authors' followers. The reason for this may be the shift from qualitative studies as cultivated by Chicago scholars in the 1920s and 1930s to positivist approaches based on quantitative surveys and statistical analysis, which dominated the social sciences for the next decades (Breckner 2007, p. 114). Only from the 1970s and 1980s onwards did researchers start to call for case-oriented studies of migration, pointing to the pitfalls for the standardised collection of data and the impossibility of grasping the complex migration phenomena with up to date dominant theoretical and methodological approaches (ibid.).

Until the 1960s, migration had mostly been explained in terms of push-pull factors. The moving of people between two regions or countries was perceived as the rational choice of individuals based on the idea of the maximization of one's own profit (King 2012, p. 13). This approach to migration was largely influenced by the neo-classical economic paradigm, which dominated the social and economic sciences at that time (ibid.). However, the push-pull models were later on the subject of extensive criticism: migration researchers criticised their simplicity, ahistoricism, functionalism, and the impossibility to explain diverse forms of migration which were not a priori based on economic reasons. Moreover, they pointed out the failure to integrate individual and family aspects in the process of migration, historical connections and power relations among regions, as well as economic dependencies on a macro and micro level, all of which shaped the migration processes (King 2012, p. 14). Thus, from the 1970s onwards a range of new theories – such as the world systems theory, dependency theory, dual labour market approach, or theory of social networks – appeared which were aimed at reconceptualising migration processes (King 2012, p. 16).[26]

Besides the efforts to explain migration processes by means of one overwhelming theory, the other stream of migration studies concentrated on the processes of assimilating migrants into mainstream society. The assimilation approach was pioneered by Chicago scholars in the 1920s and 1930s and dominated migration studies until the 1960s (Schmitter Heisler 2008, p. 83). It also experienced new popularity later on (ibid.). The main question underlying the numerous pieces of research was the adjustment or maladjustment of migrants to mainstream society. In order to explain and predict the processes of adjustment, including not only social status but also shifted habits as well as social and cultural practices, several models were developed (see e.g. Park 1928; Gordon 1964). Within these classical assimilation approaches, mainstream society was perceived as a homogenous and unchangeable unit and migration as a social problem and threat for the "receiving" society (Schmitter Heisler 2008, p. 85). This understanding of migration was connected to the major discourses on nationality and belonging, which gained in importance in the course of nation building and the shaping of national borderlines in the 19th and 20th century. Migration, which has actually been a common phenomenon throughout history, was construed as an exception and an anomaly, and therefore as a problem (Wimmer, Glick Schiller 2002; Borkert et al. 2006, § 1). From the 1960s onwards, the assimilation theories were heavily criticised. Scholars argued that the assimilation theories failed to explain the perpetuating inequalities based on ethnicity, nationality and/or skin colour. Moreover, they criticised the perception of mainstream society as a homogenous and amorphous entity and pointed out its structural inequalities and transformation processes (Schmitter Heisler 2008, p. 85). Nevertheless, despite that fact that the focus moved from "assimilation" to "integration" of migrants into mainstream society, and despite the fact that conceptualisations and models on migration changed, the main questions shaping migration research remained nearly unchanged for the next decades.

The economic crises in the 1970s changed the migration landscape. In Europe, migration politics became more restrictive and the way migrants were perceived in political and public discourse shifted (Borkert et al. 2006, § 3). The "guest worker" programs, which were common in several European countries in various forms and which were aimed at attracting workers from former colonies or other countries, were stopped. However, instead of returning to their home countries as was commonly expected, many guest workers continued to live in the various host countries and were joined by their relatives (Bukow, Heimel 2003, p. 15). These shifts had an impact on the change in focus of political and scientific discussions. In Germany, for example, the

26 For a more detailed and comprehensive overview of migration theories, see e.g. Pries 2001a; Han 2006; King 2012.

102

focus of attention moved from guest workers or temporary workers to "foreigners". Most of the discussions from 1970s onwards concerned social issues, but also the question of assimilation, return migration and the acculturation of migrants.[27] The new social realities also brought new sets of questions with them, calling for new methods of researching migration. The slowly rising impact of qualitatively oriented studies of migration across the disciplines pointed to pitfalls in the attempts to theorise migration processes using one overwhelming theory. Ethnographical, sociological and geographical qualitative studies brought the dimension of migrant experiences to the core of researchers' attention. These studies underlined not only the dependencies resulting from the macro-structural interconnections within the global economy, which were the pillars of world system theory, dependency theory and other historical-structural theories developed from the 1970s onwards, but also the role of migrants' agency in shaping the migration processes and social reality (King 2012, pp. 19, 24-25).

Ursula Apitzsch (1990) was among the first to once again take up the tradition of studying the processes of social change and migration from a biographical perspective as first introduced by Chicago scholars. With her study "Migration und Biographie" (Apitzsch 1990) she contributed to the existing discussion on the theorisation of migration and methodological tools in researching migration. Apitzsch focused her research on the educational and biographical pathway of youngsters of Italian origin in Germany. On the basis of an analysis of biographical narrative interviews with children of migrants who had come to Germany in the course of the guest worker schemes, she challenged the perception of migrants as trapped between two cultures and suffering under these conditions – which was the theoretical mainstream view within education sciences at that time – and showed that youngsters with a migrant background developed diverse forms of "intercultural disposition" which served them as a resource within their educational path and in positioning themselves in society (Apitzsch 1990, p. 376; Apitzsch, Siouti 2007, p. 12). According to Apitzsch, this "intercultural disposition" gave rise to creative biographical orientations which did not necessarily emerge solely from the context of one or another culture. Neither were they decontextualized, but developed in the biographical course of events and in confrontations with structural frameworks. Apitzsch showed that the educational path of youngsters was shaped both by family orientations, which were not passively taken over but continuously reworked in an active process of reflection, and by institutional and structural possibilities in the country of migration. She also showed that the "traditional" and "modernisation" processes were not necessarily opposites, but that they developed simultaneously and in mutual interplay. She thus argued against the assimilation approach, as

---

27 For the development of theoretical and methodological discussions within migration studies in Germany see especially Breckner 2009, pp. 21–64; Bukow, Heimel 2003.

well as against the thesis that a strong family orientation would necessarily lead to the reproduction of traditional social roles and to the failure of educational projects. She supported her thesis by finding that close – and seemingly traditional – family links of youngsters of Italian origin did not necessarily act as a hindrance, but potentially as a resource for the subject's onward biographical and career path (Apitzsch 1990, p. 345; Breckner 2009, pp. 57–58).

Ursula Apitzsch introduced the central biographical concept of process structures as developed by Fritz Schütze (1980; 1983) to migration studies. She argued that the biographical processes of trajectory were of particular relevance in researching migration, since they showed the processes of disorder and suffering in the course of migration. Schütze introduced four types of process structures – the biographical action scheme, the trajectory of suffering, the institutional expectation pattern and the process structure of metamorphosis – which describe different attitudes towards biographical and social events. In contradiction to biographical action schemes which point to the intentional agency of biographers within their possibility horizons, processes of trajectory are characterised by the "attitude of feeling overwhelmed by powerful outer forces and of just suffering through their impact. This attitude includes the basic experience of having lost the aptitude to model one's everyday encounters and one's life through personally controlled action; on the contrary, there is the feeling to be able to do nothing more than to react to the powerful outer events and just to attempt to keep some balance of handling social encounters and one's life situation. Therefore a basic feature of the trajectory attitude is that of a conditional orientation structure. Another feature is the irritation of becoming strange to oneself, since the active relationship to life is lost." (Schütze 2012b, p. 23). Apitzsch (2000, p. 62, own translation) argued that migration processes are shaped by both of these contradictory types of social action: "Far-reaching intentional action and with it the migration project itself, the force of which might even span several generations, is interrupted or superseded by unexpected new experiences, misguided assumptions regarding the host country, hostility towards migrants and the shaking up of plans as a whole due to chaotic reactions by individuals and social groups alike. It is precisely by means of the connection of these two types of action that the social construct of the migrant's biography is made". In other words, the action scheme and trajectory of suffering processes are crucial for understanding the constructions of migrant biographies, since they point out the structural constraints and the (limited) ability of individuals to carry through their biographical plans. In addition, the focus on process structures within biographical migration research enables one to analyse the emergence of creative transformation processes and biographical metamorphosis –shifted perceptions of one's self and one's own biographical path and discovering alternative possibilities of action and of self-development (Apitzsch 2000; Schütze 2001).

From the 1990s onwards, the biographical approach within migration studies developed significantly. Numerous bodies of research focused not only on migration in different time-space contexts, but developed different perspectives on migration processes. In 1999, Ursula Apitzsch edited the book "Migration und Traditionsbildung" (1999), in which the contributors once again took up the theme of "tradition building" and "modernisation processes" in the course of migration. Lena Inowlocki (1999), one of the contributors to the book, convincingly showed that tradition is not a static set of beliefs and practices which are automatically passed from one generation to another in a one-directional manner, but rather that it is a process which is recreated in everyday communication, social practices and transgenerational processes. While studying the transmission of religious practices of three generations of women in displaced Jewish families, she pointed out the role of "doing tradition" in creating continuity within families which had experienced extreme ruptures in the past as a result of persecution and forced migration. Inowlocki also introduced the concept of "family work" – the reflexive process of integrating different reference systems of traditionality among generations into family narratives (Inowlocki 1995, p. 431) – which has its theoretical origins in the biographical research tradition.

Biographical research has proven to be useful not only for investigating the passing down of information from generation to generation and tradition building in the course of migration (see e.g. Inowlocki 1993; Delcroix 2009; Apitzsch 2009a), but also for investigating the shifts in gender relations and gender orders (see e.g. Dausien 2000; Apitzsch 2003b; Apitzsch, Kontos 2008; Lutz 2009a, 2010; Lutz, Davis 2009; Ruokonen-Engler 2012). Biographical research has also been used to study work relations (see e.g. Karakayali 2010b; Satola 2010), the processes involved in educational and professional careers (see e.g. Kreutzer 2006; Tepecik 2009; Liversage 2009b; Nohl et al. 2010b), and social positioning from an agent-centred perspective (see e.g. Ruokonen-Engler 2012). Over the past decades, there have been a wide range of biographical-oriented case studies focusing on different types of migration in different time-space contexts. Of particular interest to the present study were studies setting out migration within Europe (see e.g. Miller 2012), and more concretely migration along an East-West axis (Breckner, Miethe 2000; Breckner 2009; Karakayali 2010b; Kempf 2013; Palenga-Möllenbeck 2014). These studies describe – albeit with a different emphasis and from different perspectives – the interplay of migration processes and structural societal changes in this region of Europe, the meaning of borders and border crossings, as well as the various negotiations concerning the shifted positioning of subjects after migration.

The transnational approach, which was introduced to migration studies in the 1990s, offered a new perspective on migration processes and called for the re-conceptualisation of migration theories and methodologies so far. The new set of questions put forward by the transnational approach initiated new discussions within the sphere of biographical migration research with regard to the applicability of up-to-date theoretical and methodological tools.

4.2.2 Links between the transnational and biographical approach

Positioning the transnational debate within migration studies

The discussion on transnationalism in the field of migration studies was initiated by Nina Glick Schiller, Linda Basch and Cristina Blanc-Szanton in the early 1990s. In their edited book "Towards a Transnational Perspective on Migration: Race, Class, Ethnicity, and Nationalism Reconsidered" (1992a) the authors introduced up-to-date studies which dealt with the transnational dimension of migration processes from different perspectives. In their own contribution to the book the authors outlined new challenges for migration research. They argued that the existing conceptualisation of migration did not suffice in order to grasp the contemporary migration processes. "Now, a new kind of migrating population is emerging, composed of those whose networks, activities and patterns of life encompass both their host and home societies. Their lives cut across national boundaries and bring two societies into a single social field." (Glick Schiller et al. 1992b, p. 1). The authors described this new kind of migration as "transmigration" and the migrants involved in it as "transmigrants". According to them, "[t]ransmigrants develop and maintain multiple relations – familial, economic, social, organisational, religious, and political that spans borders. Transmigrants take actions, make decisions, and feel concerns, and develop identities within social networks that connect them to two or more societies simultaneously (Glick Schiller et al. 1992b, pp. 1–2). The authors based their observations on ethnographic studies focusing on migrants from Haiti, the Caribbean and the Philippines living in New York. They observed their participation in diverse social and political organisations connected to their country of origin, the role of remittances, family networks which transgress national borders, as well as multiple senses of belonging resulting from their positioning in diverse social locations.

The authors criticised the existing migration theories which conceptualised migration in the terms of "immigration", "emigration" or "re-migration" and which studied the migrant population through the lenses of nation states. They called for the "unbounding" of the social sciences, arguing that social sciences and up-to-date migration research produced theories which took for granted the perception of societies as discrete entities which have their own separate history, economy, and culture (Glick Schiller et al. 1992b, p. 6; Faist et al. 2013, p. 13). This perception, so the authors, overlooked the migrant realities which spanned across national borders. They proposed that migrant phenomena needed to be embedded within the global arena and within the global economic system. Only within this context, so the authors, would it be possible to explore transnational fields of action, meaning and positioning, without neglecting the role of nation states and global economic systems in shaping the lives of individuals and the constructions of belonging (Glick Schiller et al. 1992b, p. 19).

The transnational approach soon became established within migration research in the USA. Numerous studies, which focused predominantly on the migratory spaces between the USA, Mexico, South America and the Caribbean, offered new perspectives on transnational interconnections and migration processes and questioned up-to-date conceptualisations of migration within migration studies (for the overview see e.g. Levitt, Jaworsky 2007; Pries 2001a). This research approach soon moved to the European context as well, and was applied in diverse projects across scientific disciplines in order to study different facets of trans-border movements, networks, constructions of multiple belongings and cultural, political and economic interconnections (for the overview see e.g. Siouti 2013, pp. 22–23; Levitt, Jaworsky 2007). Since the early 1990s, a large amount of literature and research has been produced (see e.g. Pries 1997; Smith, Guarnizo 1999; Levitt et al. 2003; Lutz 2009b; Amelina et al. 2012; Faist et al. 2013), which in turn has made some authors speak of a transnational turn in migration studies (see e.g. Amelina et al. 2013).

However, the transnational approach was also exposed to criticism. Some authors criticised the ambiguity of the central definitions of transnational research and the danger of transnationalism losing its explanatory power, since it was often used as a "catch-all-term" (Pries 2008a, p. 168). Furthermore, others argued that other forms of trans-border activity, as well as the role of nationalism and national politics, could be overshadowed by an over-emphasis on transnational movements (King 2012, p. 25; Lüthi 2005). Other critics pointed out that transnational processes were not a new phenomenon, but that cross-spatial interconnections had also been made in the past (Waldinger, Fitzgerald 2004, pp. 1187–1189).

Later scholars researching transnational migration responded to these critics by redefining certain concepts central to transnational migration research, such as transnational social spaces, anchoring their conceptualisations in the sociological theory of space and movement (see e.g. Levitt, Glick Schiller 2003; Pries 2008a; Faist et al. 2013). Moreover, they endeavoured to highlight the special character of transnational processes in relation to other cross-border movements and underlined the role of national states as part of the analysis (for the discussion see e.g. Levitt, Jaworsky 2007). Several authors also responded to the "newness" of transnational phenomena, arguing that what was new was not the existence of transnational migration per se, but the new variation of these processes linked to tightening global interconnections and dependencies, as well to new possibilities of transport and communication technology (Levitt, Jaworsky 2007, p. 133; Faist et al. 2013, p. 46). Despite the criticism, I see the strength of the transnational approach as being that it questions "methodological nationalism" (Wimmer, Glick Schiller 2002) and the dominant theories within migration research which consider migration as a linear process from one country to another, and which conceptualise migrants within binary categories of "emigration" and "immigration" (Lutz 2009b, p. 13; King 2012, p. 25). Furthermore, this perspective enables one to study new forms of migration and transnational links, as well as multiple belongings and positioning which emerges in transnational social spaces and which has been overlooked by theoretical and methodological instruments hitherto.

The concept of transnational social spaces

Transnational social spaces, or transnational social fields, are one of the central concepts within transnational migration studies, and also became the key concept for the present study. Generally, transnational social spaces refer to links, processes and practices among individuals and institutions which span across the borders of national states. They denote the shifted relation of "social" and "spatial", which bring about the rewriting of social boundaries and the establishment of new scopes of action for individuals involved in these spaces.

The concept of transnational social fields was introduced into transnational migration studies by Peggy Levitt and Nina Glick Schiller (2003). At the core of this concept lies the empirical evidence of transnational processes and the redefined perception of society, which in theoretical thinking hitherto was often congruent with nation state units. While referring to Burdieu's conceptualisation of social fields, the authors defined social fields as a "set of multiple interlocking networks of social relationships through which ideas, practices, and resources are unequally exchanged, organized, and transformed" (Levitt, Glick Schiller 2003, p. 1009). They argued that national boundaries do not necessarily have to be congruent with the boundaries of social fields. According to the authors, "[n]ational social fields are those that stay within national boundaries while transnational social fields connect actors through direct and indirect relations across borders." (ibid.) This perception, so the authors, not only challenges "methodological nationalism" (Wimmer, Glick Schiller 2002), but also the divisions between local, national, transnational or global. On the one hand, actors can be embedded within transnational social fields through their daily practices despite being bound to one local space, structured by multiple structural and institutional settings (Levitt, Glick Schiller 2003, p. 1010). On the other hand, people can often move places and be simultaneously engaged in more than one nation state (Levitt, Glick Schiller 2003, p. 1029). This approach, which recognises that "individuals occupy different gender, racial, and class positions within different states at the same time" (Levitt, Glick Schiller 2003, p. 1015), helps to understand a subject's multiple positioning and their interplay in transnational spaces. Peggy Levitt and Nina Glick Schiller distinguished between "ways of being" and "ways of belonging" in the social field. According to the authors (Levitt, Glick Schiller 2003, p. 1010), "[w]ays of being refers to the actual social relations and practices that individuals engage in rather than to the identities associated with their action." In contrast, ways of belonging describe the practices which demonstrate the subject belonging to a certain group. With their analytical division of these two dimensions the authors made it clear that participation in transnational spaces does not have to be connected to constructions of belonging to a particular group and vice versa.

Ludger Pries (2008a, p. 44) defined transnational social spaces as relatively sustainable and dense multi-local relations of social practices, symbols and artefacts which span across the borders of nation state. He argued that the transnationalisation processes are not new but that they have been increasingly gaining in importance over the last decades. Similarly to Levitt and Glick Schiller, Pries understood the establishment of transnational social spaces to be the process of uncoupling geographical and social spaces, although he developed the relation between these two dimensions and their genesis in more detail. His thesis was that in the course of societal changes and nation building over the past centuries, the "spatial" and "social" dimensions had become strongly interconnected and now overlapped each other. Geographical space, constrained by the borders of national states, became the framework within which everyday life and the social world of individuals developed. This exclusive embeddedness of geographical spaces and social spaces, so Pries (2001b, pp. 55–56), has been changing. On the one hand, so the author, the different social spaces can be "stacked" within one geographical location. On the other hand, the social spaces can also span across two or more geographical spaces (Pries 2001b, p. 57). Thus, transnational social spaces are, so Pries (ibid.), "social spaces that have a multi-local geographic link rather than an exclusive one". Within these spaces, "individual and collective biographical life projects, everyday life as well as the real 'objective' sequence of life stations span between different geographical-spatial extensions." (Pries 2001b, p. 67).

Ludger Pries (2004; 2008a) included the relational conceptualisation of "space" in his analysis. He criticised that in migration studies geographical spaces were predominantly understood to be absolutistic categories, taking for granted the existence of locations – be it cities, regions, or national states – and any associated constructions of belonging. In contrast with this view, he proposed conceptualising geographical space as a relational category, one which is always a result of meanings given to that space by individuals. The "spatial" thus always has a "social" dimension and vice versa (Pries 2004). Transnational social spaces could also be understood as new configurations of "spatial" and "social", which disrupt the mutual embeddedness of these two dimensions within the framework of a nation state.

In a similar manner, Thomas Faist, Margit Fauser and Eveline Reisenauer defined transnational social spaces as social formations which result from the social ties of individuals and other actors across the borders of national states (Faist et al. 2013, p. 2). More precisely, "[b]y transnational spaces we mean relatively stable, lasting and dense sets of ties reaching beyond and across the borders of sovereign states. They consist of combinations of ties and their contents, positions in networks and organizations, and networks or organizations that cut across the borders of at least two nation-states." (Faist 2000, p. 197). Transnational social spaces can take diverse forms, from family ties – expressed for example by regular exchanges, remittances, care arrangements and other trans-border practices – or information or business networks, to large transnational communities, such as a diaspora or church (Faist et al. 2013, pp. 56–60; see also Pries 2008a, p. 46). Transnational social spaces can be established and maintained for diverse reasons, ranging from emotional and intimate links to purely political or economic interests, and can involve both migrants and non-migrants. They are spaces within which ideas, goods, information and resources are circulated, but also "symbolic elements, such as common meanings, memories, future expectations and collective representation" (Faist et al. 2013, pp. 54–55). Transnational social spaces are also according to Faist, Fauser and Reisenauer not static formations set by predefined fixed boundaries. Rather, they are dynamic processes which are socially constituted (Faist et al. 2013, p. 60). This approach to transnational social spaces, so the authors (ibid.), enables one to study "relations and practices of migrants and non-migrants across the borders of two or more nation-states" (Faist et al. 2013, p. 53). Moreover, it enables one to observe how boundaries are transformed, redrawn, or replaced by others and how social spaces are transformed and newly established.

Although the authors above have approached the conceptualisation of transnational social spaces from different theoretical and disciplinary perspectives, their definitions point out similar features of transnational social spaces: they are not spaces which would exist per se, but they are created as part of an ongoing process by individuals or other actors. Thus, rather than being concrete geographical places, transnational social spaces are relational social spaces which span multi-locally and which are given different meanings by different individuals. The authors underlined both the biographical dimension and the role of institutional and structural settings in shaping transnational spaces. In order to grasp the emergence of transnational spaces empirically, the authors proposed a number of different research approaches, including multi-sited ethnography, longitudinal qualitative and quantitative approaches (Levitt, Glick Schiller 2003, pp. 1012–1013; Faist et al. 2013).

The alternative approach is the biographical research approach, which has gained in importance over the last few years and which seems to be particularly promising in researching transnational migration processes and the emergence of transnational social spaces. It offers theoretical and methodological tools in order to research societal processes from an agent-centred perspective. In the next chapter I shall discuss the theoretical and methodological connections between the biographical and transnational approaches.

The biographical approach to transmigration processes

The transnational approach soon became established within biographically oriented migration research. Over the last decade, several works were published which endeavoured to show the connection, both theoretically and empirically, between the transnational and biographical approaches (see e.g. Apitzsch 2003c, 2009b; Fürstenau 2004; Lutz 2004b, 2009b, 2011b; Apitzsch, Siouti 2008; Rosenthal, Bogner 2009; Karakayali 2010b; Inowlocki, Riemann 2012; Miller 2012; Ruokonen-Engler 2012; Siouti 2013; Kempf 2013). The authors investigated not only different forms of migration both within and outside Europe but also contributed to theoretical and methodological discussions concerning the constitution of transnational social spaces, transnational biographies, multiple positioning and belonging, and transnational biographical knowledge.

Biographical researchers pointed out that transnational social spaces are biographically constituted. Ursula Apitzsch, who initiated the discussion on transnational phenomena within biographical migration research with her article "Migrationsbiographien als Orte transnationaler Räume" (Apitzsch 2003c), defined transnational spaces as invisible structures of multiple transnational, legal and cultural transitions by which individuals orientate themselves and in which they are at the same time involved through their biographical and collective experiences (Apitzsch 2003c, p. 69). According to her, transnational spaces are located within the migration biographies, which are both constituted and in ongoing processes newly re-construed through the biographical work of individuals (Apitzsch 2003c, p. 65). At the same time, Apitzsch pointed out that transnational spaces are not arbitrary subjective constructions, but that they are formed by hegemonic relations and gender order (Apitzsch 2003c, p. 65, 2009b). On the basis of a comparative analysis of different migration flows both in the Asian and European context the author showed how migration regimes influence the establishment of specific gendered transnational movements (Apitzsch 2009b). They shape not only the possibilities of crossing the border and of social and cultural participation for individuals, but also the transnational "entanglements" which can span across generations (ibid.). At the same time, the author underlined the role of transnational biographical knowledge on the constitution of transnational spaces and on the development of diverse individual and collective strategies of action (Apitzsch 2009b).

From a biographical perspective, transnationality is neither an automatic result of migration processes, nor is it one-to-one transmitted to the next generation, as for example shown by Irini Siouti (2013). She based her study on biographical narrative interviews with the next generation of Greek migrants who came to Germany in the course of guest worker programs. She showed that the transnational way of life of second generation migrants developed from biographical revisions of the migration projects begun by the migrants' parents (Siouti 2013, p. 209). The author argued that the development of transmigration was an unintended consequence of coping strategies developed by migrants and their children in order to challenge the structural barriers, experiences of exclusion and alienation in both societies within which they moved. Siouti showed that the cross-border practices and links with which the migrants grew up – be it the painful experience of separation from their parents, moving frequently between countries, keeping close contacts to significant others across the borders, speaking several languages or attending both German and Greek schools – were experiences which migrants built on and re-worked in order to develop coping strategies and possibilities of action which spanned across the borders of one nation state. Such transnational links could in the process of "biographical work" carried out by the relevant migrant be turned into a resource, facilitating a transnational educational career and upwards social mobility (Siouti 2013, pp. 209–210).

Focusing on the other form of migration processes within Europe, Minna-Kristiina Ruokonen-Engler (2005; 2012) showed that transnational spaces signified not only the enlargement of the scope of possibilities for the migrant, but also the construction of biographical continuity, linking the past and new biographical experiences, relevance systems, knowledge and positioning and integrating them into the subject's biographical path and perceptions of the self. The author exemplified by means of diverse migration biographies – which she collected as part of her study of migration processes and the positioning of Finnish migrant women in Germany – how migration was connected to biographical transformation processes and negotiations of the migrant's positioning. She showed that although migration can be the continuation of transformations commenced prior to migration, it can also initiate the process of extensive inner change, whereby the author underlined the interplay of "outer" structural societal factors and "inner" biographically acquired patterns of perception and action in these processes (Ruokonen-Engler 2012, p. 357). On the basis of biographical analysis Ruokonen-Engler described the influence of hierarchical power relations, policies, social discourse, and biographical process structures on the construction of gendered and ethnic positioning and belonging (Ruokonen-Engler 2012, pp. 319–320). She showed that the establishment of transnationality is closely connected to the experience of different power relations (Ruokonen-Engler 2012, p. 350). Transnational spaces thus could be understood as biographical spaces of action which are not bound to one nation state but span beyond it. They leave open the possibility of realising biographical plans and enable one to position oneself simultaneously within diverse societies (Ruokonen-Engler 2005, p. 67, 2012).

Helma Lutz's study "The new maids. Transnational Women and the care economy" (Lutz 2011b) showed that the establishment of transnational social spaces is an ambiguous process which can represent the enlargement of the scope of possibilities and present new challenges for migrant women and men at the same time. She based her work on biographical interviews with migrants working in German households as maids, and with their employers. She investigated, amongst other things, the setup of transnational families and transnational motherhood and the associated new social organisation of family life, transformation of the gender order, new dependencies and the development of multiple positioning and coping strategies of migrants in transnational spaces. Lutz (2004b, p. 212) proposed conceptualising transnational biographies – i.e. biographies that were "entangled" within transnational processes – as "articulations". She based her conceptualisation on the theoretical thoughts of Stuart Hall who studied the relation between discourse and subject and described this relation as an articulation. According to him, an articulation, which is both produced by subjectivity and by producing it per se, expresses not only the interconnection of discourse and subject, but also any disconnections, ruptures and re-articulations (ibid.). Thus, the conceptualisation of transnational biographies as articulations makes it possible, so Lutz, to analyse the positioning and practices of individuals and social groups, which are expressed in biographical narratives, as products of disarticulation or re-articulation processes. This conceptualisation, so Lutz (2004b, p. 215), enables one to study and acknowledge different and sometimes contradictory forms of positioning and their meaning.

The aforementioned studies – which represent only a fragment of the developing body of research on transmigration processes from a biographical perspective – contributed to the question of how transnational social spaces are constituted and formed both by biographical and societal processes. Furthermore, they stirred up the debate on the role of discourses and power relations for the production of biographical narratives and for the practices and multiple positioning of individuals in transnational spaces. The authors showed that the biographical approach is a useful method for studying migration and transmigration phenomena, as well as diverse constructions of belonging and positioning, since the biographical narratives offer the possibility of accessing both the action of individuals and the "invisible but real structures of transnational spaces" (Apitzsch 2003c, p. 70). Moreover, the biographical approach enables one to study transnational phenomena on a time axis, following the process of its developments and shifts over the course of the individual's life and throughout generations (Apitzsch 2009b, p. 136).

Transnational biographical knowledge

The question of how transnational knowledge is constituted, shaped, or passed on through transnational processes has been the subject of interest of diverse interdisciplinary approaches (see especially Bender et al. 2013a, 2014). The production and re-production of knowledge, so the argumentation, cannot be studied without taking into account the increasing transborder movements of people, goods or information, as well as new forms of spaces of action and multiple senses of belonging that go beyond one nation state (Bender et al. 2013b, pp. 7–8). Désirée Bender, Annemarie Duscha, Lena Huber und Kathrin Klein-Zimmer (2013b, p. 10) distinguished three ideal types of transnational knowledge: firstly, knowledge of transnational phenomena, whereby they underlined that this knowledge is not limited only to people who actively cross the borders of nation states but also includes those who are in some other way "entangled" within the transnational network; secondly, transnational knowledge which circulates, emerges or shifts within transnational spaces, such as everyday practices of transnational families; and lastly knowledge which results from negotiations of different nation frameworks in the cross-border processes. The authors called for approaches which investigate how the knowledge emerges and "becomes" transnational in diverse social contexts, how it is acquired by individuals in the course of socialisation processes and how this is socially and locally embedded, how it is transformed during the subject's biographical pathway and over a wider period of history, how it is transmitted in intra- and intergenerational processes, and finally which functions and consequences the knowledge has, acknowledging that transnational knowledge could be both used as a resource and be experienced as a burden and the expression of power relations (Bender et al. 2013b, pp. 13–14).

Ursula Apitzsch (2003c; 2009b) concentrated on the question of how transnational biographical knowledge was linked to social practices spanning transnational spaces. Starting with theoretical assumptions concerning the conceptualisation of biographical knowledge as elaborated by Peter Alheit and Erika Hoerning (1989), she considered transnational knowledge to not just be a "stockpile" of knowledge collected on the basis of one's own or transmitted migration and biographical experiences. Rather, transnational knowledge is re-worked and reorganised in an ongoing process. This is not a static formation, but a process which is in constant change (Apitzsch, Siouti 2013, p. 150; see also Bender et al. 2013b). Apitzsch showed using diverse

114

examples how transnational knowledge is created and used by individuals and social groups in order to orientate themselves and act within transnational social spaces (see e.g. Apitzsch 2009b; Apitzsch, Siouti 2008, 2013).

Transnational biographical knowledge can be transformed, so Apitzsch and Siouti (2013, p. 150), into a biographical resource which individuals can use in order to cope with barriers set by national and transnational policies and exclusion mechanisms in the societies within which they lead their lives. The strategies they develop can take various forms, such as transnational educational careers (Apitzsch, Siouti 2008) – which can be the reaction to the exclusion mechanisms of educational system in the country of migration and which can become an alternative means of achieving educational and upward social mobility –, diverse transnational care-arrangements (Apitzsch, Siouti 2013) or "geographically mobile motherhood" (Siouti 2013, p. 215). These processes in which transnational biographical knowledge and biographical resources play a central role are, so the authors, accessible only through concepts which are not bound to the framework of one nation state but which take on a transnational perspective (Apitzsch 2009b, p. 135).

The contours of European transnational migration spaces

The migration biographies which were the subject of the present study are embedded within the specific context shaped by extensive changes in the European migration regimes. The narratives of the interviewees are structured by geo-political events such as the collapse of the bipolar world order or the enlargement of the EU in 2004, which had a significant effect on shaping the possibilities and motives for border crossings. Their biographies became part of the "new map of European migration" (King 2002), at the core of which, so Russell King, lay the new European geopolitics after the Cold War, the new time-space flexibilities, shifted international labour divisions and changed perceptions of and possibilities for self-realisation (King 2002, pp. 90, 100). An important role in the changing "map of European migration" was played by new legal frameworks within the EU, particularly the processes aimed at European integration (Recchi, Favell 2009, p. 2). These were supported by a variety of contracts among the European states, supporting for example freedom of movement, the regulation of the EU labour market and health and social insurance, the implementation of one currency throughout many European countries, and international educational opportunities. These changes led to new forms of transnational social interconnections and to a new understanding of Europe as a common frame of reference (Schütze, Schröder-Wildhagen 2012; Recchi 2014). In this chapter I will introduce several studies which tried to capture the changes within this part of Europe from an agent-centred perspective, and I depict the contours of the migration space within which the migrants act and develop their lives.

In order to describe the meaning of Europe as experienced by people who have either been on the move or who have been to some extent engaged in European cross-border activities, Fritz Schütze and Anja Schröder-Wildhagen (2012) introduced the concept of a "European mental space", which corresponds in many aspects to the concept of transnational social spaces (Faist et al. 2013). They based their conceptualisation on the large amount of data consisting of biographical narrative interviews collected for the "Euroidentities" project.[28] According to authors, the European mental space differs in many aspects from collective identities, such as national identities, which are based on the idea of "imagined communities" and on the idea of mutual loyalty of individuals towards each other. Rather than a supranational form of belonging which would lead to the explicit self-identification of individuals with Europe and which would replace the attachment of individuals to national states, the authors define the European mental space as the frame of reference which "enables the *transcending* of one's own familiar regional and national horizons", provides different approaches for comparison and imagination, and opens up new possibilities of cooperation and of establishing social contacts (Schütze, Schröder-Wildhagen 2012, pp. 258, 259).

The European mental space can therefore be understood as the framework which enlarges the orientation system of individuals and enables new forms of biographical unfolding. Lena Inowlocki and Gerhard Riemann (2012) refer to a European "potential space", which is established through biographical experiences and deals with different and unfamiliar social practices, perceptions and new forms of positioning. It functions as an enlarged sphere of possibility of action, self-development and self-perception. Of course, attempts to use the opportunity structure outside the border of one's national space can lead not only to better chances, but also to unplanned and unexpected events, such as the devaluation of one's education, knowledge or social competencies, which may lead to the subject experiencing the "trajectory of suffering" (Apitzsch 2000; Inowlocki, Riemann 2012).

The way in which migration within Europe, and particularly within the integrated EU, is experienced by migrants and how transnational social spaces develop has been the topic of a number of qualitative pieces of research. Adrian Favell (2009), for example, based his investigations of European integration processes on ethnographical observations and biographical interviews with inter-EU migrants who, according to him, embody the European idea of free movement. As Favell put it: "*Eurostars and Eurocities* sought to put flesh and blood to the theoretical construct of an ideal type European 'free mover', among a population that ranged from the young, freely mobile, individual movers in their twenties, through to older people in their thirties

---

28 The results of this project were published in the book "The evolution of European identities" (Miller 2012) and on the web page of the project: www.euroidentities.org.

and forties who might now be settling into cosmopolitan single or family lives in the three cities." (Favell, Recchi 2011, p. 69, the italics in original). He conducted about 60 interviews with migrants who were originally from other EU countries and now lived and worked in one of the three European global cities of London, Brussels or Amsterdam. He showed that "Eurostars" did not necessarily belong to mobile elite upper classes. They were often from lower and middle class families living in provincial areas. They were mostly young, well educated people who moved in order to escape family expectations and norms and institutionalised gendered careers within the local and national settings, in order to search for pathways other than those followed by their peers back home, in order to overcome diverse barriers in their countries and enlarge their scope of possibilities, or simply in order to try living in different surroundings (Favell, Recchi 2011, p. 70). According to the author, "European free movement has effectively created a new kind of regional freedom in the world, uniquely available in terms of European citizenship status rather than elite privilege. European movers discover themselves as individuals, learn to free themselves from norms they learned as nationals, to play around and instrumentalize their identities, try out new social pathways." (Favell, Recchi 2011, p. 71). Despite moving places in order to uncover new possibilities and new facets of "the self", the relative proximity to the place of origin was an important factor for considering moving and staying abroad. The possibility of enjoying transnational forms of living, commuting across borders and moving longer distances in a short space of time, were made possible because of open borders and increasingly advantageous transport options (ibid.). As Favell showed, "Eurostars" did not necessarily experience upward social mobility. Their stories revealed, however, that a "free European space" was an area in which new possibilities of self-realisation, life-style and self-perception could develop for migrants.

Favell focused his study on the newly emerging type of migration that was occurring in the course of integration and trans-nationalisation processes within the EU. The results raise further questions, however. Are the patterns of migration and social mobility also applicable to migrants from other countries, for example from Central and Eastern European countries which joined the EU in 2004 and 2007? Do they experience inter-EU migration in a different way than migrants moving from the "old" EU-countries? Adrian Favell and Tina M. Nebe (2009) tried to answer these questions on the basis of in-depth semi-structured interviews conducted with both highly skilled and low skilled Polish and Romanian migrant women and men in Germany, France, Grain Britain, Spain and Italy. The authors underlined not only the different legal frameworks – at the time the book was written, many countries still had restrictions on access to the labour market for new EU citizens – but also the different perception of these migrants from the viewpoint of political rhetoric and public opinion (Favell, Nebe 2009, pp. 205–207). The interviews were conducted in 2004, shortly after the first round of EU enlargement, although the migrants that were interviewed had already been living in the respective countries for a period of time. The analysis showed that Polish and Romanian migrants often experienced great difficulties in legalising their residence and obtaining work permits. They often crossed the borders on tourist visas and worked in irregular jobs, since the formal labour market was in their eyes difficult to access, despite the high level of education of some migrants. Moreover, they often felt discriminated against in different spheres of life because of their nationality and class positioning in the country of residence (Favell, Nebe 2009, p. 216). Their irregular status as well as different forms of discrimination led in many cases to downward social mobility. The social downgrading in the country of residence with which they were often confronted made them position themselves in society and its social structure in a new way (ibid.).

Importantly, the interviews also revealed the different value given to diplomas and qualification skills acquired in "Western Europe" and elsewhere. As Favell and Nebe put it: "[t]hose who are Eastern educated are most liable to be blocked, undervalued and thus exploited when they move – especially in highly regulated labour markets." (Favell, Nebe 2009, p. 217). For some, the possibility to work in a desirable job or to better their situation was connected to acquiring further qualifications at one of the "Western European" universities (Favell, Nebe 2009, pp. 216–217). As the research of Favell and Nebe showed, there were great differences between migrants moving East-West and people moving within the old EU-countries, such as France, Great Britain, Germany or Spain. Central and Eastern European migrants were to greater extent exposed to discrimination and prejudice based on their nationality, which was enforced by limited access to the labour market and other constraints, non-recognition of or a different value being attributed to their qualifications and skills. As Favell and Nebe conclude: "East-West migrants are more likely to find themselves in exploitative scenarios, rather than ones in which they fully benefit from their move, even in an integrated Europe." (Favell, Nebe 2009, p. 218).

The aforementioned studies showed the impact of legal and institutional frameworks as well as social discourses on migration experiences. They revealed that despite tightening integration politics within the EU, migration processes are not equal, but shaped according to nationality, gender and class belongings. There is thus not one European transnational migration space but diverse spaces which partly overlap each other and which create a map of multiple forms of migration and migration experiences within Europe.

4.3 Shifting social positions in transnational spaces

Migration is often connected to a shift in social position. While a large proportion of people move places in order to better their situation, crossing the borders may be connected with unexpected obstacles to this intention being encountered, be it in the form of legal or institutional barriers or the devaluation of their qualifications and skills. Many migrants do not experience until after migration that their ideas about the country to which they moved do not match the reality, that they have to develop new strategies in order to position themselves in society and that they often have to think over their life plans, knowledge and own resources. In order to understand these processes, it is necessary to rethink the existing ideas on social stratification and social mobility, which hitherto have been bound to the national framework. While this approach may explain the social pathways of some people, for others who cross the borders and position themselves in more than one society simultaneously, it loses its explicatory character, since it does not allow one to consider the complex and dynamic processes of positioning in multiple locations. So far we know little about the way migrants negotiate their social position across borders and make use of the qualifications, knowledge and skills they acquired prior to migration in the new contexts. Moreover, we know little about how migrants make sense of their own and sometimes contradictory social positioning in the country of emigration and in the country of immigration. In the following chapter I will outline the recent scientific discussion concerning some of these topics. I shall start by theorising on social mobility in transnational spaces and continue with the question of the transferability of skills across borders. Afterwards I shall introduce the concept of translocational positionality, which enables one to capture multiple and changing positioning of migrants and their interplay. Finally, I shall shed some light on the way migrants make sense of their positioning by including the biographical perspective to the analysis.

4.3.1 Theorising social mobility in transnational spaces

The study of social stratification – the positioning of individuals and social groups within the unequal social strata – and the study of social mobility – changes in social position by individuals or groups during the course of their life or over generations (Hradil 2008, p. 225) – have been prominent topics of sociological research. Sociologists have studied the unequal life chances of individuals and unequal access to resources in society on the basis of belonging to a certain social class (see e.g. Weber 1978a), the hierarchical distribution of power (see e.g. Mills 1959), the mechanisms and reproduction of social inequality (see e.g. the volume Lutz et al. 2011), the life situation and life style of people positioned differently along the social strata (see e.g. Bourdieu 1997, 1998a), as well as the processes of social mobility of individuals and social groups (see e.g. Sorokin 1959; Bertaux, Thompson 1997b; Breen 2004). Social scientists have argued that the individuals' positioning in modern society is shaped not only by economic property and wage, but also by their level of education, their profession and associated social prestige and, finally, by their access to power (Hradil 2008).

Probably the most prominent study of social stratification is a study by Pierre Bourdieu who investigated the positioning of individuals within French society on the basis of large quantitative surveys. He argued that individuals are positioned within society according to the capital which they possess. Pierre Bourdieu (1997) distinguished three forms of capital: cultural capital, social capital and economic capital. Cultural capital consists of skills, preferences, ways of thinking and acting, education, as well as cultural aspects. According to Bourdieu (1997, p. 47, italics in original), "Cultural capital can exist in three forms: in the *embodied* state, i.e., in the form of long-lasting dispositions of the mind and body; in the *objectified* state, in the form of cultural goods (pictures, books, dictionaries, instruments, machines, etc.), which are the trace or realization of theories or critiques of these theories, problematics, etc.; and in the *institutionalized* state (…)." In other words, the embodied cultural capital consists of one's transmitted or self-acquired habitus, such as way of speaking and thinking. Objectified cultural capital is expressed in the material objects and media one possesses. Finally, institutionalized cultural capital takes the form of any diplomas and certificates acquired. Social capital, on the other hand, "is the aggregate of the actual or potential resources which are linked to possession of a durable network of more or less institutionalized relationships of mutual acquaintance and recognition (…)." (Bourdieu 1997, p. 51). Social links one has established in the past thus not only indicate the positioning of individuals on the social strata, but they can represent a potential resource for future action. Finally, economic capital means one's economic resources, such as goods and properties, which manifest one's social status and which one can apply in order to reach one's goals (Bourdieu 1997, pp. 53–55). All of these forms of capital are, according to Pierre Bourdieu, related to each other and they can be transferred into other forms of capital in order to sustain or improve one's social position.

Most of the studies concerning social stratification and social mobility have been connected to the framework of nation states. Much like Bourdieu's investigations, theoretical considerations were in most cases based on statistical data collected on a national level. Despite the increasing amount of international comparative studies, the setting behind the analysis – defined along the borders of the nation state – has in most cases stayed the same (for the critique see e.g. Weiss 2005; Weiß, Berger 2008; Pries 2008b; Amelina

2010). This research approach defined not only who could and cannot be included in the analysis, but faded out any transnational processes which have an increasing impact on individuals and their positioning (Weiss 2005). The reason for taking the nation state as a natural unit for theorising and analysing social inequalities lies in the understanding of society as congruent with a nation state formation, which goes back to the original sociological works on society (Pries 2008b). This perspective on society shaped not only the perception of migration as an anomaly and exception as described in the previous chapter, but also influenced how the social mobility of migrants was theorised.

The study of the social positioning and social mobility of migrants goes back to classical migration works, which were concerned with the pathways of migrants to the stratification system of society to which they moved. For example, Milton M. Gordon (1964) connected the notions of ethnicity and class in his influential work "Assimilation in American life". According to him, American society was divided on the one hand by diverse ethnic sub-societies, and on the other hand by hierarchical class divisions, the major group being the protestant Anglo-Saxon middle class. In order to assimilate into this group, Milton M. Gordon defined the steps leading from the acquisition of dominant cultural patterns by migrants to the absence of discrimination and civic assimilation (Gordon 1964, p. 71). He argued that cultural assimilation – i.e. the acquisition of language and cultural habits – was relatively quick and common, whereas structural assimilation – i.e. integration into the institutions and establishing close links to mainstream society – was more difficult. In order to express the failing assimilation on a structural level and with it the persisting cohesion of ethnic groups in diverse layers of the social stratum, he introduced the concept of "ethclass" – accounting for social groups which share the same ethnic origin and same class belonging (Gordon 1964, p. 53). In the European context, the pathway of migrants to mainstream society and its stratification system was for example described by Hartmut Esser (2001). He introduced an assimilation model which consisted of a number of steps ranging from cognitive assimilation – such as the acquisition of the language of mainstream society – through the positioning of migrants within the social stratification system in the terms of education, wage and social position, to identification with mainstream society.

Both Gordon's and Esser's theories contribute significantly to the theorising of social mobility and the positioning of migrants after migration. Both highlighted the cognitive and structural barriers – be it the knowledge of a language or legal obstacles for entering the labour market – which migrants are exposed to and which they try to overcome. However, their theories also have a number of weak points. Firstly, both theories saw migration as a one-way process from country of origin to country of migration, and from one stratified system into another, neglecting potential transnational interconnections. Secondly, they implicitly assumed that migrants automatically moved to the lowest stratum in the social order after migration and then had to make their way up in the new society through various assimilation steps, whereas their different class positioning, history, knowledge acquired prior to migration, and individual strategies of negotiating their skills were not adequately taken into account. Thirdly, they portrayed the social pathways of migrants as changeable, whereas the society into which they were about to be integrated was perceived as being static and unchangeable (Amelina 2010, p. 12). Finally, they overlooked the multiple positioning of migrants in diverse social locations and associated potential new forms of stratification in transnational spaces (Pries 2008b).

Later scholars criticised methodological nationalism in studies on social stratification and social inequalities (see e.g. the volume Berger, Weiß 2008; Amelina 2010). They argued that the social divisions cannot be explained solely on a national level but have to be put into a wider global and transnational context. They stirred up the debate concerning the adequate framework for analysis and the existing theoretical tools for researching the social positioning of individuals. The authors argued that in order to understand the positioning of migrants, one has to take into account not only the context of the country of migration, but also the context of the country of origin and the position of countries in a global context. Anja Weiß (2005), for example, proposed conceptualising social positions on a worldwide scale. She argued that while a national approach might be functional for some individuals, it is inappropriate for others who move country frequently, keep contact with those left behind, receive support, and are positioned in more than one society at the same time (Weiss 2005, p. 709). These social, material and symbolic attachments spanning across multiple locations highlight the necessity, so Weiß (2005, p. 712), of including spatial relations in the analysis, whereby spatial entities can take diverse forms, from absolute territorial settings such as nation states to relatively "non-located" social spaces. Eleonore Kofman (2008, p. 109), another scholar studying social stratification, also argued that the complex patterns and structure of stratification can only be adequately understood when taking into account the positioning of individuals not only in the country of migration, but in multiple locations within which they act and their lives develop. She argued that in order to understand the complex stratification system within which migrants move and which they also (re-)produce, one needs to take into account diverse factors: the placement of respective countries within the hierarchical global system, the migration policies, which influence in different ways not only men and women per se but also increasingly people belonging to different social classes, the possibilities of migration for respective groups as well as their chances to transfer and utilise their qualifications, resources and skills after migration.

Moving the focus of the analysis beyond the framework of the nation state did not mean, however, that the role of nation states in shaping the stratification and possibilities of individuals to move within the social strata would be neglected. Michael Hartmann (2008), for example, convincingly showed that the national frameworks continued to be the main arena which structure the social position and career paths of individuals. He revealed on the example of economic elites in diverse countries the importance of national settings for their career, which developed almost exclusively within this framework. His study showed not only the continuing power of expected social mobility paths within national frameworks, but also the exclusion mechanisms affecting those coming from different class and national contexts. The role of national settings was also underlined by Anja Weiß (2005). However, she argued that the power of the nation state over individuals depends on the social class to which they belong. Taking into account the spatial relations and resources accessible to individuals, Weiß distinguished three positions of individuals on the global scale: the transnational upper classes, people positioned on the middle tier, and lastly those positioned on the lower echelons. According to this scheme, the transnational upper classes are spatially autonomous, since they have the resources enabling them to move places, without the necessity to really do so. In contrast, those in the middle tier are more dependent on the national welfare system and they are thus more bound to the nation state. The relevance of the nation state and national welfare system as a structuring force for social positioning decreases once again, however, for those positioned at the bottom of world society. According to Weiß (2005, p. 716), "[t]he lower echelons of world society tend to be 'fixed' to disadvantaged locations and are lacking state protection from a globalizing economy." In her view, it is thus the presence of the national welfare system, but also its absence that shapes the position of individuals on a global scale. In line with Wallerstein's world system analysis she argued that the position of individuals on a global scale is often structured by the position of nation states within the centre-periphery hierarchies. This unequal relation, however, has a different impact on individuals moving in different social layers.

Thus, taking on the transnational approach enables one to pay attention to both the role of nation states in shaping migrants' pathways and to analysing the processes which go beyond the nation state formation. It enables one to see, for example, that taking a low skilled job in the country of migration does not have to be connected only to downward social mobility, but it can be a means of sustaining or bettering one's social position in the country of origin (see e.g. Vianello 2014). Rhacel Salazar Parreñas (2001) described these seemingly paradoxical processes using the example of Filipina migrant women working in households in Rome. According to her (Parreñas 2001, p. 150), "[m]igrant Filipina domestic workers define their sense of self and place in the global labour market from the contentious subject-position of contradictory class mobility. This contentious location refers to their simultaneous experience of upward and downward mobility in migration. More specifically, it refers to their decline in social status and increase in financial status."

Contradictory class mobility points to the different social positions of migrants in the country of migration and in the country of origin. It shows that these social positions are not independent from each other but that they are mutually interconnected. The shifts in social position in one location can have a greater or lesser impact on the social position in the other location. Moreover, shifts in social position not only affect the person who is actually migrating, but also his or her family members and significant others, who receive remittances or support the migrants in diverse ways (Glick Schiller et al. 1992b).

Contradictory class mobility, however, expresses only one of the possible variances of social positioning and social mobility of migrants in transnational spaces. The chances to move upwards or downwards on the social ladder are shaped by diverse factors. Roland Verwiebe (2006; 2008b), for example, drew attention to the role of the cultural, economic and social capital of migrants. Starting with an analysis of biographical interviews conducted with migrant women and men living in Berlin, Germany, Verwiebe introduced five categories of migrant: "elite migrants", "higher middle class migrants", "middle class migrants", "lower middle class migrants" and finally "lower class migrants". These categories were based on the interplay of cultural capital, such as education and skills, social capital, and economic capital. For each category, Verwiebe elaborated a typical career and migration pathway and shifts in status and showed that it is not only education and skills that have a bearing upon maintaining or improving one's situation after migration, but also social contacts and economic resources. Taking another research approach, Ettore Recchi and Adrian Favell (2009; 2011) pointed out the interplay of class belonging, gender and age in shaping the social mobility of migrants. They investigated the impact of European integration processes and freedom of movement within the EU on the social mobility of "internal" migrants, i.e. people moving from one EU country to another EU country in the course of their life. The research was based on a large telephone survey conducted in Germany, Great Britain, France, Italy and Spain. The target group were migrants who moved from the aforementioned countries in the period between 1974 and 2003 and had lived in one of these countries for at least one year. The survey asked, inter alia, about the motives for migration, experiences of possible barriers, political orientation as well as how the migrants identified with Europe. The results were compared to the population in respective countries (Braun, Recchi 2008, p. 164). The analysis of the survey revealed that the proportion of migrants with a higher education rose significantly over time, as well as their active participation in the labour market (Braun, Recchi 2008, p. 170). Furthermore, the class background of "movers" was higher than that of "stayers" – the population of the respective country. With the exception of Italian and Spanish migrants in Germany and to some extent in Great Britain, the proportion of migrants that had a working class background was significantly lower than amongst "stayers", while the middle and upper classes prevailed. Mobility within the EU was, so the results of the analysis, therefore increasingly a matter for the middle and upper classes (Braun, Recchi 2008, p. 172). Authors also studied the impact of migration on intergenerational social mobility of migrants. The results showed that the intergenerational mobility of "movers" did not differ significantly from that of "stayers" in the countries studied (Recchi 2009, pp. 81, 95). However, they revealed that for example education, social class background, gender and age had a significant influence on constraints and possibilities of upward social mobility in migration processes. Generally, the higher the education of migrants, the better their chances of moving up the social ladder or reproducing their class positioning after migration. Furthermore, a comparison with the intergenerational social mobility of "stayers" revealed that migration could contribute to a greater extent towards the (mostly upward) social mobility of people from lower-middle class families. Mobility also helped to reinforce the class positioning of people from the upper social classes (Recchi 2009, pp. 84–85). Thus, so the authors, inter-EU migration could on the one hand be a means for less privileged people of improving their social position in comparison with their parents, and on the other hand a means of reproducing social positioning for the mobile upper classes. There were, however, discrepancies concerning gender and age: women and young people tended to be more socially mobile in the migration process, yet they were at a much greater risk of experiencing downward social mobility than men and people in other age categories (Recchi 2009, p. 88).

The results of this investigation show the changing role of class within migration flows over time and the impact of class, gender and age on the social mobility of migrants. They also opened further questions: could the patterns of social mobility as outlined using the example of "inter-EU movers" also be applied to people migrating from the new EU countries, from outside Europe and other world regions? As Adrian Favell and Tina M. Nebe (2009) underlined, those moving from the new EU countries which joined the EU in 2004 and 2007 tended to experience more obstacles in their social mobility, caused by more restrictive migration regimes, which lasted until 2011, the devaluation of their educational attainments and skills, and discrimination on the labour market. Thus, despite moving within the same migration space of the EU, there seem to be great differences concerning the geographical locations from which migrants move. These findings call for a deeper investigation of the role of geographical locations within social mobility. Moreover, they call for an analysis which pays attention to the interplay of class, gender, age, nationality and other social divisions both on the level of policy and structural patterns shaping for example access to the formal labour market, and on the level of people's agency (Kofman 2008). Before developing this point in more detail, I will turn my attention to the question of the transferability of qualifications, skills, resources and knowledge of migrants between different locations.

4.3.2   The transferability of skills across borders

In the large body of research on migration, migrants' skills were perceived as the property of migrants which move country with them and which they can apply in a straightforward manner in the new contexts. In criticising this predominant approach, Umut Erel (2010) used the metaphor of the "rucksack" within which cultural capital – i.e. the knowledge, skills, diplomas and so on that have been acquired – cross the borders with their holders. After arrival the rucksack can be unpacked and its content utilised (or not if it does not fit) in order to reach one's own goals and move up the social ladder. However, as Erel and other authors showed on the basis of empirical studies (see e.g. Kofman 2008; Liversage 2009b; Trevena 2013; Nowicka 2014), the mechanisms according to which migrants transfer and utilise their qualifications, skills, resources and knowledge across the borders of nation states, are more complex and deserve to be investigated in more depth.

Migration research has shown using multiple examples that migration is often connected to the processes of deskilling and devaluation of one's own skills (see e.g. Dumont, Monso 2007; Kontos 2009b; Freitas, Pécoud 2012). The impossibility of utilising one's own qualifications, professional skills and other resources acquired earlier is the result of diverse factors, which in many cases are linked. These are the restrictive gendered migration regimes (Kofman 2014), a lack of or only partial recognition of qualifications acquired abroad beforehand on the part of state authorities or labour institutions (Iredale 2005), the devaluation of work experience acquired in the country of origin or in countries other than the country of residence (Liversage 2009b), as well as discrimination on the labour market (Kontos, Voswinkel 2010). The authors showed that despite the ongoing transnationalisation of biographies and institutions, the national frameworks continue to somewhat shape the biographical and career paths of individuals and the possibilities of social mobility. Empirical research carried out in diverse contexts has revealed that the local educational and professional careers of migrants are in most instances valued more than work experience acquired abroad, whereas class, nationality, gender and the type of education make a great difference in the positioning and recognition of migrants' skills (see e.g. Kofman 2008; Erel 2010).

In researching the transferability of skills and resources from one location to another, diverse authors made use of the concepts of cultural, economic and social capital developed by Pierre Bourdieu (1997). However, they enlarged these concepts by the transnational dimension (see e.g. Weiss 2005; Kelly, Lusis 2006; Nohl et al. 2006; Verwiebe 2006; Erel 2010). With the help of this concept, the authors researched how migrants could build on the intrinsic and institutionalised cultural capital – i.e. for example knowledge of a language, accent and cultural practices, as well as formal qualifications and work experience – acquired in one cultural, legal and social setting and transfer it into another setting that is shaped by different "rules of the game" (Kelly, Lusis 2006, p. 834). Philip Kelly and Tom Lusis (2006, p. 834) described the contextual character of cultural capital: "[i]t is the objective 'rules of the game' that establish what will be prized and rewarded in any given context, what things are worth, and what is considered worthy and worthwhile. Although these rules of the game exist beyond individual control, they must also be reproduced by individuals in their social practices." Thus, the value of resources may shift according to the context and, importantly, according to who possesses them (Sen 1985).

Building on the concept of cultural capital, Anja Weiß (2005) introduced the notions of transnational cultural capital and location-specific cultural capital, which are both interrelated and shape the social pathways and recognition of migrants' skills in migration processes (Weiss 2005, p. 708). The author's research focused on a group of highly skilled migrants who possessed the relevant qualifications which were in demand on the global labour market, such as qualifications in the IT sector or in selected economic spheres. The market demand for such professionals make their skills, so the assumption, more easily transferable from one location to another. The author did not limit her observations to migration to a particular nation state but observed the movements on a global scale. She found that even though migrants came from different countries and moved differently on a global scale, they shared a social position which was not bound to a nation state framework, since their skills were mostly recognised in the country of destination and migration was often made easier for them due to migration politics reducing the barriers for these kind of experts. She labelled this kind of capital, which is recognised and transferable from one location into another, as transnational cultural capital. She also pointed out differences concerning the hierarchy of countries within which migrants moved. While those moving as expatriates – i.e. from "Western countries" to other countries, such as German migrants being sent by their companies to Asian countries – were able to profit from their location-specific cultural capital, since their "Western culture" was universalised (Erel 2010, p. 648), those moving in the other direction were hindered in their social mobility because they lacked the necessary location-specific cultural capital, i.e. capital which was connected to the local cultural specificities, language nuances and habits.

However, other authors pointed out that not only skills and resources acquired prior to the migration were decisive for the positioning of migrants, but also the new forms of cultural capital which was produced in the course of migration. Umut Erel (2010) dealt with the question of how cultural capital was made up and recognised in migration processes and how cultural capital was linked to other economic and social forms of capital. She argued that migrants not only brought cultural capital with them, but that they also created, re-created and recognised their resources in a new way, making use both of their past and knowledge and skills acquired in situ (Erel 2010, p. 649). By doing so migrants built upon power relations both in the country of origin and in the country of migration, as well as reworking them (Erel 2010, p. 642). Erel illustrated her theory using the example of biographies of women who migrated from Turkey to Germany and to the United Kingdom. She showed, for example, that some women could profit from their middle class background in order to mobilise their social networks, which in turn helped them to validate their skills and enter qualified positions. Others used their experiences as political activists in Turkey, for example, and transformed these experiences into capital in the country of migration. While some were able to validate their knowledge of the Turkish language and turn it into economic capital, others from lower classes or other cultural settings were not able to transform these cultural practices into capital. Erel therefore argued against the perception that a migrant group would share homogenous cultural capital connected to their country of origin, manifested for example by knowledge of a particular language. According to her (Erel 2010, p. 656), "cultural practices within a migrant group are differentially validated in gendered, classed and ethnic ways. Cultural practices acquire different meanings and validations according to the local, national and transnational context."

In order to understand the mechanisms of the validation of skills and resources, Magdalena Nowicka (2014) argued that it is necessary to extend the scope of the research from focusing merely on the country of migration to focusing on a wider transnational approach. She proposed that one focus not only on the context of the country of migration, but also on the context of the country of origin. In her empirical study on the positioning of highly educated Polish migrants working predominantly in low skilled positions in London, Nowicka showed that often migrants had already experienced a devaluation of their skills in their country of origin, which was linked to the restructuring of the educational and economic system in Poland in the last decades. University graduates often experienced limited chances of entering the professional life in positions which matched their qualifications, and they felt that they were underpaid (see also Trevena 2013). Nowicka (2014, p. 171) argued that the meaning and validation of skills prior to migration had an impact on the way in which migrants negotiated their skills after migration and how they positioned themselves on local labour market. In her study, the way Polish migrants spoke of their qualifications showed that they were devaluating their skills even before they entered the UK labour market, mentioning for example the lack of practice-related knowledge which was required by employers. However, while questioning their education skills, they also established new strategies of validating their position. Thus, not only the opportunity structure in the country of origin and in the country of migration need to be taken in account, but also the migrants' subjective perceptions of their resources (Nowicka 2014, p. 176).

The mechanisms of transferability of one's own skills and resources in transnational spaces are crucial for understanding the positioning of migrants within the stratified social systems within which they move, be it in their country of origin, the country of migration or social spaces that go beyond the national setting. Research on the transferability of skills and resources within these settings is still in its infancy. However, the existing body of research has already pinpointed the importance of taking a transnational approach (Nowicka 2014), the role of contexts within which skills and resources are validated (Kofman 2008), and the role of migrants' agency in transforming their knowledge, skills and resources into capital (Erel 2010). Research has shown that cultural capital is neither a "rucksack" which travels across borders with its holder, nor is it ethnically bound to certain groups of migrant; instead it is structured and (re-)shaped according to gender, class, or national belonging (Erel 2010). In the next chapter I will pay special attention to the intersection of these categories and I will introduce the concept of translocational positionality which describes the interplay of different social divisions in respect of the positioning of individuals from different theoretical standpoints.

4.3.3 Translocational positionality

As I have shown above, individuals build on knowledge, skills, or resources acquired prior to migration; they rework these and link them with new knowledge, skills or resources in the migration process. Migration from one location to another may thus start the process of an individual's re-evaluation of his or her cultural, economic and social capital, to once again use Pierre Bourdieu's concept. It may also initiate reflexive processes concerning the migrants' established perception of self and their positioning in the societies within which they move and transform. Transnational spaces become particularly important in these processes. According to Nina Glick Schiller, Linda Basch, and Cristina Blanc-Szanton (1992a, p. 12) "[t]ransnational social fields are in part shaped by the migrants' perceptions that they must keep their options open. In the globalized economy that has developed over the past several decades, there is a sense that no one place is truly secure, although people do have access to many places. One way migrants keep options open is to continuously translate the economic and social position gained in one political setting into political, social and economic capital in another." Floya Anthias (2001; 2002; 2008) grasped this question of the "translatability" of social positions from one location to another and developed it further. Before I introduce her concept of translocational positionality, which became an important heuristic device during my research, I will briefly outline the discussion on intersectionality in which this concept is embedded.

Intersectionality is an approach which examines the ways in which different socially and culturally constructed categories are intertwined on multiple levels of society and produce specific social positions and identities (Anthias, Cederberg 2006; Anthias 2008). It was established as a reaction to feminist theories, which neglected to see the ethnic and class differences among women. Black feminists in the 1970s refuted the notion of a "global sisterhood" by underlining other social divisions, such as "race" and class criss-crossing the category of gender, leading to even deeper forms of oppression of women (Winker, Delege 2009, p. 11). The term "intersectionality" was introduced by Kimberlé Crenshaw (1994) in the 1990s in order to describe the space in which different forms of discrimination intersect. She criticised approaches which ascribed individuals to one dominant category, such as gender, without neglecting the power of other social divisions, such as class or "race" in shaping the unequal positioning of individuals within groups and societies. The analogy of crossing roads which Crenshaw used was heavily discussed in recent decades. It was argued that social divisions were, in contrast to roads, always constitutive for one another and could therefore not be separated (see e.g. McCall 2005). Moreover, some scholars criticised the growing body of research on intersectionality for its descriptive nature instead of embedding it into social stratification theory, which takes into account wider hierarchical structures of domination (see e.g. Gimenez 2001; Anthias 2001).

Floya Anthias (2008, p. 14) furthermore argued that the notion of intersectionality risked constructing people as belonging to fixed categories, such as gender, colour of skin, or class, which determine their ways of acting. Instead, it is important to take into account the contexts and meanings and the changing and emerging character of social categories and positions (Anthias 2002, p. 275). To grasp the impact of social processes, practices and outcomes to social categories, social structures and individuals (Anthias 2008, p. 14), Anthias introduced the concept of "translocational positionality". The notion of positionality contains a reference to both social position and social positioning, where the former refers to social effects or outcomes and the

130

latter to a process, i.e. a set of practices, actions and meanings (Anthias 2008, p. 15). Hence, the notion of positionality includes the effects of social structure and agency.

Anthias further argued that people are situated within different locations which "are multiple and span a number of terrains such as those of gender and class as well as ethnicity and nation, political and value systems" (Anthias 2008, p. 15). Although locations are interconnected, a "dislocation" at one level, such as for example at the level of ethnicity, does not necessarily lead to "dislocations" in other levels, such as class and gender. However, when moving within social and geographical spaces, such as for instance across national borders, our social place and perception of it can be transformed. As Anthias added (ibid.), "to think of translocations opens up not only thinking of relocations but also of a multiplicity of locations involved in time and space, and in terms of connections between the past, the present and the future."

In line with the concept of translocational positionality, Minna-Kristiina Ruokonen-Engler (2009; 2012) used biographical analyses to study the migration processes and positioning of Finnish women living in Germany, and in doing so developed the notion of "transnational positionality". According to her (Ruokonen-Engler 2009, p. 251), this notion helps to overcome "the binarity of belonging and not belonging and acknowledges the ambivalence and the locality as well as the translocality of the notions of belonging and positioning." The author showed using diverse examples how transnational positionality is biographically made up and shaped by power relations. She argued that the positioning of migrant women in transnational spaces can be seen as a strategy of reassure the individuals of their agency capacity and belonging across diverse spaces (Ruokonen-Engler 2009, pp. 251–252, 2012, p. 347). As she put it (Ruokonen-Engler 2009, p. 262): "'[t]ransnational positionality' is a biographical resource as well as biographical strategy that results from the negotiations of location and dislocation in relation to social positioning and constructions of difference at the intersection of ethnicity, gender, class, nation and racialization. However, it acknowledges that some differences are more important that others in influencing the development of biographical agency. It also takes into account at least two frames of reference as a starting point of the constitution of agency and belonging: the country of emigration and that of immigration." In order to gain access to descriptions of differing or multiple positioning and belonging, Ruokonen-Engler pinpointed the theoretical and empirical tools of biographical research. It makes it possible, so the author (Ruokonen-Engler 2009, p. 263), "to deconstruct and reconstruct how different power relations and positioning intertwine with biographical processes and in that way influence the constructions of belonging and agency across the borders of nation states."

The strength of both concepts lies in the ability to grasp the complex processes of social mobility and multiple positioning and belonging of migrants, since they take into account the interplay of structure and agency, as well as "the importance of context, the situated nature of claims and attributions and their production in complex and shifting locales" (Anthias 2002, p. 276). Coupling these concepts with the analyses of biographical interviews enables one to study social positioning as a dynamic process that changes over time and has different meanings in diverse locations.

4.3.4 Making sense of one's own class positioning

As Paulina Trevena (2011) showed in her study on highly educated Polish migrants working in low skilled jobs in London, migrants often experienced difficulties concerning their class positioning after migration. On the one hand, Polish graduates often experienced a devaluation of their knowledge and skills on the transformed Polish labour market despite the high level of education and associated prestige they had enjoyed in Poland. On the other hand, they found it difficult to position themselves within the stratification system of the United Kingdom to which they migrated. Despite working predominantly in low skilled positions in London, they did not associate themselves with the low classes with which these sectors were associated. Trevena argued that even though the migrants worked in positions that were unequivocally below their qualifications, it would be incorrect to assume that they only experienced downward social mobility, i.e. a fall in their social status after migration. She showed that migrants not only felt ambiguous concerning their social position in Poland; they also often experienced their work in low skilled jobs in London as temporary and as an opportunity to learn new skills, such as language, or to earn some money for future projects. Hence, paradoxically, work in the lower sector could for some migrants be a means of moving upwards on the social stratum (Trevena 2011, p. 89).

It is interesting to observe which strategies migrants applied in order to position themselves within the stratification system of both the Polish and British society. Trevena showed on the basis of migrants' narratives that migrants compared the meaning of low skilled and manual work in Poland with that in the United Kingdom. They critically re-evaluated the perception of manual work as being at the bottom of society and as being treated with disrespect. Instead, they tried to develop a positive relation to this kind of work. However, they were also aware that they might be categorised as unskilled or unintelligent by the wider society (Trevena 2011, p. 88). Migrants' expressions, such as "I am middle class though not in the British sense", "working class. No, middle... Well no, I'm not middle class.", or "I don't know, I simply am [here]." (Trevena 2011, pp. 89, 91) point out the difficulty for migrants to position themselves within one class category. Some developed their class belonging from their social background in Poland, stating that they would count as middle class or intelligentsia. Others construed their class belonging on the basis of the work they did in London, arguing that they would belong to the working classes. Nevertheless, while they felt economically related to the lower classes, with regard to cultural capital and educational attainments they usually described themselves as being middle class. These difficulties in positioning themselves within the class stratification system seemed to be connected to a different understanding of the concepts of working class, middle class, upper class and so on by migrants. Moreover, they expressed difficulties in relating to one stratification system: is it the Polish one? The British one? Or the multicultural scene of London?

The class positioning of migrants became clearer from the passages in which migrants described their place of work in the low skilled sector. Many compared their cultural capital to that of co-workers or customers, which was often very low. The topic of the devaluation or stagnation of one's own cultural capital arose in this context. At the same time, the interviewees balanced these perceptions by pointing out the temporal character of their status. It was thus the option of moving away which distinguished them from their co-workers.

The voices of migrants invite us to rethink the notion of class as bound to one location, be it the country of emigration or the country of immigration. Moreover, they call for one to rethink the notion of class as a static and fixed formation. As I have shown above, people often experience changes in social position in very different ways in the course of migration, whereby these shifts do not have to be planned or expected. As Paulina Trevena and others revealed, migrants did not leave one stratification system and move into another, where they had to build up their position again from scratch. Instead, they endeavoured to interconnect their different (and sometimes contradictory) positioning in diverse locations. They compared the meaning of their positioning and eventually created new meanings for their work and perceptions of self.

Fritz Schütze and Anja Schröder-Wildhagen (2012) described this process of ongoing comparison of different settings, meanings, possibilities and potential life paths in migration processes in a study carried out as part of a project on the evaluation of European identities (Miller 2012). The authors argued that these comparisons are one of the features of European mental spaces – biographically established frames of reference. According to them, migration or other forms of social transnational encounter expand one's horizon in relation to social practice, knowledge and other possibilities of work and life (Schütze, Schröder-Wildhagen 2012, p. 258). However, they also facilitate the development of a critical approach to one's own familiar regional and national horizons and their opportunity structure, way of life or common discourses. Hence, the establishment of a European mental space – and I think this could also be extended to other transnational spaces – involves learning processes which not only enable one to shift one's approach from one regional or national horizon to another, but also to create by means of one's own internal "biographical work" new perspectives that go beyond the regional or national settings (Schütze, Schröder-Wildhagen 2012, p. 268).

This approach can be expanded in terms of the knowledge of diverse stratification systems in which migrants are involved. They compare it, critically question and develop new perceptions of their positioning, opportunities, ideas and resources. Biographical analysis provides the possibility of also approaching these facets of biographical work, which show the way in which individuals position themselves in the relevant societies and make sense of this positioning.

4.4 Summary: biographical approaches to migration and social mobility

In the chapter above I outlined the theoretical framework of the present study. I introduced two approaches that have been crucial for my study – the biographical perspective and transnational perspective – and complemented them with other streams of thought – social mobility and social positioning in transnational spaces. The links between these approaches enabled me to approach not only ever complex migration processes but also the ways people negotiate their positions within the social strata across diverse locations and how they make sense of their positioning.

First I introduced biographical approach. I started by giving a history of biographical research, which can be traced back to the research tradition of the Chicago school in the 1920s and 1930s. I then followed the development of the biographical approach in Europe, while pointing out its interdisciplinary and transnational interconnections and exchanges of knowledge. Subsequently, I introduced the main concepts of biographical research which became crucial for the present study. I outlined the concept of biography – which is to be understood as a social construct produced in interaction processes in the specific context – and its location at the intersection of social and individual processes. I elucidated the use of terms such as "agency" and "structure" which in biographical research are not approached as contradictory concepts but studied in terms of their mutual interplay – arguing that structures may constrain the individuals' action but may also be changed by it. The concept of biographical process structures (Schütze 1980), which I introduced afterwards, goes a step further by introducing diverse ways in which agency and structure – and individual and social processes – interplay and are experienced by individuals. Finally, I paid attention to the biographical constitution of experiences and knowledge and especially to the processes by which past experiences and associated knowledge can be transformed into a resource for use in diverse life situations.

After outlining the contours of the biographical approach, I turned my attention to the instances in which the biographical approach intersected with migration research. I outlined first approaches to biographical migration research, which can be traced back to the "Polish peasant" (Thomas, Znaniecki 1958) and which were developed in a more rigid way by biographical researchers from the 1980s onwards. The transnational approach which became increasingly influential within migration studies in the last decades offered another perspective on migration processes and questioned the existing theoretical and methodological tools of migration research. After situating the transnational approach within the wider field of migration research, I introduced the concept of transnational social spaces – referring to links, processes and practices among individuals and institutions which span beyond the borders of national states – and I outlined the links between the biographical and transnational approaches using the example of recent migration studies. I paid particular attention to the concept of transnational biographical knowledge which is crucial for understanding the action and positioning of individuals in transnational spaces. Finally, I delineated the contours of European transnational spaces within which the present study is embedded.

Next I added a third to the two approaches mentioned above, focusing on social stratification and social mobility in transnational spaces. First I outlined the theoretical framework for researching social positioning and social mobility, which did not stay bound to nation state formations as was often the case but which also grasped transnational processes. I showed that the social mobility of migrants is shaped by diverse factors, be it gendered migration regimes, (non-)recognition of educational attainments, conditions on the labour market, as well as the possibilities of migrants to validate their own skills, knowledge and resources in the course of migration. I paid particular attention to the latter, the transferability of skills across the borders in the following chapter. I showed that skills are not universal tools which could be applied or not in diverse situations, but that they were re-worked as part of ongoing processes and ascribed different meanings by individuals in different contexts. The way one's own skills and knowledge can be used after migration is structured and (re-)shaped in accordance with gender, class, or national belonging. In order to understand the interplay of these characteristics on the positioning of individuals within possibility structures, I introduced the concept of translocational positionality (Anthias 2008), which enables one to grasp multiple, fluid and ambivalent positioning across different locations. Finally, I argued that the biographical approach can allow one to access to the way migrants position themselves in the societies within which they move and to the way they make sense of their – sometime contradictory and ambiguous – positioning.

5 The research process

The way I designed the research project and approached the empirical material is embedded in the tradition of interpretative social research, which builds on the theoretical and methodological positions of symbolical interactionism, phenomenology, pragmatism and Grounded Theory. Its main principles of communication, openness, sequentiality, reconstruction and (self-) reflection guided the whole research process from formulating the research question to writing down the research results (see e.g. Hoffmann-Riem 1980; Rosenthal 2005; Riemann 2009).

The biographical approach which became the framework for my study offered me the possibility to study the migration processes on the East-West axis from an agent-centred perspective. The theoretical background and methodological tools of this biographical approach made it possible to reveal both individual and collective processes connected to the transformation of society and migration, which became part of everyday life for many people in the Czech Republic after the collapse of the communist regime and the opening up of the borders. Furthermore, it enabled me to reconstruct the structural patterns within which biographies were embedded – be it either the patterns of action transmitted within families and social locations, or migration and gender regimes – and the way the individuals reacted to them. The productiveness of this approach is demonstrated by a variety of studies in the field of migration and transmigration (see e.g. Thomas, Znaniecki 1958; Apitzsch 1990, 2002; Breckner 2009; Lutz 2008b), gender (see e.g. Apitzsch 2000, 2003b; Dausien 1996, 2004; Lutz 2004a, 2010; Lutz, Davis 2009), social mobility (see e.g. Bertaux 1997; Bertaux, Thompson 1997b) and in studies examining the impact of societal transformations on biographies (see e.g. Breckner, Miethe 2000) which are the crucial dimensions of the present study.

In this chapter I shall clarify the methodological framework within which I have situated the present study. I shall explain which methodical tools I chose and how I used them in practice. In the first subchapter I shall provide a theoretical background to biographical narrative interviews – the prime method of data collection of this study. I shall explain the principal theoretical assumptions of this method, the role of narrations within everyday communication and biographical renderings, and the mechanisms which shape the production of narratives.

In the next subchapter I shall outline the research logic and embed it within the tradition of interpretative social research and Grounded Theory. I shall show that the research process was not a linear path from development of the research question and the collection of material to verifying or falsifying the hypothesis formulated at the beginning of the research, but that instead it was a reflexive process of ongoing interactions of empirical material, own experiences and theory. Further on I shall describe the way I construed my sample according to the logic of theoretical sampling. I shall also outline the interview settings and the course of interviews. In order to enable readers to gain a comprehensive overview of all of the case studies conducted for this paper, I will give a brief summary of all interviews in the order in which they were conducted. By doing so I will briefly describe the context of interviews, i.e. for example where interviews took place and under which circumstances, and the main features of respondents' biographical pathways.

After describing the process of data collection, I shall turn my attention to the analysis thereof. The first step in the analysis was to write down ethnographical notes, i.e. first notes on the course of interviews and theoretical thoughts. The transcription of interviews, which was the next step in the research process, was the basis for my in depth analysis of selected interviews. The analytical steps I followed will be explained and exemplified in the next subchapter.

Finally, after clarifying how each of the individual cases were analysed and compared to each other, I shall reflect on the research project as a whole. First, I shall examine methodological nationalism (Wimmer, Glick Schiller 2002) and discuss the limits and potential of this method in a transnational setting. Further, I shall reflect on the role of language and translation in the research process, since both language and translation had a crucial impact on the working relationship between my interviewees and me and the research process as a whole. Finally, I shall discuss the way my own migration experiences and positioning influenced the research process, underlining once again the important role played by self-reflection in carrying out interpretative social research.

5.1 Telling the stories: the theoretical background behind the "biographical narrative interview"

The so-called "biographical narrative interview" was developed by Fritz Schütze during the seventies, a time at which the echoes of the positivist dispute were still resonating in social research in Germany (Riemann 2006b, p. 120). Schütze belonged to the group of Bielefeld sociologists who contributed to the debate concerning the translatability of empirical research and theory building. They criticised – while pointing to the tradition of structural functionalism – the genesis of universal sociological theories formulated behind the desk, distant from everyday life. They were in favour of the establishment of sociological theory which would be grounded in practice and empirically controllable (Arbeitsgruppe Bielefelder Soziologen 1976, p. 10). Furthermore, they pointed out the flaws of standardised forms of data collection which at that time were commonly used instruments for social research. Instead of data collections based on the logic of standardisation, validity and objectivity, they argued in support of communicative social research (Arbeitsgruppe Bielefelder Soziologen 1976, pp. 15–17) which would build on the rules of everyday communication and which would challenge the state of alienation between the researcher and the research participant (Riemann 2006b, p. 120), common not only in the settings of quantitative social research but also in the settings of ethnographical observations. By developing the concept of the biographical narrative interview, Schütze made great efforts to put these demands into practice.

5.1.1 Theoretical assumptions

Fritz Schütze studied sociology, philosophy and linguistics at the University of Münster and later on took up a professorship at the University of Bielefeld and Magdeburg. These three disciplines became the source of Schütze's theoretical and methodological work. While searching for the methodological instrument which would address some of the pitfalls of standardised interviews on the one hand, and open, unstructured interviews on the other hand, Schütze turned his attention to the theoretical tradition of phenomenological sociology, symbolic interactionism, and the Chicago School tradition and adjusted them from the perspectives of conversational analysis and Grounded Theory (Apitzsch, Inowlocki 2000, p. 53). The theoretical background for the establishment of the biographical narrative interview was, according to Schütze (2012a, p. 2), the assumption that "social reality is not just experienced and bestowed with meaning by individual actors with their unique life histories, but in addition that it is produced, is supported and kept in force, is endured with pain and suffered, is protested at and turned over or even destroyed as well as it is gradually changed by individual actors with their personal life histories and involved biographical identity developments." In other words, the individual actors create, maintain or transform social reality in the interaction processes. However, at the same time they are being shaped by society and living within its expectations. The avenue to social reality, so Schütze believes (ibid.), can be entered through the individual and his or her life stories – accessible neither by standardised data collections nor by other available methods.

In order to address these personal experiences and points of view as closely as possible, Schütze turned his attention to the course and structure of interaction processes. The interaction processes, in which the individual actors, despite their possibly different points of view, biographical knowledge and experiences, come to act together, do not proceed arbitrarily, but follow specific constitutive rules (Schütze, Kallmeyer 1977, p. 159). Together with linguist Werner Kallmeyer, Schütze elaborated a model of communication processes which proceeded on three levels: organisation of the talk, constitution and negotiation of action, and lastly actual presentation of the message (ibid.).[29] Before the communicative exchange takes place, it is necessary to establish the frame of communication as well as the conditions of entering and maintaining communication among the persons participating in the conversation. These frames are independent from the course and goals of communication (ibid.). Once the frames have been established and the communication partners have made contact, the action scheme or the mutual goals of communication must be negotiated. At this level it is decided whether the aim of the exchange is merely the delivery of information, the attempt to convince the communication partner of certain ideas or past events, or to exchange stories on certain experiences. The third level – presentation of the message – builds on the previous two layers. After the action schemes have been negotiated, the communication partners make decisions concerning the specific form of presentation of the content. In order to make the content of the message understandable to the listener, the narrator has to take into account not only the inner logic of the message, but also the perceptions of the listener at whom the message is directed. There are, so Schütze and Kallmeyer (1977, p. 162), specific rules – so called communication constraints – which shape the presentation of message in order to make it comprehensible to others: the theme has to be started and completed, the context needs to be explained and described whilst simultaneously depicting and selecting the most important points have from the infinite number of other events or reflections.

According to Schütze (1983; 1984; 2012a; 2012b), there are three communication schemes: narration, argumentation, and description. They are all present during everyday interactions, however, their features and functions differ. The communicative scheme of narration is the basic means of expressing and understanding the train of events experienced by the narrator (Schütze 2012b, p. 15). Unlike the scheme of narration, the scheme of description does not deal with social processes but rather with more or less stable social frames – such as institutions, everyday routines, or social relations – in which the biographical and social processes take place (Schütze 2012b, p. 15). Finally, the scheme of argumentation is applied in order to explicate the events, social frames or biographical and social changes. It

29 The original terms used by Fritz Schütze and Werner Kallmeyer for the three levels of communication process are as follows: "Gesprächsorganisation", "Handlungskonstitution" and "Sachverhaltsdarstellung" (Schütze, Kallmeyer 1977, p. 159).

offers explicative theories, searches for reasons for decision making and discusses possible alternatives (ibid.). In everyday interactions, the schemes of communication do not only shift but also penetrate each other. The scheme of narration also encompasses fragments of descriptions and argumentations, and vice versa.

5.1.2 The focus on storytelling

Schütze highlighted the role of narrations for sociological analysis. Unlike the communicative schemes of description and argumentation, the scheme of narration provides an insight into the way in which events succeed each other and which meanings they had for the narrator. On the one hand, narrations give an insight into the way the relevant social events have developed in relation to the ongoing processes, from small everyday episodes to extending socio-historical events in which the narrator has directly or indirectly taken part. On the other hand, the scheme of narration enables one to gain an insight into the way in which social events of the past have influenced, shaped and changed the individual. Thus, the scheme of narration enables one to access the individual and social processes and their mutual influences (Schütze 1987, p. 243).

Furthermore, the scheme of narration is the most important scheme for capturing and portraying biographical work (Schütze 2012a, p. 15). The reflective passages of narratives show how important events are explained by the narrator and which meaning they have for him or her. They give an explanation of reasons for and the course of certain events and their role in relation to inner changes experienced by the individual. Moreover, the reflective passages offer an insight into the way in which events might have developed differently if other decisions had been made (Schütze 2012a, p. 15). The ability to reflect and to understand the past events of one's life is not self-evident cognitive capability, but it develops, so Fritz Schütze (ibid.), during one's life. In early childhood individuals already develop the capability to narrate stories along with the acquisition of speech skills. However, it is not until later on during adolescence that the narrated stories are given biographical meaning, as reflections on past events and their meaning in relation to inner changes to the individual's identity become involved.

5.1.3 The autobiographical presentation

The autobiographical narrative interview, developed by Schütze in the study concerning the structures of municipal communities (Riemann 2006b, p. 121), is based both on the capability of recapitulation and reflection of past events and experiences and on the rules of storytelling in everyday communication. To let the narration develop without the interventions of interviewer, Schütze argued for interviews to be structured such that the interviewer gives up the role of a questioner and instead takes on the role of a listener. The interviewee should have the possibility to develop his or her story not only concerning the contents which are of relevance to him or her, but he or she should be able to decide how the story shall be presented.

The biographical narrative interview as introduced by Schütze consists of three parts: unprepared off-the-cuff narration concerning one's life or some important episodes of it, narrative questioning and lastly the part in which questions aimed at obtaining explanations or descriptions may be requested (Schütze 1983). The aim of the first – main storytelling – phase is to generate the off-the-cuff narration concerning either the whole life story or some of its specific phases that are of interest for the research. Only after the narrator finishes recounting his or her story additional questions can be posed. At first, the questions should be narrative and concern those topics explicitly or implicitly mentioned in the course of the main narration (Schütze 1983, p. 285). When all relevant themes have been covered and narrations delivered, the third – argumentative or descriptive – phase can begin. Now the narrator's own theories and explanations of certain events can be requested, or descriptions of events, relations or life phases encouraged. The reason for the methodical separation of narrative and argumentative questioning phase is, according to Fritz Schütze (1976), to avoid the irritations resulting from "scheme salad" – the mixture of different communication schemes which are based on diverse operation rules (Schütze 2012b, p. 13).

Off-the-cuff narration is a special type of text which is more or less unprepared and spontaneously created at the moment of recounting. During storytelling, so the argumentation of Schütze (2012b, pp. 12–14), the narrator once again delves into the process of recapitulation and reflection on past events. The narration is thus more than just a reproduction of events that have been experienced. The storyline with its detailed or brief presentation is created at the moment of narration, following the contours of experiences and events that have been lived through. The events that have been experienced are accorded a specific meaning in the process of narration, which are "negotiated" in relation to the present and past views of the narrator. Off-the-cuff narration thus develops on two time lines: retrospectively following the sequences of past events, as well as in relation to the narrator's current views. Autobiographical off-the-cuff presentation therefore is neither solely a reproduction of memorised past events, nor is the activity fully controllable by the narrator and his or her present views. The process of recapitulation and presentation is shaped by specific mechanisms of interaction, which Fritz Schütze and Werner Kallmeyer (1977, p. 188) have called the narrative constraints. Schütze and Kallmeyer have argued and empirically proven that these mechanisms are operative not only during everyday storytelling, but also during biographical presentation.

5.1.4 Narrative constraints

Schütze (Schütze, Kallmeyer 1977, p. 188; Schütze 2012a, p. 16) identified three types of narrative constraint which shape the biographical rendering: the constraint of completing gestalt, the constraint of condensing and the constraint of going into detail.

According to Schütze, the story narrated to the counterpart follows a specific framework: beginning, development of events, and ending. When the story has already commenced, the narrator endeavors to finish the story, even if it has been interrupted. If this is not the case, both the listener and the narrator feel irritated. Schütze calls the process of finishing the story and presenting its complete development the "constraint of completing the gestalt". The constraint of condensing is based on the assumption that the narrated story cannot be presented to include the full volume of actual events and situations, with all details and contextualization. There is neither time nor is the listener patient enough to listen to such an uncondensed story. To make the story comprehensible and able to be followed easily by the listener, the narrator thus has to select those features which seem relevant to him or her and condense the narrated story accordingly. Condensing the story makes the story and its message accessible to the listener. The features of condensing the story are important for one's analysis, since the way the story is narrated and the way in which parts of the story are selected and presented reveals a lot about the system of relevance employed by the narrator. However, the constraint of going into detail also influences storytelling. This means that the characters, situations, events and relationships between them need to be elucidated, otherwise the story would seem unreliable. These additional detailed explanations, descriptions and narrations are often presented as background constructions in biographical narratives, as the narrator feels obliged to repair those parts of the story which lack plausibility (Schütze 2012a, pp. 27–28).

5.1.5 Cognitive figures of autobiographical presentation

Besides the mechanisms shaping the production of narratives described above as narrative constraints, Schütze (1984) elaborated a system of other components by which the narrator orientates him or herself while narrating his or her story. Schütze called these orientation principles "cognitive figures". According to Schütze, cognitive figures are essential for every biographical recounting of events. They are not only necessary for the recapitulation of experiences and the train of events, but also for reflecting and making sense of these experiences and events for the narrator (Schütze 2012b, pp. 20–21). Therefore, without these principles the biographical story could not be construed and understood and the biographical work could not be set in motion. Schütze distinguished six cognitive figures (Schütze 1984, 2012b, pp. 20–25): The concatenation of narrative sections, situations or scenes of biographical importance, the story carrier, the event carrier, social frames and finally the global shape of the narration.

The first cognitive figure, *the concatenation of narrative sections*, stems from the assumption that the story presented by the narrator consists of a sequence of smaller units – sections – which correspond to the life phases as experienced by the narrator (Schütze 1984, p. 78). The way the sections follow each other reveals not only the sequence of experiences and events but also the inner changes faced by the narrator as a result of the experiences he or she has been through (Schütze 2012b, p. 21). The beginnings and the ends of sections are marked by special verbal markers. They close one unit and announce the beginning of a new one, introducing different frames in which the story carrier acts, the altered relationship between oneself and one's own biography, shifted settings for possibilities of acting and decision making and so forth (Hermanns 1992, p. 122). Furthermore, not only is the link between the sections which precede and follow each other of importance, but also the concatenation of supra-sections, indicated by special "demonstration markers" (Schütze 2012b, p. 21). They reveal not only the global shape of the story, but also the contours of biographical process structures, which I introduced earlier.

Nevertheless, the narrated story is not only the linear reproduction of a sequence of events which have some meaning, importance and emotional tune for the narrator. The narrated story also has its peaks and turning points, which are closely linked to changes in the inner state of the biographer. The situations or scenes in which the changes happen and which are therefore of particular importance to the narrator have to be more or less described in detail in order to make the changes accessible and understandable to the listener. In the narration, the situation is accorded a certain social and spatial context, the time indications, as well as indications as to the position and relevance in relation to the preceding and forthcoming sequence of narrated events and experiences (Schütze, Kallmeyer 1977, p. 180). The situation as a peak in the sequence of events may appear in a single narrative unit – presenting the events and the experiences from different perspectives, often in the form of direct speech between the biographer and other participants or between the narrator himself or herself at the time of the event and at the present time – or in the form of an episode, going through several narration units (Schütze 2012b, p. 21).

Every biographical narrative has *a story carrier*. In the off-the-cuff autobiographical narration, the story usually begins with the introduction of the story carrier: the narrator himself or herself. The story carrier thus presents the central figure across the whole development of the story. Nevertheless, he or she does not stay the same throughout the narration, but instead develops and changes throughout the course of his or her life as a reaction to events and experiences. For example, the story carrier might be introduced to the story as an active person who has his or her life firmly in his or her own hands. However, as a reaction to certain events and experiences the narrator might lose the possibility of acting and making decisions, which in turn starts a process of suffering (Schütze 1984). Changes in the narrator's inner state might be conscious, marked in the narration by inner dialogues between the person the narrator used to be and the person he or she is at present, or in other reflective ways such as self-criticism, questioning or irony (Schütze 2012b, p. 21). Nevertheless, the narrator does not necessarily have to be consciously aware of internal changes during the course of his or her life.

Schütze (1984, p. 84) distinguished between the story carrier and *the event carrier*. Whereas in autobiographical off-the-cuff narration the story carrier is identical to the narrator, the event carrier does not necessarily have to be the narrator himself or herself. Moreover, event carriers can not only be significant others or other people the narrator came in contact with, but also other non-human or abstract actors (such as communism, illness or the computer). Event carriers are often introduced to the narration with their name and a description of their characteristics. Their effect and meaning for the narrator is often commented on and evaluated by the narrator. According to Schütze (2012b, p. 21), significant others introduced by the narrator and with whom the narrator compares him or herself, enters into interaction and (directly or indirectly) consults in respect of his or her past and future biographical steps.

The last but one cognitive figure is labeled *"social frames"* by Schütze. They are necessary for putting social events, social processes and the development and changes experienced by the biographer into context. Social frames can be organizations, different sorts of social and institutional milieus, but also relationships and so forth. Social frames can both pave the way for certain biographical processes and restrain them.

All previous cognitive figures contribute to the establishment of the last cognitive figure: *the global shape of the narration*. Every off-the-cuff autobiographical story, so Schütze (1984, p. 103), has a specific global shape with its moral, emotional tune and perspective from which the story is told. In the short moments before the narration starts, the narrator develops a rough idea about what will be the theme of his or her recounting and how the story will be presented. The preamble – the introductory sentences of the biographical self-presentation – already provides a first glimpse of the global shape of the narration by the way the story is introduced and put into social and historical settings. The first lines of the story also often reveal the overall emotional tune of the story: is it a success story? Or is it the story about searching for oneself? Is it the story about loss and suffering? During the autobiographical presentation, as the story is being constructed stage by stage, the shape of the overall story becomes more specific. The structure of the global story is marked, among other things, by special verbal expressions connecting the supra-sectional units of the story. Furthermore, important indications as to the overall gestalt of the biographical presentation are often to be found towards the end of the presentation, in the pre-coda and coda – the expressions marking the end of the section and narration. During this concluding phase at the end of the presentation, the narrator in most cases summarizes, evaluates and completes the story. These are the moments which reveal how the narrator sees and explains the course of his or her life. An analysis of the pre-coda and coda also provides an indication as to the way the narrator experiences the link between past events and his or her present inner and outer state. The summary and evaluation of the narrator's life story might even give an insight into possible future perspectives as the narrator sees them. Without understanding the overall gestalt of the life story from past to present, future perspectives would also remain sketchy and unclear (Schütze 2012b, p. 19).

Narrative constraints and cognitive figures are crucial for understanding the development and meaning of the narrated stories. Their analysis helps to reveal how the biographical presentation was structured, which events and experiences were of particular importance and which had only marginal meaning for the narrator. The cognitive figures give indications as to the social spheres and their changes within the story, to the actors and their relationships with the narrator, to the inner development experienced by the narrator, as well as to the deeper meaning – both conscious and unconscious – of the biographical presentation.

In order to get access to the cognitive figures and in order to analyze biographical interviews, Schütze introduced a process of analysis consisting of five steps: formal analysis of the interview, sequential analysis and structural description, analytical abstraction, knowledge analysis and lastly contrastive comparison of diverse interview sections and of interviews overall (Schütze 1983). The analysis of biographical narrative interviews has been the subject of discussions within biographical research. Nowadays, different methods coexist. The framework I used for the analysis of my empirical material is based to a great extent on proposals by Fritz Schütze and Gerhard Riemann (Schütze 1983; Riemann 2010), since they take into account different views of the text and its production. Before I introduce in more detail the analytical framework which I applied for the analysis of biographical interviews collected for this study, I will discuss the research process embedded in the tradition of interpretative social research and Grounded Theory.

5.2 The reflexive research process

The starting point for my research was personal experience and observations connected to migration and social mobility, along with the perusal of actual literature on the topic. Since there were hardly any studies on migration processes from the Czech Republic to Germany, I turned my attention to finding out more about my chosen topic. I participated in courses and read literature on transnational migration, intersectionality, East-West migration processes and biographical approaches. The initial interviews I conducted had a significant effect on shaping my views on highly skilled migration and social mobility in general. An in depth analysis of the initial interviews led me to immerse myself once again into the available literature and search for processes which I discovered within my materials – the processes of deskilling, professional reorientation, upwards social mobility and the processes of negotiation of belonging and positioning in relation to migration and biography. Existing literature, as well as discussions within colloquia and working groups, helped me to get more out of my empirical data and to question the features which before I had taken for granted. Thus, the analysis of the interviews happened not in an isolated vacuum, nor was it a separate phase of the project. The research process did not take a linear course from the research question and collection of empirical data to analysis and verification or falsification of the previous hypothesis, but instead was a process which moved forth and back, allowing me to turn around and see, correct, develop and reflect on the phenomena being studied.

The way I approached the empirical data corresponds to research and practice embedded within interpretative social research and Grounded Theory, both of which are built on the tradition of the Chicago School, emphasising the role of discovery, communicative exchange and reflexivity in the research process (Riemann 2011). Grounded Theory, introduced and further developed by Barney Glaser and Anselm Strauss (1967), is aimed at the development of theories from empirical material. According to the authors, the analyses do not appear from the text per se. They are developed in an interactive process between the researcher and the empirical material, whereas the goal of the analysis is the generation of new knowledge (Corbin 2006, pp. 70–71). At the same time, the development of theories is not based solely on inductive logic. Theoretical knowledge is used in order to sensitise the researcher to working with the empirical material.[30] Reading and working

---

30 The role of prior theoretical knowledge for the analysis of empirical material was the reason for later disputes between Barney Glaser and Anselm Strauss. While Barney Glaser emphasised the development of new knowledge from the empirical material without any influence of existing theories, Anselm Strauss argued that theoretical prior knowledge is and has to be part of the analytical process (Reichertz 2011, p. 280).

with the material are thus not separate working steps but related to each other (Corbin 2006, p. 71). The way in which knowledge is generated from the empirical material thus follows not the logic of simple induction or deduction, but the logic of abduction, which integrates these two logic conclusions and research strategies.

As Jo Reichertz (2011, p. 288) has argued, abductive thinking is not a mere method of generating hypotheses and theories, but rather the attitude towards the empirical material and one's own knowledge. The empirical facts are the basis for further thinking. They can put prior theoretical knowledge into question and start a process of correction and reworking, which may lead to the reconstruction and further development of existing theories or to the discovery of new concepts or theories.[31] Thus, abductive thinking is based on the willingness to question, reflect and give up one's own knowledge and explanations and to search for new solutions (Reichertz 2006, p. 13). The logic of abduction allows one to discover phenomena in the empirical material which are unexpected and surprising. They are the basis of the formulation of hypotheses which, subsequently, are verified, falsified or reworked in the process of induction and deduction.

At the same time, phenomena which appear surprising and unexpected to us point out the knowledge we are acquiring, since in order to see and underline anomalies in the material, one has to relate to existing knowledge derived either from everyday life or scientific discussions (Burawoy 1991, p. 9). Knowledge thus does not grow from empirical data itself, but is produced in the course of an ongoing dialogue within the scope of the knowledge and theories that are accessible to us. This dialogue between the empirical material and theory is not bound to one specific phase of research, but occurs during the whole research process, including the moment of writing down the research results.

This approach on the interplay of empirical material and theory building influenced not only the research process, but also the way this paper has been written. I started to write down the methodology and biographical case presentations, and continued with migration contexts and theoretical approaches. These chapters were written in conjunction with empirical material. In both chapters I highlight the features which were particularly important for my interviewees and which help one to better understand their narration. The migration contexts and theoretical approaches as presented here therefore formed the starting point for their analysis and their results alike. Only afterwards did I move to the last chapter, biographies in comparison, in which the cross-case findings are presented and embedded within the wider body of theoretical discussions.

---

31   For the reconstruction of social theories through empirical work see e.g. Burawoy 1991.

5.3 Constructing the sample

The choice of interviewees for the study followed the logic of theoretical sampling (Glaser, Strauss 1967). According to this research tradition embedded in Grounded Theory, the aim of theoretical sampling is not the selection of cases which would statistically represent the studied society, but rather such selection of cases which is meaningful for the development of concepts and theories (Strübing 2006, p. 155). In contradiction to quantitatively oriented research strategies, the object of research is neither designed in advance, nor is it perceived as "given". Rather, the construction of the sample is an important empirical step, which is carried out in the course of the analysis with ongoing comparisons to other cases and with regard to theoretical questions which come up during the research process.

The focus of this research project is the migration processes of people who, at some time during their life, have moved from the Czech Republic to Germany. I decided to focus only on "new migration flows" (Lutz, Koser 1998), i.e. on people who came to Germany after the fall of the Iron Curtain. This decision was based on the assumption that migration regimes and migration patterns changed somewhat after the revolution and "opening up" of the borders in 1989. Since the focus of this study was on highly skilled migration, the next criterion for the choice of interviewees was their level of education. I interviewed predominantly those migrants who had already accomplished their university studies. The majority of my interviewees studied in the Czech Republic prior to or during migration. I did not limit the choice to migrants specialised only in certain special fields, such as engineering or science, but decided to include in the sample those who studied art and humanities, medicine, pedagogy or other subjects as well. This gave me the possibility to analyse the way in which university degrees in different fields were used and negotiated after migration. Finally, I decided to interview both women and men in order to analyse the role of gender within these processes.

When searching for interviewees, I left open in which year after the fall of the Iron Curtain people moved country. However, very early on I realised that it did matter for migrants whether they had moved before the Czech Republic joined the EU in 2004 or afterwards, since the possibilities of migration as well as legal frameworks changed somewhat. Early comparisons of interviews also revealed the role of the subject's gender within the migration processes at different time periods. While in the 1990s the only perceived opportunity for the majority of the migrant women in my sample to stay legally in Germany for a longer period of time was via an au pair visa, studies or marriage, from 2004 onwards a residence permit was no longer required. Nevertheless, restrictions on entering the labour market continued to be in place until 2011. Despite these conditions, which affected both men and women, women appeared to have more difficulties in obtaining a work permit and entering the formal labour market. Gender thus became the main criterion during the construction of a sample and overall analyses.

Furthermore, the initial analysis of interviews showed that despite the majority of interviewees already having accomplished their university studies in the Czech Republic, surprisingly many took up further studies in Germany. When searching for my next subjects and trying to discover new variations, I thus paid particular attention to the role of further education and other strategies which were important to migrants in gaining access to positions within the labour market that would correspond to migrants' expectations. Moreover, during my analysis I became aware of the role of the family within migration processes. While being single was for many the precondition for moving back and forth across borders, as well as for upwards social mobility, having children influenced their decision to stay in one place for a longer period of time. Children's future opportunities and education was one of the main deciding factors for staying in Germany, moving back to the Czech Republic or to the other relevant country. In order to also capture these experiences, I therefore researched other subjects so as to gain variety within my sample concerning family status.

I conducted interviews in two phases: the first ten interviews were carried out between November 2009 and April 2010, the next six interviews in 2011. Whereas during the first phase my choice of subjects was mainly explorative, during the next phase one year later my search became more specific in order to include within my sample those interviews which would made the sample "complete" and theoretically saturated.[32]

5.4 Interview settings

I contacted my interviewees in a number of different ways, via email, networking platforms, telephone or personally. My initial contact with the majority of subjects was in writing, mostly via email. During initial contact I introduced myself and the purposes of my study. I explained that I was interested in the life experiences and pathways of people who had moved country during the course of their life. I clarified that I would use the biographical approach in order to hear their unique biographical experiences and establish the meaning to them of border crossings. I consciously avoided using the expression "migrant" or "migration", since these terms are not free from discursive imaginations, which not only picture "migrants" as "foreign" and "not belonging to the major society" but "migration" across national borders,

---

32   As to the concept of theoretical saturation see e.g. Glaser, Strauss 1967 or Strübing 2006.

which are considered fixed natural dividing lines, as an "anomaly" (Lutz 2007, p. 79; Wimmer, Glick Schiller 2002). In order to overcome the ascriptions of my interviewees in relation to these terms, I emphasised my interest in biographical experiences and life stories. I explained that these were accessible through the biographical narrative interview, i.e. such form of interview which does not follow the question-and-answer scheme but instead lets the narrator structure his or her own story. Most of the potential interviewees were surprised by my interest in their life experiences and asked for more details. We then exchanged further emails, spoke to each other on the telephone, or met in a café in order to clarify open questions.

I contacted all my interviewees in Czech. Speaking their native language in predominantly German speaking surroundings created a special relationship between us. Despite the fact that interviews often took place in public, our common language created a protected sphere, since we could assume that that which was spoken would not be understood by others. Coming from the same country and speaking the same language eased the establishment of contact with my interviewees, as well as interaction throughout the interview. At the same time, the assumption of similar biographical knowledge and biographical experiences connected to the country of origin had an impact on thematising and de-thematising of certain experiences.

I was aware that in order to enable my interviewees to narrate their personal life story to me, I would have to create an atmosphere in which the experiences could be expressed freely and with respect. I thus let interviewees choose the time and place of the interview. I revealed my personal story and told them how it came that I myself moved to Germany and started working on this research project. Before we started with the interview, I once again explained the parameters and format of the interview in order to prevent irritations and misunderstandings at the beginning and during the interview. I asked for permission to record the interviews so that I would be able to concentrate on the narration and come back to certain passages later on. At the same time I underlined that protecting the interviewee's privacy would be of great importance in the research process. I explained that the protection of privacy would be assured by careful anonymization of all personal data and events which could lead to identification of the interviewee. In connection herewith I asked interviewees to give themselves an anonymous name. In most cases this served to create a relaxed atmosphere and prepare the ground for the narration, since many chosen names were already connected with a certain story.

The interviews took place in very different settings. I conducted them in cafés, restaurants, offices, at interviewees' homes, or at my place. During a number of interviews other family members, mostly small children and in some cases the partners or parents in law, joined us at some stage. These varying contexts shaped our interaction and the narration in different ways.

The reconstruction of the interview settings and of the interaction were important steps in the analysis of interviews.

5.5 The interview process

In order to access biographical experiences connected with migration, I used the biographical narrative interview as developed by Fritz Schütze. At the beginning of the interview I asked my interviewees to tell me their life story. I formulated it as follows: "Could you please tell me your life story? You have as much time as you wish for your narration. I will not interrupt you. When you have finished telling your story, I would then like to ask you some questions."[33] Interviewees reacted very differently to this question. Some people started narrating their life story the moment I asked them to. Others needed more time to sort out their thoughts, to clarify where they could start their life story, and to confirm again what the interests of the research were and which role they should take in the interview setting.

Off-the-cuff life stories were different in length. They lasted between ten minutes and two hours, during which I took the role of the listener. I concentrated on the narration and made only a few notes during narration. Only at moments in which the interviewee felt uncomfortable or did not know what to narrate next did I intervene. In such moments I tried to ease the situation by means of a question or comment. In some cases the interviewee asked me to stop recording the interview and take a short break. After few minutes the interview usually continued.

Despite the structure of narrations differing somewhat, they were mostly narrated in chronological order and initially followed the path which is familiar from one's curriculum vitae, i.e. naming the various stages of education and of the individual's professional career. Such structuring may be explained by the fact of interviewees already having internalised this method of telling their life history as required by diverse institutions, such as job agencies, universities or foreign offices. Despite this being the dominant structure of interviews, narrations usually became more detailed as the interview progressed, touching on areas of life other than education and work in the later sequences of the interview.

Only after the interviewees had made it clear that they had finished telling their story did I start to ask questions according to notes I had made during the narration. When I had the feeling that all of the topics were narrated

---

33 In Czech: "Ráda bych vás poprosila, abyste mi vyprávěl(a) tvůj životní příběh. Máte na to tolik času, kolik chcete. Nebudu vás přerušovat, teprve až dovyprávíte, zeptám se vás na pár věcí."

152

or when I realised that the interviewee wished to finish, I turned off the recording equipment and we spoke for a while about the interview, about our past experiences and future plans. The interviewees' reflexive biographical work thus frequently continued even after the interview had been completed (see e.g. Schütze 2012a, p. 13).

5.6 A brief summary of interviewees

My first interviewee was *Lenka*. I established contact with her through a Czech-German internet platform and met her shortly afterwards in a café in Cologne, the city in which she lived. She studied Pedagogy in the Czech Republic and initially moved to Germany as an au pair. When we met she was working as a grammar school teacher and had one daughter. Lenka introduced me to two of her friends, Zuzana and Štěpánka, who had also lived in Germany for some years. However, before I met them, I travelled to Wiesbaden to conduct an interview with Marie.

Marie was working in a public institution in Wiesbaden. She studied Czech and German in Prague. Shortly after the revolution in 1989 she had spent some years in different German towns, where she taught Czech. She continued teaching languages after moving back to Prague. She lived there until she decided to follow her husband to Wiesbaden, where he had got a job offer.

Shortly before Christmas 2009 I visited *Zuzana* in her flat in a suburb of Cologne where she lived with her husband and two children. Zuzana was originally from a small town in North Bohemia. After high school (Gymnasium) graduation in 1997 and an unsuccessful university application she went to Germany as an au pair. She moved to Cologne and besides working in a household as a cleaner and child carer for several years she studied Pedagogy there. At the time she was looking for a qualified job. She had considered moving with her family to some other European country in the future.

Since *Štěpánka* had a small baby, she invited me to conduct the interview at her flat on the outskirts of Cologne. Before going on maternity leave she had worked as a pharmacist for a health organisation in Cologne. She studied Pharmaceutics in Prague and continued with a PhD at Göttingen University in Germany, to which she had established contacts during her student exchanges. After she finished her PhD studies, she was not sure whether to stay in Germany or to go back. Her decision to stay was eased by the fact that she had a job in Cologne and had met her boyfriend, the father of her child, there.

Whilst conducting my initial interviews, I searched for other ways to access further potential interviewees. In a professional networking platform I contacted *Martin* for the first time. We exchanged several emails and arranged to meet in a Czech restaurant in Düsseldorf, the city in which he was currently living. Martin was born in North Bohemia, moved to Prague to study Economics and started a job with an international finance institution there. His former boss arranged contacts with Düsseldorf, where he has been working in the finance sector ever since.

I established contact with *Ivan* through the same networking platform. After explaining to him the purposes and focus of the study, Ivan offered to meet me in a restaurant on the outskirts of Cologne, where he worked and lived with his wife and a small child. Ivan was born in Ostrava, one of the biggest cities on the eastern border of the Czech Republic. He spent his childhood in Ostrava, studied Computer Science and had his first jobs in the IT sector there. However, since jobs were insecure and low paid, he decided to apply for a job abroad. Through a job agency he went to Cologne in 2000 and worked as an IT specialist on the basis of a work contract and later by means of a Green Card for an international company, within which he later progressed to higher professional positions.

My next interviews led me to Bamberg in February 2010. There I met Karolína, Arnošt and Linda, to whom I had established contact through Marie, one of my previous interviewees. *Karolína* invited me to her flat in the centre of Bamberg, where she lived with her husband and her small child. While sitting with her child on the carpet and drinking tea, Karolína told me her life story. She was born in Ústí nad Labem, a city close to the northern border of the Czech Republic. She went to a German-speaking high school (Gymnasium) and later on studied German and English at the University of Olomouc. In 2000 she went to Bamberg as an Erasmus exchange student. There she met her future husband. After graduation she moved back to Bamberg and one year later she started a PhD in the field of English Literature, which she completed some years later. At the time of the interview she was looking for a way to professionally use her qualifications and her knowledge of languages.

The next day I arranged a meeting with *Arnošt* at his office at the university. He was born in 1964 in Olomouc and studied History and German there. Arnošt's life story was about repeated migrations to Bamberg and other cities and about his efforts to come back to Olomouc with his family. At the time of the interview he was working as a professor at a Slavic institute in Bamberg.

Linda organised a free room at the university in Bamberg, where she currently worked as a research assistant, for our meeting. She was born in 1975 in Brno, one of the biggest cities in the Czech Republic, where she also studied History and German. During her studies she received an offer to go to Bamberg for one semester. There she met her current boyfriend. For several years after graduating she commuted between Brno, where she worked as a lecturer at the university, and Bamberg, where she was studying German as foreign language and working in restaurants and factories or as translator.

Since the commute was demanding for her, she decided to stay in Bamberg. She started to study Czech, worked on diverse research projects and completed her PhD shortly before the interview took place.

In order to conduct an interview with *Jana*, to whom I established contact via my previous interviewee Štěpánka, I travelled to Göttingen and visited Jana in her small one bedroom flat. We sat on the bed while Jana narrated her life story. She was born in Ostrov, close to the western border of the Czech Republic, and at the age of five moved with her family to Prague. She went to a secondary nursing school and afterwards studied Theology. After graduation she spent a year in Germany working as a volunteer at a hospital. Shortly afterwards she went to England and worked in an old people's home. When she returned to Prague, she took a job at a Computer Company. However, she left after several months and decided to return to Germany and to study Music. At the time of the interview she was still studying Music and working as a carer for elderly and handicapped people.

A year later I started the second round of the interviews. I met *Barbora* during a Czech event in Frankfurt. A few months later, in April 2011, I contacted her again and we arranged a meeting at a café in Mainz, the city in which she was studying Social Work at the time. Barbora was born in Teplice in 1977. She went to high school (Gymnasium) there and afterwards moved to Prague to study Tropical Geography. After university graduation she and her husband bought a house together and moved to a village near Mainz. Besides caring for her three children, she had decided to start a new course of studies which would give her new options of professional self-realisation.

I also met *Jitka* and *Tomáš*, a Czech couple, at the same event in Frankfurt. They came to Germany in 2004 and since then had lived in Frankfurt. I first interviewed Jitka at their flat, and a month later interviewed Tomáš at my flat. Jitka and Tomáš were both from the same region in the north-eastern part of the Czech Republic. Jitka was born in 1984. She grew up in Hradec Králové and went to high school (Gymnasium) there. Tomáš was born in 1983 and lived with his family in a nearby village. He trained to be an Electrical Engineer and took his leaving examinations (Abitur) in the neighbouring town. Since Tomáš's sister had lived and worked in Frankfurt for some years, Jitka and Tomáš decided to join her. At first they both took language courses and Jitka then enrolled at university. She studied Linguistics and later on German as a foreign language at the university in Gießen, a medium sized city near Frankfurt. Tomáš initially worked as a messenger. Later on he worked as a housekeeper for several houses on a self-employed basis. Their plan to only stay in Germany temporarily changed over time, and they started to plan their future in Frankfurt.

I travelled to Leipzig in order to meet *Kamil*, my next interviewee to whom I established contact through a friend of mine who had studied and worked in Germany before. I visited him in his flat. Since it was a nice summer's day, we sat on the small balcony. His wife was present throughout the majority of the interview and commented from time to time on Kamil's story. Kamil was born in 1978 in Trutnov. He was apprenticed as an electrician there and passed his leaving examinations (Abitur) in a neighbouring town. Afterwards he moved to Prague to study Electrical Engineering at university there. During his studies he spent a summer holiday in Germany as a volunteer assistant for handicapped people in order to learn German. This experience gave him the idea of studying in Germany. He thus went to Leipzig for one semester and later on participated in several university exchange programs. Kamil established firm contacts during his studies in Leipzig and, after graduating, returned to Leipzig and now works as an electrical engineer for an automobile company.

I met *Petr* at a seminar for international students in Bonn. We kept in touch and I asked him to participate in an interview with me. He agreed and visited me in my flat in the summer of 2011. We had dinner together and spent many hours talking about his biographical course. Petr was born in 1985 in Uherské Hradiště. He completed high school (Gymnasium) there and afterwards moved to Prague to study Economics. During his studies he applied for a scholarship in Munich and moved there for two years. During that time he did some internships in the financial sector, finished his master's degree and started to work for a prestigious financial institution in Munich. Shortly after the interview Petr received an offer to work a one financial company in South America, and moved there.

My last interviewee was *Adela*. I established contact with her through a friend of mine who was working with Adela in Luxemburg. Adela had only recently come to Frankfurt, where she was working for a public institution. Adela was born in 1980 in Opava on the eastern border of the Czech Republic. According to Adela, the turning point in her life was a one year student exchange programme placement in the USA when she was 18 years old. Since then she has travelled extensively and moved house regularly. She studied English, French and Public Administration in Hradec Králové. Before she moved to Frankfurt she worked for a European institution in Luxemburg for five years.

5.7 Ethnographical notes

Shortly after I conducted the interviews I noted down how they went in the form of ethnographical notes. I described the first meeting, mutual expectations, the place at which the interview took place, the atmosphere of the interview as well as our interaction and the sequential course. In doing so I tried to distance myself from the situation and to take the position of someone who observes the events and the relations between me and my interviewee "from above". This research perspective, which Gerhard Riemann described as "die Befremdung der eigenen Praxis" – the alienation of one's own practice (Riemann 2004, 2009) – made it possible for me to recapitulate the interview process, to point out ruptures and unexpected developments and to analyse the relationship between me and my interviewees. Furthermore, it enabled to me to critically evaluate my own role as an interviewer, to analyse the impact of the questions I posed and of the comments I delivered during the course of interview, thereby learning from my own mistakes.

The following excerpt from my ethnographic notes written after the interview with Kamil in Leipzig in Juli 2011 serves as an illustration of the way in which I wrote and used ethnographic notes for my study.

(…) I arrived at the house in which Kamil lived shortly before six o'clock in the evening, the time we had arranged via email. We had never spoken to one another before, which made me insecure and curious at the same time. At six o'clock I rang the doorbell of Kamil's flat and he opened the door and invited me in. Since it was a sunny and warm summer's evening, Kamil proposed that we go straight to the terrace. He offered me something to drink and invited me to sit at a small round table on the tiny terrace with a view of the green garden. We talked about life in Leipzig and in Germany in general and Kamil initiated the discussion on the cultural differences between the Czech Republic and Germany. At the beginning I had the feeling that Kamil was a bit shy and felt insecure in that situation, which was particularly visible in the way he quickly changed topics. However, this impression changed during the course of our meeting. Kamil proved to be very talkative and he was the one who decided how the flow of our conversation should develop, which topics would be addressed and which would not. (…) After about half an hour his wife Alice joined us at the table. She was German but she spoke very good Czech, which surprised me. After a few minutes Alice got up, took the rabbits to the garden which they were taking care of, and went off to prepare dinner consisting of sandwiches and tea. During dinner Kamil narrated how they met and how their wedding was. He explained that the ceremony was in Leipzig, but the celebration was on the Czech side of the border. They had both Czech and German guests and made efforts that everyone understood and that everything was translated. Alice commented on Kamil's narration, but it was mostly him who narrated. Kamil mentioned that it was very important to him that Alice learned the Czech language. They speak Czech at home. (This surprised me since most bi-national couples I met spoke either German together or another "neutral" non-native language for both of the partners, such as English. Using Czech as their common language may be Kamil's strategy of balancing the unequal and contradictory power relations concerning gender and migration status between him and his wife.) (…) While sitting at the table on the terrace and drinking tea, I placed the recording equipment on the table and again explained the way in which the interview would proceed. I asked Kamil to choose his anonymised name. He laughed and decided on the nickname he had been given during his studies. Afterwards I asked him to narrate his life story to me. He thought for a second and started to narrate from the moment of his birth in Trutnov. (…)

As this example shows, ethnographic notes allowed me not only to recapitulate the course of the interview, but also to memorise my thoughts, irritations and feelings and to formulate my initial interpretations of the particular case.

Despite reworking some of my hypotheses and assumptions in the course of further analysis, the ethnographic notes were very important in the research process since they enabled to me to analyse the biographical narration in the context of its creation.

5.8 Transcription

Before I started with the transcription of the interviews, I listened to the interviews repeatedly in order to understand the flow of the narration, its interruptions and structure. When listening to the interviews I paid attention to the sequential order of narration. Later on I illustrated the sequences in the written text by separate paragraphs. The transcription of the interviews was a very time demanding process – altogether the transcribed interviews accounted for more than 800 pages. Nevertheless, it contributed to a better understanding of the interviews, since it encouraged me to also pay attention to small details which would otherwise have stayed unnoticed.

I opted for a means of transcription which would reproduce the narration as closely as possible whilst at the same time being comprehensible to the reader. I wrote down the words and sentences in the way in which they were spoken, i.e. including all spelling and grammatical mistakes and dialects. I used punctuation not according to grammatical rules but according to the accent and melody of the voice of the speaker. I made it clear by using punctuation and other symbols whether the words or sentences were finished or interrupted. I also paid attention to the accentuation of the speaker in relation to certain expressions or the lowering of the volume of the speaker's voice in other places. I noted nonverbal expressions, such as laughing, clearing one's throat or breathing deeply, as well as shifts in the modes of expression. Furthermore, interventions, comments, questions and nonverbal expressions of the interviewer and any other persons present were noted. Despite this intense focus on verbal and nonverbal expressions and interactions, the aim of the transcription of interviews was not its exact reproduction. I perceived the transcription instead to be a process of selection, construction, interpretation and translation of some expressions into words.[34] The following table 1 shows the transcription symbols I used when writing down the spoken interview.

---

34   On the theory of transcription, see e.g. Kowal, O'Connell 2000.

Table 1: Transcription symbols

Transcription symbols	Example	Description
[I: Hmm]	And then it happened [Me: Hmm]	Nonverbal or verbal intervention by the interviewer
(laughs)	That was just crazy (laughs)	Nonverbal expressions
italics	*I did not get visa*	Quietly expressed consonants, words or sentences
–	Yeah and I – had to	Small break
(1)	I had to return (1) and	Break in seconds
Bold font	**Imagine** it!	Accentuated or loud expressions
/... (changes in the tone of voice)/	/ and I came back and I did not know (speaks slower and with deeper voice)/	Changes in the mode of expression
:	And: I applied for several jobs	Elongated expressions
-	But there was a prob-	Interrupted words or sentences

Quelle: Eigene Darstellung

During the process of transcription I anonymised all of the actual names, dates, institutions and places. I often used the names which the interviewees had given themselves. In some cases I chose similar names in order to protect the privacy of the interviewees. I also changed all of the cities mentioned by interviewees, with the exception of Prague. Although the other cities were able to be exchanged with structurally similar cities as to size and general atmosphere, there was no equivalent for Prague, the cultural, political and commercial centre of the Czech Republic. Its extraordinary position also became apparent in the biographical narrations: nearly all of the interviewees connected with Prague at some moments in their biographical course. I transcribed all of the interviews in Czech, the language in which the interviews were conducted. Not until later on did I translate some parts into German or English for the purposes of presentations at colloquia, discussions within interpretation groups and workshops, and for the purposes of publication.

During transcription I made comments in my notebook on whatever appeared to me as being unusual, striking, or unclear. I also wrote down my ideas, initial interpretation of the relevant case and possible comparisons with other cases. These initial interpretations were included in the analysis later on.

5.9 Analysis

The main advantage of biographical material is the possibility of approaching it from different perspectives and switching among them. Firstly, the biographical narrative interview makes it possible to approach the social world and events from the perspective of narrators. It gives one the possibility of seeing the world through their eyes, to see the events as they experienced them. This perspective enables one to reconstruct which possibilities they perceived as being accessible to them in order to make decisions and to act, as well as to see the barriers they experienced as limiting. It gives access to explanations of and reflections on these events by the narrators themselves. Secondly, it enables one to change the viewpoint from that of narrators to a more abstract one. It enables one to step back from the narrated events and to see them embedded within the line of events which follow each other in the biographical narration. The narrator does not have to be specifically aware of the link between and meaning of these narrated events in their specific sequence. Instead, this can be reconstructed by careful analysis of interview sequences and how they are embedded within the whole story. Thirdly, working with biographical narrative interviews enables one to see the narrative within the further social context and to compare how different narrators experienced certain events.

I decided to base my analytical framework on the recommendations of Fritz Schütze and Gerhard Riemann (Schütze 1976, 1983, 2012b, 2012a; Riemann 2006a, 2010). The analytical steps of formal and sequential analysis of the text, structural description, as well as analytical abstraction and construction of types as proposed by Schütze and Riemann involved different ways of working with the biographical material, thus enabling different perspectives on the biographical narrative interviews to be integrated as described above. I combined their recommendations with some aspects of analysis as elaborated by Gabriele Rosenthal (2005). Over the next pages I will describe how I "translated" the analytical recommendations into practice.

After transcribing the first interviews, I chose one of them in order to analyse it in more detail. Later on I included six other interviews in the detailed, time consuming analysis. The remaining interviews were scrutinised using a "global analysis" approach (Rosenthal 2005, pp. 92–94) – i.e. a preliminary rough analysis of the interview – before subjecting certain sections which were of particular interest for my study to detailed analysis.

5.9.1 Formal analysis of the text

The first step in working with the transcribed biographical narrative interviews involved formally analysing the text. At this stage I concentrated solely on the particular case at hand. I listened to the interview and re-read the transcript several times in order to identify the inner sequential structure of the interview. I paid attention to the verbal expressions, as for example "yes and then", "well", "afterwards" and so on, which marked the end of one section and the beginning of the next one. Furthermore, I considered nonverbal expressions, such as breaks in the narrative or the pitch of the interviewee's voice, whereby the end of the section was usually indicated section by a drop in the subject's voice (Detka 2005, p. 354; Schütze 1984, p. 79). Moreover, I focused on communicative schemes during the interview and their various shifts in order to understand the structure of the biographical rendering.

Differentiating between communicative schemes of argumentation, description and narration were crucial for this first step of analysis. By looking more closely at communicative schemes and their shifts within the life story, the focus of attention was moved from a sole content analysis of the message to the *way in which* the message was narrated (Riemann 2006a, 2010). The identification of communicative schemes and the analysis of their functions within the biographical presentation helped to reconstruct the meaning that diverse events and experiences had for the biographer.

Formal analysis of the text also enabled me to identify the main storyline within the narrated story, its supra-sectional structure and the additional storylines which should support, complement or confirm the main storyline and which often come in the form of background construction (Schütze 1984, p. 91; Detka 2005).

In order to gain an overview on the formal text structure, I created tables in which I noted the sequences in their consecutive order. These tables helped me to orientate myself within the narrations and to identify their inner logic. I wrote down the line numbers which marked the beginning and the end of the section and I identified the dominant communicative schemes for the respective sections. Further on I briefly summarised the content of the sections and left space for my notes, in which I marked my thoughts on the respective sequences as well as the overall structure of the narration. The following table 2 which I made on the basis of interview with Ivan collected during winter 2010 in Cologne serves as an example of the formal text analysis.

Table 2: An example of formal text analysis of the interview with Ivan

Sequence	Line numbers	Communicative scheme	Content	Notes
1.	15-18	Narration	Ivan was born in Ostrava. He spent his whole life there until he went to Germany.	Time before and after migration – the biographical division line
2.	19-26	Argumentation/ reflection	It was surprising for him that he ended up in Germany. He thought that he would spend his whole life in Ostrava.	Altered expectations and life plans, comparisons with his past self
3.	27-41	Description	Ivan has parents and one sister. They lived in a block of flats, they had a cottage and the most of the time they spent there. They went abroad on holiday from time to time, which at that time was exceptional.	"Normal" life despite communist regime
4.	42-55	Narration/ argumentation	After grammar school Ivan went to high school (Gymnasium). In his third year there was a revolution and the system radically changed. Ivan argues that his family was open and against communists' way of thinking.	Expected institutional course Construction of "close" vs. "open" regime
5.	56-62	Reflection	After the revolution the possibility opened for him to go abroad. However, he was not attracted by it at that time.	The structural changes

Quelle: Eigene Darstellung

5.9.2   Structural description

After formally analysing the text I elaborated on the structural description for the main narrative, as well as for the questioning part of the six interviews which appeared central to my project. I described the initial sections of the narrative and continued with the other sections in sequential order.

The structural description involves a detailed textual analysis focusing both on the content and on the formal presentation, i.e. the way in which the text is narrated and which linguistic expressions are used in doing so (Riemann 2010, p. 228; Schütze 1983, p. 286). The aim of this analytical step is to elaborate on the biographical and social processes which shape present and future biographical developments and possibilities of action (Detka 2005, p. 357). These processes, which influence each other and develop both simultaneously and one after the other, are expressed in the textual presentation.

The focus on linguistic expressions can thus reveal how the past events were experienced by the biographer and which attitude the biographer had towards the social and biographical events (Schütze 1984, p. 87). Fritz Schütze elaborated four main ways of reacting to biographical events and called them process structures: the action scheme, trajectory of suffering, metamorphosis and expected institutional pattern.[35] The dominant process structures as experienced in the past are expressed at the moment of their rendering (Riemann 2010, p. 229).

When describing and analysing the respective sections I paid attention to the cognitive figures (Schütze 1984) as they were expressed in the text.[36] I concentrated on the structure of the text and on the way in which respective events, situations and scenes interplayed and followed each other. I paid attention to the way in which the biographer introduced him or herself to the narration and which other "event carriers" gained in importance for the biographer. Social settings and situations were accorded particular attention too. Finally, I examined which process structures were found in the text and their impact on biographical developments. The following excerpt from the structural description which I examined on the basis of my biographical narrative interview with Zuzana, one of my first interviewees, illustrates the way in which I dealt with the extensive amount of biographical material:

„Z: I was born in Jablunkov, in North Bohemia, it is such a small town, six thousand inhabitants, [I: Hmm] and I grew up (-) there. I was actually there until I went to Germany. [I: Hmm]. I went (-) to grammar school and then to Gymnasium there, and: then I submitted a few applications to university, but I did not get anywhere (breathing) although I actually also (-) then I did not fancy going anywhere, I rather wanted to work already [I: hmm]. But: (breathing in) it wasn't so easy with work there. (Clearing her throat) I then got a job as a seamstress. In the factory, I stood it for three months there and: on the last day of my trial period I managed it (shortly laughing) and I quit. [I: hmm], and I went to Germany as an au pair [I: hmm]. Ninety six (1). (Zuzana, p. 1, l. 23-32)

In this way Zuzana begins her narration. First of all, she locates her birth and life in a specific town situated in North Bohemia prior to moving to Germany. Mentioning North Bohemia seems to be of importance to Zuzana. It is an area which is in social discursive imaginations characterised by unemployment, heavy industry and pollution. Zuzana delivers a brief description of the town and underlines its small size. She contextualises her life prior to migration in this manner, and indirectly outlines her past life perspectives and possibilities. Her statement that "I was actually there until I went to Germany" gives the impression that her life is divided along the axes of time and space: the time before migration is connected to her life in her town in the

---

35   For a detailed description of process structures, please refer to the chapter within this thesis entitled "Biographical process structures".

36   The cognitive figures have already been described above in the chapter entitled "Telling the stories: the theoretical background behind the biographical narrative interview".

Czech Republic, and the time after migration with her life in Germany. She continues to develop these divisions along national borders in the following section of the interview, in which she briefly illustrates her life in Jablunkov before she went to Germany. She concentrates on her educational experience, her failure to enter university and her job as a seamstress in a factory. Her university application could be interpreted as an effort to continue on the expected institutional route following the typical grammar school-Gymnasium-university route. However, she subsequently questions this expected institutional route and introduces her alternative biographical plan: starting work. The statement "But: (breathing in) it wasn't so easy with work there." makes it clear that her expectations concerning working were not fulfilled. She positions her difficulties of finding work in a specific place expressed by "there", which could mean the town, region or the Czech Republic in general. Working as a seamstress in a factory seemed the only alternative from her point of view. Paradoxically, Zuzana describes the moment in which she quits her job as a positive event in which her agency played a central role: "I stayed there three months and: on the last day of my trial period I managed it (shortly laughing) and I quit." With her brief description of her life until that moment she outlines the possible course her life could have taken if she had not quit her job and left to go to Germany. Migration to Germany seems to be the turning point in her biography. It not only represents a move across national borders for her, but above all opens up a new horizon of opportunities."

5.9.3   Analytical abstraction and the construction of types

Whilst considering the structural descriptions it became clear that some patterns were repeated throughout the relevant life story. For Martin, for example, it was the conviction that his biographical pathway happened by chance, which he depicted by means of detailed narration and argumentation. Lenka, on the other hand, used the expression "I took my chances" in a number of different contexts, which for her represented a strategy of finding alternative possibilities of development in limiting situations. The structural description also revealed the thematic line of the interview and enabled me to question why some events and experiences were blanked out or only partly thematised, and why others came to the foreground. These individual and structural features, which were "abstracted" from the detailed analysis, became part of the next analytical step, analytical abstraction.

Analytical abstraction is embedded in the biographical material, but also goes beyond it. The aim of this analytical step is to take a different look at the biographical material. It moves attention away from detailed analysis of separate sections to a more abstract level. It enables one to elaborate on case specific features as well as general features which apply to more than just the particular case (Riemann 2010, p. 229). Analytical abstraction provides the possibility of describing the overall structure of the life story, i.e. the sequence of dominant process structures as developed on the basis of a detailed analysis of particular sections, the interplay of biographical and social processes, as well as their biographical meanings, reflections and explanations (ibid.). Analytical abstraction is the basis for choosing other cases for detailed analysis, and for their analytical comparison.

The choice of individual cases for analysis is based on the principles of maximal and minimal contrastive comparison embedded in the research tradition of Grounded Theory (Glaser, Strauss 1967; Schütze 1983). The case that is chosen next for analysis should from a research interest point of view cover some dimensions which are in contrast with those cases that have already been analysed. Contrastive comparison of these cases provides an outline of an emerging theoretical model. This process should be repeated with other cases until the theoretical model is saturated (Glaser, Strauss 1967; Schütze 1983, p. 287; Riemann 2010, p. 329).

The three dimensions at the core of my analysis were as follows: migration processes, the development of transnational spaces, and finally shifts in social position and the significance hereof. As shown by the biographical interviews, these three dimensions were interconnected whilst at the same time influencing each other. I thus looked for interviews which would give indications as to the interplay between these dimensions, and which would reveal their different facets. I chose four cases which presented different types of migration, career pathways and social positioning within transnational spaces.

The first interview I chose to subject to a detailed analysis was the interview with *Lenka*, my very first interviewee. Lenka moved country frequently after she finished high school. By migrating, she created transnational spaces for herself which in turn signified an enlargement of her sphere of possibilities. After university graduation she went to Germany and for several years worked in low skilled jobs in Germany. Only afterwards did she manage to build up her career from the roots to become a teacher, the profession which she had initially studied in the Czech Republic. Despite all the interruptions and shifts, Lenka made an effort to maintain continuity in her biography and her career. She presented herself as someone who had crossed borders and who could translate between cultures and social contexts. Lenka narrated her story as a success story. Nevertheless, her narration revealed that her success was not recognised by her significant others back in the Czech Republic. This led me to the question of the transferability of career paths and social positions across national borders.

The next case I chose for detailed analysis was that of *Martin*. Like Lenka, he also narrated his life story as a success story. He too experienced social mobility in the course of migration, although its course and what it meant to Martin differed significantly from how Lenka had presented it. In contrast to her, for Martin migration was connected with upwards social mobility. He moved from a working class family to Prague where he studied and discovered new social spheres before subsequently moving within the same international finance company to a prestigious job position in Germany. Martin's story concentrated on describing his pathway through different social positioning and classes. He compared his biography and career to that of former colleagues in Prague, colleagues in Düsseldorf and his peers who had remained in his home town in the Czech Republic. He presented his biographical course and his class mobility as an exception and the result of luck. His narration could be interpreted as an effort to position himself in transnational spaces and classes in a new way.

The biography of *Barbora* became the third central case for my study. In contrast with Martin and Lenka, Barbora told her migration story not as a continuing event but as a "rupture" and new beginning. Her biographical and professional re-orientation played a central role in her narration. She moved to Germany after graduating in nature sciences. Since she could not find a job in her field, she enrolled to study social work after spending several years at home with her three children. Studying represented a new turn in her life, "emancipation" from her role as a mother and the opening up of new horizons and possibilities. In contrast with my two previous cases, Barbora did not manage to use her education and other resources, which she had acquired prior to migration, in the new context. Transnational links were not important to Barbora; instead, she made an effort to position herself in a new way and to construct her affiliation with Germany.

The last case which became central for my study was the case of *Arnošt*. The central theme of Arnošt's narration consisted in repeated moves with his family between the Czech Republic and Germany. Arnošt studied in the Czech Republic, obtained his PhD in Germany, and later on became a professor at the university there. He made an effort to create a dual transnational career in academia, which was unsuccessful, however, since the knowledge, skills and other resources he acquired in Germany were not recognised in the Czech Republic. Throughout his entire narration he searched for explanations as to why he lived in Germany, a country in which he had never actually wanted to live. His biography shows the difficulties that exist in "translating" knowledge and resources across borders, not only from the subject's country of origin to the country of migration but also vice versa. Furthermore, it illustrates the array of exclusion mechanisms to which migrants are exposed both in their country of origin and the countries to which they migrate.

The chosen biographies are not typical examples of migration and career paths in the statistical sense. Instead, they are cases which would easily be overlooked by statistical analysis, since they would most probably not fit in with dominant patterns according to statistical probability distribution. In actual fact, all of the stories I included in my analysis are in some regard exceptional. Lenka became a teacher with the status of a civil servant despite starting at the fringe, Martin moved from a working class milieu to a prestigious position in the finance sector, Barbora enrolled in new studies in a very different field after migration, and Arnošt became a professor in Germany and was paradoxically denied the appropriate positions in the Czech Republic because of his foreign higher qualifications. Nonetheless, despite their statistical unlikelihood, these cases are all evidence of social structure and processes in which biographies develop, as well as of the strategies used by migrants in order to position themselves and claim a sense of belonging in newly established transnational European spaces.

5.10   Reflections on the research process

5.10.1 Reflections on the research process in transnational settings

The transnational approach, which became dominant in migration studies from the late 1990s onwards, showed migration phenomena in a new light and questioned previous migration theories and methodologies. Andreas Wimmer and Nina Glick Schiller (2002) were among the first to point out methodological nationalism, i.e. the way in which nationalism formed the focus of researchers and framed their research interests. National states became, so they argued, naturalised and unquestioned units for designing research in social sciences. The focus of research was limited to migration to a priori given national units, thereby largely overlooking transnational processes which happened beyond the borders of national states. Taking the scope of national states for granted led, so the authors, to naturalising, or ignoring the power of nationalism in modern societies (Wimmer, Glick Schiller 2002, p. 301).

Wimmer and Glick Schiller initiated a fruitful discussion within the field of migration research concerning the design of studies and the methodological tools which would challenge the traps of methodological nationalism (see e.g. Amelina 2010; Amelina et al. 2012; Amelina, Faist 2012; Weiß, Nohl 2012a; Ruokonen-Engler, Siouti 2013). The authors criticised the way in which national settings and notions of ethnicity and nationality have been treated by a large part of migration studies. Considering national units as natural social contexts of migration have, so the authors, had a crucial impact on research design, the choice of methods and construction of the sample, disregarding social realities which do not suit their "container' thinking" (see e.g. Amelina, Faist 2012, p. 1710). The authors also criticised the central role of national and ethnic scope in conceptualising migration and creating the sample. They criticised the reduction of migrants to their ethnic or national origin, while paying little attention to other dimensions of positioning and belonging (see e.g. Weiß, Nohl 2012b, p. 65). This perspective often sees ethnicity and national belonging as given, instead of seeing it as a result of social and historical processes of nation building, positioning and belonging (see e.g. Rosenthal, Bogner 2009).

Migration researchers have developed diverse tools and perspectives in order to respond to ever complex migration processes and to challenge the traps of methodological nationalism (see e.g. the edited book Amelina et al. 2012). In order to challenge this methodological bias, some authors proposed widening the scope of research from national units to other contexts, such as transnational social spaces (Amelina, Faist 2012, p. 1711; Faist 2000). Other authors, such as Anja Weiß and Arnd-Michael Nohl (2012a; 2012b), proposed a different strategy – a multilevel comparative research design, which follows both the principles of country comparative and theoretical sampling strategies and analyses by means of further steps the role of diverse contexts, such as national states, transnational spaces and so forth, for studying phenomena. The other authors have underlined the importance of self-reflexivity throughout the research process as the methodical and methodological tool in order to overcome the bias of methodological nationalism (Shinozaki 2012; Ruokonen-Engler, Siouti 2013).

I argue that another way of challenging methodological nationalism is to include in the analysis the historical perspective which sheds light on the processes of nation building and construction of national and ethnic belonging over time. Looking at the changing meaning of borders and collective belonging questions the naturalised understanding of national units and belonging and enables one to see it as a process which is the result of both historical developments and constructions of society and the life stories of individuals. For this reason I have placed migration processes in this region of Europe into the historical context of mutual encounters, the changing significance of borders and border crossings and different migration modes over time. This approach made it possible for me to question the meaning of "national" while not ignoring its power in constructions of self and in shaping the possibility structures of individuals.

Furthermore, I challenged the notions of methodological nationalism by the choice of method. The biographical approach makes it possible to grasp complex transnational processes and to overcome some traps of methodological nationalism (see e.g. Apitzsch, Siouti 2007; Ruokonen-Engler, Siouti 2013; Siouti 2013). Biographical narrations create the opportunity of thematising such pathways, positioning and belonging which go beyond the expected and stereotypical biographical developments linked to a particular national state. Furthermore, biographical reconstruction enables one to ques-

168

tion the binary and static categories of "national", "ethnic" and so forth by putting forward different ways of positioning and constructions of belonging developed by biographers (see e.g. Tuider 2009).

The wide variety of studies showed that the biographical narrative interview as developed by Fritz Schütze can be used effectively in researching (trans-)migration processes (see e.g. Apitzsch 1990; Lutz 2008b; Breckner 2009; Karakayali 2010b; Ruokonen-Engler 2012; Kempf 2013; Siouti 2013). Its use in multilingual and transnational settings, however, produced a new set of issues, such as the use of language and translation in the interview and within the research process (see e.g. Tuider 2009; Lutz 2011a; Palenga-Möllenbeck 2009), the translatability of cultural meanings (Matthes 1999) as well as the impact of unequal power relations in the interview setting and during analysis. These new challenges can in my experience be solved to a large extent by means of careful analysis and (self-) reflection in respect of the interview situation and throughout the entire research process.

The process of (self-) reflection was facilitated by diverse methodical tools. Firstly, an important instrument for (self-) reflection was my book of ethnographic notes (see Riemann 2004). These notes, which I wrote immediately after the interview and throughout the research process, helped me to memorise the interview setting, how we interacted and how the interview went, as well as other important moments. Furthermore, it enabled me to remember some of my thoughts on the individual cases, on their possible comparison and on the construction of types later on. My ethnographic notes were the basis for my analysis of the interview situation, my own bias as well as the relationship to my interviewees. Notes which I wrote during the further research process often formed the basis for deeper investigation of various phenomena.

Secondly, the analytical steps which I followed and which were to a large extent based on the recommendations of Fritz Schütze and Gerhard Riemann (Schütze 1983; Riemann 2010) gave me the possibility of integrating my reflections on the interview setting, our interaction, our working relationship and the differing positioning between me and my interviewees into a clearer analytical frame. The analysis of interview sections thus did not happen in a de-contextualised space, but instead was always embedded in the overall storyline and in the context of its development (in the interview settings).

Finally, my participation in and discussions with interpretation groups (see e.g. Riemann 2004, 2011; Ruokonen-Engler, Siouti 2013) was another important setting for (self-) reflection. Discussions within these groups, which were to a large extent multilingual and cross-cultural, revealed different meanings for events and experiences and questioned the dominant position of one's own viewpoints. The process of revealing one's own "national" bias was often surprising and shocking, since it showed how strongly national structures and viewpoints influence the way in which we see and understand the world in which we live.

5.10.2   *The role of language and translation in the research process*

I contacted all interviewees in Czech, my native language and that of all of the interviewees'. This also influenced the language in which our further interaction took place. Even though I left it open in which language the interviews would be conducted, they were all held in Czech. Speaking the same native language helped in establishing a relationship of trust between me and my interviewees. I had the impression that most of the interviewees, who had all lived in Germany for some years, actually enjoyed speaking Czech. Nevertheless, some of the subjects experienced uncertainty concerning the translation of certain expressions from German to Czech when speaking to me, since German had for many of them become the everyday language, with Czech having moved to the background. Lenka verbalised these uncertainties in the following way:

L: Afterwards I got actually the possibility to apply for, to apply for the position, [I: Hmm] for a so called Planstelle, that means that I was before employed as: (1) /I will use the words in German [I: sure], because I don't know (she speaks quicker)./ I was employed as an Angestellte, yea. [I: Hmm] (-) And: because there was one free position, a so called Planstelle, I actually had the possibility to apply for the position, hmm, so I somehow- I also sent a CV to the Education Office. /I use the German words, that's terrible, because I speak German here all day long [I: It's ok (laughing)] (both laughing). That's terrible (laughing). (Lenka, p. 6, l. 180-187)

"Planstelle" and "Angestellte", or in some other interviews "WG", "freiwilliges soziales Jahr", "Studienkolleg" and so on are German expressions which cannot be translated directly into Czech, since the phenomena which they describe are not common practice in the Czech Republic and are therefore not reflected in the language. The interviewees were able to use these German words as shortcuts instead of longer descriptions of these phenomena since they assumed that I would understand the meanings of these expressions. The basis for our interaction was thus the assumption that we share cross border experiences, knowledge of the Czech and German cultural and social contexts as well as a knowledge of both languages. It was striking that interviewees used German expressions for describing life experiences which they perceived to be connected to their life in Germany and which they had not experienced in the Czech Republic. Zuzana, for example, who moved to Germany after high school graduation and subsequently studied in Germany, used German expressions in connection with her university studies. Barbora used German expressions in connection with her children, when speaking about diverse courses or the institutional career taken by her children. Lenka,

Ivan and Kamil, on the other hand, used German expressions to describe their work situation and its specificities. Use of language thus was not universal but contextualised by individuals' experiences. Zuzana expressed the difficulties in translating in the following way:

Z: And then I got an offer to do the translation. I was there only a few times, it was in Leverkusen in one agency, and it was such a bigger project. It should have taken three weeks, it took four weeks but it was day and night [I: Hmm] (shortly laughing). Seven days a week in order to finish it, because I needed to train myself a lot (deep breathing) because I did not do it, the translation, for some time. And it was (2) two thousand and six (1) I had been in Germany for ten years [I: Hmm] (1) and after these ten years things changed enormously. I had a feeling that I left the Czech Republic which was not so world open. It was, of course, officially, but (deep breathing) I am also from a small town, so not many things got there somehow. [I: Hmm] And then I got here and now these things which happened then in these ten years, especially the internet, [I: Hmm] thanks to the internet things changed enormously. People now have access to all information and: (-) I had to translate a page from an official Italian tourist office for Italy. [I: Hmm]. (-) And it was difficult because I did not know many things. [I: Hmm] There was so much about food and I did not know at all how the fish were called and how I could translate all the wines, if I should translate it at all. [I: Hmm] (Deep breathing) So I had to search a lot on the internet and it was demanding so I needed more time than the others, I was there really Saturdays, Sundays, I got up at seven o'clock which was very early for me (laughing), I returned home around ten. [I: Ahh] Yeah um. Well it finished but I was really happy there, because I really loved it, [I: Hmm] (1) and: (1) I wanted to do then (-) um (1) such work (1) translation to Czech does not exist here at all. There is no (1) how do you say (1) no demand for it. [I: Hmm] And it would probably be what I would like to do the most. [I: Hmm] To have contact with the language and to search for some expressions and to analyse that all for myself. (Zuzana, p. 10-11, l. 297-321)

The narration of Zuzana's story reveals how knowledge of a language is contextualised – in her case by national constraints, the town of her origin, class positioning, as well as by a time dimension and her biographical path. Furthermore, it underlines the importance of language and of the translation from one language into another after migration. Keeping in touch with the changing language was for Zuzana and other interviewees of biographical importance, expressed in her case by the wish to professionally translate and thus stay connected with the development of the language.

Language played a central role not only during the interview process but also in later phases of the research process. Transcriptions were written in Czech, as were most analyses. Nevertheless, since the analysis took place to a large extent within the working groups and colloquia at university, large parts of selected interviews were translated into German or English and discussed in these two languages. I tried to produce translations which would maintain the meanings given by the interviewees. Nevertheless, despite a careful translation some deeper interconnections and references to historical and cultural meanings of certain expressions were lost, since there were no linguistic equivalents. Interpretation within culturally diverse groups clarified the different meanings of expressions in respective cultural and lingual contexts. The process of translation was thus not a clear, direct transfer from one language into another but always an interpretation, in which some meanings were inevitably re- and decontextualized (Tuider 2009; Palenga-Möllenbeck 2009).

The next challenge was the translation of interview sections for the purposes of this paper. The translation into English required meanings and expressions to be reworked again and placed into a different lingual context. Again I tried to stay as close as possible to the meanings and expressions narrated in the Czech language. It was a process of imagining how something could be said by the biographer, whose language was shaped by age, gender and class positioning, in the narrated situation but in another language. In order to transfer the meanings in the process of translation, I had to look into my own unquestioned and self-evident understanding of the Czech language. In certain instances I looked up expressions in semantic dictionaries of the Czech, German and English languages and discussed some expressions with native and non-native speakers.

All of the interview sections presented in this paper have been translated from Czech into English. Words or sentences spoken in German or another language were kept in the original language and marked by footnotes. In the footnotes I also discuss the translation of certain expressions and offer a word for word translation or explanation of the meaning of the relevant passage if and when I had the impression that it could contribute to a better understanding of the text.

5.10.3 Being part of it: reflections on my own position within the field

Doing research on a topic which is closely connected to my own biography was both resourceful and constraining. Similarly to my interviewees, migration played an important role in my life as well. From the age of 18 onwards I started to discover the world beyond the borders of the Czech Republic. I temporarily lived, worked and studied in different European countries. My own migration experiences and encounters with other migrants during my various stays formed the background for my later scientific interest in migration and migration biographies. When I came to Germany and started my PhD project, I first had to learn the language and, just like my interviewees, establish new contacts and orientate myself within the social structure and new surroundings. During my research project I was able to make use of my own experiences and of my knowledge of language, as well as of historical, political, cultural and social settings in order to better understand the life situations and narrations of my interviewees. On the other hand, I also had to question my experiences and interpretations of migration in order to allow the articulation and the perception of other, in some cases very different, narratives.

Throughout the entire research process I moved between being close to and distant from my field of research.[37] When choosing the research topic and writing the research exposé, I was not aware of my own biographical dimensions which were unconsciously influencing the way in which I thought about the research subject. The necessity of reflecting on my own experiences and perspectives arose during the conversations with my interviewees in the interview sessions, during my analysis of the biographical narrative interviews and also when I was writing down the research results.[38] Every biography I "collected" and analysed, as well as every relevant study on the subject, entered into a dialogue with my own experiences, social positioning and perspectives and changed them in some ways.

The challenges posed by having an "insider" perspective became particularly apparent when analysing the interviews. The analysis of how we interacted during the interview revealed different ways in which the similarities and differences between my interviewees and me were construed. These processes became apparent on closer inspection of the structure of the interview and the way in which events were expressed. The mutual assumption of shared experiences, for example growing up with communism, experiencing the changes after the revolution, or having cross border experiences, had an impact on the manner of narration. Some interviewees limited their narration of certain topics to mere references and "shortcuts", since they assumed that a detailed description was not necessary in order for them to be understood. This was particularly true when they described their childhood during communism. In this context, the description of the social setting was often limited to short descriptions, such as "weekends at the cottage", "the impossibility of travelling abroad" or "empty shops", abstracted from everyday practice. Events which were assumed to be alien to me – introduced by expressions such as "you surely don't remember it" – were recounted in more detail.

Besides such constructions of differences on the basis of age, in some instances the interviewees also stressed differences concerning the region of origin. The interviewees often made a great effort to describe to me in detail the social, economic and cultural background of their place of origin. The comparisons and differences were addressed openly – as for instance in Martin's statement: "I doubt that you ever experienced in Prague that (...)" – and indirectly present in the narrations and evaluation passages, comparing the

37 As to the discussion of the relationship between the closeness and distance in qualitative research, see e.g. Riemann 2004, 2009; Lüders 2000; Wohlrab-Sahr, Monika, Przyborski, Aglaja 2008, pp. 58–62

38 As to the role of reflexivity in the research process in transnational settings, see e.g. Ruokonen-Engler, Siouti 2013 or Shinozaki 2012.

173

accessible possibilities of self-development in different regions of the Czech Republic. Furthermore, comparisons were also made in respect of gender and partnership status. Petr, for example, broached the issue of the difference between being a man or women from "Eastern Europe" with regard to options of starting a relationship in Germany. By doing so he indirectly compared my status – being in a partnership with a German man – and his of being unwillingly single, and explained it by means of gender and ethnic stereotypes in German society. Differences were often identified in respect of migration experiences as well. Lenka and Ivan, for example, depicted the difficulties in gaining a residence permit, working visa or insurance prior to the Czech Republic becoming a member of the European Union. They compared their past experiences to migrants arriving later on, and to some extent also to me. In addition, the length of stay in Germany was of importance when establishing the working relationship and negotiating power relations between my interviewees and me.

Reflecting on the working relationship and power relations in interview sessions and analysing the interviews showed that despite coming from the same country of origin and being an "insider", my biographical experiences, positioning, knowledge and resources differed somewhat from those of my interviewees. These differences were not self-evident, but became apparent in the course of analysis, whether at my desk or within the regular sessions of interpretative working groups of which I was part during the research process. They were crucial for me in order to differentiate my own ideas and rework some of my unquestioned assumptions and prior knowledge.

6 Biographies

Four contrastive cases became central in the course of the analysis: Lenka, Martin, Barbora and Arnošt. These cases shaped the way in which I thought about my project and about the crucial theoretical concepts. Lenka, Martin, Barbora and Arnošt came from different regions in the Czech Republic and had different social backgrounds. Their migration, biography and career also differed somewhat. Nevertheless, they all made an effort to construct transnational links and searched for ways in which to position themselves in both societies. They all dealt with the notions of recognition, national belonging and the possibility of returning or moving elsewhere, and established different strategies of dealing with them. In the following chapter I shall introduce the four biographies in detail in order to illustrate the possible facets of "new migration flows" on the East-West axis (Lutz, Koser 1998), along with possible careers and life histories and diverse responses to establishing transnational spaces and one's position within them.

To give an insight into the way in which the interviews developed, I shall first introduce the interview setting and the main features of the biographical presentation. I shall pay attention to the moment of establishing contact, and to how our meeting and the interview went. Embedding the interview into the relevant context is crucial, since the narratives were not produced in an isolated space where only the narrators' biography and recollections were involved. The narratives were also shaped by the manner of communication between the interviewee and the interviewer, their expectations and mutual interpretation of the situation (Rosenthal 2005, p. 45; Schütze 2012b, p. 42). The description of the situation, which is based to a large extent on my ethnographic notes which were written down after the interview, can shed light on the way in which the narratives were construed and influenced by the surroundings and our interaction before and during the interview. Subsequently, the main storyline shall be presented and discussed. I will outline the thematic and structural order of the narration and discuss the main themes and features of the main storyline. Next, I shall reflect on the working relationship, i.e. the interaction and interplay of mutual expectations in the interview situation between my interviewees and me. Only afterwards will I analyse and discuss the various life stories in detail. I shall introduce several interview excerpts in the individual chapters in order to let the interviewees themselves describe the events from their own perspective. The chapters, which consist of interview passages and their analysis, will follow the sequential order of the narrative. Each biographical presentation concludes with a summary in which the main features and findings are repeated and highlighted. In order to enable the reader to better understand the educational pathways of the interviewees, I briefly explain the Czech educational system in the first subchapter before turning my attention to the cases.

6.1 Background: the Czech educational system

In order to understand the educational and professional biographies of migrants, I will in this subchapter provide a short overview of the structure of the Czech educational system, which differs in some aspects from the educational structure of other countries.

The Czech educational structure can be divided into six levels which correspond to the International Standard Classification of Education (ISCED): the first and second stage of basic schools (ISCED 1, ISCED 2), the secondary education, conservatoires and post-secondary courses (ISCED 3, ISCED 4), higher educational institutions and tertiary professional schools (ISCED 5) and finally the doctoral studies programs (ISCED 6). The attendance of basic school is compulsory. Basic school has nine grades and it is usually attended by pupils aged six to fifteen. The first stage of basic school consists of five years of general education and the second stage of further four years. After successfully completing the first five (or seven) years of basic education, pupils have the possibility of switching to the eight-year (or six-year) secondary general school (gymnasium) or to a conservatoire. The enrolment procedure includes an entrance examination set by the respective school (The Ministry of Education 2011, p. 19).

After successfully finishing compulsory education, pupils have the possibility of continuing in higher education. Secondary education can be finished with a school leaving exam, an apprenticeship certificate or with vocational and practical education. About 74 per cent of secondary school leavers obtain the school leaving certificate at the end of their school studies (The Ministry of Education 2011, p. 24). The school leaving exams can be sat at secondary general schools (gymnasium), lyceums, and secondary technical schools or at conservatoires. These schools take four years and are usually attended by pupils between the ages of fifteen and nineteen. Vocational and practical schools usually take one to three years. Secondary schools are usually public and free of charge.

After secondary education, pupils who have attained the school leaving certificate can continue at university, tertiary professional school or a conservatoire. It is common practice for the majority of students who completed secondary general school (gymnasium) to continue to study at university or a tertiary professional school. University offers masters, and more recently

176

bachelor studying programs. Tertiary professional schools provide the necessary qualification for technical professions. The programs last from one to three and half years and graduates receive the title DiS. (specialist with a diploma). The enrolment procedure to most of the fields of study includes an entrance examination set by the respective departments. Each institution decides on the number of students to be enrolled and sets the admission criteria. The success of one's application often depends on one's success in the school leaving exams, on the number of applicants and limited vacancies, or the difficulty of the entrance examination. The pass rate for successful admission to university was 74 per cent in 2012 (ČSÚ 2014). Interestingly, the number of admitted students differed significantly according to gender. In 2012, 82 per cent of all male applicants were admitted, but only 61 per cent of female applicants (ibid.). The disparity between admitted men and women can be partly explained by different educational pathways and by different choices of field of studies by men and women. While the proportion of university educated women has been rising since the early nineties and in the meantime has become equal to the proportion of men, women dominate in fields such as education, arts, humanities, social sciences and health, and in the social sector (Vincent-Lancrin 2008, p. 275). Since the fields of tertiary education such as engineering and natural sciences, which are dominated by men, are accessible to a higher number of applicants, the chances of admission are higher. Tertiary education is mostly public and free of charge. Nevertheless, the number of private universities has been growing since 1999 (ČSÚ 2011a, p. 18).

The Czech educational structure is characterised by a very high proportion of people who have completed secondary education (Vavrečková 2005, p. 48). They make up approximately 80 per cent of citizens. The proportion of other educational groups is much lower in comparison with other European countries. People who have only finished their basic education (ISCED 1, ISCED 2) only make up about 8 per cent of inhabitants, whereas for example in Germany, Austria or Sweden it was about 17 per cent of inhabitants in 2004 (Vavrečková 2005, pp. 48–50). Similarly, there is a relatively low number of people who have completed some tertiary education in comparison with other European countries: while the proportion of tertiary educated people was about 25 per cent in Germany and 26 per cent in Sweden, it was only 13 per cent in the Czech Republic in 2004 (ibid.). Even though the number of tertiary graduates has risen since then and in 2009 reached 17 per cent, their proportion is still relatively low in comparison with other countries of the European Union (The Ministry of Education 2011, p. 28).

6.2 Lenka: the difficult route from private to public sphere

Lenka was the first person whom I interviewed for my project. This meeting as well as the interview significantly changed my thinking on the topic of highly skilled migration in Europe. Her story made clear that "highly skilled" are not only those who are presented as such by the media, such as economic elites, but also those who migrate through very different migration corridors. The themes revealed by the analysis of the interview with Lenka appeared again and again in further interviews with migrant women. Many of those I interviewed had experience of caring for children or the elderly abroad. So-called "care migration" was for many the gateway to further migration and status changes which often followed. In addition, the strategies for transcending status, for example by undertaking further studies in Germany or establishing new contacts in the new fields, seemed familiar to some of my interviewees. Lenka's story, which is in many ways very specific, is also representative of other stories I heard and analysed during my field work and which reveal similar migration processes, the coping strategies used by women to overcome the inequalities and structural barriers both in the country prior to migration and in Germany or elsewhere in order to alter their status and better their situation in society.

Lenka was born in 1978 in a village close to Brno, one of the biggest cities in the Czech Republic, and close to the border with Austria and Slovakia. She lived with her parents and brother in a house in the centre of the village. Lenka went to grammar school and high school (Gymnasium) in the area. Afterwards she spent one year in nearby Austria as an au pair. When she came back she started her studies in Ostrava, a city about 200 kilometres from her hometown. Following her second job as an au pair in Germany she obtained a job as an office assistant in Prague about 250 kilometres away. However, she left the job and went to Cologne in Germany, where she was living with her husband and small daughter at the time we met.

6.2.1 Interview setting and biographical presentation

The context of the interview

I came across Lenka during one of my periods of internet research. In November 2009 I was reading one of the platforms devoted to Czechs and Slovaks living abroad, in order to learn more about the Czech community in Germany. Lenka had posted a message in the discussion forum where people exchanged their experiences, searched for help, organised meetings and es-

178

tablished contacts. She was looking for other Czech or Slovak women with small children living in or nearby her city with whom she could meet up. I replied to her message, briefly introduced my research project, and asked her if she would be interested in meeting me. She answered by email the very same day and offered to discuss the particularities over the telephone. The next day I contacted her. At first I introduced myself and explained to her my interest in the life stories of people from the Czech Republic living in Germany. She sounded interested and replied by giving me a brief overview of her biography: she had been living in Germany for some time, had studied both in the Czech Republic and in Germany, had a small daughter and was currently working as a teacher. On the telephone Lenka spoke loudly and clearly, interjecting her speech with short, loud laughter from time to time, which made her seem particularly likeable to me. After she had spoken for a while she offered to meet me the following Thursday after work in a café in a shopping centre close to her residence, in order to conduct an interview.

The first interview

I arrived at the shopping centre a bit early and walked through the corridors to the elevators, where we had arranged to meet. Crowds of people were passing by in all directions and the air was filled with a mixture of sounds coming from diverse shops and corridors. Lenka was already waiting for me. We greeted and introduced ourselves and then walked together to the café. Although we had previously addressed each other formally over the telephone, we switched to a more informal address the moment we met.

It was a cosy Italian café equipped with small round tables made from dark wood placed along the walls of the small room. Several tables were situated by the window with a view of the busy corridor of the shopping mall. The walls of the café were decorated with pictures of coffee and Italian landscapes. We passed the counter and sat opposite one another at the very last table in the corner of the café. As we entered the café, the sounds and atmosphere changed. The noise from the mall only partly reached the café. The relatively calm atmosphere accentuated by music from the radio was from time to time enhanced by the grinding of coffee, voices from other tables and the clinking of spoons on cups. As we sat down at the table, Lenka mentioned that her mother-in-law was looking after her child and that she would come and join us in a while. By giving me this information she made it clear that our meeting and interview, as well the time we could spend alone, would be limited. We ordered coffee and while drinking it spoke about everyday issues, about the town and places both of us knew and liked to visit. We also spoke about work and the events of today. Lenka told me that she had had a hard day at school where she was working as a teacher. While narrating, she came to speak about the educational system in Germany. She argued that the German educational system was different from the Czech one and that it was difficult to explain it to someone who did not grow up in Germany. The pitch of her voice rose as she explained that her relatives and friends in the Czech Republic did not understand exactly what she was doing. A very similar line of argument appears in Lenka's actual interview. I will come to this aspect in more detail later on. After I told her about how I had arrived at my studies and my research project, we began with the interview. I explained the form of the interview to her. As my interests were in life stories, she was invited to narrate hers. Only after she had finished would I ask questions. I assured her of the anonymity of the whole interview and told her how it would be done. Lenka agreed and while I was searching for the recording equipment in my handbag, she started to think out loud as to where she should start: "Hm, so where should I start. I'll maybe start at the point at which I started to learn German. You don't want me to start at kindergarten, do you?" She asked, laughing. I answered that this also belonged to her life story and that I would let her decide. "No, so I will start with the German language, it is interesting." As I felt that Lenka and I were ready, I turned on the recording device and formulated the initial question:

I: So um. At first I'd like to ask you to tell me your life story. You have as much time as you wish.

L: Hmm but

I: The best, the best in details

L: The best in details, hm. But then grandma and my daughter will arrive. [Both of us are laughing]

I: I'll not interrupt you. I'll leave (-) the direction wholly up to you and I will only make notes on things that cross my mind during your narration.

L: OK. So I'll start – (Lenka I, p. 1, l. 7-16)

In this way, I explained the form of the interview to Lenka again and she ratified it by saying "OK.". However, even though I had assured her that she could take as much time as she wished, therefore trying to open up the span of time available for her narrative as much as possible, her comment concerning the arrival of her mother-in-law and her daughter, which followed my request to speak in detail, made clear her time limits for telling her story and for the interview. The time pressure may explain the way Lenka narrated her life story later on, listing most events in a brief and telegraphic way and only briefly hinting at more intimate topics. The setting presented by the café, to which the noise from the busy shopping centre resonated from a distance, seemed to contribute to the way Lenka narrated. Nevertheless, I had the impression that her choice of a café for our first interview not only reflected her busy life at that moment, but that it was also a means for her, as for other interviewees in my sample, of maintaining some kind of protective and neutral space, distant from everyday responsibilities, intimacies and decisions.

180

After this brief exchange about the form and settings of the interview, Lenka immediately started to narrate her life story. She spoke without interruption for about twenty minutes, fully concentrated on her narration. I listened to her, made a few notes and supported her by nodding and making eye contact. The fact that the recording equipment was on and that the emphasis of our conversation had moved to Lenka herself caused a change in the atmosphere. While our small talk was rather informal and relaxed, the moment the interview commenced we both became more focused and concentrated. Throughout the entire interview, Lenka continued narrating in a clear and loud voice. She sat straight opposite to me and after she finished her coffee, she continued to hold the cup in her hands and to slowly play with it. When she finished her narration, I started to ask the questions. The interview was interrupted only twice, the first time when her husband called and the second time when her mother-in-law and her daughter came into the café and joined us at the table. Shortly afterwards we left the café and made an appointment for the following week in order to continue with the interview. This time, Lenka invited me to her flat.

The second interview

Our next meeting had a very different atmosphere to the first one. At the arranged time and day Lenka awaited me in front of her house, holding her child in her arms. We greeted and embraced each other and Lenka invited me to go up. We entered a newly renovated, spacious three bed flat. Lenka gave me slippers and while we talked we continued into the bright living room where we sat at the dining table, which was separated from the rest of the room by a large bookshelf. Later I noticed that the modern room was decorated in some places with homemade lace embroidery with traditional Moravian motives and with painted honey cookies. Lenka meanwhile placed some cake on plates and put the kettle on, all the time carrying her child in her arms. We spoke about everyday things, about work, children, and studies. She mentioned, as she had already done during our last meeting, that they were baking honey cookies with her pupils. After all, Christmas was coming soon. She added that she baked at home a lot as well. However, today's cake was from the bakery, Lenka explained laughingly.

During our conversation Lenka came to speak of managing her household. She mentioned that there was a new cleaner at her flat for the first time that day. After her child was born, she could only manage to do the cleaning when her mother-in-law looked after her child. Interestingly, while beforehand the household chores had predominantly been carried out by Czech or Slovak women, Lenka laughed at the fact that now it was a German woman who was doing the cleaning at her flat. Lenka's laughing at this point may indicate that this constellation was unusual and even paradoxical to her. The normal situation, as had also been the case in her household previously, would be for Czech woman to clean the house of a German woman. With this remark, Lenka expresses the shifted power relations based on the intersections of class, gender and nationality in the course of her migration. The change in power relations only became possible because of her social mobility, moving from the position of a babysitter and cleaner to someone who could afford this kind of service herself. Social mobility was indeed the main theme of Lenka's narration, as I will show in more detail later on.

After Lenka put her child to the bed, we sat opposite one another at the dining table. We continued to drink coffee and eat cake, and when I placed my recording equipment on the table we followed up on the interview that had commenced last week at the café. The interview lasted about an hour and fifteen minutes. Just like our first meeting, the interview was very relaxed. It was interrupted only once when her husband came from work and joined us at the table. I asked Lenka the last question and turned off the recording equipment. Afterwards we stayed at the table for a while and spoke about the interview and everyday events. Lenka then saw me out, once again holding her child in her arms as it had woken up in the meantime.

The fact that the second interview took place at her home and we already knew each other from the previous meeting contributed to a friendly and intimate atmosphere. Contrary to the first interview, which was more superficial and only briefly touched on more private experiences and events, during the second interview Lenka spoke more openly about diverse topics, taking her time to narrate to me in detail some of her experiences and important events in her life. In some parts of the interview I felt a compulsion to bring some of my own experiences and memories into the conversation and to share them with Lenka. This I did several times. In other instances, Lenka openly asked to hear about my experiences, commented on them and compared them to her own experiences. My own biography thus became involved in the narration and biographical work of Lenka, and vice versa.

The main storyline and Lenka's presentation

Lenka begins her narration by considering what to narrate: "So I'll probably start with why I decided to learn German at all". In the following sentences Lenka goes on and explains in more depth the reasons for her decision to learn German: one of her uncles was a priest and another uncle ran away to Canada. Her family thus had problems with "the former government", as she reports. In order to understand the programs broadcast in nearby Austria, she therefore decided to start learning German.

The words "Yes and then: then" mark a new section in Lenka's narrative. Lenka briefly reports that she started to learn German at elementary school, continued at grammar school and then, when she failed to be admitted to university, she decided to go to Austria as an au pair. She briefly describes

182

her placement and evaluates it as a big life step. When she came back from Austria, she took up studies of Pedagogy with a focus on the German language.

Subsequently, Lenka interrupts her story of how she learnt German and goes back in time to begin telling a new aspect of her story: her first placements in Germany during her studies. She spent the summer holidays in Germany, where she worked at McDonalds. During these stays she met her boyfriend. Lenka argues that it was because of him that she decided to return to Germany after graduation in order to work as an au pair again. However, she split up with him and met someone else. As her visa expired, Lenka returned to the Czech Republic and started a job as an assistant in a company in Prague. However, she left the job after a few months and went to Cologne in Germany. She moved in with her new boyfriend and started to search for a job. She found a family where she worked as a child minder. After three years she left, while in the meantime she and her husband got married.

Lenka started to search for a job in the nursery schools, however without success. Only later did she get in to the school at which she had initially worked as a tutor and then as a teacher of German for foreigners. She describes in detail the moment of the job interview and the increase in hours and responsibility over the course of time.

At this point Lenka intersperses her narration with extensive background construction (Schütze 2012a, p. 27) concerning her studies in Germany, which were necessary in order to become a regular teacher. After explaining the reasons for her studies and the conditions thereof, Lenka mentions that she only finished her studies a year ago. She describes in detail the moment of her last examination. Further on she again picks up on the storyline concerning her professional career and explains her status as a "Beamtin auf Probe" and its position on the hierarchical ladder. Lenka then goes on to speak about her current situation: last year she was on maternity leave and afterwards she started to work again, although only on a part-time basis.

Lenka concludes her narration with a brief description of the school's Christmas market, for which she has cooked and decorated traditional honey cookies with her pupils. I begin to ask questions concerning the themes she mentioned in her narration.

Lenka narrates her story along the theme of her professional career. She begins her narration at the point at which she decided for the first time to study German, the language that is not only connected to her current residence in Germany but also to her professional career as a teacher of German at primary school. This initial decision, introduced in the first sentence of her narrative, is the moment which for Lenka stands out as being the beginning of her further development, spanning until the present day. The German language theme stays explicitly or implicitly present throughout her entire narration, either as the subject of her studies, as the means of communication during her placements abroad, as the skill required in her former office job or lastly as the language she is currently teaching. This thematic focus explains why Lenka does not introduce, or only marginally, her family members or other significant others in her narrative. The exceptions are her two uncles, whom she mentions in order to explain the problems suffered by her family in the past, her two boyfriends, who facilitated her link to Germany, and lastly her daughter, introduced towards the end of her story when Lenka speaks about the absence from work caused by her period of parental leave.

Lenka's story unfolds chronologically for the most part, with the exception of some passages in which she refers back to the past in order to add necessary information for the further development of her story, or to begin a new storyline. She lets her narrative end at the present time. The last section, in which Lenka describes the great moments baking Christmas cookies with her pupils, reflects her current situation and again highlights the success of her story, with these present events situated at the top of her career up until now.

Although Lenka develops her story as a success story in which her own activity and an action scheme dominates, the form of her presentation indicates that the course of her upwards social mobility was, especially from the moment she joined the school, not planned by Lenka and that she actually experienced it as rather surprising. The event of her joining the school, which marks the beginning of her upwards social mobility in Germany, initiated the process in which new possibilities were constantly popping up and opening up for her. The way she recounts the sequence of events within the school leading to her upwards social mobility thus reveals the process of a positive trajectory (Schütze 1983) spanning until the present day.

Interestingly, there are certain themes which are repeated throughout Lenka's story. These themes can be expressed by means of the following two phrases: "searching for alternative possibilities" and "taking a chance". They are already visible towards the beginning of Lenka's story, when she explains her motivation to learn German as a reaction to the oppression of her family during communism. Learning German and orientating herself on the other side of the border became a strategy for Lenka of overcoming the barriers she and her family had experienced. Searching for an alternative pathway in the context of limited possibilities, a theme which has its roots back in the time of her adolescence during the communist regime, is repeated in various different contexts throughout her story, be it after she failed to get a place at university and decided to continue learning German as au pair in Austria, taking the child care job in Cologne later on since other job options were inaccessible to her due to her illegal status, or picturing in detail the moment of her last examination in front of the commission in which she had prepared a "plan B" just in case. Throughout all of the structural limitations, so the message of Lenka's story, she remained an active player who managed to reach her goal and progress to her current position. The strategy of coping in spite of the barriers seems to be embedded in Lenka's family history, as I will explain later on.

Lenka's story mostly takes place outside the Czech Republic. The exceptions are Lenka's educational career, which is mentioned briefly, and later on the short explanatory remark concerning her job in Prague. The theme of crossing the border is already present – though initially only symbolically – in the first section where she explains why she started to learn German. Later, she regularly crosses the borders between Austria, Germany and the Czech Republic. Her story is thus an ongoing migration story, where the move between geographical locations also represents a move between social positions, as will be shown later on. Lenka challenges the expected institutional progression of her educational and professional career, which is connected with national settings, and makes a case for her alternative pathways which span across the border. The first time she challenges the expected institutional progression – spanning from Gymnasium to entering university – is when she moves to Austria as an au pair after she failed to gain a place at university. However, her inner dispute concerning the expected biographical course reappear later on when she decides to go to Germany to work as an au pair again after finishing her studies in the Czech Republic. In her extensive argumentation, in which she challenges the expectations concerning the institutional passage from university to a respective job in the Czech Republic, she justifies not only why she took a job which did not correspond to her qualifications, but also why she decided to take an alternative biographical path across transnational spaces. For Lenka, migration, which in this context primarily represents the enlargement of her sphere of possibilities, is the theme par excellence.

Notes on the working relationship with Lenka

The way Lenka narrates her past experiences reveals an ambiguous working relationship between us. On the one hand I represent someone with whom Lenka shares common knowledge about the past and similar migration experiences. We were both born in the Czech Republic, spent our childhood there and experienced the transformation of society. Moreover, we both migrated to Germany. The assumption of these shared experiences made it possible for Lenka and me to express ourselves in keywords and shortcuts which we both assumed to be meaningfully understood by the other. This assumption of shared knowledge between Lenka and me became more apparent during Lenka's narrative. While speaking of the sequence of events and experiences in the context of the Czech Republic, she only briefly outlined the social settings without going into detail, assuming that I would understand their specific meaning. On the other hand, although she took for granted the assumption that we had shared knowledge concerning our adolescence, Lenka made a great effort to explain to me in more detail her current life in Germany, which is of key relevance to her and her narrative. The reason for this detailed narrative and explanation of local settings may be the difference in length of our stay in Germany. In comparison with Lenka, who had lived in Germany for more than fifteen years at the time of the interview, I might be seen as a "novice" here, since at the time of the interview I had only been residing in Germany for about two years and I might therefore not know the local systems and need to be initiated into German structures. In this context, Lenka considered herself to be an expert on local settings, being able to translate her social position into different social and cultural settings, which remain of importance for her.

Throughout the entire conversation we continued to speak Czech, as this was the language in which Lenka had posted an advertisement and I had contacted her for the first time. The Czech language, which for both of us was our mother tongue, created a common ground for us. The fact that we were most probably the only two people speaking Czech in the café even reinforced the link between us. Czech remained the main language throughout the interview and afterwards, until the moment at which Lenka's mother-in-law came to join us at the café. The only exceptions were certain German expressions used by Lenka in some parts of interview, following which there often followed a discussion about her inability to speak Czech and to find the right equivalents in the Czech language. To find the Czech equivalents for German words seemed important to Lenka. However, in the course of her narration she gave up trying to find the right translations and continued to use the German instead with the comment that she did not know how to translate them. The inability of doing "translation work" seems to correspond to the missing recognition of her social mobility and her current social position as a teacher and public officer by her significant others back in the Czech Republic, as I will show later. In this context, I figure as someone who, similarly to Lenka, moves between the two national contexts and can understand these expressions and their meanings even when said in German.

The working relationship between us thus "balances" between closeness and distance, finding its expression through the use of language. Because of the similar biographical experiences, I might be seen not only as a researcher but also as someone who can understand, translate and moderate between the two social and cultural settings in which the biography of Lenka takes place.

6.2.2 Lenka's migration and social pathways

Embedding migration in her family history

L: So I'll probably start with why I decided to learn German at all (deep breath). Well it was so, because our family: had: previously, hmmm, problems during communism: with the former government, so it happened, that actually daddy, one of daddy's uncles (-) had run away to Canada, the second uncle was a priest, so our family was somehow totally written off right from the beginning [I: Um] (breath) So I (-) had decided at that time, already as a child, because we lived close to the Austrian borders and we got Austrian TV programs and I wanted to understand, so in fifth grade I started to learn German. (Lenka I, p. 1, l. 18-24)

In this opening section of her narrative, Lenka presents her decision to learn German as the beginning of her onward biographical path, the impact of which she is still feeling at present. She introduces herself in the first person in line with the "action schema" – as someone who takes decisions and makes plans about their future steps. However, when she places her decision to learn German at the time of the communist regime in which her family was disadvantaged, she switches the event carrier from the first person to her family as a whole. Lenka is introduced here not as an actor who makes active decisions about her life, but rather as part of a closely knit family – expressed by the words "our family" – which together deals with all of barriers and obstacles put in place by the former regime. This shift in event carrier indicates that the roots of Lenka's motivation to learn German and to later migrate are to be found in her family history and family dynamics, to which she feels intimately connected.

Lenka mentions her two uncles, one of which was a priest and the other who left for Canada, as the triggers of not further specified problems with the government. Interestingly, they are the first people she introduces in her narrative. The figures of her two uncles, who are not further described, embody the structural enemies of the past political system: religion and emigration. The fact that she does not further specify the roles of her two uncles in the positioning of her family during the communist regime may be due to her assumption that I, as a listener to her story who grew up in a similar political context, know the deeper meaning of these issues without her having to mention them. Through the figures of her two uncles Lenka not only outlines the obstacles her family experienced in the past, but also alludes to the religious and migration history of her family, which finds its expression in further sequences of her narration. Interestingly, some expressions like "previous times" and "former government" which refer to the past communist regime of former Czechoslovakia imply that Lenka perceives the historical events as being divided along the lines of "before" and "now", whereby the dividing point is represented by the revolution in 1989.

Possibly as a reaction to her family's position on the periphery and the disadvantages and limited chances of development in former Czechoslovakia resulting from this, Lenka found an alternative way of self-development: language. Lenka lived with her family close to the Austrian border, which was at that time highly protected and for many impossible or dangerous to cross. Nevertheless, although she herself could not go over the border – as demonstrated in more detail in the following section – , she was able to listen to the Austrian programs, which her family received and which she wanted to understand. Through learning German Lenka could symbolically cross the border to the "forbidden world", which was so close but still inaccessible. The only way to this world was through language and the media. Lenka thus developed a strategy to overcome the barriers which she and her family experienced during the communist regime by orientating herself on the other side of the border and establishing alternative ways of self-development. This strategy would not have been possible, however, if she had not had family resources on which she could build, such as contacts abroad or the possibility and willingness of Lenka's parents to watch Austrian programs. The ability to move in a space with limited possibilities and to search for alternative ways for development, which Lenka avails herself of more than once and which finds its expression in different contexts throughout her narration, seems to have its roots at this time of her adolescence.

Lenka speaks about the situation of her family during the communist regime again later on, as the answer to my asking her to tell me a bit more about her family. Lenka immediately mentions her family's problems and gives two examples – one related to the theme of religion and the second to the theme of migration – to illustrate the structural barriers her family experienced in the past. After she explains the limited educational options resulting from the religious attitude of her family, she turns her attention to unsuccessful migration efforts of her parents.

L: Because I know that my parents never got -, because erm well on my father's side, my aunt on my mother's side was in Austria and my parents always tried to get a visa to Austria. It was not possible at all. They applied applied applied but (1) never got it. Even when they wrote that their children would stay in the Czech Republic. (1) Yes and when I started to travel to Germany later on, of course my parents were on the one hand sad about that, but well, I had a brother too. [I: Hmm] And my brother stayed home and [I: Hmm] even started to repair my grandma's house which is next door, so my brother (1) seemed to stay at home for ever and / I was the black sheep of the family who left its flock and set off on a long journey (theatrically)/ (laughing) [I: (laughing)]. No, I was always more oriented to the world, so – (more seriously) [I: Hmm] (3) (Lenka I, p. 9; l. 263-273)

Lenka's mother's sister who emigrated from the former Czechoslovakia to Austria and continued living there features in Lenka's story for the first time here. Lenka's parents, who are the event carriers in this passage, made an effort to keep contact and tried to visit her. However, the repetitive process of their visa application – expressed also by the multiple repetition of the word "applied" – failed again and again. Lenka compares the impossibility of her parents to cross the border to nearby Austria to unite with family members with her own migration experiences, as indicated by the shift in her narrative from her parents as event carriers to herself. However, the parents remain present in her argumentation as critics and observers of her cross-border mobility, which became possible some years later after the change in the political system made the borders passable and accessible.

Furthermore, Lenka contrasts her migration experiences not only in a cross-generational manner, but also draws comparisons with her brother who belongs to the same generation. Contrary to Lenka, her brother stayed firmly connected to the place where she was born and where her family lives. To reinforce the argument concerning his local ties, Lenka states that he even rebuilds the house after their grandmother dies. In contrast to her, he continues the expected and intended pathway of her family and remains bound to their place of origin. Interestingly, the fact that she has a brother who stayed at home justifies – from the perspective of Lenka and her parents – her mobility and makes her migration possible. In comparison with other family members, Lenka stands out as "the black sheep" that has chosen an alternative life, one that is not firmly connected to the place of origin but which spans trans-locally.

Lenka explains and evaluates her out of the ordinary, alternative pathway in comparison with other family members as being "always oriented to the world". She internalises this attitude as always having been part of her life. However, following the sequential structure of Lenka's argumentation, it is striking that the roots of her orientation are firmly tied up in the family history of migration and obstacles experienced by her family during the time of the communist regime. Lenka's migration and orientation abroad might also be seen as the continuation of her parents' dream of crossing the border, linking up – at least symbolically – with the transnational ties which her family kept alive throughout the period of the iron curtain, taking the chances which were impossible for the earlier generation.

The opening of the borders in 1989 as a turning point

L: Now and recently I have been wondering, actually next week, the 17th of November will be twenty years since the revolution. It was erm on Monday it was twenty years since the fall of the Berlin wall, so we were watching it on TV and I was wondering, if there will be some celebrations in Prague too. I asked my brother and my brother said: "I don't know at all". (2) [I: Hmm] It would be nice if they would do something. (1) I don't know, did you watch it on Monday?

I: No, no I didn't (1)

L: It was really very nicely done. Actually many – many high schools participated. Students from high school got a block, twenty kilos, which was sort of part of the wall. They had to paint it and then these blocks were arranged behind each other and then (1) they pushed over the first block and it was – it was like dominoes falling over. It was really, the music was playing, it was beautiful, really. As if the Berlin wall were falling again after twenty years (breathing in). It was really nice. Hmm. So I think that they should do something in Prague too. (Lenka II, p. 12-13, l. 344-356)

Lenka turns to speak in more detail about the events of the revolution and the changes connected to it in our second interview, which took place in early November 2009. At that time, the celebrations and political debates concerning the twentieth anniversary of the revolution in 1989 were in full swing both in Germany and in the Czech Republic. Lenka spoke about the events of the revolution after our discussion concerning her political rights in Germany, thereby commencing the lengthy passage about the events of the revolution and the changes which followed. In the previous section is remarkable that Lenka describes the moments of the fall of the Berlin wall as a very emotional and symbolic moment. She compares the celebrations taking place in Berlin and potentially in Prague, both capital cities and centres of the revolution twenty years ago. Interestingly, Lenka mentions her brother when questioning if similar celebrations will also take place in Prague. He seems to be the one who communicates to her the events happening over the border so that she is able to stay up to date about information she would not otherwise have access to. While talking of the celebrations, she points out that the participants and "actors" involved in the fall of the Berlin wall were above all the high schools and their students. Her focus on the schools and students may be linked to her current profession as a teacher, as well as to the time of her adolescence, since she was probably of a similar age at the time of the actual fall of the Berlin wall as the students acting out the events on TV twenty years later. The image of the wall falling like dominoes symbolises the barriers which were torn down and which made it possible for the two parts that until then had been divided – East and West – to come together. The falling wall, built symbolically from heavy blocks to underline its solidity and inaccessibility, may for Lenka also symbolise the tearing down of impassable borders which had a considerable influence on Lenka's life as an adolescent.

In the following sequences, Lenka shifts from talking about the twentieth anniversary of the fall of the Berlin wall to the actual time of the revolution. After she describes in detail the changes at her primary school concerning the learning materials and the sudden emptiness of lessons – which was due to the fact that the teachers felt disoriented after the political shift and did not know what to teach – she moves on to speak about her motivation to learn the German language and her unfulfilled wish to migrate in the past.

L: I was I was learning German because I wanted to understand when we received um: the Austrian programs so I wanted to understand what Tom and Jerry were saying and so on. I also always wanted to go somewhere abroad, yes, because I never understood why we could not leave the country! [I: Hmm] But how do you want to explain it to a child, who simply, would not understand anyway. (Lenka II, p. 12, l. 361-375)

Her motivation to learn German is connected not only to her wish to understand the media penetrating from nearby Austria, but also to her wish to migrate. In her argumentation Lenka connects her wish to migrate with the impossibility of her family to cross the border. Lenka thus explains her wish to migrate as the continuation of a family project which began in the past, which she internalises as an inevitable part of her biography and which she later on accomplishes. The meaning of crossing borders is portrayed in the following section, describing the first holiday she took with her family after the fall of the iron curtain.

L: Well, we watched TV, I know that everyone was wearing the tricolour, on their lapel (1) and otherwise (1) my parents were not in Prague for the revolution. We watched everything on TV. [I: Hmm] Hmm. But it was nice because actually our first holiday was after the fall of communism, I don't know in which year it was or, I don't know exactly. However we went to South Bohemia and we went every day, we went every day for a trip to Germany. And it was simply, wow. Yes, simply across the border and now these shops and cars. The shops were full of fruit and meat, yes. All kinds of meat, everything beautifully illuminated. Not like when you came to us, to the butcher and he had two sausages hanging there and that was all (laughing). [I: (laughing)] Fruit and vegetable, apples and potatoes were always rotten and that was all that was there (laughing). [I: (laughing)] Surely you do not remember it. (Lenka II, p. 13, l. 378-389)

Just like twenty years later, Lenka watched the events of the revolution with her family on TV. While later on the centre of the celebrations being observed was Berlin, at the time of the revolution Prague played the most important role for her since it was the political centre of the country. However, the most significant change for Lenka after the revolution was the opening of the borders to nearby Austria and Germany. Lenka goes back in time and describes the exciting moments she experienced with her family during their holiday on day trips to Germany after the revolution. She depicts the easy and often repeated border crossings, which are in stark contrast with the time before the revolution. Lenka draws a comparison between the situation in former Czechoslovakia and in Germany. Interestingly, she limits her description to the most visible features concerning consumption and life style. This short sequence shows how Lenka perceived the unequal structural differences of both countries. In contrast with the former Czechoslovakia, Germany is pictured in her presentation as a rich country with "these shops and cars" offering good quality goods and a variety of choices. In the comparison with Germany, the life situation in former Czechoslovakia is portrayed as remarkably poor. These first border crossings were exciting moments for Lenka, as can be gleaned from her presentation. On the one hand, the new and until then unknown world became accessible. On the other hand, the crossing of borders facilitated a shift in perspective regarding her own until then unquestioned everyday reality in her hometown.

Lenka also speaks about her first border crossings later on. This time, she did not travel with her family but with her school.

L: So, somehow, so much changed! Because afterwards we actually had the possibility at high school (breathing in) um, to go to Austria, we had a partner school in Austria, [I: hmm] so of course it was for one week or so, when you go to Austria as (breathing in) as a student, so it was – You live in a family, so it is also great. Yes and I saw how totally backwards we are. As we were still living in the Stone Age. When you went there, only the clothing, really! We went there in our nylon suits, yes, and those trousers, and jeans, absolutely horrible, really. (laughing) [I: (laughing)]. They had their (breathing in) jeans jackets and beautiful bags, I was totally ashamed, really. (Laughing) [I: (laughing)] From the Eastern Bloc. Really. (Lenka II, p. 15, l. 463-471)

As the previous lines reveal, her stay placement in Austria made it possible for Lenka to discover not only the world behind the border, but also to reflect on the society she had left behind. Lenka uses the expression "yes and I saw how totally backwards we are" to describe the moment of realisation of the differences between the Czech post-communist society, to which she feels a sense of belonging, and Austrian society. In her comparisons she uses the constructs of East and West, where the latter represents the dominant stream which provides the criteria of being developed or not – or in Lenka's words living in the modern world or in the Stone Age. The distinctions she draws between herself and her school mates on the one hand and "them" on the other hand are hierarchical in nature. She considers herself to belong to the group which is "backwards" and undeveloped, in comparison with the "modern" and "Western" Austrian society. Moreover, she feels ashamed of being part of this group. Interestingly, as indicated by the expression "Eastern Bloc", which has a slightly derogatory meaning, she takes the side of the dominant "Western" society. These trips, looked at from Lenka's perspective these days, made it possible for her not only to discover the society across the border step by step, but also to develop a critical perspective on the social relations and situation back in the Czech Republic, both of which may have been the catalyst for her later decisions to migrate.

Nevertheless, the events of the revolution did not only bring with it the possibility of crossing the border to nearby Austria or Germany, but also opened up new possibilities for her relatives who had left the country in the past to come back to the Czech Republic after many years of emigration.

L: About two years, two years afterwards my cousins, my father's cousins from Canada began to come. [I: hmm] Well the uncle who at that time had run away through Austria to Canada had also met (breathing in) a woman, she was Czech. It was, it was also by chance. My father told me how it was. He went to church somewhere and so he stood there. Yeah. You do not know the language and you are staying somewhere, you are alone, in the foreign country, yeah. So probably, probably he was depressed so he went to church. Because he was brought up religiously, so he went to church and now, now he is standing there and now (1) the church is full and now he was standing behind a woman and now he realised that she had Czech Czech books in her hands. You know, these (1) religious books. So he had a closer look to check he had seen correctly and he addressed her and (1) then they married, yes. (laughing) [I: hmm, wow] Yes, the Czech woman, they met in Canada and had (breathing in) how many. Six children, two boys (breathing out) four girls and (1) [I: hmm] We are in contact with them. Or either my father, father is in contact with them and [I: hmm] (breathing in) it has so to say already got that far that the children of these cousins, one is teaching English in Prague, (1) [I: hmm] a Canadian woman teaching English in Prague and now my father has helped them with getting Czech nationality [I: hmm] (1) (Lenka II, p. 15, l. 449-463)

Interestingly, the figure of her uncle, whom Lenka briefly mentions in the opening sequence of her narrative, again appears in her narration when she speaks about the changes after the fall of communism. Lenka outlines his migration route which leads to Canada through the border with Austria – a border which is meaningful to Lenka – and adds a scenic narration of the moment at which he meets his future wife. As Lenka explains, this narrative is part of her family's story which has been preserved despite the uncle's long time absence. His migration experiences may play an important role in formulating Lenka's wish of migrating in her adolescence. His pathway may serve as a role model for her further biographical decisions and choices, enabled by the events of the revolution in 1989. The fact that he did not know the language and as a result suffered from depression is mirrored in Lenka's narration of her own migration experiences, as I will show later. This episode illustrates the transnational experiences of her family and the way their ties – which were reinforced after the fall of the iron curtain – were influenced by the political systems. The newly established migration politics enabled his family to rekindle family ties and transnational networks, which have continued throughout the generations, as demonstrated by the example of the Canadian cousin who is now living and working in Prague.

To summarise, the fall of the Berlin wall signifies a turning point in Lenka's biography, making it possible for her to cross the border into nearby Austria and Germany. Although she describes her first visits to Austria and Germany as a time of discovery and full of surprises and excitement, she was actually already acquainted with these countries from watching German TV with her family and from the family stories about their relatives. The closeness of the border, together with the transnational links of her family, represent a resource for her further migration experiences, enabling her to reflect on both societies from different perspectives and make use of them. The fall of the Berlin wall, to which she refers to so emotionally in her narration, is therefore important in her life as it made it possible for her to develop her transnational life path, in which the crossing of borders has become an inevitable part of her biography.

"They threw me into the deep end and I had to learn how to swim": first migration experiences

Lenka did not fully realise until some years later that her au pair placement in Austria was the "initiator" of her migration project. After finishing high school but failing to pass the entrance examinations to university as planned, the au pair placement appeared to her to be a good possibility of continuing to learn German and gaining new experiences before reapplying to university the following year. Lenka retrospectively describes her stay in Austria, which she actually shortened from one year to eight month due to disagreements with her host family, as one of her big steps in life. She depicts not only her experiences as an au pair, but also her studies of German at the university in Salzburg in Austria. This period of time was particularly important for Lenka, as she "individualised" herself from her parents' house for the first time and developed phantasies about possible further migrations, which led her to develop a possible alternative life path.

Lenka comes back to speak about her first au pair placement in more detail during the questions part of our first interview. After I asked her to tell me a bit more about her au pair stay in Salzburg, Lenka started to explain:

L: So it was actually through a teacher at high school, her daughter worked in a family in Salzburg, it was also after she did her final examinations, so to improve her German she went to Salzburg. So I decided that this would be the best possibility of learning German now. [I: Hmm] Because it is nice to learn German somewhere in the Czech Republic at school, but when you are in the country where this language is spoken, you are forced to, even more so when you are in a family that only only speaks German and they cannot tell you anything in Czech, so you are really forced to learn the language. So it was really, it was the school of life. [I: Hmm] They threw me in the deep end and I had to learn how to swim. Hmm. (2) It was actually (1) at the beginning they told me that I would be an au pair, but an au pair, it was it was the term (1) it was more like a cleaner and general dog's body. So it was like that. Although they also had a woman who came to them to clean, but (1) because I didn't know so much German at that time I couldn't verbally defend myself. (Lenka I, p. 10, l. 289-301)

As this section indicates, au pair placements were a common phenomenon in her social circle and an easily accessible practice due to her social links. When she failed to get a place at university, she decided to profit from already established migration linkages to Austria. The arrangement and organisation of her au pair stay was informal; information about the family and cross border practices was passed to her not through any institutionalised agency, but through the network of acquaintances and friends. This informal practice of organising an au pair placement corresponds to the atmosphere in the Czech Republic in the nineties. At that time, au pair placements were an already established practice of informal cross border mobility. However, the agencies which would organise the exchange and help to negotiate the conditions of au pairs were not established yet. The women had to do all the organisation and negotiation on their own, risking not only an illegal stay and work placement in the country of destination, but also mistreatment by the family they were working for. As Lenka reflects in another part of the interview, "no one knew or wanted to know about that". The illegal status also had disadvantages in instances in which the family did not keep to the au pair conditions that had been arranged earlier. In many cases, the au pairs lacked a contact whom they could approach to help them to deal with the situation.[39] This was how it was with Lenka. She was confronted with other jobs which did not conform to her perception of the content of the au pair job. However, she argues that she could not defend herself and negotiate the conditions on her own because of her language deficits. The words "they threw me into the deep end and I had to learn how to swim" expresses the learning process commenced at the time of her au pair placement, when she was alone not only within the other family but also in the different cultural and lingual context, so that she had to learn to deal with the situation on her own. Nevertheless, the feeling of vulnerability caused by the lack of language skills remained present and also finds its expression in the following scene which took place before Christmas.

L: The worst, the worst I can remember, my brother came. Because I had bought many presents for Christmas he came and wanted to help me with it and the bus, I was waiting for him and the bus came late and we came home late and it was somehow around the lunch and I had to always prepare something for lunch. [I: Hmm] Something easy but still. So we arrived and now lunch was not ready. [I: Hmm] The lady came and she started to be really angry, she started to yell at me, my brother told me, "so say something to her!" "Yeah but I don't know how to say it in German." It was the worst. Sure I went to the courses, but to say something spontaneously, [I: Hmm] it was. (1) So I started to cry and my brother told me, "oh mate why are you here." And I said "I would like to finish the German course and then then I will leave. And so I did. (Lenka I, p. 10, l. 311-320)

This section reveals the uneven power relations of Lenka and the family she was working for. Unlike the lady, Lenka was not able when in confrontation with her to mobilise the language skills which she had acquired to respond to critics, to clarify the situation and defend herself. Obviously, the position of an au pair to which she had applied and which she hoped would improve her language skills turned out to be a position of cheap labour. Lenka indirectly explains her inferior position by the fact that she did not speak German as well so as to be able to negotiate adequate conditions for herself. This section explains why language is so important for Lenka throughout her entire story. It is the instrument to defend herself, to negotiate better conditions for herself

---

39 The discrepancies between the expectations of migrant women before their arrival and the real practices of care jobs in the families is described for example by Sabine Hess in her book "Globalisierte Hausarbeit" (Hess 2009).

and to position herself in society. A lack of language skills, on the other hand, may lead to her taking on a vulnerable position, like the one she experienced during her au pair placement. In this scene, her brother takes on the role of an observer and judge of the situation who is from the outside and offers Lenka a different perspective on her position within the family. Her brother, who knew Lenka in a different context, seems to be surprised to see her in such a vulnerable position and questions her placement there, which in turn mobilises Lenka to take the decision to leave the family earlier as previously planned.

However, although Lenka did not have a good experience in her position as au pair, she was excited about Salzburg and the university, where she attended courses in German as a foreign language. Because of these experiences happening outside of the house where her au pair job was, Lenka began to develop fantasies about possibly studying at the university in Salzburg in the future. However, although her fantasies were never realised, the placement in Salzburg initiated the process of redefining her future biographical path and opened up for her new spaces of future potential development, so closely connected to migration. At the same time, the possibility of biographically keeping the connection between Salzburg and Brno, the city close to her area of origin, became important for Lenka as expressed in the section below, stressing the closeness and "connectedness" between these two areas.

Lenka's experiences in Salzburg changed her perception of her biographical path and opened up new fields of possibility for her which were not necessarily limited to one national state but which developed across its borders. Within this transnational space, which she established through her experiences, she created her new potential ways in which her biography could develop in the future. In this way, her stay in Salzburg initiated the process of metamorphosis (Schütze 2012a), not just as new life options but also by defining her relations with others in a new way. She puts her experiences in the following way:

L: But Salzburg is really, concerning the town, sights, university, it is a really beautiful city. Yes and here I had, actually one of the ideas was to go to study in Salzburg, because it was not so far from home, I live close to Brno [I: Hmm], or close, forty kilometres from Brno [I: Hmm] and the busses were going regularly every day, Brno Salzburg, so it was this idea that I would go to study in Salzburg. [I: Hmm] But then things developed the way they developed and I ended up in Cologne. [I: Hmm] Hmm. (2) (Lenka I, p. 11, l. 329-335)

Moving there and back within transnational spaces

After Lenka returned from Austria to the Czech Republic, she took up studying Pedagogy with a specialisation in the German language at the university in Ostrava, a town about hundred kilometres from the place of her origin. While describing her studies very briefly, concentrating predominantly on the

196

description of her town and the familiar atmosphere among students, Lenka depicts in her narration the seasonal migration to Germany during her studies.

Unlike her first au pair placement in Salzburg, Lenka did not migrate in an informal way, but made use of an agency. During the second half of the nineties, the first agencies arranging work placements abroad appeared on the Czech market. Student Agency, for example, one of the biggest Czech agencies promoting and organising student and au pair work placements abroad, was established in 1996.[40] Especially towards the end of the nineties and later, new agencies were popping up and quickly filled the hole in the expanding market. Lenka thus belonged to the pioneers of the cross border movement, organised by agencies, of seasonal workers passing between the Czech Republic and other European countries after 1989.

Lenka found out about the possibility to go to Southern Germany to work in McDonalds during her summer semester holiday through another student who told her about the job and described the procedure of where and how to apply. She sent the application to Prague where the central office of the agency was situated. About two months later, two weeks before the work placement was due to start, she received a positive reply and had to quickly make the decision and pack her suitcase. When she arrived at the train station in Weißarber, a town in the South of Germany, the owner of the McDonalds came to pick her and other co-workers up and took them to their lodging houses.

L: We had a lot of luck, because we were actually the first year, first year there, he had never had any students from the Czech Republic, so he took care of us. It was great. [I: (laughing)] We lived there really, really like bees in clover. Yes and the hard work, when one studies and does not work besides, so one has to get used to it. Mainly the morning shifts, we had to start at half past six, we were starting, when you tell a student that he has to get up at half past five during the holiday, so (with laughing) he does not like it very much. [I: Hmm] So something like that. (1) But I survived for three months and then I said to myself that I will try it again next year. So I returned the next year and then, that year I actually met my ex, my ex-boyfriend. [I: Hmm] Hmm. (Lenka I, p. 12, l. 365-373)

Lenka underlines that she belonged to the first generation of workers that came to Weißarber from the Czech Republic and pictures the kind treatment she received from the manager of McDonalds. However, she contracts her treatment with the hard work she had to deliver. Interestingly, while referring to the job at McDonalds, Lenka refers to herself as a student. She underlines that her co-workers who came with her were also students. Student status may help her to justify why she jobbed at McDonalds, which might be perceived as a workplace connected to a lower status. It also refers to the temporality of her placements, which were limited to the summer semester break. Seeing herself in the first instance as a student who uses cross border mobili-

---

40   See more on their web page: http://www.studentagency.cz/o-nas/profil-spolecnosti/historie-spolecnosti/

ty to better her situation during the rest of the year in the Czech Republic, Lenka challenges both the hard working conditions and the possible label of "cheap foreign labour". Furthermore, student status seems to link the different statuses and life situations in both geographical and social fields, as a seasonal worker in Weißarber in Germany and a student of Pedagogy in Ostrava in the Czech Republic, and integrate them as one into her life.

Within McDonalds, Lenka worked herself up to the position of assistant at the counter. She was also the one who trained her boyfriend for the position.

L: Hmm, he was also at McDonalds. I was training him, [I: Hmm] I was training him at the counter. Hmm. And then, when I came next year, he was already working as: the shift supervisor. So he was promoted. [I: Aha] /Hmm, well great. (with a deeper, lower voice)/ I actually knew that it is time limited, for three months, that I will earn something and that I will then come back and will have some money saved and that I will live the next nine months like a king. (2) [I: Hmm] Hmmm. That was good. (5) (Lenka I, p. 12, l. 377-382)

In contrast with her boyfriend whom Lenka trained and who had less experience of working in that position than Lenka, she was denied promotion. Lenka balances the unequal treatment with the temporality of her placements there. While reflecting on her stays there, Lenka refers indirectly to the differences in wages in both neighbour countries at that time. She uses her experience from the previous placement abroad and makes the choice which describes elsewhere as „better to work there then at home for small money". The temporality of the job, as well as a higher wage in comparison with similar jobs in the Czech Republic, makes it easier for her to overcome hard working conditions and the possibly lower status connected to the job. With these repeated and regular placements Lenka integrates migration into her life as a natural part of it.

Migration also opens up a new sphere of possibilities to her. While working at McDonalds, she met her boyfriend, who was the reason, so Lenka, for her to return to Germany again after graduation.

L: (2) And because I wanted to somehow stay with him I decided to initially try working as an au pair again, although at that time I was already twenty four. So I did another au pair placement. (Lenka I, p. 2, l. 53-55)

The only accessible possibility for Lenka to get to Germany legally was through the au pair visa status. Obviously, as her expression "I decided to initially try working as an au pair again" indicates, the au pair placement was perceived by her as a bridge to other possibilities on the labour market rather than solely a one year experience of cultural exchange.[41] She took her already

---

41 The au pair placement as a strategy to enter the labour market in Germany has also been described by other authors, such as Sabine Hess, who observed the motivations and strategies of Slovakian au pairs living and working in Germany (Hess 2009).

198

acquired experiences from working abroad in general and working as an au pair in particular and utilized them while searching for new opportunities. Her argumentation, which she uses to justify her decision to take the job of an au pair again despite her age and her status gained by graduation, indicates the conflict between "doing a proper job" in her country of origin, which she may feel to be expected from her, or taking on "lower status care work" abroad.

After her previous negative experiences, Lenka this time took the chance of going through an agency. The agency arranged for her to work for a host family with one child in a small town in the south of Germany close to the mountains. Lenka actively participated in negotiating the working arrangements and argued that, in contradiction to previous au pair placements in Austria, her language skills were at that time so advanced that she could defend herself. Once again language plays a crucial role in the positioning of Lenka in Germany. While making comparisons with her previous time as an au pair, she also outlines her inner development since that time which is closely connected to language.

Lenka describes her placement in the south of Germany as an exciting time:

L: It was also in the south of Germany, the tourist area, if you have ever heard of Pflaum-berg, Brunnen, so there, this part. There are mountains everywhere in the background, just beautiful. Beautiful nature. There I fell in love with nature and- /yes I split up with my boyfriend (she speaks quicker)/ and: I met someone else (2) with whom I stayed in contact. However, my visa expired and I had to come back to the Czech Republic, after one year as an au pair and I started work in Prague. (Lenka I, p. 2, l. 55-62)

Lenka describes several contradictions in this section of the interview. While depicting the beautiful natural scenery and her discovered love for nature, she mentions that she and her boyfriend split up. She does so quickly and – at this point of the main presentation – without any further information or comments. However, her comment about breaking up with her first boyfriend is important at this stage. Without this information, the new man, whom she met during this time, could not be introduced. Her way of presenting it indicates that the second man plays an important role in her further narration and life course as he is the one who keeps contact with Germany alive for Lenka.

Throughout Lenka's entire narration, she underlines her active planning and decision making – and so the biographical scheme of action (Schütze 2012a) – concerning her wish to migrate. However, not this time. Her return to the Czech Republic was, so Lenka, not influenced by her active decision and life planning, but by migration politics. Her visa, which was limited to au pair status for one year only, expired and she had to come back and search for a job in the Czech Republic. As I showed earlier, Lenka's aim was not to return to the Czech Republic after one year as an au pair but to use the time as an au pair to search for other possibilities or perspectives. She used her time in the south of Austria as a kind of moratorium, a time of reflexion about further possible steps.[42] During this time, Lenka found out that she could legally stay in Germany if she signed up for university. She had already found a university about hundred kilometres away from Pflaumberg, the city in which the host family lived. However, for enrolment she needed the approval of someone living in Germany who would – at least formally – act as a guarantor for and support her during her studies. She therefore asked the host family if they would be willing to do so. As they refused, the possibilities of her staying in Germany legally came to an end.

After an initial period of unemployment back in the Czech Republic, Lenka took a job as an office assistant in one of the big food chains in Prague, about 250 kilometres from her home town. She expected that she would utilise and develop her language skills, which were required for the position. However, as she puts it, "one could have put a trained monkey there too", who would repeat one sentence in German over and over again. Lenka describes why she quit the job in the following way:

L: Well on the other side I learnt many new things there. But because I am not um: really the business type that would sit in front a computer every day and fill in tables in SAP and so on, so. In the end I stayed there for nearly a year and after one year I quit because I was actually in contact with my (breathing) husband, but we wrote emails to one another and then one nice day we decided that he will come to Prague. It was in May he came to Prague, everything was blossoming, so romantic. (Laughing, both are laughing) (2) Hmm. So I showed him around Prague, yes, so we felt in love and – (laughing) (Lenka II, p. 2, l. 47-55)

Lenka uses the argumentation to justify why this job was not suitable for her and why she quit it. On the one hand, she portrays her "de-qualification" by the example of language outlined above. While she expected to use her language skills and develop them further in the job, she experienced that in reality she was over-qualified in respect of language skills for the tasks required from her. In the section presented above, Lenka positions herself at odds with the image of an "office type" doing – so Lenka – monotonous work and being tied to the work desk. In contradiction with this image, Lenka portrays herself as an active person searching for change and new tasks. Possibly, as her argumentation indicates, she has a need to once again justify why she has chosen an alternative path to the one that was expected of her.

Furthermore, Lenka connects the decision to leave the job directly with her future husband. Meeting and becoming a couple with her future husband – set against the romantic backdrop of blossoming spring in Prague – represents a break in Lenka's biography. Thanks to this contact, Lenka quit her job after one year and implemented an alternative plan. She decided to return to Germany, to Cologne where her boyfriend lived at that time.

---

42   On the moratorium phase in migration processes, see also Apitzsch 2000 or Kempf 2013.

Cologne and the difficult route from the private to public sphere

L: So I decided (louder and with a decisive voice), that I will try it again in Germany, and I went: it was actually in September 2001, I went to Cologne, I moved in to my boyfriend's place who in the meantime has become my husband. (Lenka I, p. 3, l. 67-70)

To resolve the dissatisfaction in her previous job, Lenka made a decision to move to Germany again. With this section, Lenka announces the beginning of a new life phase, which in contrast with previous phases she describes with an exact date and changed vocal modality.

After she got together with Thomas, her boyfriend, she travelled regularly by night bus every three weeks between Prague and Cologne to spend the weekend with him. She describes her first visit to Cologne in the following section.

L: And the first time I came it was somehow a strange feeling, because I arrived and I looked around and there was no one. I said "damn, now alone in Cologne, great. He is not here". So I called him, he did not answer the phone. I said "well, great." And he was already on his way. So he came then, picked me up and showed me Cologne in the morning, yes, it was at half past six, half past six in the morning, so we drove through Cologne and then, then: we actually went to his place, he went to work that day because I needed to sleep a bit anyway because of the journey on the bus, all night, I did not close my eyes at all. He came back around three, showed me Cologne, I stayed for four days and on Sunday evening I travelled back to Prague. (…) Well and so we did this for about half a year and then, because I knew that the job didn't satisfy me, so I quit it and I was thinking, so I told him (breathing) that I would like to come to Cologne for longer, if it were possible, if I could live at his place. So of course he was a bit afraid at the beginning of someone from from Eastern- Eastern Europe coming and now moving in to his place (laughing) [I: (laughing)], so of course he was a bit afraid, but then he nodded and I came in September and: and the first thing was, "what will you do", because of course I did not have a work permit. (Lenka II, p. 3, l. 69-90)

The scenic presentation (Schütze 2012b, p. 38) describing her first visit to Cologne portrays the uncertainty she experienced at the beginning in Cologne. She did not know the place, nor did she have any plans as to what she could do if Thomas did not come to pick her up. Lenka's boyfriend figures as an important person who showed her around and provided a "base" for her. He showed her the city, thereby starting Lenka's initiation into the new structures. Through the frequent visits, Lenka got to know Cologne more. It even became the place she could imagine emigrating to. She thus made a decision to quit her job in Prague and move to Cologne. However, the success of her migration was dependent on the agreement of Thomas. Interestingly, Lenka explains his indecision by using the categories of "East" and "West" and positions herself within the migration flows from East to West. However, her laughing may indicate the self-irony with which she questions these categories and the connected stereotypes.

Lenka did not have a clear idea where to find a job after her arrival in Cologne. Because she did not have a work permit, she searched for a job where she would not be seen by many people and where she would not stick out. She thus decided to work in the private sphere and searched for a family where she could care for children, a field in which she already had experience. The search was, according to Lenka, very easy as there was a large demand among families for au pairs and child minders at that time. She responded to some advertisements and shortly afterwards decided on a host family where she could work five days a week, from Monday to Friday. The host family tried to arrange a visa for her, but the application was denied after an approximately one year long procedure. Lenka later argued that there might have been the possibility of receiving a visa if they had applied not for the position of child minder for their family, but for a position within the private company directed by the man in the family. As all efforts to legalise her status failed, her host family decided that Lenka would work for them illegally and encouraged her not to tell anybody about her job.

L: And then (1) after two years, after two years we decided with my husband that we will marry. Because (1) I couldn't any more. It was always, um, I was actually insured, it also concerns health insurance. (Lenka II, p. 5, l. 150-153)

After previous efforts failed, Lenka decided to legalise her status by marriage. Marriage became the possibility for her to better not only her work opportunities but also her rights which until that time had been limited by her illegal status. She illustrates this by the example of insurance and by the difficulties to finance the necessary health treatment in Germany through her Czech insurance. The marriage to Thomas also enabled her to apply for a residence permit. However, the issue of her residence permit was not without problems, as the following section shows.

L: Afterwards as we married I went to report for and (1) I went to get the residence permit. And: (1) we went there, drew the ticket, (1) then it was our turn, the man tells us: "Well, you are wrong here, you have to go – you have to go to my colleague." So we went to his colleague, (1) he had a look, "no, you are wrong here." So finally we stayed. We did a circle, yes, they sent us from the devil to the demon43 and we finally ended up at the first one. My husband got mad (laughing). /Of course they expected there only to be foreigners coming who do not speak German. (she speaks more quickly)/ So my husband got mad (laughing), and the man was sitting behind armoured glass and as my husband bent forward and started to bitch, he backed away and said, "so here you have the ticket and now you will tell us, you will come out from this cabin and you will tell us, you will tell us immediately where we should go so we know where to get it issued". Yeah, the man did not expect my husband, my husband to speak German at all. So then he came out of that cabin and he took us to the place we needed to go to. Well and then, we sat there. At that

43 "Chodit od čerta k ďáblu", which could be literary translated as "going from the devil to the demon", is the phrase commonly used in the Czech language describing the process of being sent from one person or institution to the other in order to process one's case or issue the endless line of documents.

time, 2001, it was actually, 2003, one was still allowed to smoke in public authorities. Because we went there and the woman was sitting there at the computer, in one hand – hand a telephone, in the other hand a cigarette, and to it – no, not even in her hand, but in her mouth, and so she was writing like this (she demonstrates it) (1) yes and as she wrote and phoned like this, it happened that I have in my document um some mistakes, such as (1) I don't have a Czech passport, tschechische Reisepass, but I have technische Reisepass, (both of us are laughing), so I am not from the Czech Republic at all, but I am from somewhere in the Technical Republic. (both are laughing (3)) And I also have a few mistakes concerning my name and so on, yes, so my husband keeps telling me that "when someone checks you and has a look, they will think that that you falsified the document". So this is my experience with the authorities. Fortunately now that we have entered the European Union one actually does not need this residence permit anymore. I think. Hm. Lenka II, p. 7-8, l. 220-244)

Lenka's husband figures as an important person in relation to her contact with the authorities. She again underlines the vulnerability caused by her language skills. Although Lenka spoke German perfectly at that time, she had been positioned as a vulnerable position by being a "non-native speaker" and "foreigner". Her husband, on the other hand, is a native speaker and is therefore in a position from which he can deal on equal terms with officials. The power relations within the institution are also symbolically described by Lenka by means of her description of the solid glass panel behind which the official was situated and divided from the clients, as well as by the physical positioning of her husband, bending over the glass to the official – thereby crossing the dividing line between clients and officials and between "foreigners" and the "state authority represented by natives" – even forcing him to get up and show them the way. Lenka explains her husband's power by the fact that he speaks German, which was not expected by the officials. Thus, the power relations in the Immigration Office are described by Lenka as being based on language and, consequently, on the division between "natives" and "foreigners". Her husband is thus in an exclusive position in comparison with other clients of the Immigration Office like Lenka. Although the figure of Lenka's husband is only hinted at briefly in her main narrative, the scenic presentations which Lenka delivers during the questioning part show clearly the important role played by her husband in the process of legalising her status and in her orientation within the local structures.

After the marriage to Thomas, new job opportunities opened up for Lenka. Once she had received a residence permit, she could apply for a job not only in the private sphere but also in the public one. While still working for the host family as a child minder, Lenka started to reflect on what she could do.

L: What could I do with my qualifications as a primary school teacher, specialising in the German language (her voice drops). What could I do in Germany as a foreigner! (Lenka I, p. 3, l. 82-84)

For the first time, Lenka's qualifications feature in her reflections on her ongoing job possibilities. However, the transfer of her qualifications into a suitable position seemed to her impossible. The fact that she studied German in the Czech Republic and lived in Germany with the status of a "foreigner" appears to be a contradiction, an insuperable matter of fact. Due to this perceived barrier, Lenka decided to apply for a job not in a primary school but in a kindergarten. She hoped to connect her qualification with her experience of working with children. However, her efforts failed. She sent many applications to diverse kindergartens and received only refusals. Lenka explains her failure retrospectively by the fact that she was overqualified for the position. Lenka's failure to get a job made her frustrated and gave her the feeling that she could not overcome the invisible barrier standing between her and a job in the public sphere.

Despite this alleged barrier, Lenka later managed to get a job at a school, which in turn opened a new field of possibilities for her. She took the chance offered by these new possibilities and worked her way up step by step to a position comparable with other teachers.

Upwards social mobility within the school

In the time that Lenka was looking for a job and sending a large number of job applications to diverse kindergartens, she came across an advertisement by Caritas[44] offering a part time job as an afterschool tutor in one of the Hauptschulen.[45] She decided to apply.

L: So I decided, it was actually only ten hours per week, so I decided that I would not send my CV but that I would go there in person, to Caritas. So I took my bike and the map (laughing) [I: (laughing)] and I went, and I was very lucky because my current colleague and my former boss at Caritas um was having a very good day. She liked the way I spoke to her and that I was so brave and came and asked immediately what the job situation looked like, so she offered it to me on the spot, actually a totally different job! Hmm! (Lenka I, p. 4, l. 99-105)

Lenka explains her success of finding the job by her own initiative and changed strategy: she applied for the job in person and not just in writing as in her previous efforts. Lenka underlines her act of taking the initiative by her presentation of the way she travelled to Caritas: with her bike and a map. This brief description, suggesting that she not only planned her way there but that she also travelled to the organisation on her own, expresses her autonomy and an independent orientation within the local structures. This changed strategy together with her active performance assured her not only of a better

---

44 Caritas is a worldwide Christian organization that is active both as a charity and in arranging various kinds of job in the social field.
45 Hauptschule is a secondary school in Germany, which can be attended by children after four years of elementary schooling.

job, but also increased the number of teaching hours. The figure of her former boss, who over the course of time became Lenka's current colleague, reflects the process of Lenka's upwards social mobility within the institution. In actual fact social mobility – described by the increasing number of working hours and ongoing comparisons with her colleagues – is the main theme of her further biographical presentation.

The new work position she was offered involved her teaching German as foreign language at special afternoon classes. As she reports, this job gave her a look at the way the classes were organised and, at the same time, she got an insight into the structure of the German educational system. Her role was to teach the children not only the language, but also the necessary skills in order to orientate themselves independently about town. This seems particularly important for Lenka. At the time she came to Cologne, she was able to enjoy the help of her husband who showed her around and initiated her into the local structures. Over the course of time she developed into someone who knows the city well, can independently move within its structure and can even pass on her knowledge further. She became part of the city within which she could start to develop her new and independent biographical path. After one and half years Lenka got an offer from the director of the school to teach more hours and, at the same time, to change employer since until then she had been paid by Caritas. She agreed and her working hours increased once again.

L: So I actually nearly had a full time position, because twenty seven hours is full time for teachers. And I had twenty four. (Lenka I, p. 4, l. 125-127)

In gaining her new position, Lenka became able to draw comparisons between the position of full time teachers and her own, which was limited to a student contract of twenty, or more specifically twenty four teaching hours per week. It is striking that it was important for Lenka to underline that her status was rising and getting closer to the status of full time teachers. Obviously, the shifted position enabled her to create new perspectives on her further development and, at the same time, opened up new possibilities of social mobility for her. As she changed position, Lenka immediately became the form teacher of one of the classes.

L: And before that I actually also – in the meantime I had started to study because I found out that I had /the possibility, also as a Czech, to teach at a German school if I also complete a second subject. (She speaks slowly, loudly and in clear phrases)/ Because I studied German before and I was told that if I completed a second subject too and sat the second state exam so to speak, I would be on the same level as German colleagues who studied for five years in Germany. (Lenka I, p. 5, l. 131-137)

Lenka's further qualification became an important means and strategy for her to better her social position. It is of interest that the belonging to national categories, in the context of social mobility, presented an important dimension for Lenka definitive of access to or exclusion from certain social spheres. In her narration, the "German colleagues" serve as a mirror of her own lower situated position and development possibilities accessible to her. At the same time, they represent an important reference group to whom she draws ongoing comparisons and with whom she wishes to be equal. In this context, the further studies became for Lenka a strategy for achieving her goal and equalling her position to that of German colleagues. Her studies also became the means of overcoming the apparent contradictions of being a Czech and being able to teach at a German school.

Lenka decided to choose history as the second subject and after three years she successfully finished her studies by sitting her final examination, at which the director of her school was present as an important referee. After she graduated, she could apply for a so-called "Planstelle", which she finally obtained after some moments of insecurity.

L: So I got the position and currently I am actually a Beamte auf Probe, it will still be until April or or: until May and then: then I will take one more examination and if I pass I will be a Beamtin auf Lebenszeit. So to say the official. (Lenka I, p. 7, l. 196-199)

To describe her current status, which she reached thanks to further education and the ensuing promotion, Lenka uses the term "Beamte" (civil servant). In Germany, the school system is considered by the law as being part of the public service (Art. 7 GG). Therefore, teachers at public schools are seen as public employees and part of the "Beamtentum" (officialdom) (Art. 33 GG). The civil servant status, the different phases and hierarchical relations of which Lenka outlines, seems to have a particular importance for Lenka. On the one hand, it is connected to higher social status and relative security. On the other hand, it also means that her stay as well as employment has been recognised by the authority of the state. As she points out in another part of the interview, by obtaining civil servant status she actually became an employee of the ministry of education. The recognition of her status by the state seems to be particularly important for her, taking into account her difficulties in legalising her status after her arrival in Cologne and earlier.

To gain the status of a civil servant became possible for Lenka thanks to EU enlargement in 2004 by ten countries, one of which was the Czech Republic. Through the regulation of the free movement of persons within the EU, EU citizens gained, inter alia, the right to be employed in certain professions in the German public service sector, which until then had been reserved for German citizens. Although Lenka does not name it explicitly, the possibilities of her promotion became possible within this very context of shifted regulations (Art. 7 BeamtStG).

Lenka explains her newly gained civil servant status as a big success. She presents herself as an exception, especially because of her nationality and previous biographical and career path. The gaining of the position of "Beamte auf Lebenszeit" seems to be at the present time the peak of her social mobility: the "German" teachers, who served as the reference group with whom she compared herself, have become equals as colleagues possessing the same status. Furthermore, her language skills, which during the course of her life she experienced as the main "culprit" for inequality and vulnerability in different situations – whether not being able to defend herself as an au pair, or as a "foreigner" who is treated differently because of limited language skills at the Foreign Office – have now officially been recognised, since she received the certificate not only for teaching history and Germany as a foreign language, but also for teaching regular German language classes, i.e. just like her native speaker colleagues teaching pupils who are native speakers. This development, looking back at her biographical path, is experienced by Lenka as something paradox and extraordinary.

The relatively quick upward social mobility she experienced after joining the school was not planned and rather surprising for Lenka. Getting in to the school through the job agency has constantly opened up new possibilities of social mobility and further development for her, a process which Schütze (1983) describes as a "positive" or "rising trajectory". The success story of Lenka seems really extraordinary. However, her way of presenting it also raises the question to what extent her efforts are recognised in other socio-geographical contexts, especially through the eyes of her significant others back in the Czech Republic.

The translatability of social position across the border

Lenka's story is a story of great social mobility after migration. Throughout all of her narration she describes how she worked her way up from the position of an au pair through part time jobs and her further studies to a position as a teacher recognised by the state. However, despite her great success, Lenka has difficulties in "translating" her efforts across the border and gaining recognition in respect of her career path by her relatives and close friends.

L: So I got the position and currently I am actually a Beamte auf Probe, it will still be until April or or: until May and then: then I will take one more examination and if I pass I will be Beamtin auf Lebenszeit. So to say the official. (1) So something like this (laughing) [I: (laughing)]. Well, it is really very difficult to explain it to someone who didn't grow up in this system here and doesn't have a chance to somehow get into it. Because when I explain it to my family46 they do not understand at all what I am talking about. What – like how the official, yeah, what does it mean. How could a teacher be an official? Hmm, there it is! (Lenka I, p. 7, l. 196-203)

While picturing the success of reaching the position of a regular school teacher and the status of a civil servant, which in Germany is highly recognised, she changes perspective and offers an insight into her status from the

---

46 In the original, instead of the word "family" (rodina) Lenka uses the expression "naši", which could be translated both as "parents" and closer "family".

viewpoint of her close relatives. Lenka raises the issue of difficulties of translation of the meaning of the position she has attained to her significant others who live in a different socio-cultural context. The inability to explain the meaning of her acquired position also puts her social mobility, the theme on which she concentrates throughout her entire narrative, into question.

The difficulties of "translation work" regarding certain positions across the border also find their expression in the use of language in Lenka's narration. Although Lenka spoke Czech throughout the entire interview, she used German expressions in certain particular contexts. It is of relevance that the German expressions appeared predominantly in the narrative about her current job and in the narrative about her further qualifications in Germany.

At the beginning, Lenka made an effort to explain to me what expressions like "Referendariat" mean. Later on, as the words "Angestellte", "Planstelle", or "Beamtin auf Probe" appeared in her narrative, she gave up trying to find the Czech equivalents and commented that "I will say the words in German because I don't know" (p. 6, l. 182-183). The fact that I speak German and understand these expressions made it possible for her to overcome the explanations, which would have diverted her away from the main line of her narrative. Nevertheless, the use of German expressions in the context of her narrative concerning her work and qualification does not appear to be arbitrary. Moreover, the difficulties in "translation work" concerning these expressions and their meanings seems to correspond with her argumentation on the lack of understanding from her significant others and relatives in the Czech Republic concerning her status and the nature of her work. By her use of language she thus also expresses the difficulties in translating certain experiences across the border. The feeling of not being understood by her relatives and significant others makes her justify her social position when speaking to me and, indirectly, in the dialogue with her significant others through her narrative.

The difficulties in translatability of her social position uncover the different structural contexts of both societies. The missing recognition of her career path may be influenced by the ambiguous discussions concerning the recognition of primary school teachers in the Czech Republic. While the teaching profession is relatively highly ranked in the annual tables on the prestige of professions (Tuček 2012), teachers still suffer from unsatisfied conditions and low salaries, which are among the lowest within the EU (Ranguelov, Pejnovic 2010). Similarly in Germany, primary school teachers enjoy a relatively high reputation in the public mind (Rothland 2007). However, the relatively high reputation corresponds to higher salaries in comparison with other EU countries (Ranguelov, Pejnovic 2010). The social position of teachers thus differs accordingly in both countries.

Nevertheless, Lenka's success cannot be explained solely by discursive perceptions concerning the teaching profession in both countries. More than that, it is influenced by her biographical pathway. While in the Czech Republic her pathway would be considered to be quite ordinary taking into account her university studies, in Germany she sees her career path as a great success because of the legal and language barriers she had to overcome due to her "foreigner status". Crossing the border thus also changed her perception of the goals and possibilities accessible to her.

Furthermore, the difficulties of translatability of her social position reveal the positioning of Lenka in both societies. She moves within the national discourses and, as opposed to her significant others who stayed in the Czech Republic, can understand both of them. Once again she compares her significant others and herself while pointing to her alternative and extraordinary life path, which however suffers from a lack of recognition.

"I always wanted to be a teacher": reconstructing the continuity of one's career path in transnational spaces

When Lenka comes back in her narration to her family and to the situation during communism, she recounts an event describing her dream to become a teacher in her childhood. However, this dream seemed impossible to her because of the positioning of her family during the former regime. A similar feeling of impossibility to carry out her profession also appeared later on when she reflected on what to do in Germany and how to use the qualifications she had acquired in the Czech Republic. That she managed to get a job which corresponds to her qualifications is still surprising and not self-evident for Lenka.

Lenka's career path was not linear, but crooked, full of ruptures, searches and shifts in status and positioning. However, as her narration indicates, Lenka reconstructs the continuity within her biography by linking up her past dream of becoming a teacher and her present profession in Germany. Lenka narrates her dream of becoming a teacher in the following way.

L: My parents signed me up, for example. My parents signed me up for religion lessons and: it wasn't at that time very popular, you know. Of course when – I think it was in fourth grade. My parents went to the parents' evening and Mrs Teacher told them that I would never have any chance of studying, because of course everyone had erm: everyone had their own card and she could have a look at what was on our card, so when I constantly said that in the future, I wanted to be /"children, what do you want to be when you grow up?" (Lenka imitates the high pitched voice and claps her hands together)/"Princess" (with a high voice)/ /"President" (with a deeper voice)/ and I always said /"teacher" (normal, descending voice)/. And when this procedure was repeated every year, they wrote on my report card that Lenka wants to be a teacher. So I was told, or my parents were told that I would never have any chance of studying, that I should rethink it. Well, like this. (Lenka I, p. 8, l. 245-255)

In the event described above, Lenka outlines the religious orientation of her family and the problems that resulted from it. As Lenka depicts in other parts of the interview, the family of Lenka's father was brought up religiously. One of Lenka's uncles was a priest and the other uncle was a practicing catholic even after his emigration to Canada. However, the religious beliefs, which her parents tried to transfer not only within the family but also by means of her institutional education, were the reason for the oppression and limited chances of Lenka in her childhood under the former regime, which perceived religion as its enemy. The control of the state over the individual finds its expression in the cards which every individual had. The teacher, who represented the institution and its power, had access to these cards, which normally remained inaccessible to other individuals. The possibility of having access to individual records became an instrument of power for teachers, making recommendations concerning the future of pupils. Parents were in this situation positioned into the role of listeners and receivers of verdicts "from above", having no possibility to oppose.

As the scenic presentation shows, Lenka had a clear idea what she wanted to do in her future. Her wish to be a teacher differs from the wishes of other children, who dreamt of being a princess or president, professions which are rather unrealistic and belong to the dream world of children. Contrary to them, Lenka had a very realistic dream of becoming a teacher, which she expresses by using a normal, descending voice. Nevertheless, although her wish was so real, it seemed to be inaccessible to her because of her family background. Lenka expresses the inability to pursue her plans and wishes due to the structural limitations imposed upon her. Interestingly, this motive is repeated later when Lenka speaks about her efforts to find a suitable job after migration to Germany, and the way the migration regime formed her possibilities.

After picturing the event of denial of her desired career path, she goes on in her narration and draws a direct link to the career path of her father.

L: The same with my father. My father had to go into agriculture, he also wanted to study and they told him that no, that he had to go into agriculture. So he went at first to agricultural high school in Opava and then somehow he managed (1) to study veterinary medicine in Brno. He studied veterinary medicine, but it was totally sort of somehow through the acquaintances at that time that they made it possible for him, otherwise he wouldn't have had any chance. Yes and I studied actually thanks to the fact that in eighty nine the government fell apart, otherwise I would not have had a chance either. Hmm. So like this. (Lenka I, p. 8, 256-262)

Similarly to Lenka, her father was denied the option of pursuing his plans and wishes concerning his career path. Despite his disagreement, his career was decided "from above", by the power of the state. Nevertheless, he finally managed with the help of friends to attain the education he wanted to have. His career pathway proves similarities with the pathway of Lenka. Similarly to her father, Lenka also took an alternative and "crooked" way to overcome the structural barriers and to become a teacher, the job she wanted to do from the time of her childhood. Just like her father, Lenka was able to use the help of friends, and notably her husband, to enlarge the space of her possibilities. By drawing similarities to the career path and social mobility of her father, she reveals their similar strategy to deal with the problems resulting from the unequal position in society. The strategy of searching for alternative possibilities for self-development, which Lenka uses as a resource in different historical and cultural contexts, seems to be embedded in the experiences of Lenka and other family members acquired at the time of communism.

As Lenka states, she was able to start her studies after the changes in the political regime in 1989 in the former Czechoslovakia. She started to study Pedagogy with a specialism in the German language. By choosing this subject, she continued to learn the German language and to build on the language skills she had developed during her previous stay in Austria. However, after she graduated she did not take up a position on the labour market which would have matched her qualifications, but instead went to Germany to work as an au pair. At that time, she saw a placement as an au pair as the only possibility to stay in Germany legally. In the Czech Republic the possibilities of carrying out her profession seemed limited to her too. After a period of unemployment she took a job in an office in a city about 250 km from her hometown; unfortunately this job did not satisfy her because she felt underqualified, particularly with regard to her language skills. Her unfulfilled efforts to find a job which would satisfy her not only demonstrate the regional inequalities within the Czech Republic in which she was embedded, but also the limited chances in Germany which she experienced because of her migrant status.

The possibility of making use of her qualifications did not become available to Lenka until after the marriage to her husband, through which she was able to legalise her stay in Germany and gain access to the German labour market. She nonetheless experienced her "foreigner" status as an obstacle in searching for a job. Her statement "What could I do with my qualification as a primary school teacher, specialising in the German language. What could I do in Germany as a foreigner?" affirm the way Lenka positioned herself and which chances of entering the German labour market she experienced. For this reason, she decided to build on her previous experience as an au pair and "Tagesmutter" and take a job at one of the kindergartens. Only after her efforts failed did she decide to orientate herself differently and join a school, at first as a tutor and later on as a teacher. Interestingly, her goal of becoming a teacher was not pre-planned. As the opportunity arose, however, she decided to grab it.

Studying in Germany was very important for Lenka, which is demonstrated by the fact that she devotes a great deal of attention to this phase of life within her narration, picturing in detail the course of studies and the final examinations. They became a means of bettering her position and overcoming the inequalities between her "German" colleagues and herself. When talking about her studies, Lenka positions herself as a "foreigner" from an EU country, by which she therefore draws a distinction between more privileged EU citizens and the "others". In comparison with the "others", her diplomas were recognised and she was able to build on her previous studies without the necessity of repeating the whole course of studies or searching for another profession.

In her profession, Lenka not only interconnects the knowledge acquired in both countries during her studies, but also makes use of her cross border experiences and transnational knowledge in general. Teaching the German language and cooking with pupils at the grammar school, which is situated in a multicultural city in Western Germany where the proportion of children whose first language is not German is relatively high, makes it possible for her to use her language skills – switching to Czech for a moment, for example, in order to gain the attention of pupils who have started to speak to each other in a language which the others do not understand, thereby "irritating" the pupils and causing them to think about it – and to transmit the cultural practices which she acquired prior to her migration to her pupils. Lenka's aim to interconnect the cultural practices across the border is expressed in the following section, which also represents the final part of Lenka's story.

L: Well, otherwise, um, every year we organise the Christmas market, [I: Hmm] (-) first Advent, this year it will be at the end of November, that weekend. So I make an effort, because I also teach cookery by the way, so I make an effort um, to bake Christmas honey cookies with the pupils. And Standa saw it, how really, how Muslim children decorate the cookies. (Laughing) It is something amazing. Simply boys, I have photos! They have their tongues hanging out and they decorate fishes and stars and angels. (laughing). Hmm, well yeah. It is beautiful, really. If you could only see it. I took some photos two years ago, (1) absolutely amazing (1) hmm. (Lenka I, p. 6, l. 220-227)

By portraying the situation of baking honey cookies, which are traditional Czech pastries prepared in many families before Christmas, Lenka expresses her satisfaction of "importing" this piece of Czech tradition into the other cultural context. She expresses the different context by naming the Muslim children and boys as the main actors, which creates a contrasting picture to the practice of baking the cookies in the Czech Republic, where the baking and decorating is predominantly the task of women. As this section shows, Lenka figures as someone who can translate among cultural practices and is able to make active use of them in different cultural contexts. She sees herself as an active player within these transnational spaces, which she continuously creates and re-establishes through her cross border experiences and dealings with others.

The transnational practices of Lenka seem to be connected to her perception of her biographical and career path, spanning across the borders of national states. By constructing the continuity of her migration and career she makes sense of her past and present decisions and practices. Furthermore, it helps her to overcome the ruptures in her biographical path and establish a link to her family living in the Czech Republic and to her past in a new way.

6.2.3 Summary

Lenka's story is a success story, which developed from a situation defined by limited possibilities in the past to her present reputable position. Despite the limited possibilities of development due either to the position of her family in the time of former communist Czechoslovakia or due to her irregular status after her migration to Germany later on, she presents herself as someone who constantly searches for alternative possibilities and takes the opportunities which appear to her. The phrase "I took the chance", which Lenka repeats throughout her narration in various different contexts, may represent Lenka's overall attitude towards her biographical pathway. Hereby her pathway is not only the result of chance and lucky coincidences for Lenka – in contrast to Martin's biographical presentation – but more than that the result of her active decisions and search for alternative pathways.

Migration is the most important theme for Lenka, which extends throughout her entire story. Her motivation to migrate is closely connected to Lenka's family history. In her narration, she constructs a link between the attempts of her parents to migrate in the past and her own migration activities. Her migration thus could be seen as the continuity of a family project to migrate, which stayed unfulfilled. While constructing the links to her family history, she maintains the link to her family and justifies her alternative biographical path which spans trans-locally.

Lenka already began to orientate herself across the border during her childhood, as a result of the inequalities and limited chances of development her family experienced in the communist past. While at first she only crossed the border symbolically – through language and the media – after the revolution in 1989 when the borders opened she decided to migrate on her own. Again she responded to the lack of other opportunities in the place of her origin after she was denied access to university. The first migration experiences as an au pair in Austria played an important role for Lenka. She "individualised" herself from her family home and developed fantasies concerning her future studies and life in Austria. Although she never implemented her dreams, this experience of living in different cultural and lingual surroundings was crucial for her. Her experiences initiated the transformative processes in which she could not only define her position in a new way but, through emerging thoughts of further biographical possibilities, enlarge her space of action, taking Europe as a reference setting (see e.g. Inowlocki, Riemann

2012; Schütze, Schröder-Wildhagen 2012). Her au pair stay in Salzburg thus became the first step in creating her transnational biography.

Lenka drew on her previous migration experiences and emerging transnational space again later on during her studies in the Czech Republic, spending every summer holiday as a seasonal worker in the hospitality sector in Germany. The au pair job, which she took after her graduation, was a time of a "moratorium", in which she could reflect on her biographical development and establish new life plans. During this time, she established a plan to stay in Germany for a longer period of time. In order to legalise her status there, she considered signing up for university in Germany. However, she did not find the necessary support from her host family to carry through her plan. The opportunity of establishing a new life in Germany came later on when she met her future husband and moved to his place after she quit her office job in Prague, having found said office job after a period of unemployment but having perceived herself as being overqualified. As Lenka's story reveals, her decisions to migrate are influenced by her personal preferences and shaped by social and geographical inequalities in the Czech Republic, which have deepened in the course of the post-communist transformation of the Czech society.

Moreover, Lenka's career and migration pathway is shaped not only by structural settings in the Czech Republic, but also by the intersection of migration and gender regimes in Germany. Due to her limited legal rights preventing her from entering the public sphere, Lenka turned her attention to work possibilities in the private family sphere, which would assure her anonymity and protection from possible legal consequences. After Lenka legalised her status through the marriage to her husband, new possibilities opened up for her. She managed to mobilise her qualification as a teacher of German and worked herself up to the position of "Beamte". However, further studies and qualifications acquired in Germany were necessary for her in order to attain this status.

Although Lenka only refers to her husband briefly in her narration, it became clear during the analysis of her story that he played an important role in her social mobility. He figures as someone who, besides helping her to legalise her status through marriage, initiated her into the local structures and assisted her with communications with the authorities, in respect of which Lenka always underlined the vulnerability she felt as a result of her accent and her "foreigner" status.

Lenka's German language skills, which Lenka is constantly honing, are the means of negotiating her positioning within society. During her placements in Austria and Germany, she felt vulnerable due to her lack of language skills, her accent and her "foreigner" status when in contact with her employers and the authorities. Not knowing the language meant for her not being capable of defending her rights and being treated in an unequal way.

The fact that she nowadays teaches the German language in one of the primary schools, and that she has even become a "Beamte" herself, which means that her status has been recognised by the state, justifies not only the development of her language skills but also her belonging to German society.

Throughout her story, Lenka refers to the perceived expected institutional pathway for her education and career in the Czech Republic. The extensive argumentation which Lenka uses to justify her decisions to go to Germany and to take jobs which did not correspond to her qualifications, reveal Lenka's internal dispute. The perceived expected biographical path taking place within the national setting of the Czech Republic serves Lenka as a means of comparison with her own biographical development, which spans transnational spaces. While comparing her life with this "normal biographical development", Lenka presents herself as "the black sheep of the family who left its flock" and chose a transnational biographical pathway. Despite her efforts to "translate" her experiences and position across the border, her social mobility suffers from a lack of recognition by some of her significant others back in the Czech Republic. In comparison with her family and the significant others she left behind, Lenka presents herself as someone who is shifting the borders and social and cultural settings and who can translate and transmit among them. She uses her cross border experiences not only for her biographical path, but also in her profession as a teacher.

6.3 Martin: moving places and passing classes

M: And it was, I can remember it. It was quite paradox. Somehow the last day, I was already leaving or I was coming back to, it was-, I don't know if I was there for two or three months (in the canning factory- comment AG). And when I was going back to the Czech Republic, I went through Düsseldorf. I had time, I was there for about a half day, so I was walking around, then I sat in the park and was watching the skyscrapers and I said to myself that it would be something! It was an absolutely absurd imagination of course. I said to myself that it would be great if I could sit up here or there in the office! But it was so absurd, you know. Because at that time I didn't have any idea where I would be working after university, not at all. I didn't think about it at all, so it was absurd, you know. When I walk around nowadays, and you know I work there, I just think that it is somehow a dream. I don't want to say a fulfilled dream but it is really interesting. Well, I just remember how I was sitting there at that time. With my backpack and I was observing it and telling myself that it would be amazing to work there! You know. And now, how many years it is. Maybe five years ago, five years ago, yes. Or about that. And now I am here. (Martin, p. 9, l. 257-23)

The image of moving from the bench in the park to the office in one of the skyscrapers expresses Martin's move across social classes, which is the main theme of his narration. This section is situated in that part of the interview in which Martin talks about his temporary job in one of the can fabrics in Germany, which he took during the summer semester holidays in order to earn some money for his studies. At that time, jobs in the skyscraper seemed inaccessible from his position. And nowadays, even though he actually works as a finance consultant in one of the skyscrapers in Düsseldorf, he still perceives his career pathway as something unexpected, extraordinary and unplannable. The shift in ideas between the past and the present and between the different social positioning of Martin, as pictured in the section above, penetrate his entire narrative. They are the expression of the "metamorphosis" of his biography and of the search for his own positioning within the social spheres in which he moves and operates.

Martin was born in 1982 in the medium sized town of Most in the northern part of the Czech Republic. He was the third child of his parents, who both originated from this area close to the border with Germany. His mother was a shop assistant and his father worked as a locksmith in Most his whole life. The parents, their three sons and the grandmother all lived together in a house on the periphery of Most. Martin spent his entire childhood there. After primary school he went to business college in Most. After graduating, he moved to Prague to study and later take on a job in the finance sector. At the time of the interview, Martin was living in Düsseldorf in central Germany.

Martin's story is one of the interviews I conducted which narrate the story of geographical and upwards social mobility. As Martin's and other narratives reveal, upwards social mobility would not have been possible without an act of relocation. However, moving ones geographical and social spaces brings with it the challenge of having to position oneself afresh, not only in different national settings but also in different social classes, the significance and perception of which shifts over the course of time.

6.3.1 Interview setting and biographical presentation

Context of the interview

After I conducted my first interview with Lenka, a field of potential new female interviewees opened up to me. However, I still had no contact with any migrant men. I therefore turned to the internet and searched through diverse platforms. I made contact with Martin on a social network for professionals. In the information listed under his profile it stated that he had studied in the Czech Republic and at that time was working in Düsseldorf, Germany. I sent Martin a contact request and shortly afterwards we exchanged emails for the first time. At first I explained the purpose of my study to Martin and asked him whether he would agree to my conducting an interview with him. He replied very quickly in a friendly and informal way, agreed to a meeting immediately and proposed that we should call one another by our first names since we were almost the same age. We exchanged a few emails and agreed to meet the following Friday after work at a Czech restaurants in Düsseldorf.

At the arranged time I was already waiting in front of the restaurant and reading the menu beside the entrance. Martin arrived shortly afterwards. He was about to enter the restaurant when I approached him. We greeted each other and, as it was a cold January evening, entered the restaurant and searched for a free table where we could be more or less undisturbed. We passed the bar and found a free table at the end of the restaurant, divided from the other tables by a partition wall. Although the restaurant was only half full and relatively quiet when we entered, it became much busier over the course of the evening. Our apprehension disappeared after we ordered dinner and started to speak about life in Germany and about contact with other Czechs living in Düsseldorf. Martin told me of a number of situations in which he had by chance met other Czechs, however after a short period of time all of them had either moved to another country or left to go back to the Czech Republic. Martin was very interested in my PhD studies. He stated that he had also thought about doing a PhD after his studies of economy in Prague, but then had decided against it since "the surplus value" of a PhD was minimal for him. Interestingly, business terminology explaining certain biographical decisions such as this one appeared in various contexts throughout Martin's story and was his means of explaining biographical events.

We spoke Czech together all the time. The language and the familiar smell of the restaurant contributed to my feeling that we were transcending space and that we were in some restaurant in the Czech Republic. The atmosphere of the place also had an impact on the Martin's memories and narrative. In his story he often spoke about situations taking place in a similar context a hundred kilometres away.

After we had eaten dinner, I described to Martin the form of the interview and explained to him why I was interested in his narratives and own experiences. When I clarified to him my interest in his life story, how the events followed each other and how his biographical path had developed, he joked that after such a narrative of his there must surely come some surprising and unexpected questions. We were still laughing when we began the interview. I turned on the recording device and asked Martin to narrate his life story. After a short moment of reflection and arranging the point from which he should start to narrate, whether from the moment he moved to Germany or as early on as the time of his birth, he immersed himself into the narrative. I was very surprised how quickly he got into the flow of narration. Martin spoke calmly and relatively silently. He interspersed the narration with extensive evaluations of the biographical events and by thoughts which came to his mind while reflecting on his biography. He laughed often and repeated many times that a story like his could not happen again, that it all only became possible because of fortune and coincidences. After about an hour, when Martin's story had reached the present moment in Germany, he stated that his narration was finished and that I could start posing questions.

Before we came to the questions, we finished our beers which had remained largely untouched during the prior act of recounting, and ordered new ones. As my questions flowed, Martin once again immersed himself into a detailed narration of his experiences during childhood, studies and first work experience opportunities at home and abroad. The later it got, the more crowded and louder the restaurant and our conversation became. Unfortunately, the last part of the interview did not get recorded because the battery in my recording device was flat. We didn't realise that the recording device had switched itself off until near the end of the interview. We quickly returned to talking about normal life and spoke again about Martin's experiences, about links between the Czech and German culture and about the language in the border regions. Martin also asked me many questions concerning my life and experiences. The roles of interviewer and interviewee were thus reversed. After about four hours of talking, we left the restaurant shortly after midnight.

The main storyline and Martin's presentation

M: OK. (1) So I was born in Most, (1) in the Czech Republic, in North, (2), I have two brothers, two older brothers, so we are three boys [I: Hmm] Um- (2) from – actually from childhood I did a lot sport (he clears his throat) (1) actually I have done it a lot all my life, it is somehow important to me, to have some movement, some sport, so I played a lot of football, all – all different kinds of sport. (Martin, p. 1, l. 24-28)

After this initial sequence in which Martin names two constants throughout his life, i.e. movement and sport, Martin comes back to introduce Most in more detail. He specifies that he was born at the time of communism and describes the environmental situation and school trips to nearby mountains.

He continues by outlining his education, stating that he started grammar school but two years later changed schools. Martin speaks extensively about this step being meaningful for his life retrospectively. After this long reflexive passage, Martin comes back to his main narration and reports that after primary school he went to business college. After graduation he was admitted to the University of Economics. He evaluates his course of studies and draws comparisons to other students.

Subsequently, Martin begins to recount his experiences of living and working abroad. He names the "work and travel programs" he used for his initial travels to Germany, where he worked in a canning factory. Martin describes his work responsibilities and the conditions there. The following summer he left for the USA to work as a baker in one of the amusement parks. Once again Martin concentrates on describing the working conditions evaluating the working conditions and possibilities in the USA in general.

When Martin returned from the USA, he took on a part time job aside from his studies. At this point he interrupts the line of his narration, which until now has been in chronological order, and inserts extensive background construction (Schütze 2012a, p. 27) on the history of the various different jobs he has had during his lifetime: from construction works to sweeping streets. Only afterwards does he come to speak about how he came to join ABC Company. Martin delivers a detailed narration portraying the situation surrounding his entrance test to ABC Company. He was successful and started to work there as an intern. As Martin further explains, before starting a regular job he considered studying in the USA. However, he finally decided to stay with the company. As luck might have it, so Martin, he received an offer to go to Düsseldorf, Germany, as an intern for six months. After the initial six months Martin received an offer to stay longer. In the following sections, Martin reflects on his position within the company and by way of example describes a particular meeting.

Subsequently, after a short break searching for the right words, he reflects extensively on his relationship with Most and Prague. He disputes once again why he decided to stay in Düsseldorf, and explains how the social circles around investment banking are made up.

When Martin has finished his narration, I ask him if there is anything else he wants to add. He has a short think and then hypothesizes in the manner in which successful people speak about success, namely in terms of luck. He argues that the act of achievement is also important and reflects again on his life and his decisions while comparing himself to those of his peers who stayed in Most. Martin summarises his narration with the words: "It was, well, it was all down to luck that I got to Düsseldorf, yes" (Martin, p. 24, l. 744-745). Afterwards, I start to ask Martin questions on his story.

The opening sequence and concluding statement – coda – provide important indications as to the structure of Martin's narrative. Martin begins his narration by naming the town and the geographical area in which he was born and which is in many aspects very specific. As he later discloses, his town is not only part of an industrial area situated in the borderlands which is burdened by a polluted environment and few work opportunities. It is also a historically important place in which, according to local legend, the events of the revolution began. While starting his narrative at this location, Martin lets his story end in Düsseldorf, the city of finances, services and global networks in Germany. His concluding afterthought that „it was all down to luck that I got to Düsseldorf" confirms that his story is about his pathway to Germany, to his current position and life situation. The different places of residence along which Martin structures his narrative are closely connected to his shift in status and upwards social mobility.

At the very beginning of his story, Martin introduces the town in which he was born and names his two brothers and the fact that he was always doing sport and still does until this very day. Sport is thus a constant which runs throughout his entire life, even when the social frameworks have shifted. As Martin specifies, to him sport represents movement which he needs in his life. Moving within the sports "showground", where collective collaboration, tactics and knowledge of the rules of the game are crucial, could be seen as a metaphor for his movement within the social fields and social strata. On the "real life" showground, Martin also learns the rules of diverse social fields and how to move tactically among them while making use of his social contacts.

Martin concentrates on recounting his education and career path. He begins with his childhood, pictures in detail the transfer from one primary school to another, as well as moving on to business college and later on to university. The next part of his story concerns his working holidays placement abroad during his studies and subsequently his joining ABC Company by means of which he transfers to Düsseldorf to take up a full time job. However, although he concentrates predominantly on his career and shift in status, his family and friends stay present throughout his narration, serving as significant others and a mirror and means of comparison for his own development and position in different locations.

Right from the very beginning, Martin emphasises important shifts and extraordinary and exceptional events in his biography rather than everyday ordinary affairs: he pictures the trips and school holidays due to air pollution, the accidental transfer from his first primary school to another school with better language education, the way in which he ended up in a different school class than his former schoolmates, or meeting the boss at his job who arranges the internship in Düsseldorf for him. By emphasizing these exceptional circumstances, he pictures his pathway as extraordinary and different from that of his peers, with whom he draws comparisons.

The events which Martin depicts in his narrative and which he sees as being the most influential on his biographical path are explained by Martin in terms of luck. These coincidences, which in his view he was unable to influence, opened up new possibilities for action and new areas of decision-making. These lucky coincidences, which could not happen again the way they did, as Martin often repeats, highlight the exceptionality and success of Martin's biography. The emphasis on the exceptionality, the impossibility of planning, the individualisation and uniqueness of his biographical path, supported by luck and coincidences, push the presentation based on individual performance to the background.[47]

---

47 Similar observations were also made by Liebold 2009 who studied self-presentation and self-manifestation of elite businesspeople based on detailed analyses of published autobiographies. According to Liebold, self-presentation by elite businesspeople shows similar fea-

Martin's story is interlaced with extensive reflexive passages aimed at trying to explain the biographical developments and his experience of the metamorphosis (Schütze 2012a) of his world view, altered status and new life options. The role of luck, which Martin emphasizes, serves as one explanation for the decisive events which started the process of self-development which for him were neither planned nor intentional. The process of a metamorphosis dominates Martin's entire narrative. Moreover, his manner of presentation is full of his search for explanations for his biographical path, for new positions within emerging transnational spaces and changes in his life prospects, thereby indicating that these processes are not yet complete. His concluding sentence that „it was all down to luck that I got to Düsseldorf" describes this attitude perfectly.

Notes on the working relationship with Martin

The way in which Martin narrates his story is closely connected to our mutual expectations regarding the interview and to the relationship we established from the very first moment on. Our relationship was defined, among other things, by the place in which we first made contact, our age, similar biographical experiences and, last but not least, social class and gender.

The internet platform through which I made contact with Martin serves professionals and companies in establishing links in the labour market. Martin, like other participants, had listed basic biographical information concerning his educational and professional background. These selected biographical data were accessible to me and became the base on which I chose Martin for the interview. My choice of this platform for contacting Martin inadvertently led to my addressing primarily as a professional, even though I did not explicitly state this while contacting him. Despite the very informal nature of contact we established during our next email exchanges, the professional aspect stayed present even during the interview, since Martin tended to present himself in terms of his educational and professional career.

We also managed to establish close contact because we both belong to the same generation. This eased the informal nature of contact between us and was also the basis for our similar experiences and perceptions of changes in the Czech society over the course of time. Nevertheless, as for example his

---

tures which stress the uniqueness of the person's biographical path and confirm their position within society. Among these features are an emphasis on exceptionality, uniqueness of one's own biographical path, and the impossibility of planning ahead in advance (Liebold 2009, p. 60). However, what distinguishes Martin from how elite businesspeople, who Martin perceives as an important group of reference, present themselves is his family background. Elite businesspeople, so Liebold, tend to highlight the higher social status of their families which serves them as an important resource and reference for their own position. I will come to this distinction and its impact on the biographical positioning of Martin in detail later on.

comment concerning the outset of the revolution in 1989 indicates, the collective memory which influenced the perception of particular historical events differed regionally. Martin took time to explain to me in more detail the situation in North Bohemia and its distinction to other regions, assuming that since I am from a different geographical area in the Czech Republic, I might be missing this information in order to fully understand the meaning of his narration. To emphasize the specificity of his region, Martin gave lots of examples of German words which had found their way into everyday use in the spoken language. He distinguished this from other regions in the Czech Republic, where German words are not as commonly used as in the border regions.

The fact that he was from a different region also became visible during his narration concerning his studies. He described to me in detail his life in the halls of residence during his studies and distinguished himself from people who did not have this experience due to the proximity of their home town to the university. Living in a town other than his home town was an important experience for Martin and a source of further development. Despite these differences in our university careers, for Martin it was important that I myself had a university degree. He often stressed that people who did not have any experience with finance or more generally with university studies would not be able to understand his life story and his actual positioning. Belonging to a similar social class thus enabled Martin to present his story the way he did.

The analysis of the interview revealed that gender played an important role. Gender had an impact on the interview situation and the way the narration developed. While I usually met the female interviewees in a café or in their homes, the male interviewees mostly chose a restaurant or their office for the interview. The atmosphere in the Czech restaurant in which I met Martin had a particular influence on our conversation, as it became the transnational space where Czech was, among other languages, spoken and regional Czech food and drinks served. This atmosphere made it possible for us to transcend spaces and switch among cultural codes, the meaning of which we both understood. It was striking that, possibly as prompted by the nature of the place in which we were sitting, Martin often referred back to situations that had taken place in his local pub in Most. In his narration, most of the customers in the pubs were men, just like the people in his sports club and later in his job. Thus, gender not only shaped the interview situation but also the way in which Martin presented his story in which the "masculine order" dominated.

6.3.2 Martin's migration and social pathways

Born in the border regions

Martin's hometown plays an extraordinary role in his life. It features at the very beginning of his narration and appears repeatedly in various contexts throughout his story. At the very beginning, Martin describes his hometown as he remembers it from his childhood in the following way:

M: Yes! Most was not really nice. Um it was (1) actually it was, I was born during the time of communism, (laughing) [I: Hmm] Yes and it was just the time in which there was always smog, especially right in Most. I still remember that we often had inversion holidays, for example a day or two [I: aha], that we didn't go normally to school because there was an atmospheric temperature inversion. Sometimes there was a trip we went on- (1) there are mountains in the vicinity, it is interesting. Quasi Krušné Hory[48], which is near the border to Germany. So we always went up to that place, yes instead of school we went with our teachers (cleaning his throat) to those mountains. One could see the industrial pollution there, how it is spread across the valley like a pancake, yes, as something quite black, yes, or- Hm! (Martin, p. 1, l. 29-38)

To describe the specificity of his town, Martin goes back in time to his childhood, to the time of communism. He uses the term "communism" as a shortcut for his description of the local atmosphere and as an explanation for the "nastiness" of the town. After the Second World War and the takeover by the communist regime in 1948, Most changed considerably. North Bohemia, which after the events of the Second World War lost a significant proportion of its German speaking inhabitants, changed into an area of heavy industry. Some parts of town were demolished and rebuilt into large housing estates in order to provide accommodation for newcomers arriving to work for the most part in the industry sector. Smog, which was a side effect of the growing industrialization of the area, is an important topic for Martin. In his narration he describes how everyday "normality" was disrupted because of the polluted environment. Interruptions, such as inversion holidays at school, became an inevitable part of everyday life and his everyday routine. Martin describes the smog burdening the city through his trips to the mountains. From the top of them, he could from a distance observe the city and the smog spread over it. Furthermore, the height of the mountains enabled him to look around, dissociate himself from the city and its everyday life and develop new ideas. These altered positions and perspectives, metaphorically described by Martin's view from the mountains, are an important topic for Martin. He develops it further later on when speaking about his town and his status within different locations in the context of migration.

---

48   The mountainous area in North Bohemia.

For Martin, Most was not only a town affected by smog which disabled "normal" life. It was also place with historical significance, as Martin outlines in the following excerpt.

M: And it is actually, it is quite interesting, maybe only a few people know about it but in eighty nine so to speak on the seventeenth of November49, [I: Hmm] it actually all began in Most! All of this. It is so to speak officially confirmed, just that only a few people know about it, but (breathing) it was sometime at the beginning of November, first there were mass protests. They were not students, of course. But people who were protesting against the environment in Most, against these atmospheric temperature inversions. And these protests were already quite extensive. And – my parents told me and then I also heard it a couple of times on television, they were also speaking about it, that these were the first massive protests so to speak. (Martin, p. 2, l. 38-48)

Martin legitimises the fact that the events of the revolution started in Most by giving testimony of what his parents said, as well as quoting the authority of television. While his parents passed on to Martin the local narrative of the events of the revolution, television, which broadcast to the whole of the Czech Republic, reaffirms the validity of the narrative countrywide. Contrary to the collective memory according to which the revolution was initiated by students and centred on Prague, Martin acknowledges that local custom identifies the initiators of the societal changes as workers protesting against pollution. The town thus becomes an originator of wider societal changes. Workers and inhabitants of the town – to which Martin and his family also belong – are not only presented as mere victims of industrialisation, but above all as active contributors to social change.

Besides the industrial character of the region, there is one more feature which Martin names as being important: the proximity of the border to Germany. The proximity of the border becomes tangible not only when watching it from the nearby mountains but also when Martin describes everyday reality in his home town, where the Czech and German language coexist next to one another. Martin illustrates the Czech-German interconnections by means of his family history. One of his grandmothers was sent to Germany during the Second World War for the purpose of re-education after her mother was taken to a concentration camp. His grandmother on the other side of the family was of German origin and came to Most during the Second World War to join her husband whom she had met during his period of forced labor in Germany. The intertwined Czech-German history makes this region different from others, as the following section illustrates.

---

49 17th November 1989 is the date which is perceived as the beginning of the "Velvet Revolution". Wider protests against the government and the political system developed from student action devoted initially to the 50th anniversary of the death of Jan Zapletal, who was killed during anti-Nazi demonstrations in Prague in November 1939, leading to the closure of universities and arrests of thousands of students.

M: Yes in Sudetenland it is like this very often, yes. There are so many of these mixed marriages and I doubt that you ever experienced in Prague that for example two elderly people spoke to each other in German. Even though they were both Czech.

I: No, I didn't.

M: Yes. I remember it well. These elderly people had at that time all learnt German at school, so they simply spoke to each other, they were Czechs and they spoke German to one another for example. Or Czech woman always spoke German with their German husbands. Just, the elderly spoke to one another like this. Well, these elderly people are not alive any more, they have nearly all died already. And – it was really, it was very often. I remember that on the streets they often spoke to one another in German. And it was really often! My grandma also never learned – I don't know, yes, maybe sixty, no, well. She lived in the Czech Republic for fifty years and she never learned to speak Czech brilliantly. When she spoke, you just knew that she was not, that she was basically German. Or not that she was German, but just, the accent was there a bit and some pronunciation and that you somehow, yes? I don't know. She always for example – she couldn't pronounce, she couldn't pronounce 'ch' at the beginning of the word for example, yes, she always said for example 'kchleba', yes, not simply 'chleba'', yes, 'kchleba' (both of us are laughing). Or for example some declination, yeah, no! (Martin, p. 27, l. 844-864)

Martin grew up in a bilingual environment. The German language was present not only on the streets, but also at home. Martin gives in his narrative numerous examples of German expressions that became an everyday unquestioned part of the spoken language within his family. He did not discover the origin and meaning of these expressions until later on when he heard them in spoken German while living in Germany. Nevertheless, the section above also indicates that the language practices so typical for this area are about to change. The people who used to speak Czech and German equally belong to the previous generation which is about to disappear. Martin nonetheless considers himself to be part of the generation which still experienced the bilinguality of the area.

The lingual and cultural settings of the area had an impact on Martin's adolescence and, to some extent, on his further biographical development. The everyday presence of German language and its use within his family led Martin to choose German as his first foreign language. His second language behind German was English. His knowledge of German and familiarity with the German culture influenced Martin's decisions in respect of migration later on: it made it possible for him to apply for a seasonal job in the canning factory in Germany and, later on, to establish closer contacts with one of his bosses who arranged the job in Düsseldorf for him. Nevertheless, the lingual and cultural settings in Most not only impacted Martin's biography because of his choice of language. Living in an area in which two languages and different cultural practices were a part of everyday life made it possible for Martin to develop the ability to "translate" and "shift" from one cultural code to another, from one language to another. This ability of "translating and shifting" plays an important role in his educational and professional progression and is also at the core of his ability to integrate the different cultural and social settings in which he operates during his lifetime. From this perspective, for Martin Most does not only represent a town which is linked to the working class and burdened by a polluted environment. Instead, its multicultural character means that it also becomes a resource that Martin can tap into with regard to his later steps.

Moving school and social locations

After describing the city and its specificities, Martin narrates his pathway through the various educational institutions. He concentrates on the moves from one institution to another rather than on the description of events taking place within respective schools. In this manner he describes his social mobility, which was not planned a priori and which retrospectively appears to him as surprising and unexpected. Martin's social mobility, pictured step by step by his description of his move from one educational institution and social location to the next, was not a family project. Martin's family, which was predominantly situated in the workers' milieu, lacked any experience with studying and was unable to pass on the necessary knowledge of education and career progression. Nevertheless, Martin did not stay bound only to his family's knowledge and resources. He drew inspiration from peers and acquaintances he came into contact with while changing places and social locations.

Martin describes his move from one primary school to another as the first important step in his career.

M: Well and I don't know. Then I went to primary school, (1) two years and then, then I went to a primary school with enlarged language classes, from the third, from the third class. (1) It is actually, when one looks back, so these steps, they were – at that time maybe not so important, but then it turns out that these circumstances are sort of decisive, yes, for all – for all – for all life, yes. [I: Hmm] Because when I see for example (1) because where I went to primary school, so it was also – I lived sort of on the periphery, actually sort of in the village which was right beside the town, yes, you know, it was not independent, it was part of the town [I: Hmm] (clearing his throat) and it was also a village. And above it (clearing his throat) there was a big housing estate where the town actually began, so there was this school. And so and so such housing estate schools, where as it were, yes? Um, there were, I don't know. Now – at that time I was not aware of it. But now I see these people with whom I went to school at that time, yes, when I now look back at what has become of them, of some of them, yes. (1) It is really terrifying. [I: Hmm] (Martin, p. 2, l. 49-63)

Martin retrospectively describes his move from one primary school to another as being one of the most decisive but nonetheless unintentional moments. For him this step marks the beginning of the metamorphosis of his biography which is accentuated by extensive reflections and changes of view which stand out not only in this section but throughout all Martin's narration.

226

To explain the changes which went hand in hand with the school move, Martin concentrates on describing of locality in which the school was situated. The term "housing estate", which is not further clarified, is contrast with the „village" where he spent his childhood.[50] It differs not only in architectural style but possibly also in the social background of the inhabitants, as it is the place often associated with lower social classes and limited chances and possibilities of development because of its cheap rent and its location on the periphery of the city. Martin illustrates the structural barriers connected to this specific location by means of his schoolmates with whom he went to school and who developed in a different way from him. Retrospectively, he sees the success of his social mobility as being not primarily because he moved to a school that provided better education, but because he got the chance to leave the location for some other place. Moving location enabled him to distance himself from the district in which he grew up. Furthermore, it allowed him to develop new perspectives on his future as well as on his past life.

The impulse to switch schools initially came from his teacher who "said once that 'well there is the possibility of going there!'" (Martin, p. 4, l. 109-110). She was the one who offered him new perspectives and possibilities, which he decided to follow. However, his moving schools was also possible because of his parents, who supported him, but still let him chose which school he wanted to attend. He himself justifies the move by the fact that a girl he liked was about to change schools. He thus decided to follow. His moving schools stands out in this light as an unintentional practice based on the individual rather than a collective or family decision.

The next turn of events in his biography is described by Martin as his progression from primary school to secondary school.

M: Well and then I went (breathing out) to secondary school, (1) I actually went to business college. (1) It was actually, it was also interesting that (1) about um: or lots of people from primary school went there, but somehow I went badly, I don't know, I don't remember, but in fact I didn't end up – or not – of course I was admitted, but there were about five classes and they didn't put me in the class in which ninety percent of people who had gone there from my primary school were. They were in some other class. I ended up sort of (1) in the other class where I didn't know anyone from before and at that time I was really, really angry, yes, that I would sort of continue with my friends who I, and so I – of course there was a new class, new timetables, so with those people I didn't have such good- er such regular contact. [I: Hmm](1) And it is also. Because I have said to myself that if they had at that time put me in that class, I would have developed completely differently. (Martin, p. 4-5, 128-143)

---

50 From Martin's description it is possible to induce that the "housing estate" belongs to one of the products of socialist architecture constructed from the sixties onwards and characterized by a uniformity of panel houses, offering a large number of flats initially conceived for industry workers and their families.

In this section Martin again concentrates on his move from one institution to the next rather than on describing his pathway through the particular institutions. He pictures the way in which he happened to join a different group of people than he had planned, an event which, according to him, had a decisive impact on his further biography. Martin does not give reasons why he decided to go to business college. He simply states that most of his schoolmates went there. His group of former schoolmates, just like his new class at secondary school to which he was allocated by chance, took on the role of a "guide" and became the source of inspiration for Martin concerning his social mobility. Martin did not plan his progression through the educational institutions in advance. Rather, he developed his next steps along the way, taking as a role model and "guide" his "new" social locations. In this way, Martin let himself be guided by his peers and people who surrounded him all the way up until university.

After graduation from business college, Martin applied to diverse universities all around the Czech Republic and, finally, got in to study at the University of Economics in Prague. Martin explains it like this:

M: And: (1) many of us from secondary school didn't take the examinations there, because the University of Economics was a bit more difficult, or it was seen as more difficult and (1) I didn't think that I would be admitted there. I was sort of – well, when somehow one doesn't have this in the family, sort of (1) if one doesn't have anyone in the family who would for example study, or who would have studied at university, so now I retrospectively see that it was a kind of handicap for me in the sense that [I: Hmm] (1) one doesn't know how things work at university, um: concerning the entrance examination or or [I: Hmm] or or that one can also think the course over at university, yes. [I: Hmm] For example these things like – a semester abroad and yes? [I: Hmm] This simply (1) and I was actually, it was not only my family, right, but in the village there was (breathing out) there was sort of no one from the people I knew who would study at university. And even in Prague! (Martin, p. 5, l. 148-160)

While talking about his progression to university, Martin also mentions his group of former schoolmates. He depicts, as he has done in previous instances in which he changed school, the process of leaving one community and social location for another. However, this process of moving was more difficult for Martin because of his family background. It is clear from Martin's line of reasoning that he does not base his social mobility and his achievements on his family's resources. On the contrary, his family, which was from a working class milieu and was missing the "manual" on how to progress through the educational system, was unable to transfer any family knowledge or patterns of possible action to him, and was therefore no longer a "role model" for him in this respect. In this light, the new social locations became increasingly of importance, as they took on the role of the "guide" through social mobility, which was missing in Martin's family and Martin's surroundings. It is also interesting to note Martin's statement that "now I retrospectively see that it (his family background, comment A.G.) was kind of a

228

handicap for me", which shows that Martin's perception of social classes and positioning shifted with time. The act of belonging to a certain social class was not apparent to him before; however, it became apparent during his biographical progression in comparison with others and their lives.

By pointing to the possible disadvantages concerning his family background, he indirectly positions himself as someone who distinguishes himself from his family and the social locations of his hometown, which he transcended. He stands out as someone who managed to overcome the boundaries of social classes.

Studying and living in Prague

After Martin successfully passed the entrance exams to various fields of study at a number of universities all around the Czech Republic, he decided to join the University of Economics in Prague. He decided on that University not only because of its prestige, but also because of its location in the centre of Prague, which became particularly important for Martin.

He was commuting between Most and Prague in the first months of his studies because he did not get a room in the student halls of residence. Then, however, a room became available and by chance he moved to one of the most renowned halls of residence in Prague. Martin describes how he was the only freshman among all the other students living in that residence. Over the next few years Martin lived in several halls of residence before moving into a flat in one of the housing estates on the periphery of the city with some friends when he was in the fourth year. Step by step he moved from being a commuter and resident of temporary dormitories to becoming a relatively permanent resident of the city.

In Martin's story there are certain discrepancies concerning his studies. While in the main narration he describes school as not being very difficult, picturing himself as someone who did not have to study much during his education, later in the narration he brings up the difficulties he had at the beginning. He describes the doubts he had concerning his knowledge and depicts his efforts to learn topics which until then had been new to him. The difficulties at the beginning were acerbated by the fact that he did not know many people in Prague with whom he could exchange views. There were only a few people from his former college who went to the same university in Prague as Martin. Most of them ended up in other cities or did not take up any further studies. These circumstances led Martin to establish new contacts which eventually helped him to enter new social spheres and opened up new possibilities for his future career.

Martin compares his new field of possibilities resulting from living and being in the capital city with those of his former schoolmates who studied in different towns and cities in the Czech Republic. Migration to Prague, one of the economic and cultural centres of the Czech Republic, thus becomes particularly important, as illustrated by the following excerpt:

M: Nevertheless, all these companies are in Prague. When one doesn't have these contacts in Prague, when one doesn't reside in Prague, doesn't live in Prague, so I think that it is much higher added value than only the school itself, yeah. (Martin, p. 7, l. 205-207)

Life in Prague opened up new possibilities for him as he had the chance aside from his studies to do various kind of jobs, thereby joining the network in which job opportunities were procured. Furthermore, living in Prague enabled him to "individualise" himself from his parental home and from the city in which he had grown up. Although migration to Prague was a move within the same country and thus within one legal and cultural framework, for Martin it represented all a shift between different social locations, offering new fields of possibility. In this context, migration to Prague became an important step in his social mobility and in his further migration.

First border crossings

In the second year of his studies, Martin decided to spend the summer vacation working in a canning factory in Germany. This job has been arranged through an agency in Prague specialising in work and travel programs. Martin explains that he did not want to go straight to the USA, which was the most common destination of these programs, but rather to first try something that was closer and more familiar. For this reason, he chose Germany. At first, he wanted to go to abroad together with a friend. However, although they applied in the same way, only Martin got a work permit and was invited to go. Once again Martin stresses the role of luck and the exceptionality of his life path.

Martin spent three months working in the canning factory. When recounting his job, he again depicts the role played by luck. While others got a job on the production line and had to stand there all day and sort the fruit that passed by, he drove the trolley and transported the final products. His job was thus less monotonous and not as dirty. During this time, Martin lived in a dormitory with other men. They were from Ireland and Canada and, as Martin adds,

M: they were the only ones from Western Europe. Otherwise there were only Czechs, Slovaks, maybe some Russians, I don't know. Maybe some Russians, yeah. [...] For them it was more, you know. We were there to earn some money and for them it was more you know, to have a look and to have some fun, yeah. (Martin, p. 40, l. 1270-1276)

At that time, this job was relatively well paid compared with the student jobs he had had during his studies in Prague. Martin considers himself part of the group of workers from "Eastern Europe", for whom the motivation for working in the factory was predominantly the income. The hierarchical division

230

between East and West, which he construes according to belonging to one of these categories based on nationality, is also the division between different economic conditions and resources accessible to individuals.

Nevertheless, Martin spent his time in Germany not only earning money but also studying the language.

M: I remember when I went there, how was it. I didn't like German so much. And there I mean I mean in Germany it was for two or three months, I was buying Bild every day and I read it intensively. And I got so much better in German. So much. Especially concerning the vocabulary. And then at university I remember that in that group, you know. We always had some word and now everyone tried to (1) and I always knew it. (Martin, p. 41, l. 1302-1309)

This intensive period of self-study of German helped him later on at university where he became, so he says, one of the best in his class. Furthermore, this initial experience of living abroad had an impact on his willingness to migrate later on, first to the USA and later on to Germany again.

Martin spent the next summer holidays in the USA. He was working in a bakery at an amusement park. In describing his job, he again emphasizes the role of luck concerning the nature of his work as well as the cooperation with his colleagues. When he returned the following year, he had already been promoted and moved from the position of assistant to the position of a supervisor. Martin reflects on the flexible working conditions in the amusement park and in the USA in general. According to him, Americans working in that type of amusement park had seldom reached some higher level of education. They lived in peripheral areas and lacked the resources which would enable them to study and to cross the boundaries of their social class. Martin implicitly positions himself as the opposite of them, as someone who managed to study and to cross the borders of social class, which became possible not only because of luck and his own performance, but also because of the social frameworks enabling upwards social mobility in the context of the Czech Republic. Class belonging, which he highlights not only in his life path but also in comparison with people in his surroundings, refers to his pathway through different spheres of social class and his expertise on the relevant topic.

From sweeping streets to a job in the office

M: Well and when I came back from America, it was, it was I think, when was it. It was when I entered the fourth year of my studies. (1) Before during my studies I had one – (1) it was – or like this. I had many many different jobs. I for example, it is really paradoxical which different jobs I had. During my studies I for example, well, before I went to university, it was actually after the entrance exams, so I (1) so I had a job digging in the canalization. (Martin, p. 11, l. 329-336)

Before Martin narrates the events which led him to his office job after his placements in the USA, he again comes back to narrate his experience of diverse jobs. He lists the jobs he did in chronological order: from the canalization works through sweeping the streets to his first job in the office. He thereby presents his work history as a progression from the working class milieu to a "white collar job" in the office. Similarly, as when describing his schooling, Martin pays attention to the description of work relationships and the position of people who regularly carry out these jobs.

Martin took a job on a construction site before he entered university in order to earn some money for his studies. He describes the workload in detail and evaluates this job as hard and dangerous. Due to time and money saving efforts of most companies, safety measures were not sufficiently fulfilled. Therefore, workers hired to carry out jobs of this nature often had an insecure legal status and worked in precarious conditions. Because of this experience, Martin considers himself an expert in this field.

During his studies in Prague, Martin worked as street sweeper on night shifts together with a friend of his. Martin describes the workload and its organization in detail and emphasizes that there were mostly homeless people or people from the lowest social strata working in professions such as these. Besides Martin and his friend there were also several other young people, students, who enjoyed relatively high wages in comparison with other student jobs in Prague. Although Martin acknowledges that he worked shifts together with "homeless people", who did exactly the same jobs, he always stresses his student status as distinguishing him from the others. In contrast to his previous job in the canalization building, here Martin uses his student status to confirm his higher social position and the temporary nature of this kind of work. Even though he is working in a position which is barely considered socially acceptable and which is connected to the lowest social status, he already thinks like someone who does not belong to this social field but who has moved up the social ladder.

A few years into his studies Martin decided that it would be good to try and get a job which corresponded to his qualifications. He therefore sent emails to diverse companies. He offered to work for those companies for free, stating that his primary aim was not to earn money but rather to gain experience of working in the field of his studies. One company contacted him and offered him a paid internship. Through this short period of practical work experience, which he left after a few months due to his travels to the USA, he gained access to the circle of accounting and counseling firms. He remained in this sector after his return from the USA.

Martin devotes the longest part of his narration to how he obtained the job in finances after he returned from the USA; this shows the relevance of this event for his biography. Martin chose to apply three of four of the most prestigious companies in his field in the Czech Republic and was admitted,

232

after a long assessment process, as an intern to one of them. When Martin speaks of the assessment center process, he emphasizes the role played by luck as well as indirectly stressing the role of his own performance, as the following sequence shows.

M: Well and it was at ABC Company, there were assessment centers and as is usual in these companies, you have several rounds. And here the next coincidence occurred. I had an interview, it was already my third and it was already with the person from the department I would be working in. (1) We had at that time at university - I took a course in which we dealt with some accounting specificities concerning mergers. Concerning mergers. Accounting practices for mergers yes. These are kind of more difficult and: (1) so I had an interview with this person and: accounting practices for mergers are based on certain standards. International standards. You have some numbers somewhere and – it does not matter. And so he spoke to me and said "well and we work on such and such a project and we do so according to this standard." And now he said the number of that standard, (1) one normally does not know it. That – well, ok. One does not know it at all. (1) And so I said, he said the number of standard and I said: "Yes! Mergers. Well, ok." And his eyes started to shine [I: (laughing)] yes and he said: "Well, you – I didn't -, you know everything!" "Well" "Excellent, excellent!" [I: (laughing)] (laughing) And it was only a paradoxical coincidence. That I had taken that course. [I: Aha] At university. And that I knew these standard numbers and well otherwise I would not have known it of course. (Martin, p. 15, l. 450-467)

The interplay of coincidences and Martin's own performance and knowledge extends throughout his entire narration. He presents himself as an active player who is able to strategically use the resources and accessible knowledge in order to achieve his goals. However, the role of coincidences in his narration is crucial, as he always comes back to these unexpected moments and constructs his narration along this theme.

Martin got the position as an intern at ABC Company and worked there during the final year of his studies. When he successfully graduated, he received an offer to transfer as an intern to Düsseldorf, Germany, where he has continued to work as a regular employee until the present day.

In his narration, Martin presents himself not only as an expert in his field of studies, on economics, but also in other professions that span the entire social spectrum. He presents himself as a "border crosser" of social classes. He has moved through different social spheres and he uses the experiences acquired in different jobs and social locations as a resource for his next steps. He evaluates his jobs in the canalization building and sweeping the streets as follows:

M: Well I did not talk about this so much (laughing) [I: (Laughing)], well maybe a bit for fun. (1) But I think it is good. That one um: tries different jobs like these. That one does not only live um: when one already has some income um: that one can still imagine what work looks like from another perspective. (Martin, p. 13, l. 392-397)

Martin's social mobility and achievements become even more apparent when considered in light of his pathway through the various different jobs.

From Prague to Düsseldorf: positioning himself in transnational spaces

At the time Martin was finishing his studies, he was considering going to one of the universities in the USA to complete an MBA. This option was also offered by the University of Economics in Prague. Martin applied to the USA and after a while received an answer which stated that one place was vacant and that since he was on the waiting list he could have the scholarship. Nevertheless, Martin decided to stay in Prague.

M: And: then I decided that I would stay in this in this (clearing his throat) in this job in Prague, (1) and the next coincidence, the next big coincidence was that my boss there, one of my bosses boss was German, from Düsseldorf, who was in Prague for an exchange for about two years, [I: hm] (1) or for him it wasn't exactly an exchange, it was more about – (1) Germans were a bit further in some aspects of work, concerning some products [I: hm] and they sort of went to Eastern Europe to bring us some knowledge (1) from the big world, from the West (1). So he was in Prague and I worked a lot with him because after all at that time O spoke a bit of German, (1) German had been my other main language all my life, only seconded by English, because (1) as I am from Most, which is in Sudetenland, [I: hm] so there nearly everyone -, my grandma is German, [I: hm] yes, so, there are – or nearly everyone has in their family in some way (1) some German, yes. [I: hm] So German was so to say – (1) Because we had a choice of first foreign language, then at college there was not much German, or well yes there was some, but then at university I didn't have it much somehow, I don't know, two semesters (1) but nevertheless I could speak German, so I could speak to him in German too, yes, or English, and sometimes we phoned one another, from time to time (1) well and (1) at the time I was about to finish my studies, it was 2008, he called me and told me that he would give me the possibility of going to Düsseldorf through his connections, for a half year to be there as a sort of intern, yes. (Martin, p. 15, l. 534-554)

Martin's narration can also be read as a sequence of important coincidences which influenced his life. The story of his migration to Germany is part of this chain of coincidental but relevant events contributing to Martin's current status. Nevertheless, although Martin explains his move to Germany as a coincidence, it is strongly influenced by Martin's own activity and the use of resources, such as language, in order to enlarge his social network.

The significant person in his story is his former boss. It was due to Martin's knowledge of German, as he states, that he established closer contact with him. To explain and justify his knowledge of German, Martin recalls his hometown and the area in which he grew up. The multicultural and multilingual character of the place had an impact not only on his choice of foreign language at primary and secondary school but it also influenced Martin's attitude towards other cultural circumstances. As he points out, the German culture was not unfamiliar to him and was even part of his own family history. Through his depiction of his hometown and the specific area in which he grew up he demonstrates the transnational links which are firmly embedded in his family history and in historical events connected to his hometown. These links, which he describes as exceptional, mobilize Martin in seeking contact with his boss and using them as a resource for furthering his career. While reconstructing his links to the German language and culture, he also positions himself in a new way in the emerging transnational spaces between Germany and the Czech Republic, which increasingly gain in importance for him.

His former boss, who himself has moved in an international setting, has international connections and networks which he can utilize for himself or for the benefit of others. He is pictured as the "bearer" of knowledge fluctuating from "West" to "East". With his slightly ironic comment Martin reflects on the unequal exchange of knowledge, information and technology in establishing transnational spaces in the world of finances in which knowledge and products move in one direction from West to East. Both categories, which are characterized by different characteristics such as big (and developed) on the one hand and small (and outdated) on the other hand, are in an asymmetrical and hierarchical relationship to one another. This unequal division of power also describes the position of Martin and his relationship with his boss.

His boss is the person who gives Martin the possibility of migrating and enables him, by means of his existing international network, to enter the international finance scene, which is of importance for Martin's future career. He is also the person who makes the decisions regarding the status and time limits of Martin's stay in Düsseldorf. And again it is that same boss who gives Martin the chance some months later to stay in Düsseldorf not only as an intern, but to enter regular employment in a reputable company specialising in accounting and business counselling.

As Martin describes it, his beginnings as an intern in Düsseldorf were not easy for him. He did not know anyone and at first had problems with the language and finding a place to live. When his former boss from Prague, who in the meantime had returned to Düsseldorf, offered him some work experience in Düsseldorf, Martin agreed since he did not have any liabilities or relations back in the Czech Republic and was therefore free to go. Thus his plans to return after a few months to Prague and to enter regular employment there changed.

M: Well and I managed (1) or I was lucky again I don't know that with these people I work with, well I don't work with him as we thought at the beginning, hardly at all. (1) I work with other people who also – that I had a relatively good start. (1) Because normally one – normally I wouldn't have had a chance of getting here without these – without him yes. Because I didn't study in Germany, yes, which is really, and this job is a really really good job for Germans too. When they finish university there it really is a very good job. So without having been to university in Germany plus the German language -, even though German is our official language at work! Although it is true that the outcomes are often in English, that's true. But still. Your colleagues are mostly Germans. [...] Well so I managed to have a good start and I think I made a good impression. (1) Well, then it was easier. So I had a relatively good position, or a really good position. But again, it was all down to luck that I got here with the help of this German guy, otherwise -. (Martin, p. 18-19, l. 576-594)

Martin's former boss plays the role of a gatekeeper for Martin. He arranges and establishes contacts for him in Düsseldorf and, although they do not work together as planned, his former boss still plays a crucial role for him. Martin compares his career path, which he describes as "exceptional", to the path of his colleagues. The "normal" way of reaching this position would, so Martin reflects, be through respective studies in Germany. Other routes to attaining job positions like Martin's are perceived as unusual. Martin refers to established career paths existing within a national framework. Not only did Martin not study in Germany, the German language was not his mother tongue either. Among his coworkers who are predominantly German, he is considered as an exceptional case for two reasons: both as a "foreigner" and as someone who has completed his education in some other country. Martin's success only became possible because of his established social network. By emphasizing the role played by luck, Martin refers to structural barriers based on nationality, one's place of study (and class, as I will show later) which he would not have had the chance to cross had it not been for his connections.

His astonishment of getting to the position in which he currently finds himself is also expressed in the following section.

M: And often for example, when we have some – it is really interesting. (1) Sometimes I am thinking when I sit somewhere at some meeting for example, or – (clearing his throat) only with some German – there are only Germans and now erm there is some big company and now we are there as consultants and so (1) now you for example have the director of the company there and then some financial directors and (1) now for example a partner of ours and so, and now I am there sitting at the table for example, so I am – I always say to myself, I look back and I reflect on my life and it happened that I got here to this room! Yes! Because it is absolutely (breathing in) or I say to myself that it is totally (1) it could never happen like this a second time. (Martin, p. 19, l. 594-602)

Martin's current position is for him the peak of his career up until now. Once again he states and shows by referencing said meeting that his pathway is unexpected and exceptional for him. His colleagues figure in his description as reference persons. They are introduced through their positions and their nationality. Once again, he positions himself as the exception, getting to the meeting room by means of different career paths than the others.

In his narration, Martin is still searching for explanations to clarify his past life and changes in status. Just like his past, his visions concerning his future are unclear, unexpected and not plannable. He might return to the Czech Republic, stay in Germany or go to some other country. After all, as he mentions in another part of the interview, "Düsseldorf is not New York". His pathway thus may develop further within the transnational finance scene which he has entered by means of his migration and transnational networks.

Social mobility: being part of but not belonging to?

M: Well and I always- (1) or like this! When I then for example come home, (1) so I go for example to Prague, because I have the most friends in Prague. [I: hmm] But these are the people with whom I studied. [I: hm m] (1) It is sort of again a bit different sort of people when I come home yes. These are again two different worlds. There are simply, when I am in Prague with these friends, so there simply everyone knows what I am doing and that I can simply speak about it because – yes! Well, it is not so much about that people there are dumb or so, yeah. [I: hmm] Of course not, yeah. [I: hmm] But it is simply so specific in this world of finances that simply (1) it – it is not possible to explain it to people who have never had anything to do with finances or with university. It is simply – incomprehensible to them, yeah. I always only say well I am doing this and that and then they say well, he is doing this and that. (laughing) [I: (laughing)] (Martin, p. 20, l. 609-621)

Düsseldorf, Prague and Most represent three different places for Martin among which he moves and which each have a different meaning for him. While Düsseldorf and Prague are very much connected with his studies and work, Most is connected with his family, football club and friends from childhood. These locations – or worlds, as Martin calls them – are connected with Martin's different class statuses.

In his narration, Martin often compares the lives of people in Most with his own. While the lives of his peers who stayed in his hometown developed in an expected and routine way, he managed, despite his family background, to leave the town and to work his way up. While transcending social worlds, Martin alienated himself from the local community.

M: And actually when I for example come home so actually no one knows exactly what I am doing. [I: Hmm] Because I cannot explain it exactly. These are things which cannot be explained properly. [I: Hmm] Or I do not know. It is actually – when I would actually – when I come home, so I go for example to our local pub where I meet the people with whom I grew up, we played football for example and it is actually, concerning common topics, yes, for example. It is paradoxical that – apart from local topics, such as what happened to someone, so, but such general topics such as what one says I don't know. Politics for example, there's no way! Or topics like this. (laughing) It is really absolutely different, a different world. (Martin, p. 3, l. 77-85)

Martin still takes part in the activities of the local community. He visits the pubs, plays football for the local team and meets friends. However, he also positions himself as someone who has developed differently from the people with whom he grew up. On the one hand, he is confronted with the lack of understanding concerning his way of life and his work, since the "world of finances", which has now become part of his life, is not accessible to his family and to his peers back in Most. On the other hand, he is alienated from his peers and acquaintances due to his experiences and knowledge. The "worlds" or social locations, between which he moves, have for him become clearly divided, impervious, and firmly connected to geographical spaces. By referring to the differences, Martin confirms and re-establishes the social classes and affirms his social mobility.

When he moved to Prague, his social network changed considerably. This new group of people to which he established contact due to his studies and diverse jobs in Prague serve as the counterpart to his circle of friends in Most. His newly established social network possesses similar experiences and knowledge to him. He can therefore talk with his colleagues and acquaintances back in Prague about his current job in Düsseldorf and about the events taking part in the world of finances. However, the people whom Martin considers to be in his social circles in Prague also distinguish themselves from Martin in respect of their social background.

M: When I look (1) where I am now or where I work now, (1) where I worked for example in Prague, so there in these companies one mostly meets (clearing his throat) one often meets people (breathing in) erm: who have so to speak erm: different erm: so to speak a different background, you know. [I: Hmm hmm] That these are mostly people (clearing his throat) or children from families – I don't want to say from rich families, yeah! But these are a bit different so to speak, different different different circles and actually in our family or not only in my direct family but also with regard to uncles or aunts, cousins, so there nobody has been to university. Absolutely nobody. I am actually the only one (laughing) who has been to university, so. (Martin, p. 2-3, l. 63-73)

Martin not only figures as an exception in his hometown, he also presents himself as an exception with regard to his life path and family background in comparison with people he met at university and in his job. The new "social world" which Martin entered after migrating to Prague and starting his studies is pictured as a social space accessible exclusively to people of a similar class background. Class belonging and possibilities and expected life patterns connected with it are, so Martin observes, reproduced and reestablished in the intergenerational transmission of knowledge. In comparison with his new colleagues and friends who have built upon their family resources in order to develop their life path within the borders of their social class, Martin presents himself as someone who managed to cross from one "social world" into another. This for Martin the "entrance ticket" to the new social location was not his family, but his own performance and social networks which he acquired in the course of his life. Through his new social networks he also gained the knowledge to orientate himself and move within new social fields, resulting in new possibilities for action and development.

Martin describes a similar reproduction of social classes when speaking about the job he attained in Düsseldorf.

M: I see how it works in these investment banks, yeah. That there is sort of a closed circle of people, yeah. There are people who are sort of from the same cast yeah. Simply that – either (1) but it happens really seldom (1) either you get, I don't know. When you for example study in Princeton for example, yeah, a really super school in the USA [I: Hmm]. So you must be either extremely intelligent [I: Hmm] but really an extremely brainy man in order to get the scholarship. But really very good. (1) Or you pay for it, yeah. That means that you have the means (1) or your family has. Well and in these (1) relative – (1) I don't want to say a sect, yes, but in the circle of people in these schools, I speak here about finances, yes. So now everyone meets again in these investment companies, investment banks. [I: Hmm] These are very similar – very seldom does anyone get there by some absolutely different way. By luck maybe. (Martin, p. 21, l. 663-677)

In comparison with the "normal" career path leading to the respective job positions as described by Martin, Martin's career appears unexpected and to some extent not plannable. As he observes, these job positions are not open to everyone who has a suitable qualification, but instead are reserved for a certain group of people possessing similar resources. They follow established pathways leading from prestigious universities – accessible only to a specific group of people – to reputable positions. In this way, social classes are reproduced and reestablished. In comparison with his colleagues working in similar positions to his, Martin's biographical pathway once again appears to be an exception. While the path of others is pictured as a career pathway developing within the boundaries of class determined previously by family background, Martin positions himself as someone who crosses not only national borders but above all social class.

In his narration, Martin makes a great effort to explain his social mobility, which is closely connected with geographical mobility. In order to depict how he has passed through the social classes, Martin points out the differences between the social classes and reaffirms the hierarchical relationship between them. Class, presented as a closed circle or world, becomes a space which has an impact on one's possibilities for development and access to resources, being a space which is connected to a specific kind of knowledge.

As shown above, Martin identifies differences not only to his peers and family in Most, but also to his colleagues in Prague and Düsseldorf. He compares his individual career path to the path of others, taking place within the borders of one class. He reflects in his narration on established career paths linking his family's class background, possibilities of education and professional status. Furthermore, the career paths are construed as taking place within one national framework. The possibility of entering these paths or not depends to some extent on national belonging and the mechanisms of inclusion or exclusion connected to it. In comparison with "others", Martin gained access to the social classes not through his family background and existing career path, but due to his migration and transnational networks. While underlining the differences of social class in which he moves, he positions himself as a "border crosser" of social class rather than as belonging to one specific class with its clearly outlined borders.

6.3.3 Summary

The town and area of Martin's birth play an important role in his life. It is the first location Martin mentions in his narration and the place to which he often refers during his story. For Martin, it is a place connected with the working class milieu in which he grew up. The heavy industry which has dominated this area had an impact not only on everyday life, but also on the possibilities accessible to people living there. Martin illustrates this by way of the example of the polluted environment, which made everyday "normality" and regular impossible, and by way of the example of his former schoolmates who stayed in Most and developed differently than Martin did. Nevertheless, Most does not simply represent a place that is burdened by air pollution and limited options for development. It is also the place which because of its history and cultural background Martin uses as a resource for his further pathway. Being born in the border region influenced not only Martin's language skills, but also the ability to "translate" and "move" within different lingual and cultural spheres.

His moving from one primary school to another in a different part of town was the event which initiated the process of Martin's social mobility. His moving schools was not primarily significant because he ended up at a school which offered a better education, but rather because it enabled him to change location, integrate into another social group and to distance himself from the milieu in which he grew up. Moving location and social groups played an important role during his entire educational career. In the context of his social mobility, his move to Prague was decisive. As before, the move was important not only because he was admitted to university as the first of his family and acquaintances back in Most to do so, but because he moved to Prague, which in turn offered him new options. In the process of his social mobility Martin was not able to build on any family resources or family knowledge in order to plan his educational progression. Nevertheless, Martin learnt "on the job" from his peers and significant others how to orientate himself in the new fields and how to use the possibilities that opened up for him. One such possibility which opened up for him in Prague was the internship at one of the recognized companies specializing in finance and subsequently the possibility to transfer to Düsseldorf, Germany.

However, Martin's migration to Düsseldorf was preceded by several other migrations. They were important experiences for him which influenced his later willingness to migrate. The first important migration experience was the domestic move from Most to Prague. This move was a way for him to "individualize" himself from his parental home and the town in which he had grown up, and establish new social networks. Through his further seasonal migrations to Germany and to the USA he learned, besides the language, to orientate himself in the new surroundings. His frequent moves across the

240

border enabled him to enlarge the space of his possibilities over the borders of one national state. His previous migration experiences thus represent an important resource for him, which he actively mobilizes when establishing contact with his former boss and transferring to Düsseldorf later on.

Martin presents himself as someone who transcends social classes. In his narration, he concentrates on his moves between different social locations rather than on the description of particular locations. The "others", may it be his former schoolmates, family members or acquaintances back in Most or his new colleagues in Prague or Düsseldorf, serve as a mirror of his own biographical development and positioning. While "the others" to whom he compares himself in extensive argumentative passages throughout his entire story are pictured as individuals who stayed bound to the class they were born into, Martin stands out as the one who transcends the social classes. Because of his cross border experiences, his pathway is construed as unique, unrepeatable and exceptional. Martin's story reveals not only the possibilities one has of crossing the borders of social classes. It further reveals the social structure in which the classes are reproduced. Martin's difficulties in positioning himself within the classes he moves between are connected to the discourses and practices concerning the particular classes in both societies, Czech and German. In attaining his current job position Martin not only took a different career path from that of his colleagues, who studied at similar schools and had similar experiences. He was also unable to base his belonging to a respective class on his family and social background, as "the others" had been able to. Throughout his story Martin searches for a way to position himself across classes and places he moves between.

6.4 Barbora: a story of reorientation

The interview with Barbora was my eleventh interview. I conducted it about one and half years after my first interview with Lenka. When I met Barbora and listened to her story I was impressed by the way she talked about her new professional orientation after migration. Her interview came to my mind again and again and over time became of my central cases.

Barbora was born in 1977 in Teplice, a medium sized town situated in North Bohemia. She lived with her parents and her sister, who is seven years younger than her, on the outskirts of town close to nature. Her father worked his whole life first as a miner and then as a dispatcher in the mines. Her mother worked as an assistant in an old people's home. Barbora went to primary school and high school (Gymnasium) there. After graduation she went to Prague and to study. After finishing her engineering degree she decided to go to Germany to be with her husband.

Barbora's interview is one of those in which the biographical twist and professional reorientation considerably changes the individual's positioning in society. In contrast to Lenka's and Martin's biography, Barbora did not succeed in using the initial qualifications and knowledge acquired back in the Czech Republic. Migration meant a rupture not only because the social frames shifted but also because she could not continue with her initial career. Not until much later did she start to build up her career again from scratch in a very different field. Her story illustrates how reorientation can be used as a strategy for emancipation and positioning oneself in a new way in society. Furthermore, it shows how migration and gender regimes shape biographical and career pathways.

6.4.1   Interview setting and biographical presentation

Context of the interview

We came into conversation while sitting beside one another in a café in the centre of Frankfurt. We had both come from the same event where Czech language courses for children had been introduced and discussed. I had been to the event with two friends of mine who had small children. The event, which was the first of its kind in Frankfurt, was attended by more people than expected, most of them young mothers who spoke Czech and wanted to pass the language on to their children. When the meeting finished, we decided to go to a nearby café with some of the other participants. Among them was Barbora. The conversation around the table was mostly about experiences of living abroad and difficulties in passing on the language to children. At some point, I came to speak about some impressions from my project and interviews. When I mentioned that I was still looking for further interviewees, Barbora immediately offered to meet me again to share her experiences with me.

I contacted Barbora by email about four months later, in April 2011. She answered the very same day and suggested a few possibilities when we could meet, all of them in the break between her courses at university. These were, she argued, the only possibilities she had to talk, since she had to divide her time among her three children, studies, the household and work. We agreed that I would come to Mainz, where she was studying, on Wednesday morning and that we would then go to a café of Barbora's choice.

On the arranged day we met in front of a shopping centre in the centre of Mainz, and from there walked together to a nearby café. Barbora explained that she had frequented the café now and then because it was not far from the university and they served quick snacks and breakfast there. As we entered, we passed the breakfast buffet and sat at a table at the very end of the room.

242

In contrast to sunny day outside, the café was dark and furnished with dark brown tables and massive black leather chairs. Barbora ordered breakfast immediately. She explained that she had not had the chance to eat yet, although she had already spent two hours at university. Having time for breakfast is a luxury, Barbora laughed. In the next hour we talked a lot. We spoke about places both of us knew, both in the Czech Republic and Germany, about our studies and everyday life. After finishing breakfast, I explained the interview process to Barbora and the reasons why I had decided on conducting biographical narrative interviews. Barbora said that she would just get some food from the buffet which she would eat later – after all she would not have time for food until the evening – and we could start the interview then. I placed my recording equipment on the table, turned it on and asked her to tell me her life story. Even before finishing my question, Barbora asked me where she should start. I answered that she could start wherever she wanted. She laughed and wondered what she should say. However, after a moment she started to narrate. She briefly mentioned the sequence of life events which had brought her to Germany and after a few minutes she asked me to ask her some questions. The atmosphere, which had changed after I had turned on the recording equipment, became more relaxed again as a result of the questions. This time Barbora took her time and told me in detail about the events which she had only mentioned very briefly in her previous narration.

The interview with Barbora lasted about one and half hours. Then it was time to go because she had to go back to university. We paid and I walked with Barbora to the university where we said goodbye.

The main storyline and Barbora's presentation

B: Well, I was born in the winter thirty three years ago. Uhm (2) Jesus, it is somehow (laughing) what should one say (laughing). (1) Uhm: when I was born I was (breathing) very small (laughing) and: always very ill as a child. But (1) somehow one developed quite well I think. (Barbora, p. 1, l. 19-23)

This is how Barbora begins her narration. She continues by outlining her educational pathway: she went to grammar school and afterwards to high school. At that time, she always reflected on what she could do. Her dream was to study Veterinary Medicine, Barbora continues, however, she did not pass the exams. As she was interested in exotic countries, she discovered – more or less by chance, as she adds – the studies of Tropical Geography. She also passed the exams to study Ethology, but was not admitted.

Thus, she started to study Tropical Geography. At this point Barbora interrupts her narration and asks if I would like to hear more about her studies or more of her life. I nod and Barbora starts to list her interests: she was always interested in nature and animals. Her biggest life dream was and still is to go to Africa and observe mountain gorillas there. She played the piano and did sports: swimming and volleyball. She laughs and adds that there is a lot to say but she doesn't know how.

Subsequently, she comes back to talk about her studies. When she started to study, Barbora recounts, she met her future husband. They lived in a long distance relationship for five years. After three years they got married. It was the year she sat her bachelor exams. Afterwards she continued studying for two more years and completed her studies by means of a thesis.

"Coming back to my husband, erm, at the time we got married we bought a house here in Germany." This event describes a new phase of life for Barbora, bound to the house where they have continued to live until the present day. Barbora introduces her husband next: he also has a university degree but in Electrical Engineering, a completely different discipline. Barbora comments that they are actually people with completely different interests.

After finishing her studies Barbora moved to Germany to be with her husband and to find a job. However, she was not successful. She worked for a while in a veterinary clinic, but it did not fulfil her expectations, Barbora says.

Barbora recounts that they planned on going abroad. However, "everything always turns in different directions" and they did not leave. Instead, they decided to start a family. After a year of Barbora being in Germany her son was born and three years later her daughter. Until then, so Barbora states, nothing special happened in her life. It was not until after her daughter was born that Barbora started to teach Czech, which she has continued to do until the present day.

Two years after her daughter, her second son was born. At this time, she was thinking about what to do because, as she argues, the role of being a mother did not fulfil her. At that time she was still teaching Czech. It was through this experience that she got the idea of studying Social Work, which she started two years ago. Barbora says that these studies have opened up new horizons for her, adding that this is an ideal job for her. With the words "So that was somehow it in a nutshell, I don't know if it is enough for you or if you want to hear more", Barbora concludes her narration. I then start to ask questions. We speak about her love for nature, her family, her school career and her decision to go to university, her beginnings in Germany, her past and future plans, as well as citizenship and nationality.

In the introductory sentences, Barbora already mentions the main theme of her narrative – an immense personal development from a "very small" and "ill" child to a grown-up woman. As the structure of Barbora's narration indicates, her professional orientation, which is in ongoing transformation, plays a central role in Barbora's positioning and in her perception of herself. Her story is the story of a metamorphosis of the self.

Barbora's story concentrates on her education career. She describes not only the institutions she actually attended, but also her dreams and wishes which remained unfulfilled in the past. The interplay of unfulfilled dreams and real life extends throughout her entire narration. New options which she chose, such as an alternative field of studies or starting a family instead of travelling, were not planned a priori but came to her "by chance". Her educational and biographical pathway thus appears unplannable and subject to ongoing changes, which she can only influence to a certain extent. Her words "everything always turns in a different direction" illustrates this attitude well.

Interestingly, migration is not an explicit topic for Barbora. Nor does she name and describe the place of her origin, or pay attention to the places she migrated to later on. Nevertheless, migration plays an important role in her biography. After she moved country, Barbora experienced a rupture. Her plans to find a job after gradation failed, thereby causing the expected institutional pathway along which she had construed her biographical narration until then to be discontinued. She therefore decided on an alternative plan: to start a family. She considered looking after her children and managing the household as a "bridging period" until she could again gain access to the professional life. Nevertheless, "everything turned in a different direction again" and Barbora began a new course of studies in a completely new field.

Notes on the working relationship with Barbora

Barbora narrated her story very briefly without delving into details. She seemed a bit stressed and overtaxed by the task of talking about the course of her life. Turning on the recording equipment also appeared to affect the atmosphere, which had been very relaxed during our previous conversation. At that moment, our roles shifted: I turned from being someone with whom she could talk to about diverse topics into an interviewer, and Barbora into an interviewee. Whilst telling her story, she often asked whether her narration was what I expected from her. These questions revealed her insecurity. Nevertheless, the situation eased again in the questioning part.

Barbora's way of narrating may have been influenced by the lively atmosphere in the café and the time limits she set for our meeting and her narration. Her busy schedule made it impossible for her to take her time and delve into her memories. Barbora's current reorientation and redefinition of her position also had an effect on the way she narrated her story. In Barbora's life situation, which is currently subject to considerable changes, the biography still needs to be re-construed and re-interpreted in order to make sense to Barbora again.

6.4.2   Barbora's migration and social pathways

"Everything always turns in a slightly different direction"

B: Well, I was born in the winter thirty three years ago. Uhm (2) Jesus, it is somehow (laughing) what should one say (laughing). (1) Uhm: when I was born I was (breathing) very small (laughing) and: always very ill as a child. But (1) somehow one developed quite well I think. (Barbora, p. 1, l. 19-23)

Barbora starts her narration at the moment of her birth and early childhood. She does not give details concerning this time, just mentions that she was very small and often ill. The statement "but somehow one developed quite well" indicates a process of metamorphosis of the self over the course of time, which is the main theme of her narration.

Contrary to other interviews, Barbora does not at the beginning of her narration introduce the place where she was born and where she grew up. What is more, the places to which she migrated only indirectly remain present in Barbora's narration. They only appear in connection with her educational career, her move to be with her husband and her attempts to find a job. Nevertheless, migration plays an important role in Barbora's biography, since it represents both chances and barriers for her.

After the section quoted above, Barbora continues her narration by outlining her education:

B: I went to grammar school as usual and: after grammar school I went to high school (1) and I was always thinking about what I would like to do. My dream so to speak was to study veterinary medicine after high school. However, I did not get there. And I was always attracted by tropical countries, (deep breathing) so I more or less by chance came to the studies which I later studied, tropical geography. [I: Hmm] (1) Well and there I went. (Barbora, p. 1, l. 23-30)

Barbora outlines the expected institutional pathway through her educational career. She underlines that, despite her "unusual" start as small and ill child, she developed "normally". The stress on the "normality" also appears later on in her narrative when she speaks about the time prior to her migration to Germany.

She did not have a clear idea of what she wanted to study. Nevertheless, she was clear about wanting to study something. Later on Barbora explains that she actually did not want to go to high school but to a secondary school specialising in veterinary medicine, which was in another city about a hundred kilometres from her home town. As her parents were against it, she decided to go to high school (Gymnasium) and subsequently go on to university, as was common practice.

In order to continue the expected institutional pathway and pass from high school to university, Barbora had to move cities because there was no university in Teplice, the town of her origin. Her move to Prague was an important step for Barbora. She evaluates her time there in the following way:

B: Uhm: (1) it was actually (1) one of the best five years of my life so to speak because (1) you move out of your parents' place, even to some other city, to a big city, (1) you are alone there, no one tells you what to do. You enjoy the freedom. I think – it was something beautiful. I love to think about this time. Sure, everything wasn't easy, (breathing) but this freedom, those five independent years were absolutely amazing. It was the kind of freedom one would love to always have. (Barbora, p. 13, l. 394-401)

Moving to Prague meant for Barbora that she had to "individualise" herself from her parents' house and from the known surroundings. It was also a time of discovering not only a new city but also new ways of life. Barbora speaks about the time of her studies in detail in the questions part. She concentrates predominantly on describing the events she experienced with the friends she met in the halls of residence where she lived. She recounts three people who stayed in her mind, although she does not have contact with them anymore. They were from countries in Asia, Africa and South Africa, and studied the same subject as she did. Interestingly, they all led some kind of "adventurous" life, travelling a lot and living an unconventional way of life. Sometimes Barbora compares her life path with theirs and reflects on the possibilities she lacked ten years ago in the Czech Republic to go abroad and fulfil her dreams. As she argues, meeting people from other countries opened up new perspectives to her and was important for her further development and for understanding "other" cultures.

Before she started university, Barbora met her future husband Oliver during one of her summer stays at her aunt's in Germany. They stayed in contact and continued to keep in touch during Barbora's studies in Prague. After a three year relationship Barbora and Oliver got married. For the next two years, Barbora stayed in Prague and continued studying Tropical Geography. After she graduated, she then decided to move to Germany. As she explains, "I wanted to have a proper relationship at last. Five years of a long distance relationship was enough." (Barbora, p. 17, l. 518-519)

B: After my studies I then moved to be with him in Germany [I: Hmm] and: I tried to get a job (deep breathing) which unfortunately was not in my field of study – and additionally tropical geography is not really sought after [I: Hmm] so I didn't manage to get a job. I worked for a while uhm: in a veterinary clinic [I: Hmm] (1) unfortunately it did not fulfil me as I had thought (1) yeah! (-) What happened next. Then we were also thinking of moving to another country. [I: Hmm] We planned China, [I: Hmm] but of course (laughing), one always somehow, how it is, everything always turns in a different direction. (Deep breathing) There was nothing from China (1) for personal reasons and (1) well we decided to start a family. (Barbora, p. 3, l. 66-76)

Barbora switches in her narration between unfulfilled dreams, such as travelling and seeing faraway places, and her actual life path, contrasting these with one another. New options which she chose after the initial plans failed, such as an alternative field of studies or starting a family instead of travelling and taking up a suitable job, seem unplannable and unpredictable to her. Her words "everything always turns in a different direction" describe the course of her life as developing in ongoing changes with the impossibility to plan and control her next steps in advance.

New beginnings in Germany

After graduation, Barbora migrated to Germany. She moved to the house which she and her husband had bought shortly after their wedding, and started to search for a job, yet without success. Barbora comments retrospectively on her first year in Germany in the following way:

B: I have to truly say that I was afraid of it. (1) But as I had already got to know Germany as a child and the country was not unfamiliar to me, I didn't have such uhm- it wasn't anything new for me. (1) Uhm: I was really the most afraid of (1) will I find a job or not. It was probably the most important thing to me, and what somehow interested me the most – or what I was somehow the most afraid of. (1) Of course you leave your family, friends, the country which you know and you know how things work there, and (1) you have to (1) find new friends again, and basically you have to get to know the other mentality (1) other products so to speak, simply everything. Everything. Another style of life. Really, one has to change many things, yes. And (1) but (1) I cannot say that it would be (1) one got accustomed to it somehow, really. Although the first year was really hard because I did not know anyone here. [I: Hmm] My husband was always at work so I was often alone at home. (Breathing) I cried a lot because I said to myself I will not stand it here, I want to go back. (1) I kept asking myself what will you do what will you do -" (Barbora, p. 16, l. 498-512)

Barbora experienced her migration as a biographical turn. On the one hand, she argues she knew the country and did not feel foreign there. On the other hand she pictures the new and unexpected scenario containing new structures, different and unknown goods and missing social contacts. In order to find a new place and to "accustom" herself to her new life in Germany – to use Barbora's words – Barbora had to make an effort to learn the social structures which were unfamiliar to her. Additionally, she had to change herself and her life perceptions. The things which appeared unquestioned and "normal" before were put into question through the act of migration. The inability to use her knowledge and action patterns after migration led to a personal crisis and to the perception of a rupture in her biography. The missing knowledge about social structures made it difficult for her to plan her life, make new decisions and use her resources, such as her skills and university degree:

B: Hm: and when I then went to Germany, I have to truly say that I did not have a plan. Because I absolutely did not know German structures, how does it work here, uhm: which possibilities I had in Germany with my studies (1) well and when I then started to look around, everything was fifty, a hundred and fifty kilometres away. [I: Hmm] And: (1) I also did not believe in myself at that time after finishing my studies, also because of the

248

language, and I kept saying to myself, you just cannot apply for such a position, (1) when they hear your German they would not hire you anyway. Well, so I stood in my own way a bit. (Barbora, p. 14, l. 447-454)

Barbora explains the failure of finding a job by her personal deficiencies, such as insufficient language skills and lacking self confidence in applying for a suitable job. Interestingly, she does not take into account possible structural barriers, such as difficulties in the recognition of her diploma and possible discrimination on the labour market because of her origin and language skills. Once again, for Barbora potential success was only possible only in connection with personal change.

Moreover, the choice of possible job offers for Barbora was limited to the area where she lived: their house was situated in a small town in the middle Germany about 30 km from the main city in the region. Most of the options thus failed because of the need to commute. The image of the house binding her firmly in one place also appears later on in her narrative. The house, for example, is one of the reasons why Barbora and her husband decided not to go travelling after her studies and to start a family instead. However, while she presents herself as firmly bound to one place, her husband on the other hand has stayed mobile and frequently travels around the world in his job as a mechanical engineer. As I will show later, Barbora instead "converted" her desire to travel into her new studies, which for her represent – similarly to travelling – a newly gained independence and a means of self-development.

B: And then (1) I had been here in Germany for about one year, our son was born, the first son, (1) and at this time uhm: that that: he was born and after – in little less than three years later our daughter was born, so at this time I was busy more or less only with looking after the children and: (1) the house and (breathing) family, [I: Hmm] so nothing interesting happened in my life so to speak. It wasn't until after our daughter was born that I started to teach the Czech language. (Barbora, p. 3, l. 77-83)

Later on Barbora explains that one of the reasons for deciding to have children was her age. As she argues, the idea that she would establish a family in her thirties was at that time unthinkable for her. Nowadays, she continues, she sees it totally differently. Moreover, her decision to start a family was also connected to the fact she had not found a job in Germany and did not have any contacts there. It was because of her children that the situation changed:

B: Well and thanks to the children it became – it all got under way, (1) that one acclimatised here, made acquaintances, friends and today (breathing) one is here (1) really (1) well integrated. Today I for example cannot imagine living in Ger- the Czech Republic again. [I: Hmm] That I would live in the Czech Republic again. [I: Hmm] Yes. (Barbora, p. 17, l. 528-533)

Life with her children started the metamorphosis in Barbora's biography. As she explains further on, her children not only helped her to integrate into diverse groups but they were also what initiated her inner changes. Since she felt responsible for her children, for whom she had "to fight" and arrange diverse issues, she became more self-confident and courageous, Barbora says.

To summarize, migration to Germany and starting a family represented a turning point in Barbora's life. Because of changed social structures, she had to rethink her life plans. Following a period immediately after migration which she experienced as a "rupture", new social fields and new possibilities opened up to her through her children and later on through her job as a teacher of the Czech language. She started to plan her life again from the beginning.

Studies as a means of gaining independence

B: It wasn't until after our daughter was born that I started to teach the Czech language. It was through the Volkshochschule51 and I still do it a bit nowadays, but currently it's not possible to manage it because of time. Well and then two years after our daughter our son was born, third son, or – third child, son (laughing). It wasn't somehow planned but (deep breathing) but well he is simply our sunshine. (Breathing) And one would say that after having a third child one would be even less inactive and wouldn't know, but the role of being a mother didn't completely fulfil me (breathing) uhm I was always thinking what will you do what will you do, actually as I also said erm: I was still teaching the Czech language (1) well and then I somehow decided what will you do next, and thanks to my teaching Czech I got the idea of this subject which I am studying at the moment, social work. I started to study two years ago, which means that the smallest one was two years – less than – yes. No. He was three years old. Three years, yes. And I am still studying it today. (Barbora, p. 3, l. 81-94)

Barbora's first step towards building up her professional career was through her experiences as a teacher of the Czech language. It was her husband who gave her the idea. He was himself attending Czech language courses in a nearby city. He kept saying to Barbora, "what this lady does, you can do as well" (Barbora, p. 21, l. 665-666).

Interestingly, in searching for a job she did not use her diploma or the prior knowledge she had acquired through her university studies as a resource, but rather her native language. The language which before had been perceived as a barrier in her search for a job now became a resource which she could utilize. Her husband is the one who introduces the idea to her, thus initiating the process of Barbora's reorientation.[52] A different perception of

---

51   Adult education centre
52   As to the transformative processes and discovering one's own skills in the course of migration, see also Inowlocki, Riemann 2012.

her language skills opened up new options for her – such as teaching and translating – and gave her the idea of enrolling for further studies.

B: I was always thinking what. And of course the work (breathing) well it wasn't really easy and teaching the Czech language was not very lucrative and because I had got into this area of uhm "Erwachsene Bildung"53 [I: Hm] I will say it from time to time in German [I: Yes sure] because I don't know some expressions (breathing) So I started to inform myself as to how I could get into this area. Erwachsene Bildung. Yes. And when you want to work in this field you have to have a university degree in this field, (breathing) and the only area was "soziale Arbeit", social work. And I said to myself, yes why not, you can try it, it will either work or not, so I started to be interested. (Barbora, p. 22-23, l. 703-713)

For Barbora, entry into the field of adult education was possible only by starting a new course of studies in Germany. Barbora also spoke about her decision to start studying social work when we left the café and walked slowly to university. Barbora argued that Germany does not give people any chances. One has to study a certain subject in order to be able to work in the field related to it. Otherwise, the companies do not hire anyone and all the doors stay closed. She compares this with her former fellow female students who all stayed in the Czech Republic and now work in a field other than the one they studied, without the necessity to take up a new course of studies. Her comment reflects the different use of university degrees in both countries. Additionally, it reveals the common social practice of changing occupation in order to adjust to gendered conditions on the labour market. Barbora uses this strategy in a different context after migration and expresses her willingness to start from the beginning.

When she had the idea of starting to study again, she went to the student centre at the nearby university in order to find out about possible courses, Barbora goes on. As she hadn't studied in Germany before, she had to get all her diplomas translated and get a certificate proving that she was able to speak German. The very same day she therefore went to the language centre at the university, where her language skills were immediately confirmed without her even having to pass any exams. Her language skills were at that time so good that the employees at the language centre at first did not believe that she had never studied in Germany before. Shortly after Barbora sent off all the application forms, she received the notification that she had been admitted. As she states, it all went so quickly that she did not have any time to think about it. "It was destiny", concludes Barbora.

Barbora turned her focus from natural sciences to social sciences. This shift not only resulted in different study content, but also involved completely different organisation. While her previous studies were more theoretically oriented, in her new field practical application was the priority. Practical application was of particular interest to Barbora, as she did not want to waste

53   Adult education

251

time on "normal" studies after which she would need some years of practical experience in order to succeed on the labour market. At thirty three years of age she already felt quite old to start studying a new subject. Nevertheless, after she started to attend classes she realised that she was not the oldest student by far.

As with her initial studies in Prague, Barbora connects her new studies with her regained freedom and independence.

B: Well it was really a jump for me into this absolutely different world. To get into an absolutely different field of studies. And: uhm: what keeps me at these studies – I dropped out of such a world, only children and family, mothers with a family, you don't know any other world, and now you are simply among younger people, students as I mentioned. It is suddenly such a different kind of freedom, independence which one has again, you learn something different. So this is what keeps me somehow. And I think that it gave me energy, yes. That I am more energetic (breathing) even though I have more work, even though I sometimes don't have a rest during the day, but you have something to go for again. You have a goal in your life. (Barbora, p. 25, l. 785-795)

Barbora describes the new beginnings initiated by her new studies. For her they represent the possibility of self-realisation and self-development. Because of her studies, she started to actively plan her life and her next steps again. Moreover, the new studies are her means of re-defining her own position within her family and in society. While her studies in Prague signified above all the "individualisation" from her parents' house, her new studies serve as a means of going beyond the role of being a mother. Furthermore, Barbora's studies represent a gateway to new possibilities which were unexpected and unplannable.

B: I wanted at first to only do the Erwachsenen Bildung but now during my studies – as I have said. New directions have opened up for me and I shall try it somehow. Which area I shall get into. (Barbora, p. 26, l. 811-814)

Not only is Barbora's story a story of a metamorphosis of the self. It is also the state in which Barbora finds herself at the time of the interview. At the point in her life where diverse options are open to her and she is deciding which direction to take.

Rethinking belonging

After her migration, Barbora experienced a change of direction. Instead of starting a job in her profession, she initially took a job for which she was overqualified after several months of job hunting. Soon afterwards she quit the job to start a family. Barbora experienced her first time in Germany as a rupture in her life. Not until later on, when her children had started to grow up, did she start from scratch to up build her career in a very different field. The new orientation and metamorphosis of Barbora's biography goes hand in hand with the redefinition of her sense of belonging. To reconstruct her sense of belonging to Germany, Barbora goes back to the history of her family.

Barbora introduces her family into her narration for the first time in the questions part of the interview in response to my question: "Could you tell me something about your family". At first, she speaks about her parents and her sister. Barbora lists her family members one after the other and briefly outlines each of their careers. Then, her grandparents are introduced briefly. She states the year of their death, adding the age of her grandmother if she were still alive. After a short break she goes on and for the first time reveals the ethnic origin of her grandmother. This, as the following section reveals, plays an important role in Barbora's positioning within her family and society after her migration.

B: That could maybe also be interesting for your work. My grandma on my father's side, grandma and grandpa, or more or less only my grandma is a Sudetendeutsche. That's why I basically have a connection with Germany and with Germ - so to speak with the language, with German. I know that my grandma and grandpa only spoke German to each other. So I always had access to German and I listened to that language and also basically nearly all of my family lives in Germany, the family on my father's side I mean. So I have always had from childhood so to speak a connection with Germany and uhm: one part was in former East Germany and: my aunt, the sister of my father uhm: they emigrated in nineteen sixty eight to West Germany so I basically always had some contact both to East Germany and West Germany. So basically (1) Germany is not unfamiliar to me so to speak. I basically know both sides from childhood, East and West. Also the language is not unfamiliar to me. I never spoke it though, not until later. It's a pity that my father never spoke to me in German when I was small. Well, but I learned it anyway. (Laughing) And: I basically have German roots, yes. (Barbora, p. 6, l. 165-183)

Barbora makes use of the history of her family in order to construct links with Germany and to the German language. She rediscovers the origin of her grandmother, who spoke German not only to her husband but also to her son, Barbora's father, and outlines the family line in which the transmission of the German language was interrupted.

To explain in more depth her relationship with Germany, Barbora in turn introduces her wider family who migrated to Germany in 1968, the year of turbulent political changes ranging from the political liberalisation known as the "Prague Spring" to the entry of "Warsaw Pact" troops and subsequent "normalisation"[54]. Through her cross border contacts with her family which she kept alive after migration, Barbora became "an expert" not only on the "East side" but also on the "West side". The fact that she uses the division of East and West in her narration reveals their different meaning in her narration. As she explains in another part of the interview, she often spent her

54 "Normalisation" means the time after the entry of "Warsaw Pact troops" to Czechoslovakia in August 1968. Relative political liberalisation was replaced by censorship, cleansing in the party, massive dismissals from work because of one's political views and the abolition of diverse social and political organisations.

holidays with her relatives in Germany. During one of these visits she met her future husband. Her transnational networks and knowledge of how to move between the countries were for Barbora a resource for her further migration. For this reason, Barbora does not perceive the borders as a boundary per se, since she knew both countries and languages from her childhood.

Barbora creates the link to Germany in order to present her sense of belonging to the place in which she is currently living. Seeing herself as the follower of "German" traditions in her family makes it possible for her to position herself within "German" society not as a "foreigner" but as someone who belongs there. At the same time, she is rethinking her sense of belonging to the Czech Republic.

B: Uhm: (1) when I come to the Czech Republic, I really the first -, it occurs to me sometimes that I am a foreigner there. I feel foreign there. After a longer period of time I acclimatise myself there again and (breathing) I ask myself well how it would be to live there again. Well it is not so unimaginable but when I am here I cannot imagine going back again. Or to be in the Czech Republic. (…) (1) I feel absolutely different there then when I am here. I cannot even describe it. I don't know why. I don't know why. (1) You know the language, you speak it, you know the town, you find your way around, but still you feel alien there. This is bizarre. (1) Sometimes I am sorry about it because I say to myself, Jesus you were born here and you are Czech, but still I feel like a foreigner. (Barbora, p. 38, l. 1204-1221)

After Barbora migrated to Germany, she had to learn the new structures and, as she herself says, to change herself a lot in order to find a new place in society. Her new experiences, knowledge and personal change had an impact on her positioning back in the Czech Republic. Even though the town and language stayed the same, her perception shifted. Because of her development, knowledge and new orientation, the familiar turned into "foreign" and she became a "foreigner" in the country and culture she knew so well. In Germany on the other hand,

B: When I speak to someone, they mostly do not realise that I am a foreigner. Which on the other side puts such pressure on me because I say to myself Jesus Christ, when I make some grammatical mistake they must say Jesus Christ, she is really stupid. She cannot even speak German. Uhm, well, I put such internal pressure on myself. (Barbora, p. 38, l. 1185-1189)

Mastering the language is the decisive factor for national belonging for Barbora. Not only does she feel "accustomed" – to use her words again – but she is also recognised by others as a German national because of her language skills. Barbora's positioning has also had an impact on her considering to apply for German citizenship.

B: But what I should also say is that I am considering after ten eleven years getting German citizenship. But somehow I still don't feel absolutely like doing so, although last time I heard that I could keep the Czech passport. (1) If I decided to get German citizenship and I had to hand in the Czech passport, I wouldn't do it. I still probably feel too Czech to hand in the Czech passport and take a German one. To do so I probably still have not lived here for long enough and for it I am still very much Czech in my heart. But if it is really true that I can have both a Czech and German passport, so I will probably apply for German citizenship next year. Yes. (Barbora, p. 39, l. 1222-1230)

Barbora describes her sense of national belonging as a process. The longer she lives in Germany, the more she becomes "German" and vice versa. Taking on German citizenship would mean an acknowledgement of her sense of belonging not only by "others" but also by the state and legal framework. Her considering applying for German citizenship is connected to her biographical experiences after migration. Moreover, the dynamics of her family need to be taken in account. Her husband is German; also her three children have German nationality and speak German, which in turn is the "family" language. On the other hand, her argumentation concerning handing in her Czech passport reveals her ambiguous relationship with her sense of national belonging. The Czech passport symbolises Czech national belonging to her. Handing in her Czech passport would mean losing Czech citizenship, which she refuses to do. Dual citizenship would mean that she would gain full recognition of her status and sense of belonging in Germany, but still retain her connection with her country of birth, her social circles back in the Czech Republic and her past.[55]

Barbora's story of reorientation

Barbora introduces the family members into her narration in the same way as her own biography: she concentrates predominantly on their professional career and changes in it.

I: Can you tell me something about your family?

B: About my family. Uhm. (1) (Loud breathing) So: my mum is a physiotherapist. Nevertheless she works as a social worker at the moment. So there are maybe some small – maybe some genes (laughing) [I: (laughing)] in this area because I am studying this profession at the moment. She works with old people in a home and organises their day there so to speak. Dealings with the authorities and such things. And it is uhm: caring for people. When someone lives outside such a home for the elderly, and homes and such things. My father he is – he has worked in the mines all his life. He actually when I say so he also worked himself up from being a worker to uhm the position of – he worked as a transport supervisor all his life [I: Hmm]. However, after thirty six years in the company he was fired. But luckily despite the fact that he was fifty six when he was fired he got a new job, also in the mines but in a different mine so luckily he still has a job, but yes! Well and I have a sister, she is seven years younger than me, well, she is a nurse but at the moment

---

55 According to the Czech Citizenship Act (Zákon č. 40/1993 Sb.), which was in force between 1993 and 2013, at the moment of acquiring the citizenship of some other state, one would automatically lose Czech citizenship. The exception was the acquisition of another citizenship due to birth or marriage, as was the case with Barbora. Barbora thus could keep both citizenships, Czech and German.

she works at a dentist's and she lived out of town for some time, but now it must be a year since she came back, although she still works, she has to commute about fifty kilometres to work, yes. (Barbora, p. 5, l. 140-160)

As this section reveals, Barbora was not the only one in her family who experienced a change of profession. Both her mother and sister work in a profession which does not correspond to their initial qualification. Her father is the only one who has stayed in the same field all his life and moved up on the social ladder within one institution. The necessity of a professional shift as well as the need to commute to work reflects the situation in Northern Bohemia where Barbora is from. The region where her family lives has the highest rate of unemployment in the Czech Republic, regularly attaining about 13% (ČSÚ 2012). Furthermore, women are more affected by unemployment in this region (ibid.). This could be explained by the fact that most job possibilities in the region are in the mines or the automobile industry, which are positions that are traditionally occupied predominantly by men. From this viewpoint, Barbora's career shift is not an exception. Nevertheless, what differentiates Barbora from other family members, is that her "new beginning" was influenced not by the structural shortage of job possibilities in the region but by her migratory pathway.

After she migrated, she had to redefine her position in society, her skills and resources in a new way. The shift from natural sciences to social sciences which she underwent after her migration seems not to be arbitrary, but structured by the conditions of the gendered labour market in which migrant woman find more and more working possibilities in "female" professions, such as in the care sector, catering and education (see e.g. Kontos 2009b). In her search for new possibilities of professional self-realisation, Barbora made use both of her experiences and her knowledge of German in the labour market. The professional reorientation theme which is repeated within her family and which represents a strategy of responding to shortages in the labour market, applies to Barbora in a very different context after her migration. Her reorientation opens up new horizons for her, as she points out.

6.4.3 Summary

"Everything always turns in a different direction" is the sentence uttered by Barbora which summarises her story well. The introductory sentences of her story are already indicative of the theme of her story: metamorphosis of the self and personal development. Moreover, it is a story of biographical reorientation after migration.

Migrating to Germany and starting a family represented a turning point for Barbora. She experienced the time after migration as a rupture in her life. She did not know the social structures and practices and lacked social contacts. The missing knowledge of "how things work" prevented her from using her skills and resources. However, new social fields and new possibilities opened up to her through her three children and later on through her job as a teacher of the Czech language. The Czech language, which at first she experienced as a boundary, later became a resource for her. Her altered different perception of her language skills led her to her teaching activities and to the field of adult education which she studied later on. Her new area of studies became a means of self-development and self-realisation for Barbora. Through her studies, which she describes in terms of independence and freedom, new horizons of unexpected and unplannable possibilities opened up to her. She started to rethink her life plan and began to build up her life again from scratch.

Moreover, Barbora began to redefine her role in the family and in society in general. The new orientation and metamorphosis of Barbora's biography had an impact on her redefinition of the sense of belonging. Based on her family history, in which the German language was transmitted from generation to generation, she reconstructs her links to Germany and the German language in a new way and presents herself as someone who in fact has "German roots". At the same time, her perception of belonging back in the Czech Republic shifted. Her thoughts of acquiring German citizenship are connected to these changes in her sense of belonging.

After migration Barbora not only redefined her sense of belonging but also her skills and resources. She turned her focus from natural sciences to social work, a turn around which is structured by dominant discourses about migrant women and the conditions on the gendered labour market. In her search for new possibilities of professional self-realisation, Barbora made use both of her experience and her knowledge of the German labour market. Professional reorientation – which is a theme which is repeated within her family as a strategy of responding to shortages in the labour market – for her signifies a means of overcoming structural barriers after migration, enabling her to start again from scratch.

6.5 Arnošt: living in "exile"

The interview with Arnošt has a special position within my empirical material. It is one of three interviews I conducted with people working in academia. Academia has a different structure then other areas of the labour market. As the example of Arnošt shows, the various steps on the professional career ladder in this field, such as gaining a PhD or passing the "habilitation" (postdoctoral qualification) or professorship procedures, are to a great extent constrained and structured by the relevant national setting. The difficulties in transferring "diplomas", skills and work experience across the border is paradoxical, taking into account the ongoing emphasis on the internationalisation of most of the academic and scientific fields.

Arnošt was born in 1964 in Olomouc, one of the biggest cities in the Czech Republic. His parents were both academics. His grandfather was the owner and manager of an influential company, which in the course of "nationalisation" was taken over by the state in the early fifties, whereupon his grandfather was forced to leave the country. Arnošt grew up in Olomouc and also went to grammar school, high school and university there. After graduation he left for Prague, the capital city of the Czech Republic. During this time he got married and his first child was born. Six years later, his second child was born. At the time of the interview Arnošt was living in Bamberg in the south of Germany, and working as a professor of Central and Eastern European history.

Arnošt's biography reveals a difficult process of establishing and maintaining the transnational spaces in which his career and life path is developing, as well as the process of transmitting transnational links to future generations. The biographical reconstruction shows the chances and challenges associated with border crossings and an effort to position himself within both societies.

6.5.1 Interview setting and biographical presentation

Context of the interview

I established contact with Arnošt through Marie, one of my previous interviewees. After we had conducted the interview she mentioned that she knew some other Czechs living in Bamberg. She offered to arrange for me to get in contact with Arnošt and to some other former colleagues of hers at university. About a week later she wrote me an email with Arnošt's email address and said that he had agreed to meet me and be interviewed. We then exchanged further emails with Arnošt in which I explained the topic of my research and the interview process, and we agreed on a time for the interview.

I went to Bamberg in February 2010. I planned to stay for three days and meet two further interview partners who were introduced to me by Arnošt. I met Arnošt the very same day. We arranged a meeting at his office at the university in the early afternoon. I arrived at the university a bit early and therefore had time to have a look around and find my way through the labyrinthine university corridors. Surprisingly, the university seemed relatively empty and silent, even though the semester was still in progress.

I knocked at the door of Arnošt's office. He opened it and called me in with a friendly smile. It was a small, cosy office. The walls were covered in shelves full of books. Above his table hung some pictures, among them a photo of the former Czech president Vaclav Havel. Opposed the entrance door was a huge window offering a view partly of the massive grey university building and partly of the surrounding fields and the city. Arnošt invited me to sit opposite him at his desk and asked me to give him a moment to finish an email he was in the middle of. During this time, the telephone rang twice. After the second call he switched off his mobile telephone, turned to me and said that we could start. I again explained to him my research interests and described the biographical narrative interview. Arnošt nodded and mentioned that he knew the format from his own research practice. We spoke briefly about the research project in which biographical narrative interviews were used.

Before beginning with the narration, we discussed the anonymisation of the interview. Arnošt agreed to choose his own anonymised name – the name of his father. Subsequently I asked Arnošt to tell me his whole life story. Arnošt seemed surprised by my request:

A: Well, my whole life story is really long at my age (laughing). But I think that you are more interested in the phase of my leaving to go abroad. This is the core of your thesis. But to give you some background information. (Arnošt, p. 2, l. 40-43)

Arnošt made it clear that he was prepared to steer the direction of the interview. He was the one who was about to decide which topics would appear in the narration and which would stay unspoken. His comment concerning my research interests made it clear that his narration would cover not only his interests but also my presumed research focus, which we had already discussed during our initial contacts via emails and later on when we met for the interview.

The interview lasted more than one hour. Despite his clear idea of what he wanted to narrate and what not, he often got deep into his narration and enriched his story with many details and situations which revealed the history of his family. The interview was interrupted three times: once when someone knocked at the door and brought Arnošt some documents, once when the telephone rang and finally when the battery of my recording equipment ran out and I had to replace it. These interruptions irritated Arnošt and the flow of his narration. Nevertheless, he always managed to pick up the line of his narration again and continue his story. Towards the end Arnošt kept looking at the clock and became shorter in his narration. He mentioned that he had a meeting afterwards and had to finish the interview. When I turned off the recording device and packed my bag we were still talking about migration and possible explanations of his life path. Furthermore, he recommended some research projects to me which might be interesting to me. In the doorway I thanked Arnošt for the interview and we said goodbye. His telephone rang again and he went back to his desk.

The main storyline and Arnošt's presentation

Arnošt begins his narration with the statement that he is from a "normal Czech family". He was born in Olomouc in 1964. Arnošt mentions that his parents lived there too. He completed all schooling in Olomouc –primary school, high school (Gymnasium) and university. After explaining the reasons for choosing the German language and history for his studies, he comes to speak about his move to Prague where he gained a one year scholarship at the university. However, the revolution came and there was a chance to go abroad, says Arnošt. In 1991 he went to Hamburg in Germany for one year and in 1994 he handed in his dissertation and passed his PhD viva there. Since he had not establish any contacts in Prague, he and his wife decided to return to Olomouc, where he took a job a as lecturer at the department of history. He stayed there for five years. During this time, so Arnošt, he worked on his university "habilitation" (post-doctoral qualification). Since he had obtained his PhD from Hamburg, Arnošt argues, he had the courage to apply for a position in Bamberg. Arnošt unexpectedly got the position. He moved to Bamberg and about six months later the professorship post was ready for him. Nevertheless, Arnošt decided to renounce the call and come back to Olomouc.

"Well and then it got complicated", Arnošt narrates further on. He returned to the job he had had before he left to go to Bamberg, but since he was only paid a basic salary, he was not able to get by. He thus decided to move to Bamberg again. "And from that time onwards I have been here in Bamberg. This is my life story", concludes Arnošt, laughing. After a small break Arnošt picks up the line of his narration again and describes in detail the motives for his decision to return to Bamberg. Arnošt says that they did not want to stay in Germany, but they planned to come back. He commenced the procedure of applying for a professorship in the Czech Republic and in 2006 they were prepared for the return. Arnošt adds extensive argumentation explaining the motives of his family to return. Nevertheless, as a result of diverse considerations, they decided to stay in Germany after all. Arnošt concludes his narration with the statement: "Well, it was such a complicated case of leaving, returning and leaving". After he finishes his narration, I start to ask questions on his childhood in Olomouc, life in Prague and Hamburg, his beginnings in Bamberg as well as his connections to Olomouc and in Bamberg.

Arnošt's story is one of professional development and his attempt to establish a "dual" academic career in both countries. He concentrates on his academic career and his migration pathway. His story describes a process of reaching his position and living in Bamberg in Germany, which was neither planned nor intended.

Arnošt structures his narration by his various stays in different places both in the Czech Republic and in Germany. He initially names Olomouc, the city in which he was born and where he lived until university graduation. The next life phase is framed by his life in Prague, another city in the Czech Republic, and his return to Olomouc. From Olomouc he and his family moved to Bamberg in the South of Germany. Nevertheless, from Bamberg he repeatedly visits Olomouc and even though he is living in Bamberg at the time of the interview, he has not excluded returning to Olomouc one day. Leaving and returning is the main theme of his narration.

Arnošt's decisions to move back and forth were not based solely on his personal interests. They were shaped by structural conditions, such as the impossibility of starting a job because of his family's political orientation or later on because of his family's economic situation and discrimination experienced by his children after returning to the Czech Republic. The decision to migrate was never made by Arnošt alone but was a product of family discussions. Arnošt perceives the transnational spaces which they have actively established by their repeated border crossings and biographical experiences both as an opportunity and an obstruction.

Arnošt's story is full of theoretical reflections. He includes large argumentative passages seeking the answer for their departures and returns. In most passages he delivers well-structured and partly scientific arguments summarising the reasons for particular biographical decisions. The way he abstracts everyday events and explains them with the help of scientific terms corresponds to his position as a professional and intellectual.

Notes on the working relationship with Arnošt

The atmosphere in Arnošt's office, his position and our interaction from the moment of our initial contact all had an influence on the manner of Arnošt's narration. The office was relatively quiet at the time of the interview. Nevertheless, the books, computer, recurring telephone calls and time pressure reminded Arnošt and me that we were in a working office. This atmosphere contributed to the topics of Arnošt's narration: the course of his professional career and the process which led him to hold the professorial chair and his current position as a professor in Bamberg.

Retrospectively, his university title also influenced the way in which we established contact. Arnošt was the only one of my interviewees who asked for the exact theme and theoretical background of my project. I described the design of my projects to him in one of the first emails we exchanged. I felt the necessity to explain the theoretical background to Arnošt in more detail in order to win him over for the interview and to justify the relevance of my research project. We had thus already entered a discussion on a theoretical level at the initial email stage. We did not meet as "migrants" – as was the case with some of the other interviews – but as "academic colleagues". To some extent, the theoretically based reflections which created the large part of Arnošt's narration responded to our previous discussion and our presumed mutual expectations.

6.5.2 Arnošt's migration and social pathways

Olomouc

A: I come from a normal Czech family, not a mixed family. So there was no motivation for migration besides the personal one, or in my case personal one. (Breathing) And I was born in Olomouc in 1964 uhm, I grew up in Olomouc and also my parents both lived in Olomouc even though they were born in some other place. (Arnošt, p. 2, l. 43-49)

Arnošt begins his narration with a theory. With his statement "I come from a normal Czech family" he rejects the assumption that his motive to migrate might be connected to the cultural background of his family. With these few introductory sentences Arnošt indicates that the actual theme of his narration is the search for explanations for his repeating migrations. The family presents a starting point for his biography and a basis influencing his further decisions and steps.

Olomouc, the city in which he was born and grew up, plays an extraordinary role in his biography. Arnošt justifies his sense of belonging to the place by naming his parents as residents of the city. The justification of his belonging to Olomouc seems connected to his future exclusion experiences in Olomouc and consequent migrations, as I will develop later.

Arnošt's biography is shaped by the history and positioning of his family during communism. He comes to speak about his family in more detail later on when he describes the situation in Olomouc during his childhood and youth. In the course of nationalisation in the early fifties, Arnošt's grandfather lost the company which he owned and directed, and had to leave the region. Despite his skills and university education he was forced to work as an unskilled labourer in a factory. He was not permitted to return to the region. Arnošt's mother was also about to start a job as an unskilled labourer. She was refused to right to study and even to learn a profession. Only because of the involvement of her mother, Arnošt's grandmother, was she able to start training to be a glassmaker in another region. Later on she even managed to graduate from university. Nevertheless, in the late sixties she lost her job. One of the reasons was the fact that her sister emigrated and "she did not distance" herself, explains Arnošt. Being "expelled" from the region where one lives is a theme which is repeated not only in the grandfather's and the mother's biography, both of which Arnošt introduces briefly, but also in the life of Arnošt himself.

Arnošt lived in Olomouc until the age of twenty four. He finished primary school, grammar school and university in Olomouc. The history and social status of his family had an impact on Arnošt's educational pathway and the way he perceived it.

A: Well (breathing out slowly) and I experienced my education as a little bit stressful because my mum kept telling me from childhood (breathing) I had always, during all my education I only once got a B.56 It was in my fourth grade (at grammar school, comment A.G.). And when I came home in fourth grade with a B (breathing) so my mum said to me with a serious face – she looked at me and said: "Well Arnošt, you know which family you are from. If you don't only get A's (laughing) you won't get anywhere. Only like this will you have at least a very small chance of getting somewhere". (Arnošt p. 14, l. 424-430)

Politics also played a role for Arnošt when choosing a foreign language and, moreover, his university studies. As he argues, it was his mother who chose the German language for him. She was the one who made most of the decisions since her parents were divorced. After high school he chose to study History and German not because of some special motivation for the language but because of his family's political background. As his chances to enter university were limited, he strategically chose the combination of History and German since there were relatively few applicants for this combination and the chances of being accepted were thus higher. At university Arnošt belonged to a circle of people who organized seminars and lectures in private flats to which they invited professors from abroad, distributed "forbidden" texts and, because they experienced their education as insufficient, educated themselves in self-learning groups.

After Arnošt finished his studies he was about to start a job as a lecturer in the Department of history. However, at the very last moment the offered position was denied to him. Arnošt argues that it was because of the "bad family profile" and his refusal to enter the party. Consequently, he moved to

---

56 In the Czech Republic, marks awarded at grammar and high school range from 1 to 5, with 1 being the best mark and 5 the worst. In the Czech original Arnošt speaks about getting "dvojka", "2", the equivalent of which in English is a "B".

Prague where he started a one year internship. Arnošt had very similar experiences of exclusion as in Olomouc caused by the job rejection and limited further chances of self-development later on in life when returning from Prague and some years later from Bamberg to Olomouc as a lecturer and a professor.

Prague and Arnošt's first border crossings

In 1988 Arnošt moved to Prague and applied for a PhD position at the Department of history there. However, he was not admitted. Arnošt argues that the positions were already given out in advance. Nevertheless, a new position was created for him: a one year scholarship. He wrote articles and educated himself and in 1989 he switched to the Department of German Cultural Studies. He used his "alternative" contacts from his circle of friends in Olomouc in order to better his situation and gain access to "alternative sources and structures", as he explains, without having to enter the party.

In 1989 the revolution happened and with it changes at the university. The university became the place for discussions and planning the next protests and steps in the reorganisation process. Arnošt actively took part in the organisation of student meetings and discussions. Arnošt reflects on the changes at university as follows:

A: I perceived very intensively the change at university. There was a student strike, lots of people left for political reasons, but also lots of people came back because of the political vindication. Especially at the Department of German Studies lots of people left because of their insufficient qualification, or rather as the collaborators of State Security, and so on. It was a very current topic. (Arnošt, p 15, l. 470-477)

During the year of the revolution Arnošt got married and shortly afterwards his first child was born. The marriage took place in the city centre during a week of turbulent demonstrations. The moment of his marriage reflects the uncertainty at this time in which power relations were about to change.

A: My brother was always joking that I wanted for the last time to breathe fresh air while I was still single and I therefore opened the window, and that people started to gather around and were waiting for me to speak to crowds. (laughing) Really, there were armed forces everywhere, well I don't know now. It was really a thrilling moment. (Arnošt, p. 16, l. 509-513)

The political shift meant the beginning of a new life phase for Arnošt both for his professional and private life. New possibilities which had been inaccessible to him beforehand because of his social positioning were now available to him and his family, such as the possibility of going to abroad.

A: I had already got a short scholarship in the spring of 1990. It was a state scholarship which was initially given to – it was still to the former GDR so I was in Hamburg, I lived in the same block with one of the student leaders (laughing) and: it was actually a state scholarship sponsored by the Czech side and it was initially given to a differently qualified colleague who then suddenly became unqualified because his political qualification was not enough. (Arnošt, p. 18-19, l. 576-584)

The shift in political and social structures went hand in hand with the re-definition of qualifications and skills. Arnošt's qualification and skills gained in value because of the changes at university, and he became able to mobilise them to a greater extent than before. The fact that he went abroad with a Czech scholarship is meaningful for Arnošt, as it reveals a newly gained recognition of his abilities by the authority of the "state". Two years later Arnošt was again given a chance to go to Hamburg with his family, this time on a German scholarship. As he narrates,

A: We made use of it. We were in Hamburg, we lived -, we established contacts, we developed well with regard to the language and the profession, one made some work progress (breathing), I inhaled the absolutely different literature and atmosphere. (Arnošt, p. 19, l. 590-593)

Arnošt stayed in Hamburg for one year. He says he had an offer to stay even longer because his scholarship could be extended, but he was asked to return to Prague and continue his job as a lecturer there. Nevertheless, despite his return he still nurtured the contacts he had established in Hamburg. He also handed in and sat the viva for his PhD thesis there. The social networks, new knowledge and intercultural competencies he acquired there were important resources for his next migrations.

After his return from Hamburg, Arnošt stayed in Prague for about a year before moving to Olomouc. As he explains,

A: I did not manage to create such good relationships in Prague and my wife missed Olomouc. We both went to Prague at that time, in 1988 (breathing) so we went back to Olomouc. In Olomouc it was not possible to get a job at the Department of German studies so I switched to the position that had initially been offered to me before the revolution when there was no possibility to start a job at that time. So I started at the Department of History in Olomouc. (Arnošt, p. 4, l. 103-110)

The use of social networks is crucial for his career. It was because of his connections in the "underground scene" that he moved to Prague and started a job there despite his "bad family profile". Keeping the network links to Olomouc enabled him to come back and to start a new career there. Moreover, social transnational links which he established during his placement in Hamburg, Germany, also helped him to move to Bamberg later on.

From Olomouc to Bamberg

Arnošt stayed in Olomouc for five years.

A: And after five years my habilitation was finished. And: because I had also done a PhD in Hamburg I actually had the courage to apply for a position here in Bamberg. I came here for the competition uhm: for this competition not because I wanted to go to Germany (laughing) but because in Germany I had learned the strategy of negotiating the position and that one could negotiate one's wage and: because – because my wife (breathing) we already had our first child at that time and she had not returned to work because of some problems so we – in order to earn a bit more money I thought that if I applied for a position there and I was successful that I could negotiate something better for myself. (Arnošt, p. 4, l. 112-122)

While applying for a job in Bamberg, Arnošt used his transnational experience and knowledge acquired during his previous stays in Germany. He made use not only of his PhD which he had obtained in Germany, but also of his knowledge of "how the things work". His experience of living and working abroad became a resource for him which he could draw on while searching for a possibility of overcoming the economic problems back in Olomouc.

Arnošt was unexpectedly awarded the position. Shortly afterwards he moved to Bamberg and started his teaching and research activities. He recalls the beginnings in Bamberg in the following way:

A: When I came here I remember that it was actually a shock for me, because (breathing) back in the Czech Republic I held lectures for eighty people, ninety people, and now when I came here I had lecture for three students! Things have changed today that I have I don't know, twenty five forty students. But still, the role of – and the position of Central and Eastern European History is different in Germany. German studies are a key discipline here (breathing) and: and: these people are perceived as scientists even in different branches and they have a different resonance here (breathing). Like Czech history has in the Czech Republic. (Arnošt, p. 7, l. 226-233)

Arnošt describes the move from teaching a "central" discipline to a "peripheral" one in the course of his migration. On the one hand, he improved his position and financial situation. On the other hand, however, he experienced less recognition of his scientific activities. His different positioning within the scientific community also had an impact on the different level of participation of students in his lectures. As Arnošt explains further on, in addition to the decrease in the number of students attending his lectures, the target group of his lectures shifted as well. His students did not study only history, as was the case back in Olomouc, but came from diverse scientific fields. Therefore, he had to extend his knowledge and train himself to know about other fields, such as linguistic and cultural studies.

After six months in Bamberg he was offered a professorship post. Nevertheless, Arnošt turned down the professorship and returned to Olomouc. He argues that one of the reasons for rejecting the professorship in Bamberg was the fact that he did not want to live abroad. In addition, so Arnošt, he wanted to spend time with his second child who was born at this time and lived with the rest of his family in Olomouc. However, after his return to Olomouc Arnošt faced unexpected difficulties. As he recalls:

A: Nevertheless, it became a bit complicated because my colleagues (in Olomouc, comment A.G.) thought that I earned too much money in Germany and the boss who employed me had actually already been replaced by some other boss and he thought that in six months I earned so much money in Germany that – that I lost all personal benefits, I only got a basic wage and we were absolutely not able to get by. And at the same time (breathing out) I received a revised offer from here. (Arnošt, p. 4-5, l. 134-140)

Arnošt's expectations concerning his return to Olomouc were not met in reality. While in Germany he was able to negotiate his wage and working conditions, as he had learned during his stay in Hamburg, in the Czech Republic he was not able to use the same strategy and was given a basic salary. As he states further on, his decision to return to Bamberg again was very quick. When he moved to Olomouc, the university tried to fill the position of professor for Central and Eastern European History in Bamberg with someone else, however to no avail. They thus contacted Arnošt again and asked whether he would not rethink his decision. Arnošt agreed to take the job. Shortly afterwards he left again for Bamberg, with his family joining him about six months later.

Arnošt explains extensively the reasons for their renewed migration. He argues that the economic problems were not the only reason for their move to Bamberg. He liked the open attitude towards students which he had already got to know in Hamburg, Arnošt explains. He also appreciated the library and the overall atmosphere surrounding "doing science". Moreover, the decision was influenced not only by Arnošt's personal motives but also by the potential benefits for other family members.

A: The plan was – or our idea was not that we would like to come here permanently, but we actually planned to only stay for three years. And after three years – three years is a standard period for which for example lecturers leave to go abroad (breathing) so there was already some kind of tolerance towards it. (Breathing) So we had a feeling that we both would learn something, that our children would learn something (breathing) (Arnošt, p. 6, l. 174-181)

As in his previous narration, Arnošt justifies his willingness to return to Olomouc. The idea of returning was an inseparable part of his migration project and also shaped the future perspectives of Arnošt and his family. However, during his stay in Bamberg his plans changed again.

From Bamberg to Olomouc and back

A: However, in the course – in between changed – as one develops one's opinions so my perspective changed and I got used to the fact that I am independent, that I did not have to ask anyone if I can do this or that (breathing) so I did not want to return to Olomouc only as a lecturer. (Arnošt, p. 6, l. 181-190)

Returning to Olomouc meant that Arnošt would have to accept a position for which he was overqualified and start to build up his career from scratch. In order to get a professorship in Olomouc, Arnošt had to start the professorship application procedure again there. He argues that his habilitation and professorship were not acknowledged across the border. The whole procedure had to be done again. Arnošt worked on his monograph which was one of the conditions for getting the professorship. After he submitted it he was nominated for the professorship of Czech History in Olomouc. The whole procedure lasted longer than expected: three years until their planned return became six years. In 2006 he was ready to move back.

Arnošt lists the motives for returning to Olomouc:

A: There were more reasons for returning. Firstly, we, as Czechs, did not want to stay permanently in Germany. We have also never applied for citizenship even though we could because I have a permanent residency here and a job for an unlimited period of time and so on. So it never attracted us or maybe we even did not think about it. We did comparative tests for the Czech language with our son so that he could always return to school "normally", so he could start "normally" and would not have any problems. And the third reason was surely that as a historian I was a bit remote from the resources and from the events and affairs. (Arnošt, p. 7, l. 216-224)

Arnošt names his sense of national belonging as the first reason for considering returning. Not applying for German citizenship supports Arnošt's perception of his Czech sense of belonging, which he ascribes to himself and other family members, as exclusive and as opposed to a German sense of belonging. The positioning of himself and his family as "others" in Germany serves Arnošt as a justification for their positioning within the Czech society and their return to the Czech Republic. Refusing German citizenship may also be connected to the experiences of social isolation in Germany which Arnošt alludes to later on. According to Arnošt, the second reason for returning to Olomouc was the Czech language. Czech was the main language spoken within the family. Arnošt and his wife made efforts to teach their children the Czech language in order that they could pass the exams supported by the Czech Educational Act (Zákon č. 561/2004 Sb., §38).[57] The efforts of Arnošt and his wife to transmit their native language and to enable their children to move between the Czech and German educational systems are crucial for their potential return to the Czech Republic and, moreover, for the transmission of transnational spaces which they are about to create to their children. In order to explain the role of language in their return in more detail, Arnošt elaborates his story with background construction (Schütze 2012a, p. 27) concerning the language difficulties of their son at high school in Bamberg. As Arnošt explains,

---

57   The exams can be sat twice a year in one of the schools situated in the territory of the Czech Republic or in the consulate. Teaching for the additional exams is done mostly at home by parents and relatives.

A: When we came here he was eight nine years old and it means that he was relatively old and: (breathing in) in order to learn the language we let him repeat the second class. The transit took relatively long (breathing) nearly one year, or even more than one year until he actually integrated concerning the language. And: at school he did not have any special problems because of the language. He moved up normally to high school (breathing) but when he – when English started he did not have any particular problems. When Latin started he did not have any particular problems. But at the moment he got – when he started to learn the second language through the other foreign language – German was for him still not very self-evident and: despite that he knew – despite learning the grammar perfectly, despite learning the vocabulary perfectly, he did not manage nuances of translation from Latin to German. He thus got into difficulties which also had an impact on other subjects and so on. Therefore one of the reasons for returning was that we also saw the return as the solution for the problems of our son with the language. (Arnošt, p. 8-9, l. 251-267)

As a result of diverse considerations which Arnošt summarises above, Arnošt's wife and two children moved back to Olomouc in 2006. Arnošt was about to follow when the last ambiguities considering his job were clarified. His wife and children moved into the house they had built in the meantime and Arnošt began to commute between Olomouc and Bamberg. The professorship was offered to him one year later, in 2007.

A: Well! Nevertheless, you see me here (laughing)! So the commuting was an inconclusive situation for me. Well, I don't know. Personally, concerning my family, emotionally, me for myself, professionally, because I commuted once every two weeks (breathing) but the connection to Olomouc was bad so I travelled most of the time by car there and back uhm: ten hours (breathing in) I was tired, twice a month, the loss of twenty hours of actual time, it is a huge blackout time, which one could use for something else. So we saw it as absolutely essential that I would come back. (Arnošt, p. 9-10, l. 284-297)

Despite all of the preparations for the return, Arnošt and his family once again changed their minds.

A: However, at the time of the job negotiations in Olomouc it again became apparent that some practices from abroad (breathing in) (1) well that I had written some books here, besides those for which I was nominated, but that I had published a whole range of papers or that I had plenty of projects or some other different things, these qualifications did not have any impact on the salary. I would get the ordinary salary for professors plus some minimal personal appraisal and the rest I would have to build – win again. (Arnošt, p. 10, l. 297-306)

As Arnošt argues, his own experiences, knowledge and qualifications acquired abroad could only be partly used when he moved back to Olomouc, which in turn would mean a step back in his career. At the same time, the perception of the quality of the Czech educational system in comparison with the German system changed. Arnošt and his wife came to the conclusion that their children would get a better education and better possibilities studying in Germany.

A: To this came a relatively surprising fact, actual verbal bullying (laughing) to which our children were exposed. The schoolmates called them German and shut up you German and things like that. (Arnošt, p. 11. l. 329-333)

On the one hand, Arnošt positions himself and his other family members as "Czechs". On the other hand, his children experienced being called names and excluded from "Czechness" by their schoolmates in Olomouc because of their long term life in Germany. Moreover, the "othering" (Hall 1994) came not only from schoolmates but also from teachers who claimed that his children had a German accent, which Arnošt denies. The discrimination experienced by his children because of their cross border experiences, as well as the impossibility of transferring his professional abilities across the border, and the wish to provide better educational opportunities for their children, were all reasons that contributed to the redefinition of future perspectives for himself and his family and led to the renewed move to Bamberg. As Arnošt summarises,

A: So there were more motives for the departure, coming back and again in my case the end of commuting and for my family a new- new arrival in Germany. And it was I don't know, such a mixture of different reasons. There were without a doubt (breathing in) (1) many reasons. Economic, professional, personal, personal uhm a lot – In the first place the questions of- or they had always played a role, education and the possibility of self-realisation (breathing in) to which economic appreciation also belongs. But probably education for the children or the possibilities for the children- (breathing in). During the first departure it was all about our self-realisation, possibilities and qualification. We had grown older in the meantime so one thinks more about the qualifications and possibilities for one's own children. Well, it was quite a long summary, but but but it was such a complicated example of a departure, coming back and departing. (laughing) (Arnošt, p. 11-12, l. 345-359)

Living in "exile"

After Arnošt's family returned to Bamberg, they started to organise their life there again. Arnošt continued his professorship at the university in Bamberg and his children returned to primary school and high school there. Nevertheless, Arnošt did not disrupt the social links to his family and colleagues back in Olomouc but made an effort to keep them alive. As he argues,

A: I still have some contacts but it takes extra energy. Not only that I am running between two disciplines but this keeping up the contacts (breathing in) costs lots of time, because I actually have PhD students in Olomouc too and so on. It costs energy and it is actually – what frustrates me. I often think that that that – when people left before the year eighty nine they knew that they had to integrate and so on. They knew that they cannot look back. This possibility to come back is maybe (breathing in) maybe also – actually also this duty, it is difficult for our children too. We practise the Czech language with them and (breathing in) we make an effort so that they also have the possibility of potentially coming back. So we work on their bilingualism, also with writing (breathing in) which migrants before eighty nine did not have and maybe it is better for their integration because we spend lots of time – lots of holidays there and we spend lots of time there because of family as well, we try to keep contact with family and professionally (breathing in) so it is at the expense of the integration here. (1) Of us. For our children it is something different, or for our younger son. I think that our older son is not well integrated (breathing in) and our younger son is perfectly integrated, but I think that – I think that we are not well integrated, socially, or humanly, or concerning the social networks because (breathing in) we are not a mixed family, we are solely a Czech family (breathing in) and: our family actually repeatedly looked back and (1) we are a family which has also partly been back and which actually still doesn't exclude the possibility of returning. You are the sociologist so you know that when you build or keep a network somewhere it costs time and energy and you don't have time somewhere else, isn't it. That's how it is (laughing). One always tries to find some optimal in-between course (laughing). (Arnošt, p. 23-24, l. 722-749)

The option of returning and "looking back", according to Arnošt, is the most important feature which distinguishes today's migrants from the previous generation of migrants. The turning point is the revolution in 1989 which signified different structural conditions, possibilities accessible to migrants and different experiences of crossing the border, living abroad and coming back. Arnošt uses the possibility of "looking back" to describe newly established transnational links between Germany and the Czech Republic. They represent the possibility to travel between two countries, the possibility to keep contact with one's family, friends, or colleagues over the border, as well as the possibility to live and plan one's future in both places or at least to keep the possibility of doing do open.

However, according to Arnošt the possibility of establishing transnational links and a transnational way of life brings with it new challenges, such as keeping social networks alive and passing on one's native language to the next generation. Learning the Czech language abroad is a prerequisite for the successful return of Arnošt and his family to the Czech Republic, since the institutionally recognised knowledge of the Czech language is necessary for enabling his children to take part in the Czech educational system. Language is also an instrument which keeps the option of living in the Czech Republic open for his children in the future. As shown by the example of his children being labelled as "others" and excluded from being "Czechs" because of their supposed German accent in Olomouc, language plays an important role in the perception of belonging and positioning within the Czech society. The transmission of the Czech language is thus crucial for establishing and keeping alive the transnational spaces and enabling his children to have equal opportunities in both societies.

While at the beginning of his narration Arnošt introduces his family as a "normal Czech, not mixed family" in order to preclude that his potential migration motives might be based on his family's cultural background, towards the end of his narration he raises this topic again, this time in relation to his own core family. "Being a solely Czech family" living in Germany distinguishes them not only from other families with different cultural and national backgrounds, but also from families which are "mixed". The perception of social exclusion which Arnošt explains by the fact of "being a solely Czech family" supports the impression of his story being narrated from a position of "exile": in respect of his sense of national belonging, social networks and even his scientific activities the centre of which is situated across the border.

Arnošt's narration is based on extensive arguments that try to explain the reasons for his family's migration to Germany, a country in which he never actually wanted to live. The necessity to explain and justify their decision to live in Germany is connected to Arnošt's positioning in both societies and the perception of exclusion both in the Czech Republic and in Germany. At the beginning of his narration, Arnošt justifies his belonging to Olomouc, the city where his family lived and he grew up. The experiences of exclusion and limited chances of self-realisation for him and later on for his children led him and his family to repeated migrations. Nevertheless, the idea of returning to Olomouc, which has never been fully quashed, has stayed present in Arnošt's past and future perspectives. The transnational links which he actively creates and try to keep alive in his private and professional life for both himself and his children are experienced both as opportunities, because they open up new possibilities and new life perspectives, and as restraints, since in Arnošt's opinion they result in their being insufficiently integrated into the social structures in Germany. Furthermore, the necessity to explain and justify the decision to live in Germany is connected to the perception of national belonging for Arnošt. While he considers himself and other family members as "Czechs", they are exposed to "othering" (Hall 1994) both in Germany and the Czech Republic because of their cross border experiences. His statement: "One always tries to find some optimal in-between course" illustrates the act of planning his future perspectives and positioning in transnational spaces as an active and as yet unaccomplished process.

6.5.3   Summary

"It was such a complicated example of leaving, returning and leaving" is how Arnošt summarises his narration. Indeed, the various repeated migrations and returns dominate his story. From the very beginning of his story, Arnošt searches for explanations of these processes and of the fact that he now lives in Germany, a country he never actually wanted to live in. His story is a story of "living in exile".

Olomouc, the city in which Arnošt was born plays a central role in his biography. His family history had an impact on Arnošt's relationship with the city. Arnošt's family suffered under the former communist regime and also Arnošt's childhood and education were to a great extent influenced by the position of his family during this era. Arnošt's grandfather and mother suffered from the loss of their jobs and from limited access to education because of their class status and political orientation. They were both forced to leave the region and move elsewhere in order to continue or establish a new educational and professional pathway for themselves. Arnošt lived in Olomouc until university graduation. After the promised job at the university was denied to him, he moved to Prague. Just as it did for Arnošt's grandfather and mother, migration was a strategy for Arnošt for dealing with experiences of exclusion and limited chances of personal development. After his migration to Prague in the Czech Republic, and later on to Bamberg in Germany, Arnošt repeatedly tried to return to Olomouc, yet his long term return was never fully implemented.

The political turn in 1989, which occurred when Arnošt was living and working on a scholarship holder at the university in Prague, signified a biographical twist for him. New possibilities which were before denied to him opened up and he was able to use his qualifications and skills to a greater extent than before. One of the new possibilities, which he took advantage of, was a study placement in Hamburg, Germany, shortly after the revolution. He established new social networks there and even decided to change PhD supervisor from one in Prague to one in Hamburg, where in the end he completed his PhD. His PhD studies in Germany, as well as intercultural competencies and social networks established during this time, were crucial for Arnošt's future migrations to Germany. The transnational spaces which he created and later on mobilised enabled him to continue his career across the border when he was not able to hold on to the initial career he had commenced in Olomouc.

Initially, Arnošt considered migration to Bamberg as a means of overcoming the economic problems of his family in Olomouc, where he was now employed as a lecturer. He won the competition and gained a professorship position in Bamberg. However, after a few months he gave up the professorship and returned to Olomouc. Nevertheless, the economic situation led Arnošt to consider once again moving to Bamberg. The short term migration project turned into a long term stay during which Arnošt again took up a professorship in Bamberg. In order to return to Olomouc after several years in Bamberg, Arnošt started a professorship application procedure in the Czech Republic. Despite obtaining a professorship in the Czech Republic as well, in the process of moving places it became apparent that the transfer of skills and professional experiences across the border would not be possible and that Arnošt would have to start to build up his career again from scratch. He thus decided to stay in Bamberg. Arnošt nonetheless made an effort to keep his transnational social networks alive, thereby keeping open the potential possibilities of return.

Migration to and from Germany to the Czech Republic was a family project, even though Arnošt's career played an important role in the decision making. While at the beginning the motives to move to Germany or to return to the Czech Republic were based on the interests of Arnošt and his wife, as their children grew up it was mostly them and their education, self-development and future perspectives which had an impact on the border crossings.

While living in Germany, Arnošt and his wife made an effort to create and to keep the transnational spaces alive for themselves and for their children. In order to enable their return to the Czech Republic, they worked hard at teaching and passing on the Czech language to their children. The Czech language was necessary in order for the children to pass the additional exams required by the Czech Educational Act and to enable them to participate in the Czech educational system. Furthermore, language was the crucial instrument governing the positioning of his children in both societies, as shown by the exclusion experiences of his children in Olomouc because of their supposed German accent. Through extensive "transnational work", consisting of the passing on of language skills and keeping transnational links alive, Arnošt and his wife made an effort to keep the potential options, future perspectives and equal chances in both societies open for their children.

Throughout his entire story, Arnošt searches for explanations of his migrations and returns. The necessity to explain and justify the decision to live in Germany is linked to the migration history, perception of national belonging, and positioning of Arnošt and his family in both societies. His narration can also be read as an effort "to find some optimal in-between course" and position oneself in a new way within the complex matrix of power relations, positions and meanings in transnational spaces.

7 Cross-case comparisons and findings

In this chapter I shall elaborate in more detail some central findings which resulted from case comparisons. By doing so I will refer not only to the four biographies which I introduced in the previous chapter, but I will also include the narratives, evaluations, explanations and perspectives of other interviewees.

During the analysis it became clear that the changing face and meaning of the border played an important role across narratives. The interviewees pointed out multiple interconnections and divisions which can be traced back to the historical developments in this region of Europe. Their biographies cannot be understood without referring to these division lines within which migrants were entangled, which they reflected on and which they to some extent biographically reworked as well. Hence, I will first turn my attention to the biographical reflections on history, borders and border crossings – both geographical and mental. Next I will look at the role of migration within the biographies. I will point out the role of structural inequalities within the Czech Republic and draw a link to and between internal and international migration. I will show how the first border crossings shaped other migration and how the decisions to move within the newly established transnational spaces were negotiated. In addition, I will pay attention to transnational links and to the meaning given to them by the biographers. In the last chapter I will have a closer look at the links between spatial and social mobility. I will point out the structural settings shaping the possibilities and, consequently, the ways in which migrants negotiate their skills, knowledge and qualifications within these frameworks. Finally, I will reflect on the question of "translatability" of social positions across the borders and on the role of their recognition in transnational settings.

7.1 Biographical reflections on borders and border crossings

The borders and border crossings were central themes in most of the narratives. The migrants put into words the changed face of the border, dividing not only two nation states, but also drawing a line between "East" and "West". Despite the geographical borders almost disappearing in the last decade, the mental borders remained strong and became the subject of biographical reflections. In this chapter I will pay attention to the role of borders, border regions, East-West divisions and biographical reflections on the history of this region of Europe, which is marked by contradictory processes of nation-building and transnational and transcultural interconnections.

7.1.1 Borders and border regions in biographical renderings

The borders were an important theme in my interviewees' biographical renderings. Since most migrants were from the border regions – which turned out to be not by chance but a result of specific socio-cultural constellations in the border regions, as I will show later – the presence of the border became part of everyday life. Martin, for example, told me the following:

I: Could you tell me about- how you grew up. If you remember an event from your childhood. (1)

M: Well I grew up in a village (2) where (1) I had an advantage- (1) I had quite a good childhood. I lived close to the border. There was a playground close to my house, I spent a lot of free time there. I played either sport or we played games or I was at my grandma's, as I already said, she lived about one kilometre from my place, yes, there were also other children with whom I played games, so I think it was quite good. (Martin, p. 31, 1. 979-988)

The proximity of the border was often expressed in narratives concerning subjects' childhood and adolescence, although it was usually mentioned in passing, as Martin's example illustrates. Since all interviewees were born and grew up during the Cold War, they experienced the absolute character of the border, which was highly protected and difficult to cross. Lenka, who like Martin lived close to the border, reflected as follows for example:

L: I was I was learning German because I wanted to understand when we received erm: the Austrian programs so I wanted to understand what Tom and Jerry were saying and so on. I also always wanted to go somewhere abroad, yes, because I never understood why we could not leave the country! [I: Hmm] But how can you explain it to a child, who simply, would not understand anyway. (Lenka II, p. 12, 1. 361-375)

Lenka's narrative shows how the presence of the border shaped the biographies of individuals – in her case it was the decision to learn German and, after the revolution in 1989, to cross the border on her own. She put into practice the family project of migration, which had been planned several times by her family before, but which had been repeatedly denied to them by state authorities.

The impossibility of crossing the border during the Cold War and the slackening of border regimes after 1989 was a topic which was repeated across the narratives. The latter was often described by means of the expression "the borders opened" and complemented by short narrations about the first border crossing of the individuals themselves or other family members. The newly acquired possibility of movement was thematised as the most significant change after the collapse of the Iron Curtain. Jana, for example, described the way in which the revolution changed the life paths and possibility spaces of individuals in the following way:

J: Actually many things changed after the revolution, also concerning values. [I: Hmm] Until that time normal life was built differently. [I: Hmm] And I grew up in it a bit, still at the beginning of secondary school I still had this feeling. That life should go like this, you know. But then after the revolution so many things changed, and suddenly: everything was different! [I: Hmm] (1) Until the revolution you (1) studied, (1) married, had children (laughing) and: (1) because you could not go anywhere anyway! [I: Hmm] Because (1) there was no competition. Concerning work. You could not say, ok, I will be really good at work and: you just couldn't have a career! (1) It didn't exist. You got the same salary (1) and when you belonged to the communist party so maybe you were a bit better off. But: healthy competition, there was none at all. [I: Hmm] (1) It meant that everyone's life was already set out in straight lines. Well and (1) suddenly thousands of possibilities opened up after the revolution! You could choose whether to travel there, there or there and (deep breathing) you could do as you wished with your life. It was not until then. [I: Hmm] I was a bit delayed at understanding it (1) and: (2) if I had lived in Germany from childhood for example, I would probably also have decided differently. [I: Hmm] (1) I started at nursing school and I even thought that I would do it a while (laughing) (clearing her throat) but then I realised that it wouldn't be enough for me somehow, that I wanted to study. And during my studies I understood that I would actually like to go abroad. [I: Hmm] (1) That it was part of me a bit. The travelling and- (1) If I had spent my whole life living under communism as my parents did, I would never have got the idea. Because I couldn't have done it anyway. Only because I was able to try it did I discover that it was good for me. (Jana, p. 21, l. 852-871)

Jana, like other interviewees, linked migration directly to the transformation processes of Czech society. In her view, the revolution signified the opening up of new possibilities, which she described as „you can travel there, there and there". Migration, which appeared as a possible option during the transition processes, became for her the means of biographical metamorphosis (Schütze 2001), as well as the alternative to "standardised life paths" (Pařízková 2011b), which developed almost exclusively within the setting of the one-nation state. As I will show later, Jana and others drew comparisons between their alternative – or transnational – biographical pathway and the biographical pathway of those left behind – living "standardised" life paths within one nation state and seeing their everyday world through this one-dimensional perspective. This perception of migrants points out certain paradoxical processes in Czech society in the course of the transition process: the pursuit of nationalism formed by politics and public discourse both before and after the revolution (Holý 1996), as well as transnational processes, resulting from the opening up of the borders and the integration of the Czech Republic into wider global structures (Uherek 2003).

For most migrants I interviewed as part of the present project Germany was the first country they moved to after the fall of the Iron Curtain. These first stays, which also shaped further migrations as I will show later, had very different purposes – be it visiting relatives living in Germany, au pair placements, student exchanges, seasonal work in a factory or agriculture, or volunteer programs. The choice of Germany as the country of migration had several reasons – the geographical closeness, the accessibility of work or study opportunities, or/and knowledge of the German language.

Despite the fact that English was the first foreign language taught at grammar and secondary schools in the Czech Republic from the early 1990s onwards, the German language, which was generally the second foreign language learnt after English in most regions, remained the dominant foreign language in Western and Northern Bohemia (Průcha 1999, p. 259), the Czech-German border regions. The role of the German language in Northern Bohemia, the region of his origin, is also reflected upon by Martin:

M: All my life German was my main language, the second was English, because actually (1) as I am from Most, it is in Sudetenland, [I: hm] so there nearly everyone- my grandma is German, [I: hm] yes, so actually, there are- or nearly everyone has in their family in some way (1) some German these, yes. (Martin, p. 16-17, l. 542-546)

In order to explain the choice of foreign language – and consequently his migration to Germany –, Martin outlines the history of his family and the role of the German language and culture in his region of origin. The bilinguality and transculturality of the area where he grew up had an impact on his biographical pathway, influencing the choice of language and possibilities of moving country later on. Moreover, being from the border region became a resource for him, since very early on he developed the ability of "translating" and "shifting" from one cultural code into another, and from one language to another. The German and Czech languages did not only co-exist beside each other in the border regions, but they mutually influenced and formed each other. This is what Kamil said, for example, who lived with his wife in Leipzig at the time of the interview:

K: My father- you know, since I am from Sudetenland, there are lots of words which are somehow germanised. [I: Hmm] For example fusekle! Do you also say fusekle?

I: Fusekle. My grandma. (laughing)

K: Socks, yes, fusekle. Or šnuptychl. [I: (laughing)] Well yeah. So you then become aware of it. (…) You know then you find out that there are suddenly so many of these words! [I: Hmm] Dekl. (1) Or what else. Hajzl, no. [I: Hmm] They are all taken over from German. Yes and these things are- we have about six dictionaries and we are always searching for the origin of these words. [I: (laughing)], (deep breathing) and we laugh so much while doing so! (1) Ajzlboňák, isn't it. Someone who works on the railway. And my grandma used it (breathing in) because (1) I should say something about my family, well it is such a dramatic story (breathing in) the parents from both sides come from Germany, or they have

German origin and (1) actually the place where we live- we are the only family which was not displaced. All others were displaced. (…) (Kamil, p. 20, l. 615-625)

Both Martin and Kamil did not start to reflect on the cultural heterogeneity of their place of origin – which actually contradicts the scientific and public discourses on the "ethnic homogeneity" of the Czech society in the second half of the 20th century – until after migration. They underlined the specificity of their region, inter alia by drawing comparisons to my biography as interviewer, – pointing out the differences between the border regions and Prague, where I am from. Martin and Kamil, like other interviewees, re-construed their family history in the course of migration and drew links to their actual positioning in Germany. As their examples show, to speak about Czech-German interconnections in this region was not possible without mentioning their family history, which was often marked by deportation, displacement, and the process of nationalisation in Czechoslovakia after World War II (Markel 2006). Despite a large proportion of my interviewees telling me – often not until the latter part of interview and with the comment that "maybe it is also important" or "I should also say" – that some close family member actually had German origins, the German language had in any case not been passed down to them. Jana, for example, reflected on the failure of her family to pass on the language to her as follows: "actually my father was half German and half Czech. Actually his mother was German. So, theoretically, I should have been able to speak German fluently from a young age!" (Jana, p. 23, l. 842-844). Drawing links to their family history made it possible for some interviewees to again establish biographical continuity which was in some cases put into question by migration processes.

7.1.2   Becoming an "Eastern European" after migration

When moving country, migrants not only crossed the Czech-German border, but also the border between "the East" and "the West". Interestingly, it was not until after migration that migrants were confronted with being labelled "Eastern European". However, they developed different strategies of challenging this ascription which had mostly negatively connotations. Martin, for example, states as follows:

M: I am always very surprised that they don't know anything about us, although they are our neighbours, so it sometimes surprises me, they say that when they learnt about the East- they learnt the history of East Germany. And that was all. Eastern Europe was for them East Germany. They learnt about the East, but just about Germany. Nothing more. (1) Of course I am- one is sometimes pissed that they put you at the same- erm same level as for example Romanians, yes, that they see Eastern Europe so you are- but there is basically a big difference, there is big difference, Romania, Bulgaria, it is absolutely- yes! It pisses me off that they compare us to Poland! But the Czechs don't have, they don't even have a reputation of any kind, when I speak to Germans! (1) Poles for example, yes, that they steal cars, that the car is always found in Poland. But Czechs? They don't have even an opinion about them! (Martin, p. 30-31, l. 957-977)

Martin de-constructs the social construction of "Eastern Europe" which has been construed as a counterpart to "Western Europe" and which has been perceived as an undifferentiated social, cultural and political unit. The divisions of "Eastern Europe" and "Western Europe", which are in a hierarchical power relationship to one another, were radicalised during the Cold War and still continue to shape the "mental map" of Europe (Stölting 2000). In addition, Martin also brings up the "invisibility" of the Czech Republic in public discourses in Germany and the lack of stereotypes concerning Czechs, which point towards the unequal power relation between these two countries, be it because of its political and economic power, the actual size of these two countries or their respective histories. The meaning of "being Czech" and "being Eastern European" in Germany was also put into words by Petr:

P: I think there are still some prejudices. [: Hmm] That Eastern Europe is seen here as (breathing out). [: Hmm] But I try not to perceive it or not to care about it. Because it doesn't make any sense to occupy myself with it. [: Hmm] And I think that it is surely not a plus point being from the Czech Republic here. When you want to work or establish contacts. [: Hmm] Maybe for women it's easier, but for a man it is not an advantage.

I: Why do you think so?

P: Well I think- there are some- (1) it is interesting. How many couples do you know where the man is Czech and the woman is German? And how many do you know where the opposite is the case? [: Hmm] You know what I mean? (Petr, p. 40, l. 1280-1286)

Besides the processes of "othering" (Hall 1994) based on a person's "Eastern European" origin and the disadvantages resulting from such as ascription, Petr pointed out the gender dimension of this division. His observations concerning men's and women's chances to establish social contact and relationships is also clearly reflected by statistics, which show that there were about 18 times more marriages among German men and Czech women then other way round between 1995 and 2007 (ČSÚ 2007). This phenomenon, however, can be partly explained by the higher percentage of women moving from the Czech Republic to Germany (Statistisches Bundesamt 2014d). The narratives of interviewees, however, revealed likewise that the gender dimension became crucial not only concerning establishing contacts, but also when crossing the border and entering the labour market. They showed that discourses about "Eastern European men" and "Eastern European women" remained a powerful force in integrating Europe as well.

7.2 Migration as an enlargement of possibility spaces

In most of the biographies I collected for the present paper, migration became the means – both planned and unplanned – of enlarging the scope of one's own possibilities. In this chapter I will pay attention to the processes connected to the development of these new spaces of action spanning across the borders of one nation state. In the first subchapter I will give an insight into the way migrants experienced inequality among the regions within the Czech Republic. I will show how the structural inequalities shaped the decisions to migrate both within the Czech Republic and over its borders. In the next subchapter I will describe how the first migration experiences during adolescence, which were not necessarily connected to work, opened up the space of action for individuals and, in the majority of cases, acted as a catalyst for repeated migrations. In the next part I will pay attention to these repeated migrations, to their structure and to the decisions of migrants as to whether to move, stay, return or move elsewhere. Subsequently, I will outline the processes of development of transnational social and cultural links by migrants, through which they tried to keep access to their home culture and language and which they tried to pass on to the next generation.

7.2.1 Experiences of inequality in the region of origin

The geographical location of one's origin played a crucial role in developing individuals' motives for migrating. As the narratives show, one's home town was confined by specific opportunity structures, shaped by the accessibility of schools, extracurricular education, social networks, as well as work opportunities. These opportunity structures were, furthermore, structured along gender and class divisions. The first moves, which were not necessarily across borders but to other parts of town or nearby cities, allowed for the individual to develop new perspectives on their own possibilities, abilities, biographical and career pathways and alternative ways of life. For instance, Martin, who was born in a working class family in Northern Bohemia, described in detail these shifts from one location to another, for example from one school to another in a different part of town, which did not only represent a shift in geographical location, but above all a shift in social space – being connected to other expectations and new opportunities, which were limited in his original location. His migration to Prague later on was especially important for him not only because of his starting to study economics there, but also because of the simple fact of getting to Prague – the centre of culture and finance, which offered him a variety of new opportunities. Similarly to Martin, Marie, who was born in a village in Southern Bohemia and lived with her parents on an agricultural farm, also underlined the move from one school to a language orientated secondary school in the nearby town, and later on her move to Prague where she studied Czech and German. These were important biographical steps for her, since she was able to "individualise" herself from her parents' house and develop alternative career paths to those related to her place of origin.

Migration within the Czech Republic because of education and work was a very common feature within my sample. Karolína, for example, moved from Ústí nad Labem, a city close to the Northern border of the Czech Republic, to Olomouc in order to study English and German. Kamil, who was born in Trutnov, a small town in the North-Eastern part of the Czech Republic, moved at first to a nearby town to gain an apprenticeship to become an electrician and later on to Prague where he studied electrical engineering. Arnošt, for example, also moved to Prague in order to continue his scientific career because this was denied to him in Olomouc, the city in which he had lived and studied until then. These moves within the Czech Republic – which very often preceded a migration abroad – had different meanings for different interviewees. They moved in order to get a better education, to individualise themselves from their parental home and to try out other ways of life, or in order to overcome limited opportunities for career development in the place of their origin. One cannot overlook the role of large urban areas, and especially Prague, in the narrations of my interviewees – the majority of them studied there, worked there for a period of time, or argued that they might move there when returning from abroad someday. The large urban areas thus became an alternative for living abroad, since they offered wider opportunity structures for work and self-development, which were neglected in a number of regions of origin.

The theme of inequality among the regions in the Czech Republic concerning access to education and employment was explicitly or implicitly expressed in various biographical renderings. The interviewees often addressed the structural changes in their regions – be it for example changing work opportunities or unemployment which affected either the interviewees themselves, other family members, or their peers who did not migrate but continued living in the places of their origin. Barbora, for example, spoke about the restructuring and partial closure of the mining industry in Northern Bohemia which caused her father to lose his job, and the willingness of her mother and sister to re-orientate to professions other than what they were actually qualified in in order to fit in with the demands of changing labour markets. Interestingly, Barbora was able to build on this strategy to challenge the limited work opportunities by means of professional reorientation, which was a common pattern of women in her region, and also later on after moving to Germany. These changes were the results of the restructuring of the economic system from a command economy to a market economy, which affected certain sectors particularly badly, such as the heavy or textile industries.

282

Some regions, such as Northern Bohemia, Southern Bohemia, or Northern Moravia, were particularly hit by these changes (Drbohlav, Rákoczyová 2012), since these industries were the most important employers there. The interviewees reacted very differently to these "objective" structural inequalities, and they also developed different strategies to overcome them. While some moved places within the Czech Republic, others considered moving abroad.

Notwithstanding the fact that studies have pointed out a relatively low level of mobility of people within the Czech Republic (Novák et al. 2011; Drbohlav, Rákoczyová 2012), my cases revealed the opposite. Those who migrated abroad had very often already moved places within the Czech Republic. There was thus a direct link between internal and international migration. When moving places within the Czech Republic, migrants acquired new abilities, such as the ability to independently orientate themselves in new surroundings, which they were able to apply later on for further migration projects not only within the Czech Republic, but also when moving abroad. Martin, for example, whose biography I introduced above, experienced the move from Most – a medium-sized city in Northern Bohemia – to Prague as a bigger step than moving later on from Prague to Düsseldorf. This was not only due to the fact that migration to Prague was his first independent move, but also because he "moved worlds" – i.e. social spaces from a working milieu to the financial sector.

Zuzana addressed the limited opportunity structures in her town of origin, which led her to migrate to Germany, in the very first sequence of her narrative:

Z: I was born in Jablunkov, it is in North Bohemia, such a small town, six thousand inhabitants, and I grew up there. I lived there actually until the moment I went to Germany. I went to grammar school there, then to high school, and then I submitted some applications to university, but I was not accepted anywhere, (deep breathing), but actually I didn't want to go anywhere, I actually wanted to start working. But (deep breathing) concerning work- it was not so easy there (clears her throat). I then got a position as a seamstress. In a factory. I stood it for three months and on the very last day of the trial period I resigned. And I went to Germany, as an au pair. Ninety six. (Zuzana, p. 1, l. 23-32)

As Zuzana narrated later on, working in a sewing factory was one of the few opportunities of getting a job in her region. She described in detail the hard working conditions and discriminatory treatment of her and other – mostly female – workers by the supervisors which, however, she only questioned much later. In order to escape the social decline, devaluation of her education, which was of no use in her place of work, and limited opportunities, Zuzana considered going to Germany. She evaluated her decision to move to Germany in the following way:

Z: I felt a bit sad when I travelled by train, when I stood there and changed trains somewhere, I was already a bit sad in Prague. That there is no return [I: Hmm] (laughing, 2).

Then in Munich I had to change trains again and it was (shaking shoulders) I didn't want it. It was a decision which emerged from all these things. It was not really (deep breathing) planned. It was probably mostly because of work. Or that I did not get into university. (1) That I said to myself that I have nothing to lose. That I have nothing to lose in the Czech Republic. So I would do so. (2) But I knew that I wanted to go abroad, to learn something else. [I: Hmm] (1) And Germany was- maybe it was because of that advertisement that it was Germany. And that it was not so far. [I: Hmm] (1) That I did not for example go to England. (1) Even though I spoke much better English. So maybe that's why it was like that. (Zuzana, p. 25-26; l. 798-810)

Zuzana's narration points out the way in which the opportunity structures in her region, as well as the possibilities of migration, were shaped by gender. She experienced work in a sewing factory and moving abroad as an au pair, which was a common social practice for women in her surroundings – as is apparent from her explanation: "and as an au pair. Because it was normal, wasn't it. There were plenty of agencies, which started to do so" (Zuzana, p. 25, l.786-788) – as the only possibilities accessible to her. Despite the fact that it was not planned, her decision to move country was for her, as for many other interviewees, crucial for her further biographical and career path, since it opened up a new space of possibilities for her.

7.2.2 Discovering new possibility spaces through initial border crossings

Notwithstanding the fact that the migration of highly skilled people has been almost exclusively investigated in terms of labour migration, the narratives collected as part of the present project show that although work played an important role in all cases, the initial motives for crossing the border were varied and took on diverse forms. The initial moves across the border, which in the majority of cases preceded other multiple migrations, were often motivated not a priori by getting a qualified job in the profession of the relevant migrant, but in order to learn a language, to overcome structural barriers in the region of origin, to individualise oneself from one's parents' house, to discover new places, possibilities and new views, to stay in touch with relatives, or to escape the standardised life paths (see also e.g. Pařízková 2011b, 2011a). These initial migration experiences, which I will present in this chapter, were crucial for considering migration in the future, since they were the basis for the establishment of "potential spaces" (Inowlocki, Riemann 2012) spanning the borders of one nation state. In many cases, they were also relevant for the individuals' future educational pathway and professional career. These biographical developments were very often unintended and changed in many ways the migrants' perceptions of their possibilities, abilities and viewpoints.

284

Kamil, for example, decided to go abroad for the first time to learn the German language, since he had failed his exams at the University of Prague where he had been studying electro-engineering. In order to overcome the removal from university, he searched for options to learn German during the summer break as quickly as possible, yet without success initially.

K: So I was so disappointed with it, I said to myself, well I don't know now what to do (deep breathing) and I have been lucky many times in my life and now I was lucky again, because I met a friend of mine who is physically handicapped (deep breathing) Lenička, (1) and she told me that if I didn't want to go- that she would make contact with a centre for physically handicapped people and if I didn't want to go to Germany during the summer holidays in order to look after a handicapped person, that I would learn German there. So I said – well yeah! (1) That was fantastic! (…) Well so I wrote my first letter in German (breathing in) that I would like to go (laughing) and that I would look after a handicapped person, that I didn't want anything, only some food and somewhere to stay the night. [I: Hmm] Well and they wrote back to me that I didn't have to worry, that I could go. So I jumped on the train and I went. (…) They picked me up, everything went well (deep breathing) and they took me to their place. There I met Karl, whom I was to look after. He was at that time about thirty. And I was at that time twenty. [I: Hmm] Well yeah! Twenty. Well and I was there for a few days and now I can sum it up, the great advantage was that he was physically handicapped, but mentally he was very well. (…) So he cared for me very well! He explained things to me and – the village Buchholz, there was a Saxon dialect. [I: Hmm (smile)] And when I went there I did not understand anything. (deep breathing) But because he took care of me so much, I got better. Much better. (…) So I was there for six weeks, I came back to the Czech Republic, I got the best grades (1) (both of us are laughing), she (the teacher, comment A.G.) was absolutely amazed! She was so surprised! She said I cannot believe that! I will mention you as an example to all! (Kamil, p. 2-4, l. 51-101)

It was also Karl who gave him the idea to continue studying in Leipzig, Germany, later on:

K: And when I was leaving, I had not yet sat the exams at university, so Karl told me, hey, you learnt German so fantastically in such a short time, why don't you go to study in Germany! [I: Hmm] (1) It was 1998. Well so I returned to the Czech Republic and: I found out that I was really good at German. I always thought that I was a technician, that I was not good at languages. They all pushed me to learn languages even though I studied electro-technical engineering. At that time I very much changed my mind and I started to participate in the exchange programs between Prague and a number of universities. (…) And everywhere I learnt German! (Kamil, p. 4-5, l. 110-131)

The six week placement in a village close to Leipzig initiated a metamorphosis in Kamil's biography. He discovered his ability to learn languages and used these in the student exchange activities. He was also the first person to move to Leipzig as an Erasmus student from Prague and to establish contacts among universities. After his studies he moved to Leipzig and started to work there for a company specialising in automobile production to which he had established contact during his studies.

Zuzana, who initially came to Germany at the end of the 1990s as an au pair, found out from her host family that there was a possibility of studying there. Although she planned to return to the Czech Republic after a one year stay in Germany and to use her newly acquired language skills for university entrance examinations there, she decided, after her efforts had repeatedly failed, to change her plans. She moved to Cologne instead and started to study psychology and adult education there. Thus, her studies in Cologne enabled her to reach the goals which had been denied to her in the Czech Republic, and also to stay legally in Germany.

Similarly to Zuzana, Adela also moved abroad as a young person but in a different way and with different resources than Zuzana:

A: And life was somehow constantly same at high school and at grammar school. The first turning point came when I was seventeen. I went to America for one year, [I: Hmm] my parents actually paid for me to do a placement at a high school in America. In order to improve my English, I lived with a host family, I was there for a year. It was actually the first time I had been abroad. (1) And I returned, finished the last year at gymnasium and then I left my parents' house. (Adela, p. 1, l. 22-28)

Adéla initially planned to go to Germany, however, in the end she went to the USA because the family with which she should have lived in Germany cancelled her placement at the very last moment. After she returned, she moved from Opava to Hradec Králové, another city in the Czech Republic, and started her studies of languages and public administration there. Afterwards, she moved country frequently and, in the end, took up a job at a European Institution in Luxembourg – making use professionally of her cross border experiences and language skills.

All of these stories, which are simply examples of other migration motives, forms and outcomes, reveal how the new biographical experiences acquired by migrants during their mostly relatively short stays abroad during their adolescence initiated the reflection processes on their biographical pathway up until that time, as well as on their own possibilities, knowledge and skills, which until then had been confined almost exclusively to their region of origin or the borders of one nation state. Kamil, for example, discovered his ability to learn languages, which beforehand he had brushed aside, since, in his words: "I am a technician; I am not good at languages". Through his experiences and his success in the exam at university he reworked this perception and became active in diverse exchange programs, giving his knowledge of languages a new value and meaning. Zuzana, on the other hand, entered the care sector following migration. She utilised the knowledge acquired in this field for her further migrations, while putting her previous education aside for the time being. Similarly to Zuzana, Adéla described her first migration as the turning point. When living with the host family in the USA, she developed new perspectives on the dynamics in her own family, which was "far from being ideal", and decided to move out of her parents' house. Moreover, she drew on these experiences for her further educational and career path, which in the end lead her to the European institution in Luxemburg.

Very similar processes of establishing transnational "potential spaces" during adolescence were described by Lena Inowlocki and Gerhard Riemann (2012), who based their study on the analysis of the biographies of former exchange students and their further participation in European cross border cooperation. As their analysis revealed, migration experiences in adolescence helped to redefine the experiences, practices and – often unquestioned – perceptions of belonging prior to migration. Moreover, these first cross-border encounters became in many cases an important resource, on which the individuals were later able to build during their educational and professional career. Hence, they initiated – through the processes of biographical work – the enlargement of their own possibility spaces spanning across the borders.

7.2.3   Moving back and forth in transnational spaces

The initial migration, as I showed above, often instigated the process of repeated border crossings, which took diverse forms. Migrants most often moved country because of education, work, in order to gain new experiences or in order to reunite with partners whom they had met during their initial stays abroad. In most cases, the reasons to move country were numerous and changed over time. As I showed, the initial migration experiences often opened up new possibility spaces for migrants. During their first period of travelling across the border – be it to visit family living abroad or for the purpose of student or work placements – they often came in touch with alternative possibilities of development and ways of life. These essentially biographical experiences were the basis for the development of transnational spaces – links, practices, and spaces of action which go beyond the framework of one nation state and which were biographically established and then progressively reworked (Apitzsch 2003c; Inowlocki, Riemann 2012). These spaces, however, were not arbitrary or free of barriers of any kind, but structured by migration policies, institutional frameworks as well as the positioning of migrants according to gender or class divisions. Hence, when taking decisions as to whether to stay, move, return home or move to another country, the opportunity structures relating to the individuals themselves – and very often to other family members too – in diverse locations were always taken into account.

Migration policies, which have changed somewhat over the last decades in which migrants moved to Germany, had a crucial impact on the way people moved country. In my sample, the year 2004 was often experienced as a turning point for migrants, since Czech citizens were able to profit from the European agreement on free movement and needed no residency permits. Despite the fact that they were obliged to have work permits until 2011, many narrations indicate that there was a partial release of constraints here too.

The restrictive migration policies, as well as demands on the labour market, which were strongly gendered, shaped the possibilities of migrants to continue the education and professional career they had commenced in the Czech Republic. Migrant women who came to Germany prior to 2004 were particularly affected by restrictive migration policies and labour market conditions. Those who did not come to Germany as exchange students or with job contracts that had been obtained prior to migration – very often connected to the teaching of the Czech language – found employment in catering or more frequently in the care sector – usually in the private sphere. I will come to the interplay of migration and gender regimes in more detail later on.

The opportunity structures shaped not only the possibilities of migrating, but also the possibilities of returning or moving elsewhere. Zuzana, for example, argued that:

Z: It is also difficult there now concerning work. (1) Maybe it is also why it is more difficult to return. Because if I returned to the Czech Republic, I could not- I could not go to Prague. [I: Hmm] It isn't the home I remember or as I would like it to be. (1) And there is no work there (in Northern Bohemia, comment A.G.); everyone commutes somewhere anyway. [I: Hmm] They have to commute. (Zuzana, p. 24-25, l. 766-770)

While Zuzana did not perceive returning as an option because of limited work opportunities in her region, others repeatedly returned to the Czech Republic before moving away again. Marie, for example, returned to Prague after her two year stay in Regensburg, where she taught the Czech language, and started work as a lecturer of German at the university there. Lenka and Jana also returned to the Czech Republic after they both failed to obtain a visa to stay in Germany; both of them took office jobs, which did not fulfil them, however. One of the reasons was the devaluation of the skills they had acquired abroad, as I will explain later on. Linda, just like Arnošt, commuted for several years between Brno, where she worked as a lecturer at university, and Bamberg, where her partner lived and where she had started a new course of studies. As she narrated:

L: And this commuting lasted in fact until the year 2000 or 2001, I don't know exactly, however, it was four years, maybe even more. And at that time I had completed my follow-up studies (takes a deep breath in) [I: Hmm] well and here: and in Brno I taught part-time; and in Bamberg I did plenty of diverse activities, from working in a restaurant, or should I say a pub, to working in a factory, (deep breath in) to giving courses in Czech, but also in the German language [I: Hmm] to doing translations and interpretations, it is probably what all girls who are here will also tell you (deep breath in); and well then I could not manage it, this commuting, also because- I had to pay rent here and in Brno, I earned about

288

three thousand gross [I: Hmm], so it was not possible at all. So I decided to leave and move here. (Linda, p. 3-4, l. 92-103)

Since her commute between the two cities became very time consuming and expensive, she made a decision to resign and move to Bamberg, where she managed to reduce the "plenty of diverse activities" she had been taking part in to concentrate on translation work and her studies. Over the course of time she became a lecturer at the university in Bamberg and completed her PhD in Slavic studies there. A return to the Czech Republic in the future was an option for other interviewees, for example Arnošt or Ivan, who both bought a house there to which they planned to move some day. Ivan, for instance, had to decide whether to move to the Czech Republic, since he had got a job offer there, or to stay in Germany in his current position as an IT specialist:

I: So I had actually three job offers at one point in time and now I had to decide, so I decided with my wife that we would stay here for a bit longer and (1) that we would (1) return to the Czech Republic in the future. We would like to return to our home town, Ostrava, my wife is actually from Zlín, they lived there. Coincidently we have bought a row house there, so we have a base, a magnet influencing us to return there. (Ivan, p. 15-16, l. 480-487)

However, he also expressed uncertainties concerning the work opportunities in Ostrava, the city to which they planned to return.

I: And I don't know how it will be. (2) I really don't know. I will probably try in three years, I will try to find a job there and I will see. When I find something it will be better [I: Hmm] (1) and we will really move there, if not it might be worse and we will have to solve it. I would maybe leave them in the Czech Republic and I would commute or I would go to Prague, and I would commute to Prague which is closer. [I: Hmm] (1) So. but I'm not worried at the moment. I never plan much. What will be will be. It is difficult to plan, since no one knows what will happen. (Ivan, p. 39, l. 1232-1240)

As these stories indicate the decisions on where to live, how to move and for which purposes are for the most part a subject of family negotiations, in which the educational pathway of children and the professional development of partners are the principal criteria in accordance with which decisions are taken. Most of the migrants I interviewed for the current study migrated for the first time on their own during their adolescence or early adulthood. Only a few of them moved country with their partner or other family members – such as Arnošt or Jitka and Tomáš, who moved to Frankfurt together. Over time, however, crossing the border increasingly became a family affair, since most migrants either found a partner in Germany or they were joined by partners whom they had met during their stays in the Czech Republic.

Being single or not had a fair amount of influence on individuals' aspirations and motives to move country. Martin, for example, reasoned that his decision to stay in Germany after his short internship in the finance sector, which was offered to him by his former boss in the financial company in

Prague where he worked before, was influenced by the fact that he was single at that time:

M: Well and because I was not bound in any way to the Czech Republic, it was- it was- it was actually (1) the main- the big reason why I in fact stayed. Because (1) when I for example saw my colleagues who were there on work exchanges, they both had partners, so they commuted, I don't know. They travelled home nearly every weekend. So they couldn't stay here. Because- if it had been the same for me at that time, I myself would not have stayed either. I would also have returned. Well and because I did not have a partner, so I said to myself, well why not. So I decided that I would stay here. (Martin, p. 18, l. 567-575)

Being single was for Martin, just as for Petr or Adéla, one of the conditions and reasons to move away since they did not feel bound to one location. Petr and Adéla in fact moved again shortly after the interview took place: Petr left for South America and Adéla went back to the Czech Republic. If one had a partner, the decision as to where to live was a matter of mutual negotiations, as illustrated for example by Kamil, who told me how he met his future wife through teaching each other German and Czech, and about their decision to move together from Leipzig to Prague:

K: And I was still convinced that it was only because of the German, and then a friend of mine told me that Alice did not come to my place only because of the German, or because of the Czech, well so I somehow got the idea too (laughing) [I: (laughing)] well and: we got together. (1) Well and an important factor was that Alice had already told me at the beginning that she would like to go to Prague. [I: Hmm] Before she even started to date me. She was convinced that she would go to Prague (takes a deep breath). And I was at that time a well paid employee here and I was doing very well. However, that euphoria of being in love, I said ok, when you go to Prague I will go with you (deep breath). Well and it was, she told me sometime in July, or in May, no she told me in May. In May 2008, wasn't it. (1) Well! Yes. In May 2008. We were dating then and in April of the following year Alice went to Prague. (Kamil, p. 13, l. 393-407)

Shortly afterwards Kamil resigned from his job in Leipzig, where he worked as an electrical engineer, and followed Alice to Prague. Nevertheless, she repeatedly lost her job and was exposed to discrimination because of her German origin. After about a year they therefore decided to return to Leipzig. "To find a common place to live" – as expressed by Marie – was a process in which different factors were involved: knowledge of the language of both partners, the possibilities of self-realisation and education, the work opportunities, the differences in salary, general wellbeing, as well as the closeness to one's parents' house – which became particularly important when the parents of migrants and their partners were getting old and needed to be cared for. When one had children, the children became – passively or actively – involved in the decision making. In most cases, it was education and the self-realisation of the individuals' children which became central to decision making. The stories of migrants reveal that the decision as to whether to stay or move away became increasingly complex over time, especially when other family members and their viewpoints became involved. Arnošt put this into words:

A: During the first departure it was our self-realisation, possibilities and qualifications. As one gets older, one thinks more about the qualifications and possibilities for one's own children. (Arnošt, p. 12, l. 356-359)

When negotiating where to live, some interviewees underlined the role of the proximity to the Czech Republic. Some interviewees even considered moving eastwards within Germany in order to be closer to the border. Marie expressed it as follows, for example:

M: Well, I could imagine living closer to the Czech Republic. It is here somehow (4) I would love to live a bit between these two countries! [I: hmm] Yes. I mean closer, so I could sometimes go – for example in Munich or Dresden there is a Czech centre so I could go there to see a movie and (takes a deep breath), then on the other hand in Prague for example to the German theatre. Yes. [I: hmm] Yes, that would be the right combination for me. To always be able to "plunge" into the perspective of the other country. [(Marie, p. 28, l. 953-959)

For her, living "a bit between these two countries" signified both mental and geographical interconnections, characterised by the accessibility of cultural events and the possibility of transcending and connecting the cultures within which she lived and moved.

7.2.4 Doing "transnational work"

The migrants I interviewed for the present project cannot be unambiguously labelled as transmigrants, who "would be characterised by the fact that their work, housing and life trajectories (and time horizon) span between different locales in multi-local transnational social spaces" (Pries 2001b, p. 61), "move frequently between countries" (Pries 2001b, p. 60) and "live in several societies simultaneously" (Glick Schiller et al. 1992b, p. 11). As I have shown, the aim of establishing a dual career in both the Czech Republic and in Germany, as well as commuting between these two neighbouring countries, often failed due to the relatively time consuming nature of travel and the associated financial expenses. In some cases, moving (temporarily) back to the Czech Republic was a priori precluded because of limited chances in the region of origin, or due to unexpected events, such as the devaluation of skills acquired during migration, or discrimination towards family members in schools or in the work place in the Czech Republic. Hence, while moving frequently between countries was an option for some, others preferred to imagine staying in Germany long-term or moving to another country altogether.

Nevertheless, the migrants maintained and developed – to a greater or lesser extent – dense familial, social, organisational, economic and cultural links with their country of origin (Glick Schiller et al. 1992b, p. 1). These links, which the migrants kept alive through frequent trips to the Czech Republic, telephone calls, by following Czech political and cultural events, or establishing contacts with other migrants living abroad, evolved over time and had different meanings for different individuals. In the following chapter I will pay attention to the development of these links and their meaning. I will start with the act of drawing "comparisons between here and there and now and then", which were the expressions of the biographical work of individuals linked to their migration experiences and shifted positioning. Subsequently, I will describe the ways of doing "transnational work" – efforts to maintain and develop transnational links through the biographical work of individuals (Apitzsch 2003c), and how to pass them on to the next generation as well.

Comparisons between here and there and now and then

As outlined above, the initial migration experiences often opened up new spaces of action for individuals later on. They initiated processes of reflection on one's own skills, knowledge and resources and led, in some cases, to the development of new ones. These processes of biographical reflection were often expressed in comparisons between the self before migration, between the self and the society left behind, and between different societies in which migrants were involved. Fritz Schütze and Anja Wildhagen (2012) argued that the process of drawing comparisons was at the core of the establishment of so-called "European mental spaces" – spaces which emerge from biographical reflections on transnational and transcultural encounters, and which transcend the settings of one nation state. They signify, inter alia, the ability to take on the perspective of others, which might put into question one's existing dominant perception of oneself and of the society left behind. These experiences were put into words by some of my interviewees.

Jana moved to Germany for the first time for one year in order to work at a hospital after studying at nursing school and afterwards graduating in theology in Prague. She describes the way in which this experience changed her as follows:

J: And: (2) I would say that I probably (clearing her throat) (1) didn't know what to do with myself at that time. I needed to find some direction and I knew that a stay abroad could somehow help me. [I: Hmm] (1) To become more independent in life, to rely on myself and to learn many things. (breathing in) (1) To leave my parents for the first time for a longer period of time. I would say that that was the biggest motivation. [I: Hmm] (1) Well. (2) It was a year full of changes. Big changes. Such an impulse. For life. (1) Well (3) it was (breathing in and laughing) (1) this feeling (1) I had this feeling that- what I managed in my personal development in five years in the Czech Republic happened here in five months. At such an incredible speed. [I: Hmm] Ehm: (1) (laughing) Well yes. I changed a lot I would say. After that one year. So it was good. (Jana, p. 22, l. 730-741)

Jana, like other interviewees, underlined the process of individualisation from her parents and developing an independent way of life. Living in Germany and working at the hospital opened up new possibilities of self-development for her, which she had lacked in Prague. Moreover, she developed new perspectives on her existing life path and Czech society in general.

J: Because I changed through it, I had an absolutely different life experience than my (breathing in) former friends. [I: Hmm] I really felt it when I came back. That I was completely somewhere else and they had different worries and- there was suddenly this feeling of alienation. (3) Also (1) concerning the Czech Republic (1) now it is different again but at that time I had the feeling that I had crept out of my own village and now saw many things (1) more objectively. A bit from a distance. (1) Suddenly you see the life you have lived there and also the Czechs a bit from a distance and (1) it shapes you somehow, yes. Then you come back and you see that people do not have this. [I: Hmm] (Jana, p. 48, l. 1312-1319)

"This" is, according to Jana, the ability to see the unquestioned everyday way of doing things and one's own past from a different perspective. In contrast with her "former friends", she underwent certain migration experiences which changed her perception of her past and her possible future developments. The comparison with "others" became a means of articulating these changes in her biography. Like Jana, other interviewees often drew comparisons with those who stayed behind. Interestingly, it was very often peers and siblings who were presented as a counterbalance to the migrants' own development. They were the ones who continued living in the place of origin. Thus, the biographical pathways of peers or siblings presented the potential developments which those who had migrated might have experienced had they stayed in the Czech Republic. Zuzana, for example, put it this way:

Z: And I have a brother there. Well, he is at home. And: he was in England for three months, but he is completely different to me (laughing). He knows that he could not live somewhere else. [I: hmm] He has not even moved to a big city. Now he has bought a house, (1) five hundred meters from my parents (laughing). [I: aha] and: this house was his dream. To have somewhere-, but he is alone. He is thirty, but he is alone. And it is really hard for him. To be alone in such a small town. [I: hmm] He is still looking, maybe it will happen via the internet, [I: hmm] but it is also-, for example here in one's thirties, it somehow- but there a lot of people who already have children when they are thirty and they are already with someone. Hm, it has somehow shifted. The age is shifted there and time is shifted there too. (Laughing) (Zuzana, p. 40, l. 1254-1262)

When the interviewees drew comparisons with those left behind, they implicitly also compared the typical biographical pathways associated with their place of origin – be it the village or town of origin or the relevant nation state. In doing so, they presented themselves as exceptions, since they "disrupted" these expected developments and established alternative ways of life. Alena Pařízková (2011a) described these processes using the example of Czech migrants living in the United Kingdom, whereby she used the concept of the de-standardisation of life paths. According to her, biographical pathways which became strongly standardised during the communist era in Czechoslovakia – since the borders were shut and society turned to conform to a way of life restricted by politics, limited chances of professional development and civil participation – have diversified over the last two decades. Migration has become one of the alternatives to "typical" biographical and career paths in the Czech Republic, even though migration is still seen as an exception to common practice and bound to one nation state. Some interviewees challenged this perception of one nation state as the dominant sphere in shaping possibilities of action and the perceptions of individuals. Karolína, for example, argued that:

K: There are certain moments which I would never have experienced if I lived in the Czech Republic. It is such an enlargement of one's horizons. And one can distance oneself from things! From the Czech Republic. From that one-nation way of life. Erm: which actually my family lives, some of my friends live it and plenty of other people who complain about things; they only see things in that one dimension. And over the course of time you become such a Czech theorist, because you know it or you only know it from narrations or you don't even know at all how the Czechs live. (Karolína, p. 26, l. 818-826)

The interviewees, however, did not only negotiate their position in relation to others that were left behind in their home towns, but also to their significant others in the country of migration. Zuzana explains it like this in another part of the interview:

Z: I often compare how it is here or how it is- [I: Hmm] Even though my husband- we are exactly the same age and my husband grew up here completely differently than I did. I grew up in a small town and he grew up in Cologne and in Germany. He for example has coloured photos from his childhood and I only have black and white ones. [I: Hmm] (deep breath) And: (-) but I am very happy that I grew up the way I grew up, that we did not have as much as they did, because I have a feeling that I still can value things. [I: Hmm] Because I did not have so much. That we fought (breathing in) if someone had jeans at all, we all wanted to have the same jacket, that one from Severka (laughing) [I: Hmm (laughing)] and only the person whose mother worked there got it. (Zuzana, p. 17, 512-519)

In this sequence, Zuzana drew comparisons with her husband not only in terms of national borders, but also in terms of different life experiences connected to life in a small town and life in a big city. Moreover, she addressed the differences in socio-economic status and the history of both countries, which had an impact on their biographical pathways. These ongoing comparisons not only with her husband but also with her children, who have grown up in Germany and thus in different historical, cultural and economic constellations, were crucial for her in negotiating her position within the family and within society. She tried to interconnect her past experiences and viewpoints and integrate them into her life, be it in the form of a criticism of consumption spending or transnational cultural practices.

294

Z: Because I already know that there is not only one truth. You know? That people can live completely differently. So I try to gain from it what I would like and not be so stark in my habits. To watch how others do it; and maybe it is better, or- (Zuzana, p. 39, l. 1232-1235)

To summarise, comparisons became a method for individuals to position themselves within the societies in which they live or to which they can relate, to express the changes in their biography, and to criticise the dominant discourses in society. They were the expressions of the biographical work of individuals, initiated by migration processes. Moreover, they pointed out the "transnational work" of individuals – the mental acts of transcending the setting of one nation state.

Maintaining and establishing transnational links and practices

When moving country, social contacts, everyday practices and ones relationship with language and culture changed for the interviewees. Keeping in touch with family, friends and cultural, social or political events became more demanding because of the geographical distance, and required other means of communication – such as email, online social networks, telephone calls and more or less frequent visits. Despite these new challenges, migrants endeavoured to varying degrees to keep transnational social and cultural links alive. They were the means of constructing links with one's past and establishing biographical continuity (see also e.g. Ruokonen-Engler 2005), the means of keeping professional possibilities open, as well as a means of intergenerational transmission. The narratives which I collected for the current study revealed different forms and facets of transnational links. In the following part of this study I will introduce some of the aspects which became particularly important: the maintenance and re-establishment of social contacts in the place to which migrants moved and across the borders, keeping links to the language and other cultural practices and goods, and transferring transnational links to the next generation.

Since Czech community organisations were practically non-existent in Germany, or the migrants did not have any interest in joining them for whatever reason, the migrants tried to establish other means of contact. Interestingly, these were not only Czech or German but "international" ones – sharing with them the same experiences of living in another country for a period of time. Karolína explains it as follows:

K: Well, (2) (breathing out) (1) I have many friends who are (1) international. It is somehow important. Now we were somewhere over New Year's Eve and there were only Germans there. Me and fifteen Germans. And it was- it was terrible. [I: Hmm] Suddenly we were discussing (breathing in) why people steal cars in the Czech Republic. Well, I don't know, what should I say, you know. [I: Hmm] But: some years ago we were with people over New Year's Eve who are (breathing in) a Czech women and a German man or a Czech women and an American man, so you actually don't have to discuss why cars are stolen in the Czech Republic. This first discussion becomes unimportant. You can already communicate normally, so I think that it is also important. [I:Hmm] To stay in contact with people who somehow have similar experiences. Erm: of living abroad. That you are always a foreigner. That you will always be noticed when you speak. [I: Hmm] Erm: or maybe someone's German is so good that you do not recognise them as a foreigner. But of course the majority do not speak it that well. The vocabulary and the small nuances are still there (breathing in). So you live in this- also when you fall out with your husband, isn't it, Te-rezka (she turns to her one year old daughter) so you find out that you make mistakes and you feel embarrassed [I: Hmm. Yes.] But, on the other hand, you can say much more when you speak the foreign language. (Laughing) So you can swear so nicely (laughing)! (Karol-ína, p. 6-7, l. 190-208)

Links forged with other Czechs living in Germany were for most interview-ees occasional or based on close friendships established either before migra-tion or during their time in Germany. As witnessed by some of the interview-ees who came during the 1990s, the Czech community in Germany shifted somewhat over time. While during the Cold War the Czech community was relatively strong, it dissolved in the course of the 1990s, since many of the "emigrants" who were active within the Czech community moved back to the Czech Republic. Those who came after 1990 did not usually create new communities, nor did they carry on the social circles set up by the former Czech "emigrants". Nevertheless, despite the lack of institutionalised Czech communities in Germany, migrants established individual forms of keeping links with the Czech language and other cultural practices. Jitka and Tomáš, for instance, narrated the following:

J: You know. My father is passionate about making preserves. He cooks everything possi-ble (1) so always – they have a small garden. It is actually only- you know. They live in a prefab, but they have a small garden in an allotment. Well – it is a plantation! He grows all kinds of things. [I: (laughing)] (laughing) And my father built a greenhouse. But it is not just an ordinary greenhouse! This greenhouse also has blinds. [I: (laughing)] (laughing) So that the peppers wouldn't get to much sunshine. [I: (laughing)] And he also built a smoke house. It is such a masterpiece, we were all staring at it, because we asked ourselves /well where did he learn that? (with a lower, pondering voice)/ It is really beautiful. (…) So whenever we are in the Czech Republic, we pack up all this stuff. And we are like a retail store. (laughing) [I: (laughing)] Because it's really a lot. We always get plenty of sausages, some smoked meat, some preserves, at least three jars of every kind, you know, so that we will survive until the next time (laughing). Tomáš's grandma regularly makes us the dough for langoš because we loved to eat it when we still lived in the Czech Republic. So when-ever we go she already has the dough ready for us. She gives it to us in a plastic bag, so we travel with some langoš dough in a plastic bag. (laughing) [I: (laughing)] So it is nice. Well and we also get a cake, home-grown eggs, so we can survive. And at Christmas, we always get so many pastries, it is crazy. Actually in the past when we were here at the beginning, our parents always took us to a shopping centre, to Hypernova so that we could shop for these basic things. Nowadays we don't do that anymore, we only buy special things, such as tatarka, pribináček, (laughing) [I: (laughing)] [I: Hmm] polohrubá a hrubá mouka, one cannot buy this here. Then zlatý oplatky a koka: a: (-) these (-) lázeňský oplatky, (1) so we always pack everything up and we survive until the next time. So we are well equipped. (laughing) [I: (laughing)] (Jitka, p. 35, l. 1540-1571)

Food consumption became a transnational practice for Jitka and Tomáš, just as it did for some of the other interviewees. When preparing meals, they combined both Czech and German products. In order to have access to Czech products, they established networks within which Czech products were circulated. The role of food in "doing the culture" was also highlighted by Zuzana, who moved to Cologne more than ten years ago with her best friend from her town of origin:

Z: This Czech friend of mine also has a child so we have gone through our various developmental phases together. (both laughing), from being single to married with children. So it is nice. And my best friend from the Czech Republic is in Leverkusen, so that is not far. So we try to see each other whenever possible. (1) Recently we had a Czech party here. (laughing) We try to "do the culture" (laughing) like dissidents (both of us are laughing, 2), we cook goulash and someone bakes a bábovka and we drink Czech slivovitz, (laughing) [I: great (laughing)], we listen to Olympic (laughing, 4). (Zuzana, p. 14-15, l. 443-451)

The expression "we try to do the culture" points out to efforts made to symbolically establish a link to the past and to the Czech culture as she and her friends remember it and as it is accessible to them through material goods. Very ordinary things, such as eating goulash or bábovka (sponge cake), become festive occasions. Also in her case "doing the Czech culture" is done in private rather than in public institutionalised settings.

For some of my interviewees, living in Germany gave them another perspective on the Czech language. Karolína, for example, says that:

K: And it is true that I always spoke German here and I wrote my PhD in English, so I had a kind of need for the Czech language. For expressing myself in written Czech. [I: Hmm] So I started to write book reviews on books which are produced at home, and that novel which I wrote is also a "breakout" of that need for the Czech language. [I: Aha] Because one has here – I have Czech friends but this is my way of having contact with (1) the roots, through the language. Yes. (Karolina, p. 4, l. 111-118)

Her writings became a means of staying in touch with the language, which she did not use as frequently as before migration, a means of staying active within the Czech cultural scene, as well as a means of establishing links to the past – "the roots". Interestingly, the theme of her present and planned novels is transculturality – living at the intersection of different cultural spheres and "translating" among them.

Zuzana's story also points out to the new meaning given to language and other cultural practices in the course of migration. Zuzana expressed the importance of maintaining the Czech language and social links to the town of her origin in the Czech Republic in the following way:

Z: I try to read a lot and I try to read more Czech books, which I did not do so extensively before, but I've realised that my vocabulary is getting smaller. I forget words. Or I realise that when I see a word in a fairy tale, I don't know what it means any more. [I: Hmm] (1) And I don't have any illusions that my children will ever be able to understand some of the fairy tales by Božena Němcová, because they are difficult. [I: Hmm] (1) (Breathing in)

And I try to watch Czech movies, I always bring over some periodicals, in the Czech Republic I watch TV in order to absorb it so much that it lasts for a while. And- it has become much easier with the internet. [I: Hmm] /a baby cries in the background/ Now I am in contact with some former schoolmates vie Facebook, so it is great. [I: (smiling)] Even though I don't use accents when writing there (both are laughing, 3). Hm, that's how it is. Now we will be in the Czech Republic over Christmas so I will have a chance to see more people. I can organise everything via Facebook much more easily. (Breathing in) Hm, otherwise I try to invite people here but for most of my family it is hard to get here. It is financially completely different to come here from the Czech Republic than to go there from here. Everything has to be organised differently somehow. (Zuzana, p. 14, l. 419)

While Zuzana's social contacts shifted over time, as she alludes to in another part of the interview – "I already have more friends here than in the Czech Republic. In the Czech Republic everything has somehow been torn down, the bridges." – she tried to re-establish social links with her acquaintances from her region of origin through new media forms, such as Facebook. This platform made it possible for her to reach people to whom she had lost contact in the past, be it because of her own migration, the migration out of the region by others or simply because of their different life paths. Moreover, she made an effort to maintain links to the language and culture by "absorbing" through TV, periodicals or books. Social contacts, as well as the language and other cultural practices, were not given facts for her but instead a process on which she actively worked. Re-establishing social and cultural links gained particular importance for her when she had children, to whom she tried to transmit these transnational links:

Z: Hmm, I still feel that I am Czech. (Laughing) Also my children have Czech citizenship, too, German and Czech, it was very important to me erm (2) I don't know. So they also have it somehow written down on paper. [I: Hmm] So they also have another erm, I don't know. So that they wouldn't have any problems buying a house or something like that in the Czech Republic. [I: Hmm] (Breathing) Erm. I talk Czech to them at home, my friends are Czech (laughing) now we have erm, I was looking on the int- internet, I was searching for someone, because there are so few Czechs here. [I: Hmm] Or they are somewhere really well hidden, they are very well integrated into society (laughing) so [I: Hmm] it is difficult. Erm. And with Lenka we then – Lenka put up erm – an advertisement I don't know- an advertisement on the internet, which was really very difficult for me to find. [I: Hmm] Erm, in Munich there are some Czech things, in Berlin there are Czech things, in Cologne there is simply nothing. So at least there is this now. At least I have found these pages and: we see one another from time to time. Not often, but still. It is nice when one has a child to know that someone else has a child too, who is trying to erm bring them up the way you are. At least for instance with the language or (breathing) so that he still at least has some relation to Czech culture or to the fairy tales and (1) songs-. (Breathing) Even though with a small child it is still ok, but with a three or four year child who already goes to kindergarten it is really difficult. It is really a pity. Because- maybe that's why I try to have them go to the Czech Republic often. (Zuzana, p.13, l. 384-399)

Zuzana tried to transmit her transnational links to and to establish access to the Czech legal system based on citizenship for her children. Whereas having contact with other Czechs living in Cologne was irrelevant to her before, she

298

later started to establish a social network with other Czechs living in Germany who would have the same aim: to transmit at least a piece of cultural belonging to their children and to establish for them a kind of micro-world in which Czech would be spoken. By establishing transnational links for her children and herself, she kept open for them the possibility of living in the Czech Republic one day. Moreover, by doing so, she created links with her own biographical and migration experiences.

As these stories show, migrants created very individual social and cultural links spanning across the borders. Moreover, they also revealed that these links were not self-evident but actively established by migrants (see also Pape, Takeda, Guhlich 2014). In most cases, they understood themselves as the pioneers of migration – the first generation of migrants who sought to transmit at least part of their transnational links to the next generation. As Karolína argues, "we are the ones who will maybe create the roots for someone one day".

7.3 Linking spatial and social mobility

According to Daniel Bertaux and Paul Thomsen (Bertaux, Thompson 1997b), scholars whose work was devoted to diverse processes of social mobility, the life history approach is especially useful in studying the processes and patterns of social mobility, since it enables one to have a deeper insight into specific contexts and their opportunity structures, the perception of the possibilities and chances of individuals, their future plans and dreams, as well as the relations to others and their chances over the course of time. In this chapter I will pay attention to the framework of opportunity structures shaped by the intersection of migration and gender regimes, and to the way migrants perceived their chances and possibilities. Subsequently, I will describe the ways in which they negotiated their skills, knowledge, and qualifications when crossing the border between the Czech Republic and Germany and, in their minds, other countries as well. I will then thematise the question of the translatability of social position and the role of recognition in transnational spaces.

7.3.1 Biographies at the intersection of migration and gender regimes

As I have already shown, the reasons for moving country are manifold and the manner of migration differs. In this chapter I will pay attention to the intersection of migration and gender regimes (Lutz 2008a, p. 2) in shaping the biographies of individuals, their possibilities for development and the way in which they make use of their skills, knowledge and qualifications.

The migrants I interviewed for the present research project moved to Germany sometime after 1989. My sample therefore includes people who moved to Germany directly after the revolution in 1989, as well as those who migrated to Germany for the first time after the Czech Republic joined the EU in 2004. Since 1989, migration regimes have changed considerably. Despite the constant changes in the work agreements between the Czech Republic and Germany (Meduna 2004), the biggest change came in 2004 when the citizens of the Czech Republic gained the right of free movement within the EU, and in 2011 when Germany removed all barriers for new EU citizens to enter the labour market. Until 2004, migrants could only stay in Germany for up to three months on a tourist visa; if they wished to stay for longer, they were supposed to apply for a residence permit which in most cases was connected to a work permit or student visa. The issuing of a visa was often time consuming and demanding for interviewees, as shown by the example of Jana, who went to Germany for one year in 2000 after completing secondary nursing school and studies of theology in Prague:

J: erm: (1) after studying theology (1) erm: I had the feeling that I would like to go abroad somehow (1) [I: Hmm] so I arranged a Freiwilliges Soziales Jahr, [I: Hmm] in Germany (1) and: in between I worked, I worked in the health service [I: Hmm] (laughing). (1) and then I left for one year (3) and: then after my Freiwilliges Soziales Jahr erm: (-) then I actually wanted to study (2) but it was a bit complicated (1) erm: it was complicated somehow at that time: (2) so while I was still in Germany I actually sent some application forms to some universities (breathing in) but they told me that they would not prolong my visa [I: Hmm] and that I would have to return back to the Czech Republic. [I: Hmm] (1) And: (-) then they told me that if I would like to study medicine I would have to go to a Studienkolleg, [I: Hmm] (1) that means that (1) well at that time I couldn't imagine going home again and applying for a visa again from there, [I: Hmm] that I would wait another year or I don't know how long, maybe half a year, (breathing in), that I would go back to Germany again then and that I would have to attend the Studienkolleg which was every day, and it would be difficult to do it at the same time as working. [I: Hmm] (1) Well and actually when you come here with nothing, you don't have any money and you don't have any acquaintances and you cannot speak German properly, well you speak it a bit but- [I: Hmm] erm: (-) so it is difficult- the beginnings, how do you say, to "einleben" oneself, (laughing) [I: Hmm] (Jana, p. 1-2, 25-41)

Since Jana experienced the possibility of starting to study in Germany as "unimaginable" because of difficult procedures of getting a visa and starting her studies, she decided to change her plans. She returned to the Czech Republic and soon afterwards moved to England, where she worked for few weeks as au pair and then "ended up" as a caregiver in a house for the elderly on the outskirts of London. When she returned to the Czech Republic, she tried to establish a "normal" life and took a job as an assistant in a computer company.

J: And: so I said to myself, well, I cannot always run away. So I will give it a go at home, I will try and organise my life somehow (laughing) [I: Hmm] even though I actually erm: (-) now I know that it was somehow everything for me. [I: Hmm] That I needed to go abroad. [I: Hmm] Or (deep breathing) that it is important for me. [I: Hmm] To be all over the place (laughing). (Jana, p. 3, l. 81-86)

After about a year she decided to leave her job since, in Jana's words, it was not for her, and decided spontaneously to start again in Germany where she enrolled to study musical sciences. However, it was not clear until the very last moment whether she would get the visa she needed in order to study and work.

J: It was funny with visas! I ran to the German embassy in Prague (3) and they told me this. And then: then I worked for a short amount of time, it was only some part-time job in a gaming house. Some of my acquaintances had some- well. (1) And now I don't know what but once I wanted to go to solarium. Yeah. [I: Hmm] (laughing) Otherwise I never went there and I never went to the fitness studio that was there either. [I: Hmm] It was really just a coincidence. And once I went there and (1) there was a woman behind the desk and beside her there was a man (3) ey: (1) I heard him speak German! (1) He said something in German. And I said to him- I just mentioned something, one word one sentence, you know for fun, just "Spass", yes. (2) And he immediately reacted, how how how how was it that I spoke German and so. And I told him well- (3) yes and he was German! So I told him. Hey you Germans, you don't want to give me a visa! (laughing) And he said 'why! I work in the embassy! And I said 'huh'? (1) And he said. Where is the problem. And I told him that I had just been there and that it was taking so long and that I needed to start work, erm:. (1) And he said: 'So bring me these papers and I will try to ask around.' (1) It was such a coincidence or what have you! [I: (laughing)] It was providence which helped me. [I: (laughing)] (1) I was in shock that there in some fitness studio, somewhere I go once in a lifetime, that there I meet a man who works at embassy! (both are laughing) (1) And: (2) and the next day he told me to meet him, that he would ask and he immediately – and he came and said, yes, I have found these specific telephone numbers (breathing in) so you have to call there and everything should be fine. (1) And he was really, really nice and somehow- so natural, I don't know- at that moment somehow willing to help. [I: Hmm] (1) I was surprised and he was probably also surprised (both are laughing) (1) and then we simply said thank you and good bye, and it finished. It was a very quick meeting and somehow very bizarre. [I: Aha] It doesn't normally happen like that. Mostly the man wants- I don't know. (1) That he tells you if you don't want to go for coffee with him. You know? [I: Yes] (breathing in) But this one, I don't know. Maybe he just wanted to do something nice. [I: (laughing)] (1) And: then I wrote him a postcard to the embassy telling him that I was already in Germany and that I wanted to thank him. And so this contact ended. (1) Well (1) it was such an interesting experience, such an interesting experience. (Jana, p. 8-9, l. 345-378)

In contrast with Jana, who obtained a visa at the very last moment – which she describes as luck and "providence" rather than self-evident – and was therefore able to go to Germany in order to start her new studies and her part-time job as a caregiver for the elderly, Lenka did not manage to legalise her status as a child-carer during her stay in Cologne in 2001. Almost immediately she found a job as a child minder in a family and worked there, without a visa, for three years. When looking for a job, she was not only able to make use of the high demand for "Eastern European child minders" (see also Lutz 2008d), but also of her previous experience as an au pair in Austria and in Bavaria, where she moved after graduating in pedagogy. Lenka explained the failure to legalise her stay in the following way:

L: I wasn't actually an au pair, I was- what do they call it. A full-time Kinderfrau. [I: Aha] – And at that time it was not possible to legalise it somehow. I don't know why, for which reasons. I know that it was possible, I know I had a look then, it was possible to get- to get a family where someone was handicapped- I know that there were plenty of people from Poland and from the Eastern Bloc who did this, who got visas. Or if you worked in hospitality you got a visa for one year and then if your employer wanted to keep you for longer, he could prolong your contract by a year, and when your contract had been prolonged twice you could actually stay here. [I: Hmm] So we actually wanted to do something like this, but unfortunately he wrote in that letter that he needed someone for a household to look after children. [I: Hmm] And it was not possible at that time. We did not know it. We only found out on the basis of the refusal. Because they sent us a letter with a list of all the recognised occupations. And that one was not on it. So it was quite hard, yes. (Lenka II, p. 5, l. 137-150)

Despite great efforts to legalise her status, Lenka was not successful and therefore worked for a family without a work or residence permit for three years.[58] Her status precluded her from looking for other work possibilities outside a private household. She only managed to legalise her status when she married her German partner (see also Lutz 2008d, p. 45). Only afterwards was she able to make use of her initial education and qualifications as teacher, as I described above.

Ivan moved to Cologne at the same time as Lenka, but faced very different legal frameworks. Ivan had lived and studied computer sciences in Ostrava, an industrial city on the eastern border of the Czech Republic. He decided to move to Germany in 2001 after the companies in which he worked got into financial difficulties. He contacted a job agency in Prague which arranged a job for him working for an international company situated in Cologne. He moved there with other male IT specialists from the Czech Republic. They were issued a work permit for one year, with the possibility of extension. One year later he obtained a so-called "Green Card" which allowed him to stay and work for the company for the next five years. Interestingly, when talking about his beginnings in Cologne, he described everyday life and his experiences and those of his co-workers who moved with him to Cologne both within and outside the work place. He told me how he and his colleagues met other Czechs – especially Czech au pairs since, he claims, there were many of them at that time – and how they did trips together or visited restaurants. This notion is interesting, since it points out the gendered division within the

58 The profession of 'Kinderfrau" (childminder) was not regularised in Germany until 2004. Until then, contracts were negotiated solely in the "private sphere" and it was thus not possible to gain an officially recognised work permit for this kind of work (Glaeser 2014).

Czech community in Cologne at that time, where men often moved there with work visas gained prior to migration, whereas women went as au pairs and babysitters in spite of their actual qualifications.

Like Ivan, Kamil also managed to get a work permit after his graduation in Prague and start work in the automobile industry in a small company close to Leipzig. He says he was lucky, since the company was looking for someone who spoke Czech in order to communicate with costumers in the Czech Republic. However, in contrast with Ivan, the procedure of getting a work permit was very time consuming and expensive for Kamil.

K: Now the problem was (cleaning his throat) that I had to pay for it all. (1) Erm: I had to pay rent here, I had to pay health insurance, social insurance (breathing in) (…), so I got heavily into debt because I was still waiting waiting waiting and I went from here to there erm: from one office to another office (1) well and then finally it was all good, I started to work for that company, it was not exactly in Leipzig, it was about twenty kilometres outside Leipzig (1) and: (-) the work was interesting but it was not well paid. [I: Hmm] (1) From my viewpoint yes, but after one year the employment office of the city was already starting to push the company, saying that I was cheap labour and that I didn't have the average wage I should have in comparison with normal German employees. [I: Hmm] So it got- (1) and because it was a small company, I understood that for such a small company- one foreigner is quite a big problem. Because they had to always go to the authorities, they had to write diverse letters and I was a burden, so the company (breathing in) (Kamil, p. 9, l. 257-275)

As he narrated further on, one of his flatmates gave him the idea of applying for a job at an international company in Leipzig itself. He passed the assessment centre and was admitted, however only for night work shifts initially. In the course of the crisis in the automobile industry during the following years, he returned to the Czech Republic. After he returned he started to work for the same company again and he managed to shift from night shifts – which were the starting point for beginners and "foreigners" – to day work shifts.

These stories point out the different ways in which policies and demands on the formal and informal labour market shaped the biographies of individuals and their possibilities of making use of the skills, education and knowledge they had acquired prior to and during migration. Like Jana, Lenka and Kamil, other interviewees also thematised the difficult procedures of gaining student and work visas. They depicted repeated time and money consuming journeys to the embassy in Prague, uncertainty about the success of the procedures, and long waits in the queue at the embassy, not to mention degrading situations at the German "Ausländerbehörde" (the German foreign office). However, even though some of them succeeded in acquiring a student visa, they found themselves in a precarious situation, since they got into debt due to the limited amount of hours which students could work, and having to pay back amounts they had had to prove they had in their bank accounts before starting their studies. Furthermore, they thematised their – mostly temporary – precarious position outside the German welfare system.

Like Kamil, Lenka and others stayed insured in the Czech Republic for a period of time and travelled to the Czech Republic in order to see the doctors and manage certain social issues, since they could not enter the German welfare system because of their status. The interviewees, especially women employed in private households for a period of time, often mentioned difficult transactions between the German and Czech health systems, for instance when they had to use the healthcare system in Germany in an event of urgency. This situation eased when the Czech Republic joined the EU in 2004 and, subsequently, when the European health insurance system was adopted by the new EU countries. Furthermore, a residency permit was no longer required. Jitka and Tomáš who moved to Germany together in 2004, as well as Petr who went to Munich in 2008 for a two year scholarship, and Adela who moved to Frankfurt in 2009, experienced very different conditions than as described by those migrants who arrived earlier. Although the transitory measures protecting the local labour market were still in force until 2011, the interviewees found it easier to settle in Germany and get work permits. Marie, who migrated for the first time in the early 1990s, expressed the changes as follows:

M: Well suddenly you were being pigeonholed completely differently [I: hmm]. Suddenly you were no longer a problem! [I: hmm] Yes, when I was in Regensburg it was (3) I was not really much of a problem because I had a contract with the university in Regensburg, I had work (breathing in). But despite this (2) erm, I think it took much longer at that Ausländerbehörde, everything took much longer. [I: hmm] And I had to go there two or three times. However, here in Wiesbaden, I went there and I got a permit for three years straight away. [I: hmm] Yes. Which was also connected to the fact that we were already in the European Union! [I: hmm] Yes. And these are the things one needs to be aware of. Because before 2004 we needed a visa for a period over three months. This was annulled from 2004, wasn't it. (Marie, p. 24, l. 820-829)

Besides the time dimension, the narrations and migration paths differed considerably in terms of the gender dimension. Despite the small number of contradictory cases within my sample, there were some visible tendencies which pointed towards gendered migration corridors and positioning (see also e.g. Williams, Baláž 2005; Kofman 2009b). While the men in my sample often improved their social position through migration – despite its ambivalence which I will discuss later – women very often experienced a period of devaluation of their actual skills and qualifications by taking low skilled jobs in the care sector, hospitality or factories.

Linda studied history and German in Brno and after graduation moved to Bamberg to study German as a foreign language, while at the same time commuting to Brno for several years where she lectured at university. Linda revealed the following gendered experiences:

L: and in Brno I taught part -time and in Bamberg I did plenty of diverse activities, from working in a restaurant, or should I say in a pub, to working in a factory, (takes a deep breath in) to giving courses in Czech, but also in German language [I: Hmm] to translations and interpretations, it is probably what all the girls who are here tell you (deep breath in) (Linda, p. 3-4, l. 95-100)

Her comment that "it is probably what all the girls who are here tell you" makes it clear that her experiences were not an exception, but rather a common pattern among migrant women. Linda came to speak about this later in the interview and evaluated it in the following way:

L: As I said I don't like to think about it, that's true (breathing in) because it was bad, I also had some (breathing in) (1) debts, because it was also another time, we were- the Czech Republic was still not in the European Union [I: Hmm] and I didn't have a work permit (1) not for work nor for residency [I: Hmm] I would not even say it to this erm: Gerät (she points to the dictaphone) (breathing in) ey: so (breathing in) I was partly enrolled as a student and then you have permission to work certain hours, [I: Hmm] how was it, you can work x hours, at such a scale and at such and such time erm: but in order to get a residence permit you had to prove that you had enough money in your bank account. So of course I didn't have it and I had to borrow it, so I made an effort to pay it back and it was all somehow- it was all difficult. (Linda, p. 15, l. 468-479)

Her narration points out the intersection of shifting migration and gender regimes. Because of the legal frameworks in Germany, which prevented her from legalising her status and starting a job within the formal economy, and the small amount of money she was paid for lecturing at the university in Brno, she became trapped for several years within low paid jobs in order to pay back her debts. Like most of the other female interviewees, she was educated in fields such as the humanities, art, social sciences or education, which these women found difficult to utilise in the relevant other location. This is in contrast to the predominantly technical qualifications of migrant men, who in some cases were able to benefit from eased procedures of gaining long term work permits, such as the "Green Card" (see also e.g. Kofman 2012). Especially striking for Linda and other interviewees was the dilemma of how to apply the German language studies they had completed in the Czech Republic in Germany. I will come to the diverse methods developed by migrant women in order to challenge this dilemma later on.

Besides the hospitality sector, working in factories or doing the occasional translation as mentioned by Linda, the other important sector for highly educated migrant women in my sample was the care sector – and particularly child care, caring for the elderly or working in households. The private households within which women often worked for a period of time were places which assured relative anonymity and protection from possible legal consequences. It was thus a possibility of dealing with one's irregular status and staying economically active. Women in my sample found it relatively easy to find a household where they could work as cleaners, childminders or caregivers for the elderly, since there was great demand for this kind of labour performed by migrant women (Lutz 2008a; Williams, Gavanas 2008).

"Eastern European women" – as these women were often labelled after their arrival in Germany –, often found a niche in the care sector (Lutz 2008a, 2008d). Coming to Germany as a caregiver during the 1990s and in the following decade was very common among Czech, Slovak and Polish women (see e.g. Hess 2009; Karakayali 2010b; Satola 2010). Entering the care sector was often made easier by public opinion stereotyping and reducing migrant women – especially those from "Eastern Europe" – to "typically female" care positions without any regard to their actual qualifications and skills (Lutz 2008a, 2008d). Their origin, which was often connected to the seemingly "traditional" socialisation of women, was often perceived as a sufficient qualification for entering this field. Their opportunity of entering other sectors, however, was limited.

The narrations of my interviewees revealed various ways in which the possibilities for and positioning of migrants in the country of migration were shaped by migration policies, demands and changes in the labour market, the (non-)recognition of formal qualifications, as well as gender regimes and the stereotyping of "Eastern European migrant women". However, they also showed diverse strategies developed by migrants in order to respond to these shifting structural frameworks.

7.3.2 Negotiating one's own possibilities, skills and knowledge across borders

Research on the transferability of skills and knowledge across borders showed that the skills which migrants possess are not valuable per se and applicable (or not) in diverse locations. Rather, they are continuously reworked in the course of migration, put into question and complemented by other skills and knowledge acquired "on the way" (see e.g. Erel 2004, 2010; Weiss 2005; Kofman 2008; Nowicka 2014). Furthermore, research also showed that it does matter who possesses the skills and which resources are accessible to that person, spotlighting in particular the role of gender, class and ethnic divisions in these processes (see e.g. Kofman 2008; Erel 2010). In this chapter I will pay attention to the ways in which migrants interviewed for the present study made use of their skills, education, knowledge and experiences in another location. I will follow their migration pathways from the Czech Republic to Germany and, in some cases, back to the Czech Republic or elsewhere. By doing so I will identify the structural barriers to which migrants were exposed in various locations, as well as to their strategies for responding to these settings and giving value to their skills, knowledge, formal education and experiences in a new way.

The negotiation of skills after migration

Despite the difficulties in using actual qualifications and knowledge acquired in the Czech Republic, either because of their irregular status, non-recognition of their certificates, or general difficulties of finding a job, migrants developed diverse strategies in order to enter or continue their professional life. They tried to utilise their knowledge of the Czech language and of their country of origin, to turn their "care experience" in the private sphere into a resource in order to enter the formal public sector, to start new or additional studies, to set up their own business, or alternatively they considered moving elsewhere. I will introduce these strategies one by one.

Making use of the Czech language and country-related knowledge

As I have already mentioned, moving country was often connected to a reflection on one's own skills, possibilities, resources and knowledge. Above all, migration changed one's perception of elementary skills, such as speaking the language. Although speaking the Czech language was unquestionably normal for migrants, when moving to another country they often found that they could use it as resource, since knowledge of the Czech language was relatively unusual in Germany. Karolína, for instance, recounts how she made use of her Czech language skills when moving to Bamberg during and after completing her studies of German and English in Olomouc.

K: Well and: probably the most important event for my current life was that in my fourth year of studying at university I went to Bamberg as an Erasmus student. Erm: since I had studied German, I planned to visit some seminars on German studies in Bamberg. So I went there /(to her child:) Did you hit yourself on the head, my dear?/ So I went there and met Stefan in the student dormitories. Erm: he lived on the same floor and (breathing in) that was the summer of 2000. And: (1) so somehow (1) we did not plan that we would stay together or that we would have a family or that we would buy cars or houses or whatever together, (breathing in) [I: Hmm] so I went back to Olomouc as planned, finished university there, because I still had one year to go, [I: Hmm] and we stayed in contact via email somehow, and we visited each other and: then: erm: when I finished university I already knew that I would like to go to Bamberg again. So I went back as a tutor through a language program /her child babbles/ [I: Aha] Er: so I taught Czech and Landeskunde and those things here for a year. (breathing in) but I actually studied English and German. So Czech was not my field, you know. It was not my goal, but actually during my university studies because I studied English I was already interested in English more than in German, so I knew that I wanted to do it after graduation. That I would like to write a PhD. However, in Olomouc it was at that time not possible to do a PhD in literature because there was no professor for it. So if I wanted to do a PhD in the Czech Republic I would have to go to Prague. (breathing in) [I: Hmm] And: since I was here and I taught Czech I had established contact with the English studies programme here and I realised that I could also do it here. (Karolina, p. 2-3, l. 58-86)

Despite having studied German and English, she utilised "being a native speaker" for establishing contact with the Czech institute in Bamberg and teaching the Czech language in order to earn money for her future projects.

K: Well and in order to live here and somehow finance my life, I stayed in contact with the Czech institute where I had taught Czech before [I: Hmm] and: (-) I later taught some courses there. [I: Hmm] And I also taught at the Volkshochschule in Bayreuth, which is about fifty kilometres from Bamberg, (breathing) later on I also taught Czech at the Volkshochschule in Bamberg, so it was teaching Czech that made it possible for me to do the PhD. [I: Hmm] /the child babbles/ So I was able to live here normally and I didn't have to do any work that was not my thing. And actually the teaching- (breathing in) I planned that I would teach English or German as foreign languages and instead I did Czech as a foreign language. (Karolína, p. 3, l. 93-102)

Thus, teaching the Czech language was not a priori planned but became a resource for her by means of which she was able to finance her PhD studies – which served her as well as means of legalising her status – without having to do "any work that was not my thing." Besides turning it into economic capital, it was also a means of staying in touch with the Czech culture. She even wrote a novel in Czech, which she planned to publish. Since she had finished her PhD in English studies and then went on maternity leave with her first child, she was making plans to interconnect her knowledge of all three languages in her professional career in the future.

K: And: (1) now I applied for a position, which is related to English studies, so I would like to give value to my PhD somehow, and I know two foreign languages well and we live here in the border regions so I would like to make something of it. [I: Hmm] And (1) so: (1) erm: (1) we will see if it works and: when I can free myself a bit from this- getting up at night and when my mind is clearer, I would love to do some more English studies. But it is also true that I have started to flirt with the Czech institute here, with literature (Karolína, p. 5, l. 136-150)

Living in the Czech-German border region turned out to be important for Karolína both personally – living in a place in which German and Czech culture and languages coexist, as they do in her family and in her private life – and professionally, since she was able to utilise the Czech language for teaching and other projects. Like Karolína, knowledge of the Czech language was also valuable for Kamil because he was able to get his job in the automobile industry in Leipzig precisely because it distinguished him from other applicants. Marie, who taught the Czech language in Regensburg, and Linda in Bamberg, both profited from the proximity of the border. Zuzana, however, had a different experience: she looked for a job in Cologne after graduating in pedagogy, yet to no avail. Her idea of using the Czech language in a professional job failed, since in Cologne there was no demand for it. She thus had some occasional jobs in which she could use the Czech language, such as translation and interpretation, but she did not manage to turn it into a long-term resource. According to her:

Z: Well and I wanted (1) there is no work here where I could translate into Czech. There is absolutely no erm: how do you say. Demand. And that is what I would love to do most. [I: Hmm] To have some contact with the language and to search for expressions and to analyse it all for myself. Then I started to have a look around if there it would not be possible to at least do translations for Spanish. To study translation. [I: Aha] And interpretation. But there is nothing here, I would have to commute about a hundred kilometres for Spanish. And it is not possible with the child. (Zuzana, p. 10-11, l. 317-325)

These experiences point out the difference in significance of the Czech language in the border regions and further away from the border. While the border regions were places of cultural encounter and economic cooperation in which knowledge of the language was crucial, the further one got from the border the less important the Czech language became. In addition, while Karolína was able to mobilise and expand the connections with the Czech institute in Bamberg she had already established back in Olomouc, Zuzana lacked this possibility. The strategy of turning one's knowledge of native languages into economic capital was also identified by other studies (see e.g. Liversage 2009b; Nohl et al. 2010a). However, as the narratives collected for the current study showed, it matters which native languages one speaks and how these can be given value in local, trans-local and global economies.

Efforts towards giving value to "care experience" in the public sector

Another strategy of using work experience and turning it into a resource was to translate and use know-how acquired in the care sector in the course of migration or even earlier in the public sphere.

Zuzana, who came to Germany at the end of the 1990s as an au pair and worked for several years as a child minder and cleaner in order to finance her life and studies in Cologne, considered using her knowledge from the care sector after finishing her studies when she was looking for full-time employment. At that time, her first child was about two years old. As she recounted:

Z: Fanynka was still in crèche so it was good. So I had time for everything and: then I started to search for work. And I said to myself that as a recent graduate I would first look for an internship, (1) erm and I also wanted to work in an HR department. [I: Hmm] I thought that if I aim low in order to gain experience it won't be so difficult. And I got about three- three erm Absagen. [I: Hmm] It didn't work. [I: Hmm] So I started to reduce my demands a bit (1) and then I wanted to go somewhere to an office, so it would- something what would satisfy me. And then erm: despite having concentrated in pedagogy on adult education, I also submitted an application to an organisation which had a kindergarten and creches. That I would go to work in a crèche. [I: Hmm] (1) But there I would also have to start from zero because I didn't have any education as a nurse, [I: Hmm] but I was only a graduate, [I: Hmm] and it was not enough for them, so I would not have the right competencies for the crèche. No one responded to me; it was clear from the beginning that they would not even respond to me. (Zuzana, p. 9-10, l. 280-297)

Since other possibilities seemed unrealistic and inaccessible to her, Zuzana had the idea of using her care skills again in order to enter the formal labour market. She found out, however, that while her "Eastern European origin" and migration status had often been sufficient for starting a care job such as she had done in the private sphere for years, in the public sphere she needed special education. Lenka had very similar experiences of being simultaneously over and under qualified in the specific field. After three years' experience as a childminder for three children in a household in Cologne and after marrying her husband, she started to search for a job in the public sphere.

L: I got married to my husband in between. It was actually in 2003. After the marriage- I actually still stayed there. But in between I was already looking for work and thinking about what would interest me. /What could I do with my qualifications as a grammar school teacher specialising in German (her voice sinks)/, what could I do in Germany as a foreigner! [I: Hmm] So what occurred to me first was that- since I like to work with children I could try something in Kindergarten. [I: Hmm] So that was the first idea. /Then, afterwards I sent about (1) eighty to ninety CV's to diverse kindergartens and (her voice sinks)/ I got nothing but rejections, so I started to think what am I doing wrong! [I: Hmm] And then later I spoke to a colleague of mine and she told me that they were afraid of you, when they saw that I had a university education, that I studied here and here, 'they were afraid of you when they read your CV, that you will immediately take their position. So they thought it was better not to even invite you for an interview.' That's how it was! [I: Hmm] Because at the time she worked as a sociologist at a kindergarten [I: Hmm] and she said that that was one of the reasons. She said that if she were to hold my CV in her hands, she would do the same. (Lenka I., p. 3, l. 80-94)

While Zuzana's and Lenka's knowledge in the care sector was acquired in the course of migration, Jana was able to draw on her prior experience. She studied at a secondary nursing school and, after studying theology in Prague, she worked as a nurse for a year at a hospital in Germany; nonetheless Jana points out that her status was below that of regular nurses since, despite having undertaken a longer period of educational training, her diploma from the Czech Republic was not recognised. Since she did not obtain a visa for starting a further course of studies, this time in medicine, she went to England where she worked as an au pair and subsequently as a caregiver in an old people's home. When she moved to Germany a year later, she once again made use of her extensive experience in the care sector. She moved into a house with two elderly women who she colloquially referred to as "grannies" and who she looked after in exchange for housing. This arrangement made it possible for to her to save money for her studies of music and bridge the period of time at the beginning when she did not have a job.

J: And: there were plenty of things going on in my head (2) and: (1) then I met these elderly women and they were amazing. (1) And: I was really happy. For them. [I: Hmm] And I spent four years with them, I lived at their place, [I: Hmm] (1) and: they helped me- at the beginning they tried to find me a job, it was very touching (laughing) (breathing in) And: (2) then I met a girl who told me that there was a company that arranged care for people who had various different disabilities and who lived at home. [I: Hmm] (1) So I ran there immediately (1) and I got a job with them, yes. (1) Well and I am still working there at present. [I: Hmm] (1) But this was sometime in the spring, (1) and I came here in October and so until March I did not have a proper job. Or a regular job. (1) That means that it was a few months during which-, it actually always takes at least half year if not more (deep breathing) in order to recover and (laughing) [I: Hmm] one is able to start something, yes. (3) So during that time I was not absolutely healthy, I had various health problems (1) er: it was a lot, it was a lot at once. [I: Hmm] (Jana, p. 8, l. 271-282)

Interestingly, in contrast to attempts by Zuzana and Lenka to enter the public sphere, Jana gained access to both jobs through her social contacts. The job looking after elderly women was communicated to her through a friend who had studied in Göttingen beforehand and returned to Prague shortly before Jana came. The other job – caring part-time for handicapped people in their own homes – was introduced to her through other social contacts. Moreover, Jana was able to make use of her professional qualification as a nurse, practical experience of working in a hospital and extensive experience in various fields of the care sector. She was able to turn her work experience into a resource on which she could rely when taking on the physically and emotionally demanding job of caring for physically handicapped people who in some cases had difficulties to move and had to be carried around by her. For Jana, care work became a constant in her life and an important resource on which she could build after migration. It became a means for her for making the important turns in her life happen, such as moving to Germany and "recommencing her life again".

Professional reorientation after migration through new studies

J: And I think for example that many people somehow do not understand, erm: (-) those who haven't experienced it, ey: how it is to start. [I: Hmm] (1) In a foreign country. Absolutely from nothing. [I: Hmm] (1) That it is really quite difficult. [I: Hmm] Even though Germany is next door to the Czech Republic and ey: it is actually not that far. And it is also not such a cultural shock [I: Hmm] erm: (1) it is not so bad actually. (1) But anyway, (1) to disrupt that life one has lived until then in the Czech Republic, (breathing in) all contacts and suddenly you flop yourself down somewhere else and now everything starts from the beginning again. [I: Hmm] I knew that no one would be interested there whether I had already studied or not and: (laughing) [I: Hmm] that I would have to learn German and that at the beginning I would be happy to do some cleaning or whatever here. (1) And: (2) that I would have to fight everything out, yes. (1) [I: Hmm] That I would surely have to fight at the beginning in order to survive, and (1) [I: Hmm] erm: (2) yes. (1) So it was difficult, yes. (Jana, p. 9-10, l. 310-322)

Jana's beginnings in Germany, to where she returned for a second time in 2002, were for her connected to her reorientation in a new professional sphere. Despite having studied theology in the Czech Republic, she decided to start a new subject after migration: music sciences. This decision was linked to a metamorphosis within Jana, which started not with her current migration but much earlier after having finished her studies in Prague. At that time she did not know "what to do with herself". During her travels abroad she discovered that she needed to live abroad and to be "all over the place".

Thus, her spontaneous decision to start a new course of studies in Germany was a result of biographical reflections which had started in the past.[59] Thus, her decision to put aside the qualifications she had already acquired was connected both to her reflections on her options in Germany and to the processes of a new positioning and of searching for new and alternative ways of life. She herself understood her migration as the turning point in her biography and as a new beginning.

While for Jana these reflexive processes on her biographical development had begun prior to migration, of which her reorientation from one professional field to another was part, for other interviewees it was the act of migration which led to shifted perceptions on one's own possibilities and chances to utilise qualifications, knowledge and skills. Barbora, whose biography I introduced above, decided to change her professional orientation from natural sciences to social work. Her decision was connected to difficulties in using her initial qualifications and knowledge in Germany and repeated failure to get a job. She chose social work, or more precisely adult education, after gaining a temporary job as teacher for Czech language, which was introduced to her by her husband. Through this field new perspectives and chances opened up for her. In addition, starting a course of studies was a means of entering the public sphere and emancipating from her role as a mother and homemaker.

Linda also started a new course of studies in Germany after she discovered a new field in which she wanted to be active, namely translation and interpretation.

L: Well and: so I started again to eliminate these (breathing in) restaurants and factories (laughing) [I: Hmm], and I finally managed it, well and then I went to some courses and so on; so I learnt German relatively well and [I: Hmm] I was able to translate and also interpret [I: Hmm] and: (breathing in) then I got a chance actually here at university, I attended some seminars in Slavic studies here, [I: Hmm] and then I actually: I found out that the most of my: working: working time was connected to the Czech language. [I: Hmm] But I didn't study Czech, (breathing in) and because when I was in the Czech Republic I criticised people, for example Americans, who didn't study the language but just went somewhere and taught it, and pretended how much they understood everything, so I didn't want to be like that [I: Hmm] so I decided that I would study something else here, Slavic studies. [I: Hmm] So it is a bit paradoxical that in Germany: (breathing in) that I started to study Slavic studies here in Bamberg. [I: Aha] And: (-) I finished in, I don't know, but it probably doesn't matter for you, 2005 I think, (1) as a bachelor. (Linda, p. 4, l. 104-119)

Paradoxically, Linda's interest in the Czech language did not develop until after she moved from Brno to Bamberg. Her contact with the language and the possibility of using it professionally for translating, interpreting and teaching, gave her the idea of starting another course of studies, namely Slav-

---

59 As to the theoretical connection between biographical transformation processes and migration see e.g. Apitzsch 2000; Ruokonen-Engler 2012.

ic studies, after she had completed her history and German degree in Brno. By doing so, she was able to interconnect her knowledge of the German language and the Czech language and use it as resource for her further professional pathway. The studies had a twofold meaning for her: on the one hand it was a means of professional reorientation, which resulted from her biographical reflections concerning possible career paths, and on the other hand it was a means of getting a residency permit at that time.

While some of my interviewees decided to start a new course of studies after migration – both as a result of biographical transformation processes started prior to migration or in the course of migration – others built on their initial studies and complemented them by further studies in Germany. Lenka, for example, carried out additional studies of pedagogy which enabled to her to gain the same status and rights as a teacher educated in Germany. She thus drew a link between her previous studies and her studies in Germany. So did for example Arnošt, who did his PhD in Germany. Despite it being unintended and unplanned, he relied on the qualifications he had acquired in Germany later on when he applied for a research position at the university in Bamberg and was appointed a professor there.

Even if they had not undertaken an additional course of studies in Germany, most of my interviewees profited from student exchange programs when searching for a job in Germany later on. Petr, for example, established contacts with a reputable financial institution during his scholarship in Munich, where he later started an internship and subsequently got a regular job. Similar connections were used by Kamil, who after graduating in Prague joined the company in Leipzig at which he had undertaken an internship and written his diploma thesis. Štěpánka, on the other hand, was able to exploit the experience and social contacts she had gained during her Erasmus exchange year in Göttingen in order to do her PhD and subsequently start working for an international pharmaceutical company there.

The importance of studying in Germany was obvious in my sample: of the sixteen interviews I conducted, only three interviewees – Martin, Adéla and Ivan – did not undertake any additional or full-time studies in Germany. Interestingly, they all moved to Germany through international companies or, as in the case of Ivan, through a job agency. Without these structures and social contacts, interviewees found it difficult to utilise the university diplomas they had acquired in the Czech Republic, be it because of a lack of recognition, migration policies or exclusion mechanisms on the labour market preferring those who studied in the country of migration and could give proof of work experience there (see also e.g. Liversage 2009b; Baghdadi, Riaño 2014; Kontos, Voswinkel 2010).

Self-employment: turning transnationality into a resource

K: Well and: (1) it was my first more serious contact with Germany and: I wanted to go to England then because of my dissertation, to a library, so I went there and I was actually there for four months, (breathing in) erm: and: (1) I got to know Germany very well in the meantime. Me and a friend of mine made plans that we would like to establish a travel agency, [I: Hmm] and we already worked for an American agency and we carried out trips in the Czech Republic [I: Hmm] and then we made contact on that trip with a family that wanted to do the same kind of trip to Bavaria. [I: Hmm] And: so we travelled around the place here and we planned everything, it was for fourteen days, we started in Frankfurt where they arrived, then we went to Bamberg and we drove along the so-called Romantic Road to Füssen, Neuschwanstein, through Berchtesgaden, Regensburg, Passau, and back [I: Hmm] so I got to know Bavaria very well. And I know that I bought a pen with the Bavarian flag on there for the first time. [I: Aha] (-) With these blue and white lozenges' [I: Hmm] and that I suddenly felt that I belong here. Because I learnt things here much better, I did not only know Bamberg or Ingolstadt, Stefan comes from Ingolstadt, (breathing in) but I learnt things here much more and I actually got the chance to present things here as if they were mine, you know, it was important. [I: Hmm] This trip. And: I don't know whether there might be some more work for this travel agency, if we can continue, but we would definitely like to sell this trip somehow. Because there was plenty of work involved, a lot of knowledge gained and it would be a pity if it only stayed on the computer or in photos, yes. [I: Hmm] We will see. (1) And we would like to connect it erm: Bavaria and the Czech Republic, to do a historical tour- about Bavarian-Czech history. We already have it sketched out but we don't have people yet. We need to find some tourists who would like to travel it with us (laughing) (Karolína, p. 15-16, l. 477-500)

When reflecting on the possibilities of using their own skills and knowledge, some interviewees came up with creative ideas which emerged from the transnational knowledge they had developed in the course of migration. They made use of their language and translation skills, as well as intercultural competencies. Karolína, in addition, made use of her knowledge of geography and her interest in history when coming up with the idea of opening a travel agency which would go across the border. The idea of linking Czech and Bavarian geography and history not as separate units but as one space bound by a common history, is closely connected with Karolína's biography. Both in the Czech Republic and in Germany she lived in the border regions. Thus, she learned very early on to mirror "the others" and to translate among cultures. Her aim of linking these transnational influences in her private life is reflected in her professional life too. She searched for the ways of turning her transnationality into a resource.

Moving elsewhere

Moving elsewhere to another country became an option for some interviewees. It was an option when other possibilities to start a profession failed in Germany, but also an imagined option which presented an alternative to other

314

imagined or real possibilities of development in Germany or in the Czech Republic. Zuzana expressed her desire to move to another country in the following way:

Z: Hmm (1) and: (1) I don't know with the (1) second child it was again a bit different, di-different. (1) Erm. We still would like to have a look somewhere else. (1) Erm: (2), (breath) erm: I don't know. Here I am here I am in fact- somehow very satisfied, but: (1) I perhaps still need some other erm – some other influences to affect me. I already feel really at home here. In Germany. (laughing) [I: Hmm] Or in Germany, in Cologne. (Breathing) And: what I would (1) like to change is – I would like to go to another country. And my husband too. [I: Hmm] Not that we would erm (breathing) move somewhere in Germany but – to a completely different place. [I: Hmm] (1) (…) (Breathing) and we don't even have an idea where. It is all the same to us. Just that we get a bit out of here again. (breathing) With the option that we would probably come back here someday. Not that I would give things up – completely here (1) for me it is- well I have- (breathing) erm (-) For instance, I have here more friends than in the Czech Republic, in the Czech Republic everything is somehow torn down, the bridges. (Breathing) (Zuzana, p.12, l. 360-375)

For Zuzana, moving to another country was connected to new "influences" and, indirectly, with new possibilities which turned out to be inaccessible to her in Germany. Her desire to move country becomes clearer when embedded in her overall biographical presentation. For Zuzana, migration always meant the opening up of new possibilities, new perspectives and "influences". She moved to Germany for the first time in her adolescence, since other options of self-development in her place of origin were inaccessible to her. However, some years later, after graduating in Cologne and unsuccessfully looking for employment, she found herself in a similar situation. She thus applied the same strategy as before: to move country, to gain new possibilities again – which were ascribed with "influences, which would affect" her – and develop new perspectives on her life and on possible ways of self-development. Nevertheless, moving country would not mean that she would disrupt any links established in Germany. Like when she moved from the Czech Republic to Germany some years ago, she wanted to keep them and again enlarge her own scope of possibilities in new transnational spaces. Very similar ideas of moving elsewhere and back were also expressed by Jana. Like Zuzana, she could also imagine to move elsewhere in the near future:

J: I don't know. I can imagine that I might do some work which would make it possible for me to somehow be internationally (laughing) active, but which would enable to me to always come back to Germany. [I: Hmm] Well yes. The return. (1) That would be great. (1) And of course contacts with the Czech Republic! (laughing) [I: Hmm] Hmm.

I: And what do you mean- to the Czech Republic?

J: That I could travel home often to see my family, yes. [I: Hmm] (1) Somehow. To have enough money for it. [I: Hmm] It is probably about the money (laughing). So first I have to think about the money (laughing). (Jana, p. 61, l. 2511-2519)

Her dream would be to link her music studies with her knowledge of languages and her desire to stay geographically mobile. Like Zuzana, Jana emphasized the possibility of returning to Germany and keeping the social links to the Czech Republic alive. Hence, moving elsewhere would also mean the enlargement of her possibilities in newly established transnational spaces. However, she also underlined a very pragmatic feature of keeping transnational links alive, namely financial resources, which would make moving back and forth in transnational spaces real.

The negotiation of skills after returning

As I have shown previously, migration from the Czech Republic to Germany was in most cases not a simple one-way process, but instead involved several moves back and forth, which were influenced by restrictive migration policies or which resulted from ongoing family negotiations. When moving back and forth, migrants sought of ways in which to validate the skills they had acquired across the border. Allan M. Williams and Vladimir Baláž (2005) showed in their study on the return migration of skilled Slovaks back to Slovakia after a stay of more than three months in the UK, that returnees could largely profit from migration in a number of ways, even when they had worked in low skilled positions. According to them, migrants were able to valorize their language skills and professional knowledge, which in turn some of them could apply directly in their profession back in Slovakia, social networks and social competencies, as well as important "know how" – knowledge about the structures and function of organisations and businesses. They showed how this knowledge and these skills could be used creatively in order to start businesses, such as language or student agencies which were at that time booming in post-communist Slovakia, and in some cases used for professional promotion and salary increases.

In accordance with these findings, some of my interviewees' stories indirectly evidenced the successful valorization of cross-borders experiences, skills and knowledge. Ivan, for example, told me that his colleagues who returned to the Czech Republic after a few years in Germany, made use of the knowledge in the IT sector which they had acquired abroad. They established their own IT companies or got well paid jobs in already established – often international – companies situated mostly in Prague or Brno, the two biggest cities in the Czech Republic. Hence, they managed to transfer their knowledge of languages and professional skills from one location into another. In this sense, their cultural capital became "transnational cultural capital" which could be applied trans-locally (Weiss 2005).

Other narratives, however, revealed some counter-evidence. Lenka, for instance, narrated how the language skills which she had improved in Germany as an au pair and while working in the hospitality sector, and which she wished to valorize after returning to the Czech Republic, were devalued. She returned from Germany to the Czech Republic since her au pair visa expired. This was in 2000.

L: So I had to go back, [I: hmm] and I actually initially returned to my parents' house in Moravia, and at the beginning I was unemployed and I looked for a job, (1) and I was thinking what could I do. And I thought that since it was quite difficult to get a job at our place, in Southern Moravia-, I said to myself that one of the possibilities was to go to Prague. (1) So I sent CV's to Prague and I was at some job interviews and finally they took me on at a trading company. I worked there as an assistant in the trade department. (1) [I: hmm] Well (laughing) the best thing was that they told me at the beginning that they would need someone who spoke German perfectly. So I said: 'That will be great! I will speak German all day! Amazing!' Well, finally it turned out that (breathing in) our main director came and he always asked for my boss who was not in the office. 'Wo ist Frau Vlastíková?' And the only answer I gave was 'Sie hat eine Verhandlung.' (laughing) [I: (laughing)] So one could have put a trained monkey in that position too. (laughing) That was the only sentence I said in German nearly every day. Hmmm. So I was sorry about that. Well and on the other hand, I learnt plenty of new things, but because I am not really a business type who wants to sit in front of a computer all day and fill in SAP tables and similar things, so- I stood it there for nearly a year [I: hmm] and after that one year I left because (breathing in) I was already in contact with my (breathing in) husband, but we were only writing emails to each other at the time, and then, one fine day we decided that he would come to Prague. /It was in May, he came to Prague, everything was blooming, it was very romantic (poetically)/ (both are laughing, 2). So I showed him Prague and we fell in love and- (laughing) (Lenka II., p. 2, l. 33-55)

Since she did not have much work experience after graduating in the Czech Republic, she sought to valorize her language skills, yet felt undervalued in her job position. It was the devaluation of her university education and of her very good German skills, as well as the fact that she fell in love with her future husband, that made her decide to return to Germany and start there again as a childminder. Her experiences, which have been repeated in different settings by other – mostly female – interviewees as well, match the findings of some researchers who have focused on the transition processes and economic crisis in post-communist countries (see e.g. Křížková, Formánková 2011; Trevena 2013; Nowicka 2014). They showed that as a result of the transformation of the economy and educational system in the last decades, university graduates often experienced a devaluation of their university education. This was especially noticeable amongst university educated women, who to a much greater extent accepted less qualified jobs in order to overcome the possible threat of unemployment (Křížková, Formánková 2011).

Besides the devaluation of skills and knowledge, other interviewees were exposed to the process of "othering" (Hall 1994) due to their cross-border experiences:

M: I was always fighting a bit with Prague. Erm, now when I am here I miss Prague and [I: hmm] I like Prague very much and I would love to go back there (smiling) [I: hmm] But on the other hand, it is such an ambivalent relationship somehow. [I: hmm] Erm, when one-erm, I have the feeling that once you've been away and come back people see you completely differently. They perceive you differently. [I: hmm] When I started to teach at the language centre in Dlouhá street, erm, my colleagues told me: 'hey wait a minute, you can't copy as much here as you were used to in Regensburg'. [I: hmm] And there I actually felt – aha, ermmm. [I: hmm] They saw me- I was for them someone- a bit strange you know. That I came from that country where everything was possible. [I: hmm hmm] And: (2) so (1) I have this feeling that when a Czech person returns after a longer period of time abroad he or she is perceived by other Czechs as- something hostile, a bit like competition, erm, yes. (Marie, p. 20, l. 680-693)

Marie describes a process of "being made different" after she returned from her two year stay in Regensburg, where she taught the Czech language, to her initial position at the German institute in Prague. This construction of difference (Ruokonen-Engler 2009) was based not on ethnic background, but on the biographical experiences of living in another country. These were from the point of view of others related to stereotypical images of life in Germany, the country "where everything is possible". Arnošt also had very similar experiences. Despite receiving an offer of a professorship in Bamberg, he decided to refuse it and return to the Czech Republic to his initial position as lecturer at the university in Olomouc:

A: And so I returned home again with my wife after six months, and in the meantime our second child had been born. [I: Hmm] Erm: one of the motives was that I wanted to be with my child and not to commute between Germany and the Czech Republic (takes a deep breath). Well but it got a bit complicated because my colleagues thought that I had probably earned too much money in Germany and my boss, or rather the new boss since the boss who had taken me on had already been exchanged by another, she thought that I had earned a lot of money in Germany during that six month stay (breathing in) so I lost all my personal benefits and I was only given a basic salary and: we were absolutely not able to get by. And at the same time an offer came from Bamberg saying that they had rethought things and (…) that they had tried to fill the position but that they did not like anyone as much as me, so they were offering me the professorship again. (Arnošt, p. 4-5, l. 129-151)

When returning to Olomouc, Arnošt experienced the devaluation of the experiences he had acquired abroad. This devaluation, which was expressed in terms of the lowering of his salary to a minimum, was just as for Marie based on stereotypes relating to the imagined high standard of life in Germany, which was also thought to signify a high level of wages. Because of his cross-border experiences, he became "the other" and was then treated differently than before his migration. Arnošt also experienced difficulties in integrating his experience, knowledge and additional qualifications acquired abroad into his career path in the Czech Republic later on. This was, inter alia, based on the procedures surrounding career progression in academia which are to a great extend bound to the framework within that particular nation state.

To summarise, when returning to the Czech Republic, migrants experienced very different opportunities of valorizing their skills, knowledge and qualifications acquired abroad. While some were able to profit from cross-border experiences and turn them into economic capital and better social positions, others had difficulty giving value to their "other" experiences. They were confronted with discriminatory practices in the labour market which affected men and women in different ways, by stereotypes concerning life in Germany to which these were related and in terms of which the differences were construed, as well as by national procedures within academia and some other fields of the economy, which disregarded experience, qualifications and knowledge acquired abroad. These experiences of devaluation and lacking recognition were often the basis for decisions to move country once again.

7.3.3 The question of translatability and recognition of social positions across the border

"Transnational social fields are in part shaped by the migrants' perceptions that they must keep their options open. In the globalized economy that has developed over the past several decades, there is a sense that no one place is truly secure, although people do have access to many places. One way migrants keep options open is to continuously translate the economic and social position gained in one political setting into political, social and economic capital in another." (Glick Schiller et al. 1992b, p. 12)

In one of the previous chapters I showed how migrants created transnational social and cultural links in the course of migration and how these shifted over time. Despite the fact the social links spanning across borders took on different forms, intensity and meaning for migrants, they all tried to keep them alive in some form or another, be it through telephone calls, visits, emails, online social networks or letters. While some migrants did so in order to stay in touch with other family members or friends, others tried to keep links alive in order to keep the possibilities of professional development in the other location open. These biographically established transnational spaces became spaces within which goods, cultural practices, information, knowledge, emotions and intimate links circulated. Hence, family members, close friends and certain institutions across the border stayed important significant others to which migrants felt related.

I also showed that as well as opening up new spaces of action, migration also initiated a shift in perspective regarding everyday practices, culture, societies and one's own biography. These shifted perspectives were, inter alia, expressed in comparisons drawn by migrants between their country of origin and country of migration, between their own present and own past, between migrants and their significant others back in the Czech Republic, between themselves here and their imagined selves there, but also between different opportunity structures and social stratification systems. These processes of comparison were expressions of the biographical work of individuals (Schütze, Schröder-Wildhagen 2012). It was through these that migrants tried to make sense of their life paths and of their current positioning.

I showed that migration also initiated processes of reflection on one's own possibilities, skills, qualifications and knowledge as shaped by other opportunity structures, since in most cases they could not be directly "translated" or applied in another location. Barbora, for example, explains that when she moved to Germany: "I absolutely did not know the German structures, how things work here, erm: which possibilities I had in Germany with my studies" (Barbora, p. 14, l. 448-449). After several unsuccessful attempts at finding a job in Germany she found out that her knowledge of "how things work" and her patterns of action had to be rethought. It was through these biographical reflections – "what will I do what will I do-" (Barbora, p. 16, l. 512) – and her new experiences as a Czech language teacher, a job which she had later through her husband, that she got the idea of starting a new course of studies in Germany. Her decision was, inter alia, shaped by newly acquired knowledge: "if you want to work in this field you have to have a university education in this field" (Barbora, p. 23, l. 710-711). She in part reworked the patterns she already knew from the Czech Republic. Not only had her sister and mother worked in a field other than that in which they were educated, but so had most of her former fellow students. Hence, while using the same strategy of reorientation as other female members in her family, which was also a strategy of staying economically active in their region of origin, she complemented it by her newly acquired knowledge of social and institutional structures in Germany. Starting new studies in Germany signified a turning point for Barbora in her personal and professional development, since she emancipated from the household, gained new independence, and changed her views of herself and her future possibilities. It was also through her new studies that she gained more self-esteem and social recognition.

Similarly to Barbora, Martin also described, reflected and evaluated different opportunity structures across locations within which he moved. His narration included large argumentative passages in which he compared different possibilities of development not only for himself, but also for people whom he met while moving places. He drew comparisons between his biographical pathway and that of his peers who had stayed in his home town, between himself and his co-workers in Germany and in America, where he had a summer job in a canning factory and in a bakery, and later between himself and his colleagues in the finance sector in Prague and Düsseldorf. In doing so, he reflected in a similar manner to Barbora and other interviewees on the importance of studying in Germany and the role of institutionalised career paths in one location in order to access certain social positions. He presented himself as an exception who, unlike others, gained access to the finance sector in Düsseldorf not through any special qualifications or social background, but through a social contact – his former boss in Prague. As he argued:

M: Because normally one would not have a chance of getting there directly [I: Hmm], without these- without these- without him so to speak. [I: Hmm] Because I didn't study in Germany and yes, it is also a good job for Germans, a really good job. If they studied at university there then it is a really good job. (Martin, p. 18, l. 580-585)

Martin develops his argument further on in another part of the interview by outlining the institutionalised education and career pathways leading from prestigious universities, which are only accessible to a certain group of people who can afford them, to positions like his in finance. As he observed: "now everyone meets again in these investment companies, investment banks. These are very similar- very seldom does someone get there by an absolutely different way." (Martin, p. 21, l. 676-677). For Martin, as for other interviewees, it was important that his social position – and thus his biographical development leading to this position – was recognized by his significant others across the border. Although this was possible in Prague where he still kept close friendships with some his former colleagues and fellow students, in Most, where he was from, "no one knows exactly what I really do" (Martin, p. 3, l. 77). He explained this by means of class differences and the impossibility of others to envisage his social pathway. As he put it: "it is not possible to explain it to people who have never had anything to do with finance or with university. It is simply- incomprehensible to them, yeah." (Martin, p. 20, l. 617-619). However, even though his position and social pathway was incomprehensible to his significant others, he was able to "translate" – as indicated by Nina Glick Schiller et al. in the quotation above – his position into economic capital by supporting the family he left behind and "buying really good presents" for them (Martin, p. 20, l. 636).

The question of the "translatability" of one's own position and social pathway in transnational spaces and the associated (non-)recognition was also addressed by Lenka. Like Martin, she narrated her story as a success story: how she worked herself up from the private sphere in Germany, where she worked for several years as a childminder, to the public sector. After she legalised her status, she managed to get a job at a grammar school, where she initially worked as a tutor. Through additional studies and her active commitment she reached the same status as her German colleagues, with whom she compared herself and to whom she wanted to equal. The fact that she became a "Beamte" – a public servant – was important to her, since this meant that after many years of struggling she gained not just social recognition but also legal recognition of her position by German authorities. However, despite her successful story, she experienced difficulties in "translating" the meaning of her newly acquired position in Germany across the borders. Since the civil servant system in Germany is not comparable to that in the Czech Republic, it was difficult for her significant others back in the Czech

Republic to imagine and to understand. The "untranslatability" of her social position was linked to a lack of recognition of her efforts. Lenka summarised her life path towards the end of interview like this:

L: Well I can say that when I imagine how I began here (1) as a Kinderfrau and I don't know, that I cleaned flats and then: I was able to start studying (…) I can say that I worked myself out of there to where I am, so I am satisfied. Hmm. Well, it is not, one could say-nothi-. When I tell people that I teach in Germany, so "a teacher, oh well, I don't envy you." (Lenka II, p. 26-27, l. 863-869)

Lenka offers two perspectives in her reasoning: the first one is her own perspective on her successful development and the second one is the perspective of "others" who disrespect her profession and therefore also her social pathway. From their perspective, her development might be seen as ordinary, taking into account her initial studies of pedagogy. However, since she moved to Germany and the perception of her possibilities and resources shifted, inter alia because of the legal and institutional barriers she had to overcome, working in her initial profession turned out to be an exception and a great success. These two perspectives on her success, which have been negotiated in transnational spaces and which have been of biographical importance to Lenka, are visible throughout Lenka's biographical narration.

The subject of a lack of recognition of his career path also pervades Arnošt's narrative. However, it was not the lack of recognition by his significant others that he sought to solve by means of repeated moves back and forth, but rather by the institution or more accurately the university department in Olomouc at which he wanted to pursue his career but where he was exposed to multiple exclusion mechanisms. While his knowledge and efforts were recognised in Germany, not least as a result of his attaining a professorship, he struggled for professional recognition in the Czech Republic. During these struggles he found out that some of the qualifications, work and experience he had acquired across the border were not recognised, which resulted in him having to "work out his career again".

These stories highlight the question of the translatability of social positioning across borders, the role of the recognition and – multiple and sometimes contradictory – perceptions of success in the course of migration. As the narratives of Martin, Lenka, Arnošt and others reveal, social positioning is not solely a static point on the social strata, but it is connected to diverse meanings given to it by individuals. Moreover, every social position has a story behind it which is connected to opportunity structures in one location, outlined, among others, by institutionalized educational and career pathways leading to it, which migrants reflect on, negotiate and towards which they position themselves (Anthias 2008). These complexities make it difficult for some to translate their social position into another location, shaped by "other rules of the game" (Kelly, Lusis 2006, p. 834). In view of the fact that their social world spanned transnationally, "translation work" was nonetheless important for some, since they sought recognition of their social pathways by significant others living across the border. Axel Honneth (1995) underlined in his theory of recognition the human need for recognition of one's own abilities and achievements. According to him, self-realisation and self-esteem – i.e. "a practical relation-to-self in which one's distinct traits and abilities (which are not shared by all) are valued" (Brink, Owen 2010, p. 14) – can only be achieved in intersubjective processes through recognition by significant others. The disregard of recognition, as shown for example by Arnošt's narrative, is experienced as harmful and as an act of exclusion – paradoxically in the society from which that person is from. Hence, the experience of exclusion and inclusion across locations is also shaped by perceptions of success by migrants.

Nina Glick Schiller et al. indicated in the quotation presented at the beginning of this chapter that migrants tried to keep their options open across location by "translating" the economic and social position they had gained in one location into diverse forms of capital in another location. On the basis of biographical narratives I pointed out these processes of "translation" across the border. Moreover, I showed that migrants sought to translate not only the social position they had attained in one location into economic and other forms of capital in another, but also their social position and its meaning in itself. Nevertheless, the narratives also revealed the limits in "translating" meanings from one location into another and their impact on the subject's perception of the self. It was within these complex transnational spaces that the question of one's own positioning and success was continuously (re-)evaluated.

8 Conclusion

The present work concerns the migration and social pathways of highly educated people moving East-West in Europe – a group which, over the last decades, has increasingly gained importance within migration flows (see e.g. OECD 2013), yet which has largely stayed under the radar of public and scientific discussion. The aim of the present research is to contribute to the knowledge of the complex processes of migration and social mobility and their mutual interconnections in general, and of the way migrants negotiate their qualifications, skills, and knowledge in diverse locations in particular.

The landscape of European East-West migration, within which the present work is embedded, changed remarkably over the last three decades as a result of massive political and social shifts. Migration from the Czech Republic to Germany, which has been investigated for this study on the basis of diverse documents and biographical narrative interviews, serves as a "textbook example" of these processes. The two neighbouring countries, which were once separated by the heavily protected "East-West" border, have been united within the EU since 2004. In 2011, Czech citizens – alongside those of other new EU member countries – gained full access to the German labour market. These events, which diversified options for cross-border migration patterns (see e.g. Morokvasic, Rudolph 1994), are also seen as a precondition for the establishment of transnational interconnections, concerning not only the political and economic areas, but also the everyday lives of people living in this region of Europe (see e.g. Smith, Guarnizo 1999).

Theoretically and methodologically, I position my work at the intersection of "gender sensitive" migration and biographical research. This enables me to investigate possible links of migration processes with wider societal changes, the establishment of transnational processes in this ever changing context, as well as the processes of social mobility in the course of migration. In doing so, I drew from the transnational approach, which allows to investigate dynamic transnational linkages as well as complex and sometimes contradictory processes of social positioning in transnational spaces.

The biographies I collected for the present research project belong to the "transition generation" (Williams, Baláž 2005, p. 463) – the generation which experienced extensive changes in the Czech society in the course of their adolescence or early adulthood as a result of the fall of the Iron Curtain in 1989. These changes became part of biographical narrations and reflections, and for some signified a biographical turn, since patterns of action and the possibilities of self-development, self-realization and self-perception shifted.

The possibility of movement across borders, which had been restricted for several decades prior to 1989, became an essential part of these processes.

Even though the migration of highly skilled people has so far been investigated almost exclusively in terms of labour migration, the narratives collected as part of the present study showed that although work played an important role in all cases, the motives for moving country were manifold. Migration – both internal and international – became a means of discovering new places and life styles, learning new languages, pursuing one's educational or professional careers, or overcoming economic depression in one's home region.

In the course of transformation processes, some metropolitan areas in the Czech Republic, namely Prague or Brno, strengthened their position by becoming prosperous economic centers. Some other areas, however, such as border regions, were hit especially hard by economic decline and growing unemployment. These structural inequalities led to increasing migration of young people out of these regions – either to the metropolitan areas in the Czech Republic or outside of the country. Nevertheless, as the analysis revealed, the border regions – which unintendedly showed to be the place of origin for the most of interviewees –, featured not only unemployment and social decline, but also presented an important resource for migrants. Czech-German bilingualism and the transcultural nature of the area were often reconstrued in the biographical recapitulations as a meaningful dimension with an impact on migration processes. The interviewees thematised the presence of the German language in the everyday lives of people living in this area, while also pointing to the fact that spread of the language had been changing and slowly disappearing with older people passing away. Hence, the (passive or active) knowledge of language, as well as the ability to "translate" between the "cultural codes", became an importance resource for some in order to move the borders and move up the social ladder. Furthermore, the interviewees often introduced their German relatives into their narrations – be it grandparents or parents. Despite German mostly not being directly transmitted from one generation to another, these very biographical interconnections were important for migrants in order to re-construe the linkages to Germany after migration and to negotiate their belonging in a new way. Hence these results show an important role of the border regions, the regional and family history, as well as the meaning of the Czech-German bilingualism in the process of migration. Moreover, the bilingualism and transculturality of certain areas in the Czech Republic which were unveiled by the analysis put into question the discourse concerning Czech ethnic homogeneity since the second half of the 20th century, which has been perceived as a cultural norm and which has dominated the Czech public and scientific discussions since then.

For most of the interviewees, Germany was the first place of destination after the "Velvet Revolution". They moved across the borders as au pairs, within social or educational programs, in order to work as seasonal workers in agriculture, industry or catering, or in order to meet relatives. The motives for these very first migration were diverse – to learn the language, overcome structural barriers in the country of origin, individualise oneself from one's parental home, discover new places, possibilities and points of views, or escape the expected institutional patterns concerning education, career and one's family pathway (see also e.g. Pařízková 2011b, 2011a). In the course of the analysis it became apparent that these very first moves across the Czech border in the course of migrants' adolescence or early adulthood initiated further multiple migrations in both directions (see also e.g. Inowlocki, Riemann 2012). These very biographical experiences were the basis for the development of transnational spaces – links, practices, and spaces of action which go beyond the framework of one nation state and which are biographically established and continuously reworked by the migrant in question (Apitzsch 2003c; Inowlocki, Riemann 2012). These spaces are, however, not arbitrary and free of barriers but structured by gendered migration policies, institutional frameworks and local opportunity structures. Hence, when taking decisions as to whether to stay, move, return or move on to another country, the opportunity structures for oneself – and very often for other family members too – in diverse locations are always taken into account. For the majority of migrants, migration was not a one-way process but comprised multiple border crossings, which were often the result of complex family negotiations.

Disregarding the initial motives to move country, after moving to Germany the migrants endeavoured to make use of the skills and qualifications they had acquired in their country of origin. Nevertheless, many had to find out that their initial qualifications were of no use after migration – be it due to restrictive migration policies, as a result of a lack of recognition of certificates, or difficulties in entering the labour market in particular fields of the economy. Until 2004, Czech citizens needed a visa to stay in Germany for longer than three months. After that, a residence permit was no longer required, but a work permit was still obligatory until 2011. While some interviewees managed to obtain work permits, others – mostly women – remained trapped in jobs in the informal economy for years, mostly employed in hospitality or the private care sector. Not until they managed to legalise their status – often through starting new studies in Germany or marrying a German citizen – did they look for ways of entering the formal labour market and utilising both their initial skills and qualifications and any new ones acquired in the course of migration. Nevertheless, despite obtaining residency and work permit in Germany, some migrants still experienced difficulties to valorise their formal qualification acquired in the country of origin due to the lack of, or only partial formal recognition of their certificates. Furthermore, they found it difficult to "translate" their qualification and work experiences acquired abroad into jobs related to their level of qualification, since they lacked the necessary social network and the knowledge of local social structures.

The life stories collected as part of the present study revealed the important role of gender within the migration processes of highly educated people (see also e.g. Kofman et al. 2000a; Kofman, Raghuram 2005; Kofman 2009b; Riaño 2012). On the one hand, migration and social pathways were shaped by gendered restrictive migration policies, demands in the informal and formal labour market, and stereotyping of migrant "Eastern European women", reducing them to "traditional female jobs" in hospitality and the care sector in the country of migration (Lutz 2008a, 2008d). On the other hand, they were structured by gendered passages to education and the professional life in the country of origin. The migration and social pathways of migrants largely reflected the general statistical tendencies, pointing out different educational and career trajectories of men and women in the Czech Republic (Křížková, Formánková 2011). Whilst men were predominately educated in technical spheres – which can be more easily utilised in the global economy as "transnational capital" (Weiss 2005) – women dominated in the fields of education, humanities, social sciences and health (Vincent-Lancrin 2008, p. 275). Hence they experienced greater difficulties in "translating" these qualifications across borders (Kofman 2000, Liversage 2009a, 2009b).

The difficulties of highly educated migrants to valorise their skills and formal qualifications after migration showed that national frameworks continued to be the main arena which structure the social position and career paths of individuals. Nevertheless, migrants were not only exposed to these structural frameworks, but they also responded to them and developed diverse strategies for entering or continuing their professional lives. They tried to utilise not only their formal qualifications but also other skills such as knowledge of languages. Knowledge of the Czech language, in particular, turned out to be a resource for some who utilised it for teaching, translating and interpreting, or for establishing professional contacts back in the Czech Republic. However, there showed to be differences concerning the usability of the Czech language in the border regions and in areas further from the border, where demand for the Czech language was much lower. The strategy of turning one's knowledge of the native language into economic capital after migration has been identified by other studies (see e.g. Liversage 2009b; Nohl et al. 2010a). However, as the narratives collected for the current study showed, it matters which native languages one speaks and how this can be given value in local, trans-local and global economies.

Another important strategy of entering or continuing professional life was to start new studies in Germany. While some of my interviewees built on their initial studies and complemented them by further studies in Germany, others decided to start new courses of studies after migration. This decision was a result of extensive biographical reflections and the evaluation of opportunity structures both in the country of origin and in the country of migration. New and additional studies helped migrants to fully recognise their prior qualification and to start a job in their initial profession, to legalise one's status through enrolment, to re-qualify for other professions and to establish the necessary contacts in order to enter the local labour market. In some cases, the decision for new studies was a result of biographical transformation processes started prior to migration or in the course of migration. New studies were retrospectively perceived as a kind of moratorium phase (see also e.g. Apitzsch 2000; Kempf 2013) – a time of extensive biographical reflections and evaluations of new options.

Furthermore, since the efforts to make use of one's own university diplomas acquired in the country of origin often failed, migrants tried to make use of other skills they had acquired in the course of migration. Some women, for example, tried to turn "childcare experience" obtained in the private sphere into a resource in order to enter the formal public sector and start work in crèches or kindergartens. These efforts, however, mostly failed due to their lack of formal qualifications in this field. Hence, migrants experienced being paradoxically both overqualified for the position in question, since they possessed a university degree in some related field of studies, such as education, and underqualified, since they lacked the specific qualification.

Moreover, migrants tried to make use of their transnational experiences and transnational knowledge (Apitzsch 2009b; Apitzsch, Siouti 2013), either in the form of translations between the languages and cultures or in the form of diverse business plans – such as starting a travel agency specialising in transnational and transcultural encounters. Hence they searched for creative ways of transforming the transnational experiences and knowledge which they acquired in the course of migration or earlier as the part of family and regional history of the place of origin into a resource and economic capital.

Notably, migrants did not try to negotiate and valorise their skills, qualifications and knowledge only one-directionally when moving forth, but also when moving back to the Czech Republic. While some of them profited from their cross-border experiences and turned them into economic capital and better social positions (see also Williams, Baláž 2005), others experienced difficulties in giving value to the professional experiences and other skills, such as a knowledge of languages, acquired abroad. They were confronted with discriminatory practices on the Czech labour market affecting men and women in different ways. In addition, they themselves or their family members were affected by the processes of "othering" (Hall 1994) based on their cross-border experiences and – actual or ascribed – national belonging, resulting in some cases in discrimination within educational institutions, on the labour market and in everyday interactions. Moreover, some migrants were confronted with specific national procedures within academia and some other fields of the economy which disregarded experiences, qualifications and knowledge acquired abroad. These experiences of devaluation and lacking recognition in the country of origin were often the basis for decisions to move country once again, either to Germany or elsewhere.

Here again it shows that the decisions as to where and how to live were not made within the setting of one or two nation states but rather in transnational spaces, created by migrants through their biographical experiences and kept alive by maintaining transnational social, cultural and economic links. These more or less intense links had a range of meanings for migrants, which changed over time. While some kept contacts alive in order to keep the possibilities of professional development in another location open, others tried to establish biographical continuity through them by keeping in touch with the language, culture and close family members, and by passing these links on to the next generation.

It was within these transnational spaces – within which goods, knowledge, emotions, meanings, and cultural practices were circulated – that migrants tried to make sense of their biographical pathways and their positioning. They did so by means of ongoing comparisons with those left behind, with themselves prior to migration, and their imagined selves in other locations (see also Schütze, Wildhagen 2012). Moreover, they constantly compared different opportunity structures and social stratification systems across locations and tried to position themselves within and beyond them. They tried not only to "translate" the social position acquired in one location into economic or social capital in another location (Glick Schiller et al. 1992b, p. 12), but also to "translate" the meaning of their social position and of their social pathway itself, while also noting the limits to "translatability". The "translation" of the meanings of social positions and of social pathways were of importance for some migrants since they sought recognition of their possible success by significant others, to which they felt related, living across the borders. In some cases, the disregard of recognition was experienced as harmful and as an act of exclusion. Hence, the manifold and sometimes contradictory perception of one's own success in the course of migration was connected to experiences of inclusion and exclusion in diverse locations.

These findings show that migration and social pathways in today's Europe cannot only be studied from the perspective of one (or two) "draining" or "gaining" nation states. Instead they should be approached within a wider transnational frame. The transnational approach allows to focus on opportunity structures, roles of gender and other social divisions, possibilities of self-development and the positioning of migrants across a range of locations and societies. When combined with a biographical approach, it enables the researcher to see shifts in structural frameworks over time, and to observe the strategies developed by migrants to respond and overcome them. Moreover, it allows to grasp the multiple and sometimes contradictory positioning of migrants across diverse locations, as well as their meanings and interrelations (Anthias 2008; Ruokonen-Engler 2012).

In addition, this research approach allows to see the complex processes of negotiating one's own knowledge, skills, qualifications and resources across diverse locations and their specific opportunity structures. In accordance with findings of other authors (see e.g. Erel 2004, 2010; Nowicka 2014), the presented life stories showed that skills and qualifications were not valued per se, but their value was related to the context in which they were acquired. When moving places, their usability and meaning might shift somewhat. Nevertheless, these skills, knowledge and qualifications were not only applied (or not) in another location, but they were also re-evaluated, re-worked, replaced or complemented by other knowledge, skills, or qualifications acquired in the course of migration (see also e.g. Erel 2010). The knowledge of native languages, for instance, which in the country of origin were perceived as unquestioned and self-evident, were re-evaluated in the course of migration and in some cases turned into a resource which migrants tried to "translate" into economic or other forms of capital after migration. These strategies of re-evaluating one's own skills, knowledge, or resources were linked to inequalities resulting from the devaluation of initial qualifications, and from the positioning of migrants along complex ethnic, social and gender divisions. These inequalities were internalised by the majority of migrants. Despite often becoming an unquestioned and everyday part of lives, they were present in the narratives as "invisible but very real structures" (Apitzsch 2009b, p. 132) of the societies within which they lived and moved. These inequalities show that even though educational and other institutions – and with them the individuals' life pathways – have become increasingly inter- or transnational, the various national frameworks still continue to considerably shape the possibilities and biographical, educational, and professional pathways of individuals living within them.

Research on the translatability of skills, qualifications, and knowledge of highly educated people across borders is still in its beginnings. However, the developments within Europe and world-wide indicate that this topic will become ever more important in the future, taking into account the ever rising number of highly educated people within migration flows (OECD 2013). While statistics still refer to them in categories such as "brain drain" and "brain gain", their life stories show that their realities go far beyond these terms. They give insights into the complex mechanisms of negotiating skills, qualifications and knowledge not only within the country of migration, but also in the country of origin or elsewhere. In order to understand these mechanisms, more research is needed, which would take into account different locations within which migrants move, different statuses of migrants, the different kinds of skills they possess as well as different resources accessible to them. There is a need for both gender sensitive quantitatively oriented studies to show statistical tendencies concerning the usability of formal qualifications after migration, and qualitatively oriented studies which focus on the mechanisms of de-valuation and re-valuation of skills in the course of migration from an agent-centred perspective. A lot has already been done to improve the mechanisms surrounding the official recognition of qualifications acquired abroad (see e.g. Bundesregierung 2009), however there is still a lot of work to do in the political and social field. In future policy making, knowledge of the actual problems and migrants' coping strategies for "translating" their skills into other countries should unquestionably be taken into account.

Bibliography and references

Ackers, Louise; Gill, Bryony (2008): Moving people and knowledge. Scientific mobility in an enlarging European Union. Cheltenham, UK, Northampton, MA: Edward Elgar Publishing.

Alheit, Peter (1990): Biographizität als Projekt. Der „biographische Ansatz" in der Erwachsenenbildung. Werkstattberichte des Forschungsschwerpunkts „Arbeit und Bildung". Band 12. Bremen: Universität Bremen.

Alheit, Peter (1992): Biographizität und Struktur. In Peter Alheit, Bettina Dausien, Andreas Hanses, Antonius Scheuermann (Eds.): Biographische Konstruktionen. Beiträge zur Biographieforschung. Werkstattberichte des Forschungsschwerpunkts „Arbeit und Bildung". Band 19. Bremen: Universität Bremen, pp. 10–36.

Alheit, Peter (2009): Biographical learning – within the new lifelong learning discourse. In Knud Illeris (Ed.): Contemporary Theories of Learning. London and New York: Routledge, pp. 116–128.

Alheit, Peter; Dausien, Bettina (1990): Biographie. Eine problemgeschichtliche Skizze. Werkstattberichte des Forschungsschwerpunkts „Arbeit und Bildung". Band 14. Bremen: Universität Bremen

Alheit, Peter; Dausien, Bettina (2008): Biographieforschung in der Erwachsenenbildung. In Heinz-Hermann Krüger, Winfried Marotzki (Eds.): Handbuch erziehungswissenschaftliche Biographieforschung. Wiebaden: VS Verlag für Sozialwissenschaften, pp. 431–457.

Alheit, Peter; Dausien, Bettina (2009): ‚Biographie' in den Sozialwissenschaften. Anmerkungen zu historischen und aktuellen Problemen einer Forschungsperspektive. In Bernhard Fetz (Ed.): Die Biographie – Zur Grundlegung ihrer Theorie. Berlin and New York: Walter de Gruyter, pp. 285–315.

Alheit, Peter; Hoerning, Erika M. (Eds.) (1989): Biographisches Wissen. Beiträge zu einer Theorie lebensgeschichtlicher Erfahrung. Frankfurt am Main: Campus-Verlag.

Amelina, Anna (2010): Scaling Inequalities? Some Steps towards the Social Inequality Analysis in Migration Research beyond the Framework of the Nation State. No. 91. COMCAD Arbeitspapiere - Working Papers. Universität Bielefeld.

Amelina, Anna; Faist, Thomas (2012): De-naturalizing the national in research methodologies: key concepts of transnational studies in migration. In Ethnic and Racial Studies 35 (10), pp. 1707–1724.

Amelina, Anna; Faist, Thomas; Nergiz, Devrimsel D. (2013): Methodologies on the move. The transnational turn in empirical migration research. New York: Routledge (Ethnic and racial studies).

Amelina, Anna; Nergiz, Devrimsel D.; Faist, Thomas; Glick Schiller, Nina (Eds.) (2012): Beyond methodological nationalism. Research methodologies for cross-border studies. New York: Routledge (Routledge research in transnationalism, 24).

Amelina, Anna; Vasilache, Andreas (2014): The shadows of enlargement: Theorising mobility and inequality in a changing Europe. In Migration Letters 11, pp. 109–124.

Anthias, Floya (2001): The Concept of 'Social Division' and Theorising Social Stratification: Looking at Ethnicity and Class. In Sociology 35 (4), pp. 835–854.

Anthias, Floya (2002): Beyond feminism and multiculturalism: Locating difference and the politics of location. In Women's Studies International Forum 25 (3), pp. 275–286.

Anthias, Floya (2008): Thinking through the lens of translocational positionality: an intersectionality frame for understanding identity and belonging. In Translocations: Migration and Social Change 4 (1), pp. 5–20.

Anthias, Floya; Cederberg, Maja (2006): State of the Art: Theoretical Perspectives and Debates in the UK. FeMiPol. Available online at http://www.femipol.unifrankfurt.de/docs/working_papers/state_of_the_art/UK, checked on 25/6/2015.

APERIO (2011): Český trh práce optikou genderových statistik. APERIO. Společnost pro zdravé rodičovství. Available online at http://www.aperio.cz/data/1/APERIO_Cesky_trh_prace_optikou_genderovych_st atistik.pdf, checked on 25/6/2015.

Apitzsch, Ursula (1990): Migration und Biographie. Zur Konstitution des Interkulturellen in den Bildungsgängen junger Erwachsener der 2. Migrantengeneration. Habilitationsschrift. Bremen.

Apitzsch, Ursula (1994): Migrationsforschung und Frauenforschung. In Senatskommission für Frauenforschung (Ed.): Sozialwissenschaftliche Frauenforschung in der Bundesrepublik Deutschland. Bestandsaufnahme und forschungspolitische Konzequenzen. Berlin: Akademie Verlag, pp. 240–254.

Apitzsch, Ursula (Ed.) (1999): Migration und Traditionsbildung. Opladen: Westdeutcher Verlag.

Apitzsch, Ursula (2000): Migration als Verlaufskurve und Transformationsprozess. Zur Frage geschlechtsspezifischer Dispositionen in der Migrationsbiographie. In Bettina Dausien (Ed.): Migrationsgeschichten von Frauen. Beiträge und Perspektiven aus der Biographieforschung. Bremen: Universität Buchlandlung, pp. 62–78.

Apitzsch, Ursula (2002): Biographien in Europa. Neue Dimensionen des Sozialen. In Franz Hamburger (Ed.): Gestaltung des Sozialen – eine Herausforderung für Europa. Opladen: Leske + Budrich, pp. 199–225.

Apitzsch, Ursula (2003a): Biographieforschung. In Barbara Orth, Thomas Schwietring, Johannes Weiß (Eds.): Soziologische Forschung: Stand und Perspektiven. Opladen: Leske + Budrich, pp. 95–110.

Apitzsch, Ursula (Ed.) (2003b): Migration, Biographie und Geschlechterverhältnisse. 1st ed. Münster: Westfälisches Dampfboot (Kritische Theorie und Kulturforschung, 6).

Apitzsch, Ursula (2003c): Migrationsbiographien als Orte transnationaler Räume. In Ursula Apitzsch (Ed.): Migration, Biographie und Geschlechterverhältnisse. 1st ed. Münster: Westfälisches Dampfboot (Kritische Theorie und Kulturforschung, 6), pp. 65–80.

Apitzsch, Ursula (2009a): Die Macht der Verantwortung. Aufstiegsprozesse und Geschlechterdifferenzen in Migrationsfamilien. In Martina Löw (Ed.): Geschlecht und Macht. Analysen zum Spannungsfeld von Arbeit, Bildung und Familie. Wiesbaden: VS, Verlag für Sozialwissenschaften, pp. 81–95.

Apitzsch, Ursula (2009b): Transnationales biographisches Wissen. In Helma Lutz (Ed.): Gender mobil? Geschlecht und Migration in transnationalen Räumen. 1st ed. Münster: Westfälisches Dampfboot (Forum Frauen- und Geschlechterforschung, 26), pp. 122–140.

Apitzsch, Ursula (Ed.) (2010a): Care und Migration. Die Ent-Sorgung menschlicher Reproduktionsarbeit entlang von Geschlechter- und Armutsgrenzen. Opladen: Budrich.

Apitzsch, Ursula (2010b): Care, Migration, and the Gender Order. In Ursula Apitzsch (Ed.): Care und Migration. Die Ent-Sorgung menschlicher Reproduktionsarbeit entlang von Geschlechter- und Armutsgrenzen. Opladen: Budrich, pp. 113–126.

Apitzsch, Ursula; Fischer, Wolfram; Koller, Hans-Christoph; Zinn, Jens (2006): Die Biographieforschung — kein Artefakt, sondern ein Bildungs- und Erinnerungspotential in der reflexiven Moderne. In Wolf-Dietrich Bukow, Markus Ottersbach, Elisabeth Tuider, Erol Yildiz (Eds.): Biographische Konstruktionen im multikulturellen Bildungsprozess. Individuelle Standortsicherung im globalisierten Alltag. Wiesbaden: VS Verlag für Sozialwissenschaften (18), pp. 37–60.

Apitzsch, Ursula; Inowlocki, Lena (2000): Biographical analysis: a 'German' school? In Prue Chamberlayne, Joanna Bornat, Tom Wengraf (Eds.): The turn to biographical methods in social science. Comparative issues and examples. London, New York: Routledge, pp. 53–70.

Apitzsch, Ursula; Kontos, Maria (2003): Self-employment, Gender and Migration. In International Review of Sociology 13 (1), pp. 67–76.

Apitzsch, Ursula; Kontos, Maria (Eds.) (2008): Self-employment activities of women and minorities: their success or failure in relation to social citizenship policies. Wiesbaden: VS Verlag.

Apitzsch, Ursula; Siouti, Irini (2007): Biographical Analysis as an Interdisciplinary Research Perspective in the Field of Migration Studies. The University of York.

Apitzsch, Ursula; Siouti, Irini (2008): Transnationale Biographien. In Hans Günther Homfeldt (Ed.): Soziale Arbeit und Transnationalität. Herausforderungen eines spannungsreichen Bezugs. Weinheim, München: Juventa-Verlag.

Apitzsch, Ursula; Siouti, Irini (2013): Die Entstehung transnationaler Familienbiographien in Europa. Transnationales biographisches Wissen als zentrales Schlüsselkonzept zum Verständnis von transnationalen mehrgenerationalen Migrationsprozessen. In Désirée Bender, Annemarie Duscha, Lena Huber, Kathrin Klein-Zimmer (Eds.): Transnationales Wissen und Soziale Arbeit. Weinheim: Beltz Juventa, pp. 144–157.

Arbeitsgruppe Bielefelder Soziologen (Ed.) (1976): Kommunikative Sozialforschung. Alltagswissen und Alltagshandeln, Gemeindemachtforschung, Polizei, politische Erwachsenenbildung. Arbeitsgruppe Bielefelder Soziologen. München: Fink (Kritische Information, 48).

Astier, Isabelle (1995): Du récit privé au récit civil: la construction d'une nouvelle dignité? In Lien social et Politiques (34), pp. 121–130.

Astier, Isabelle; Duvoux, Nicolas (Eds.) (2006): La société biographique: Une injonction a vivre dignement. Paris: L'Harmattan (Collection Logiques Sociales).

334

Avato, Johanna (2009): Dynamics in Highly Skilled Migration: A European Perspective. Dissertation. Eberhard-Karls-Universität Tübingen, Tübingen. Wirtschaftswissenschaftliche Fakultät.

Bade, Klaus J. (2000): Europa in Bewegung. Migration vom späten 18. Jahrhundert bis zur Gegenwart. München: Beck (Europa bauen).

Baghdadi, Nadia; Riaño, Yvonne (2014): Familie und Beruf vereinbaren? Vorstellungen und Strategien hochqualifizierter Migrant/innen. In Passagen (Ed.): Vielfältig alltäglich: Migration und Geschlecht in der Schweiz. Reihe Geschlechterfragen. Zürich: Seismo, pp. 36–57.

Bahlcke, Joachim (2001): Land und Dynastie: Böhmen, Habsburg und das Temno. In Walter Koschmal, Marek Nekula, Joachim Rogall (Eds.): Deutsche und Tschechen. Geschichte, Kultur, Politik. München: C.H. Beck (Beck'sche Reihe, 1414), pp. 57–66.

Baker, Paul J. (1973): The Life Histories of W. I. Thomas and Robert E. Park. In American Journal of Sociology 79 (2), pp. 243–260.

Balmer, Brian; Godwin, Matthew; Gregory, Jane (2009): The Royal Society and the 'Brain Drain': Natural Scientists Meet Social Science Notes & Records of The Royal Society.

Bartley, Allen; Beddoe, Liz; Fouché, Christa; Harington, Phil (2012): Transnational Social Workers: Making the Profession a Transnational Professional Space. In International Journal of Population Research, pp. 1–11. Available online at http://www.hindawi.com/journals/ijpr/2012/527510/, checked on 25/6/2015.

BeamtStG: Beamtenstatusgesetz vom 17. Juni 2008 (BGBl. I S. 1010), das durch Artikel 15 Absatz 16 des Gesetzes vom 5. Februar 2009 (BGBl. I S. 160) geändert worden ist.

Beaverstock, Jonathan V. (2002): Transnational elites in global cities: British expatriates in Singapore's financial district. In Geoforum 33, pp. 525–538.

Bender, Désirée; Duscha, Annemarie; Huber, Lena; Klein-Zimmer, Kathrin (Eds.) (2013a): Transnationales Wissen und Soziale Arbeit. Weinheim: Beltz Juventa.

Bender, Désirée; Duscha, Annemarie; Huber, Lena; Klein-Zimmer, Kathrin (2013b): Transnationales Wissen: Eine Spurensuche aus Sicht der Sozialen Arbeit. Einleitung. In Désirée Bender, Annemarie Duscha, Lena Huber, Kathrin Klein-Zimmer (Eds.): Transnationales Wissen und Soziale Arbeit. Weinheim: Beltz Juventa, pp. 7–18.

Bender, Désirée; Duscha, Annemarie; Huber, Lena; Klein-Zimmer, Kathrin (Eds.) (2014): Orte transnationaler Wissensproduktionen. Sozial- und kulturwissenschaftliche Schnittmengen. Weinheim: Beltz Juventa.

Berger, Peter A.; Weiß, Anja (Eds.) (2008): Transnationalisierung sozialer Ungleichheit. Wiesbaden: VS Verlag für Sozialwissenschaften.

Bernat, Joan Sefari; Viruela, Rafael (2011): The economic crisis and immigration: Romanian citizens in the ceramic tile district of Castelló (Spain). In Journal of Urban and Regional Analysis 3 (1), pp. 45–65. Available online at http://www.jurareview.ro/2011_1_1/a_2011_1_1_4_bernat.pdf, checked on 25/6/2015

Bertaux, Daniel (Ed.) (1981): Biography and society. The life history approach in the social sciences. 1st ed. Beverly Hills, Calif. u.a: Sage Publ. (Sage studies in international sociology, 23).

Bertaux, Daniel (1997): Heritage and Its Lineage: A Case History of Transmission and Social Mobility over Five Generations. In Daniel Bertaux, Paul Thompson (Eds.): Pathways to social class. A qualitative approach to social mobility. Oxford: Clarendon Press, pp. 63–97.

Bertaux, Daniel; Thompson, Paul (1997a): Introduction. In Daniel Bertaux, Paul Thompson (Eds.): Pathways to social class. A qualitative approach to social mobility. Oxford: Clarendon Press, pp. 1–31.

Bertaux, Daniel; Thompson, Paul (Eds.) (1997b): Pathways to social class. A qualitative approach to social mobility. Oxford: Clarendon Press.

Black, Richard; Engbersen, Godfried; Okólski, Marek; Pantîru, Cristina (Eds.) (2010): A continent moving West? EU enlargement and labour migration from Central and Eastern Europe. Amsterdam: Amsterdam University Press.

Blumer, Herbert (1979): Critiques of research in the social sciences. An appraisal of Thomas and Znaniecki's "The Polish peasant in Europe and America." With a new introduction by the author. With statements by William I. Thomas and Florian Znaniecki, a panel dicussion, and summary and analysis by Read Bain. 1939th ed. New Brunswick, NJ: Transaction Books.

Borkert, Maren; Martín Pérez, Alberto; Scott, Sam; De Tona, Carla (2006): Einleitung: Migrationsforschung in Europa (über nationale und akademische Grenzen hinweg) verstehen. In Forum Qualitative Sozialforschung / Forum: Qualitative Social Research 7 (3).

Bourdieu, Pierre (1997): The Forms of Capital. In Albert H. Halsey, Hugh Lauder, Phillip Brown, Amy Stuart Wells (Eds.): Education. Culture, economy, and society. Oxford: Oxford University Press, pp. 46–58.

Bourdieu, Pierre (1998a): Praktische Vernunft zur Theorie des Handels. With assistance of Hella Beister. Frankfurt am Main: Suhrkamp.

Bourdieu, Pierre (1998b): Teorie jednání. Praha: Karolinum.

Bourdieu, Pierre (2000): Die biographische Illusion. In Erika M. Hoerning (Ed.): Biographische Sozialisation. Stuttgart: Lucius & Lucius, pp. 51–60.

Brandi, M. Carolina (2001): Skilled Immigrants in Rome. In International Migration 39 (4), pp. 101–131.

Braun, Michael; Recchi, Ettore (2008): Keine Grenzen, mehr Opportunitäten? Migration und soziale Mobilität innerhalb der EU. In Peter A. Berger, Anja Weiß (Eds.): Transnationalisierung sozialer Ungleichheit. Wiesbaden: VS Verlag für Sozialwissenschaften, pp. 161–183.

Breckner, Roswitha (2007): Case-Oriented Comparative Approaches. The Biographical Perspective as Opportunity and Challenge in Migration Research. In Karin Schittenhelm (Ed.): Concepts and Methods in Migration Research. Study Group "Cultural Capital during Migration" - Conference Reader, pp. 113–152.

Breckner, Roswitha (2009): Migrationserfahrung - Fremdheit - Biografie. Zum Umgang mit polarisierten Welten in Ost-West-Europa. 2nd ed. Wiesbaden: VS, Verlag für Sozialwissenschaften.

Breckner, Roswitha; Miethe, Ingrid (Eds.) (2000): Biographies and the division of Europe. Experience, action, and change on the "Eastern side". Opladen: Leske und Budrich.

Breen, Richard (Ed.) (2004): Social mobility in Europe. Oxford: Oxford University Press.

Brettell, Caroline (Ed.) (2008): Migration theory. Talking across disciplines. 2nd ed. New York u.a: Routledge.

Brink, Bert van den; Owen, David (2010): Introduction. In Brink, Bert van den, David Owen (Eds.): Recognition and power. Axel Honneth and the tradition of critical social theory. 1. paperback ed. Cambridge: Cambridge University Press, pp. 1–32.

Brouček, Stanislav (2003): Etapy českého vystěhovalectví. Praha: Etnologický ústav Akademie věd České republiky.

Bukow, Wolf-Dietrich; Heimel, Isabel (2003): Der Weg zur qualitativen Migrations-forschung. In Tarek Badawia (Ed.): Wider die Ethnisierung einer Generation. Beiträge zur qualitativen Migrationsforschung. Frankfurt am Main: IKO - Verlag für Interkulturelle Kommunikation, pp. 13–39.

Bukow, Wolf-Dietrich; Spindler, Susanne (2006): Die biographische Ordnung der Lebensgeschichte. In Wolf-Dietrich Bukow, Markus Ottersbach, Elisabeth Tuider, Erol Yildiz (Eds.): Biographische Konstruktionen im multikulturellen Bildungsprozess. Individuelle Standortsicherung im globalisierten Alltag. Wiesbaden: VS Verlag für Sozialwissenschaften (18), pp. 19–35.

Bulmer, Martin (1984): The Chicago school of sociology. Institutionalization, diversity and the rise of sociological research. Chicago: University of Chicago Press.

Bundesministerium für Arbeit und Soziales (2009): Kompetenzen wahrnehmen, anerkennen und fördern. Vorschläge des BMAS für ein Gesetz zur Anerkennung ausländischer Qualifikationen. Available online at http://www.migration-online.de/data/2009_06_18_eckpunktepapier_auslaendische_arbeitskraefte 1.pdf, checked on 25/6/2015.

Bundesregierung (2009): Eckpunkte zur Verbesserung der Feststellung und Anerkennung von im Ausland erworbenen beruflichen Qualifikationen und Berufsabschlüssen. 9.12.2009. Available online at http://www.bmbf.de/pub/eckpunkte_anerkennung_berufsabschluesse.pdf, checked on 10/6/2015.

Burawoy, Michael (1991): Reconstructing social theories. In Michael Burawoy (Ed.): Ethnography unbound. Power and resistance in the modern metropolis. 2. Dr. Berkeley u.a.: Univ. of California Press, pp. 8–27.

Campani, Giovanna (2007): Irregular Migration and trafficking: Controversial Concepts and Changing Contexts in Southern Europe. In Erik Berggren, Branka Likic-Brboric, Gulay Toksöz, Nicos Trimikliniotis (Eds.): Irregular Migration, Informal Labour and Community: A Challenge for Europe. Maastricht: Shaker Publishing, pp. 66–84.

Campani, Giovanna (2008): Migration inside the Union after its enlargement: Consequences of the European Democracy. In Helga Rittersberger-Tiliç (Ed.): Rethinking global migration. Practices, policies and discourse in the European neighbourhood: GLOMIG Project conference procedings. Ankara: METU; KORA, pp. 47–55. Available online at http://www.kora.metu.edu.tr/glomig/GLOMIG_Conference_Proceedings_Book.pdf, checked on 25/6/2015.

Castles, Stephen (2007): Twenty-First-Century Migration as a Challenge to Sociology. In Journal of Ethnic and Migration Studies 33 (3), pp. 351–371.

Chamberlayne, Prue; Bornat, Joanna; Wengraf, Tom (Eds.) (2000): The turn to biographical methods in social science. Comparative issues and examples. London, New York: Routledge.

Collins, Randall; Makowsky, Michael (1998): The discovery of society. Boston: McGraw-Hill.

Conradson, David; Latham, Alan (2005): Transnational urbanism: Attending to everyday practices and mobilities. In Journal of Ethnic and Migration Studies 31 (2), pp. 227–233.

Corbin, Juliet (2006): Grounded Theory. In Ralf Bohnsack, Winfried Marotzki, Michael Meuser (Eds.): Hauptbegriffe qualitativer Sozialforschung. 2. Aufl. Opladen: Budrich (UTB), pp. 70–75.

Crenshaw, Kimberlé Williams (1994): Mapping the Margins: Intersectionality, Identity Politics, and Violence Against Women of Color. In Martha Fineman, Roxanne Mykitiuk (Eds.): The public nature of private violence. The discovery of domestic abuse. New York u.a: Routledge.

Csedő, Krisztina (2008): Negotiating Skills in the Global City: Hungarian and Romanian Professionals and Graduates in London. In Journal of Ethnic and Migration Studies 34 (5), pp. 803–823.

CSO (2008): Census 2006. Non-Irish Nationals living in Ireland. Central Statistics Office. Dublin. Available online at http://www.cso.ie/en/media/csoie/census/documents/NON,IRISH,NATONALS,LIVING,IN,IRELAND.pdf, checked on 25/6/2015.

CSO (2012): Population and Migration estimates. Central Statistics Office. Dublin and Cork. Available online at http://www.cso.ie/en/media/csoie/releasespublications/documents/population/2012/popmig_2012.pdf, checked on 25/6/2015.

CSO (2014): PEA02: Estimated Population Migration (Persons in April) by Sex, Origin or Destination, Country and Year. Central Statistics Office. Cork. Available online at http://www.cso.ie/en/statistics/, checked on 25/6/2015.

ČSÚ (2005): Vnitřní stěhování v České republice. ČSÚ. Praha. Available online at http://www.czso.cz/csu/2005edicniplan.nsf/t/5A003110D9/$File/402905a1.pdf, checked on 25/6/2015.

ČSÚ (2007): Sňatky cizinců v ČR podle vybraných státních občanství - vývoj v letech 1995-2007. Czech Statistical Office. Praha.

ČSÚ (2011a): Historie a vyvoj soukromého školství 2010. ČSÚ. Praha. Available online at http://www.czso.cz/csu/2011edicniplan.nsf/p/3316-11, checked on 25/6/2015.

ČSÚ (2011b): Význam vzdělání pro trh práce v ČR (analýza). Edited by ČSÚ. Praha. Available online at http://www.czso.cz/csu/tz.nsf/bce41ad0daa3aad1c1256c6e00499152/b16fed228a28a92ac1257959002e92e8/$FILE/analyza_vzdelani.pdf, checked on 25/6/2015.

ČSÚ (2012): Nezaměstnanost v Ústeckém kraji v 1. čtvrtletí 2012. ČSÚ. Praha. Available online at http://www.czso.cz/xu/redakce.nsf/i/nezamestnanost_v_usteckem_kraji_v_1_ctvrtleti_2012_, checked on 25/6/2015.

ČSÚ (2014): Úspěšnost při přijímání ke studiu. ČSÚ. Praha. Available online at http://www.czso.cz/csu/2012edicniplan.nsf/engt/F0003691CF/$File/1413123305.pdf, checked on 25/6/2015.

Currle, Edda (2004): Migration in Europa. Daten und Hintergründe. Stuttgart: Lucius & Lucius (Forum Migration).

Dausien, Bettina (1996): Biographie und Geschlecht. Zur biographischen Konstruktion sozialer Wirklichkeit in Frauenlebensgeschichten. Bremen: Donat (IBL-Forschung, 1).

Dausien, Bettina (Ed.) (2000): Migrationsgeschichten von Frauen. Beiträge und Perspektiven aus der Biographieforschung. Bremen: Universität Buchlandlung.

Dausien, Bettina (2004): Geschlecht und Biographie. Annerkenung zu einem vielschichtigen theoretischen Zusammenhang. In Ingrid Miethe, Claudia Kajatin, Jana Pohl (Eds.): Geschlechterkonstruktionen in Ost und West. Biographische Perspektiven. Münster: Lit Verlag, pp. 19–44.

Delcroix, Catherine (2009): Two Generations of Muslim Women in France. Issues of Identity and Recognition. Söderstörn Lectures 3: Söderstörn University.

Delory-Momberger, Christine (2011): Herausforderungen, Widersprüche und Risiken der „biographischen Gesellschaft". In Heidrun Herzberg, Eva Kammler (Eds.): Biographie und Gesellschaft. Überlegungen zu einer Theorie des modernen Selbst. Frankfurt am Main: Campus Verlag, pp. 29–42.

Detka, Carsten (2005): Zu den Arbeitsschritten der Segmentierung und der Strukturellen Beschreibung in der Analyse autobiographisch-narrativer Interviews. In ZBBS Zeitschrift für qualitative Bildungs-, Beratungs- und Sozialforschung 6 (2), pp. 351–364.

Directive 2005/36/EC (2005): Directive 2005/36/EC of the European Parliament and of the Council of 7 September 2005 on the recognition of professional qualifications. Available online at http://www.aic.lv/bolona/Recognition/dir_prof/Directive_2005_36_EC.pdf, checked on 25/6/2015.

Directive 2013/55/EU (2013): Directive 2013/55/EU of the European Parliament and of the Council of 20 November 2013 on the recognition of professional qualifications. Available online at http://eur-lex.europa.eu/legal-content/EN/TXT/PDF/?uri=CELEX:32013L0055&from=EN, checked on 25/6/2015.

Docquier, Frédéric; Rapoport, Hillel (2007): Skilled Migration: The Perspective of Developing Countries. Discussion Paper No. 2873. June 2007 IZA, pp. 1–28. Available online at http://ftp.iza.org/dp2873.pdf, checked on 25/6/2015.

Domnitz, Christian (2011): From underground to the official sphere. Narratives of Europe on the eve of 1989. In Swen Steinberg, Daniel K. W. Trepsdorf, Christoph Wielepp (Eds.): Nach dem Umbruch. Transformationen in europäischer und globaler Perspektive. Berlin: WVB (Impulse, 2), pp. 39–54.

Donato, Katharine M.; Gabaccia, Donna; Holdaway, Jennifer; Manalansan, Martin; Pessar, Patricia R. (2006): A Glass Half Full? Gender in Migration Studies. In International Migration Review 40 (1), pp. 3–26.

Drbohlav, Dušan (2000): Die Tschechische Republik und die internationale Migration. In Heinz Fassmann, Reiner Münz (Eds.): Ost-West-Wanderung in Europa. Wien: Böhlau, pp. 163–181.

Drbohlav, Dušan; Rákoczyová, Miroslava (2012): Social Impact of Emigration and Rural-Urban Migration in Central and Eastern Europe. Final Country Report. Czech Republic. European Commision. Available online at

http://ec.europa.eu/social/main.jsp?langId=en&catId=89&newsId=1778&further
News=yes, checked on 25/6/2015.

Dumont, Jean-Christophe; Martin, John P.; Spielvogel, Gilles (2007): Women on the Move: The Neglected Gender Dimension of the Brain Drain. In IZA Discussion Paper Series (IZA DP No. 2920), pp. 1–24.

Dumont, Jean-Christophe; Monso, Olivier (2007): Matching Educational Background and Employment: A Challenge for Immigrants In Host Countries. International Migration Outlook: SOPEMI 2007 Edition. OECD. Available online at http://www.oecd.org/migration/internationalmigrationpoliciesanddata/41561786. pdf, checked on 25/6/2015.

Duvell, Franck (2007): United Kingdom. In Anna Triantaphyllidou, Ruby Gropas (Eds.): European immigration. A sourcebook. Aldershot u. a: Ashgate, pp. 347–359.

Engbersen, Godfried; Okólski, Marek; Black, Richard; Panţîru, Cristina (2010): Introduction. Working out a way from East to West: EU enlargement and labour migration from Central and Eastern Europe. In Richard Black, Godfried Engbersen, Marek Okólski, Cristina Pantîru (Eds.): A continent moving West? EU enlargement and labour migration from Central and Eastern Europe. Amsterdam: Amsterdam University Press.

Erel, Umut (2004): Migrantinnen zwischen Anerkennung und Abqualifikation (Migrant Women between Recognition and De-skilling). In Hito Steyerl, Encarnacion Gutierrez Rodriguez (Eds.): Spricht die Subalterne deutsch? Migration und postkoloniale Kritik (Does the subaltern speak German? Migration and postcolonial criticism). Münster: Unrast Verlag, pp. 108–128.

Erel, Umut (2010): Migrating Cultural Capital: Bourdieu in Migration Studies. In Sociology 44 (4), pp. 642–660.

Esser, Hartmut (2001): Integration und ethnische Schichtung. Mannheim: MZES (Arbeitspapiere / Mannheimer Zentrum für Europäische Sozialforschung).

European Commission (2008): European Employment Observatory Review: Autumn 2008. European Commission. Luxembourg.

European Commission (2013): Tertiary education attainment. Brussels: European Commission. Available online at http://ec.europa.eu/education/dashboard/tea/tea_en.htm, checked on 25/6/2015.

European Commission (2014a): Employment and Social Developments in Europe 2013. Brussels: European Commission (Social Europe).

European Commission (2014b): Services: tapping the potential for growth and jobs. Commission contribution to the European Council of 20-21 March 2014. Brussels: European Commission.

European Union (1997): The Treaty of Amsterdam. Amending the Treaty on European Union, the Treities Establishing the European Communities and Certain Related Acts. Available online at http://www.eurotreaties.com/amsterdamtreaty.pdf, checked on 25/6/2015.

Eurostat (2014a): Immigration by sex, country of birth and broad group of citizenship. European Commision. Available online at http://ec.europa.eu/eurostat/data/database, checked on 25/6/2015.

Eurostat (2014b): Tertiary education statistics. European Commission. Available online at http://epp.eurostat.ec.europa.eu/statistics_explained/index.php/tertiary_education _statistics, checked on 25/6/2015.

Faist, Thomas (2000): The Volume and Dynamics of International Migration and Transnational Social Spaces. Oxford: Oxford University Press.

Faist, Thomas; Fauser, Margit; Reisenauer, Eveline (2013): Transnational migration. Cambridge: Polity Press.

Fassmann, Heinz; Münz, Reiner (1994): European East-West Migration, 1945-1992. In International Migration Review 28 (3), pp. 520–538.

Fassmann, Heinz; Münz, Reiner (1995): La migration d'Est en Ouest en Europe (1918-1993). In Revue européenne de migrations internationales 11 (3), pp. 43–66.

Favell, Adrian (2003): Games without frontiers? Questioning the transnational social power of migrants in Europe. In Archives Européennes de Sociologie 44 (3), pp. 106–136. Available online at http://www.sscnet.ucla.edu/soc/faculty/favell/aes-games.pdf, checked on 25/6/2015.

Favell, Adrian (2008): The New Face of East–West Migration in Europe. In Journal of Ethnic and Migration Studies 34 (5), pp. 701–716.

Favell, Adrian (2009): Eurostars and Eurocities. Free movement and mobility in an integrating Europe. Oxford: Blackwell.

Favell, Adrian; Feldblum, Miriam; Smith, Michael Peter (2008): The Human Face of Global Mobility: A Research Agenda. In Michael P. Smith, Adrian Favell (Eds.): The human face of global mobility. International highly skilled migration in Europe, North America and the Asia-Pacific. 2nd ed. New Brunswick, NJ: Transaction Press (Comparative urban and community research, 8), pp. 1–26.

Favell, Adrian; Nebe, Tina M. (2009): Internal and external movers: East-West migration and the impact of EU enlargement. In Ettore Recchi, Adrian Favell (Eds.): Pioneers of European integration. Citizenship and mobility in the EU. Cheltenham: Edward Elgar, pp. 205–223.

Favell, Adrian; Recchi, Ettore (2011): Social Mobility and Spacial Mobility. In Adrian Favell, Virginie Guiraudon (Eds.): Sociology of the European Union. London, pp. 50–72.

Fechter, Anne-Meike; Walsh, Katie (2010): Examining 'Expatriate' Continuities: Postcolonial Approaches to Mobile Professionals. In Journal of Ethnic and Migration Studies 36 (8), pp. 1197–1210.

Findlay, Allan M.; Li, F.L.N; Jowett, A. J.; Skelton, R. (1996): Skilled international migration and the global city: a study of expatriates in Hong Kong. In Transactions of the Institute of British Geographers 21 (1), pp. 49–61.

Fortney, Judith A. (1970): International Migration of Professionals. In Population Studies 24 (2), pp. 217–232.

Freitas, Any; Levatino, Antonina; Pécoud, Antoine (2012): Introduction: New Perspectives on Skilled Migration. In Any Freitas, Antoine Pécoud (Eds.): Skilled Migration and the Brain Drain. Diversities 14 (1), pp. 1–8.

Freitas, Any; Pécoud, Antoine (Eds.) (2012): Skilled Migration and the Brain Drain. Diversities 14 (1).

Fuchs-Heinritz, Werner (2005): Biographische Forschung. Eine Einführung in Praxis und Methoden. 3rd ed. Wiesbaden: VS, Verlag für Sozialwissenschaften.

Fürstenau, Sara (2004): Transnationale (Aus)Bildungs- und Zukunftsorientierungen. Ergebnisse einer Untersuchung unter zugewanderten Jugendlichen portugiesischer Herkunft. In Zeitschrift für Erziehungswissenschaft 7, pp. 33–57.

Gaillard, Jacques; Gaillard, Anne Marie (1997): Introduction: The International Mobility of Brains: Exodus or Brain Circulation? In Science, Technology and Society 2 (2), pp. 195–228.

GG: Grundgesetz für die Bundesrepublik Deutschland in der im Bundesgesetzblatt Teil III, Gliederungsnummer 100- 1, veröffentlichten bereinigten Fassung, das zuletzt durch Artikel 1 des Gesetzes vom 23. Dezember 2014 (BGBl. I S. 2438) geändert worden ist.

Giddens, Anthony (1991): Modernity and self-identity. Self and society in the late modern age. Cambridge: Polity Press.

Gimenez, Marta (2001): Marxism and Class, Gender and Race: Rethinking the Trilogy. In Race, Gender & Class 8 (2), pp. 23–33. Available online at http://www.colorado.edu/Sociology/gimenez/work/cgr.html, checked on 12/3/2014.

Glaeser, Janina (2014): Assistant(e)s maternel(le)s d'origine étrangère et politiques de la petite enfance: une comparaison France-Allemagne. In Catherine Delcroix, Daniel Bertaux (Eds.): Vers une société du care? Revue des sciences sociales (52), pp. 54–61.

Glaser, Barney G.; Strauss, Anselm L. (1967): The discovery of grounded theory. New York: de Gruyter.

Glick Schiller, Nina; Basch, Linda; Blanc-Szanton, Cristina (Eds.) (1992a): Towards a Transnational Perspective on Migration: Race, Class, Ethnicity, and Nationalism Reconsidered. Annals of the New York Academy of Sciences 645.

Glick Schiller, Nina; Basch, Linda; Blanc-Szanton, Cristina (1992b): Transnationalism: A New Analytic Framework for Understanding Migration. In Annals of the New York Academy of Sciences 645, pp. 1–24.

Gordon, Milton Myron (1964): Assimilation in American life. New York: Oxford University Press.

Gorzelak, Grzegorz (1996): The regional dimension of transformation in Central Europe. London: Kingsley (Regional policy and development series).

Gould, William T.S. (1988): Skilled International Labour Migration: an Introduction. In Geoforum 19 (4), pp. 381–385.

Guth, Jessica (2007): Triggering Skilled Migration: Factors Influencing the Mobility of Early Career Scientists to Germany. In Focus MIGRATION, policy Brief (6).

Guth, Jessica; Gill, Bryony (2008): Motivations in East–West Doctoral Mobility: Revisiting the Question of Brain Drain. In Journal of Ethnic and Migration Studies 34 (5), pp. 825–841.

Hall, Stuart (1994): Rassismus und Kulturelle Identität. Hamburg: Argument-Verlag.

Han, Petrus (2006): Theorien zur internationalen Migration. Ausgewählte interdisziplinäre Migrationstheorien und deren zentralen Aussagen. Stuttgart: Lucius & Lucius (UTB).

Hanses, Andreas (2011): Biographie und Subjekt — Annäherungen an einen komplexen und widerspruchsvollen Sachverhalt. In Heidrun Herzberg, Eva Kammler (Eds.): Biographie und Gesellschaft. Überlegungen zu einer Theorie des modernen Selbst. Frankfurt am Main: Campus Verlag, pp. 333–350.

Hárs, Ágnes; Sik, Endre; Tóth, Judit (2001): Hungary. In Claire Wallace, Dariusz Stola (Eds.): Patterns of Migration in Central Europe. New York: Palgrave.

Hartmann, Michael (2008): Transnationale Klassenbildung? In Peter A. Berger, Anja Weiß (Eds.): Transnationalisierung sozialer Ungleichheit. Wiesbaden: VS Verlag für Sozialwissenschaften, pp. 241–258.

Hermanns, Harry (1992): Die Auswertung narrativer Interviews. Ein Beispiel für qualitative Verfahren. In Hoffmeyer-Zlotnik (Ed.): Analyse verbaler Daten. Opladen: Westdeutscher Verlag, pp. 111–142.

Hess, Sabine (2009): Globalisierte Hausarbeit. Au-pair als Migrationsstrategie von Frauen aus Osteuropa. 2nd ed. Wiesbaden: VS Verlag für Sozialwissenschaften (Geschlecht &amp Gesellschaft, 38).

Hoerning, Erika M. (1989): Erfahrungen als biographische Resourcen. In Peter Alheit, Erika M. Hoerning (Eds.): Biographisches Wissen. Beiträge zu einer Theorie lebensgeschichtlicher Erfahrung. Frankfurt am Main u.a.: Campus-Verl, pp. 148–163.

Hoerning, Erika M. (2000): Biographische Sozialisation. Theoretische und forschungspraktische Verankerung. In Erika M. Hoerning (Ed.): Biographische Sozialisation. Stuttgart: Lucius & Lucius, pp. 1–20.

Hoffmann-Riem, Christa (1980): Die Sozialforschung einer interpretativen Soziologie - Der Datengewinn. In Kölner Zeitschrift für Soziologie und Sozialpsychologie 32 (2), pp. 337–372.

Holocaust Education and Archive Research Team (2013): The Jews of the Sudetenland. Bohemia & Moravia. Available online at http://www.holocaustresearchproject.org/nazioccupation/sudetenland.html, checked on 25/6/2015.

Holý, Ladislav (1996): The little Czech and the great Czech nation. National identity and the post-communist transformation of society. Cambridge: Cambridge University Press (Cambridge studies in social and cultural anthropology).

Holý, Martin (2013): Vzdělanostní migrace v česko-německém prostoru v 16. a raném 17. století. In Stanislav Brouček (Ed.): Navzdory hranici. Migrační procesy na česko-německém pomezí. Trotz der Grenze. Migrationsprozesse im tschechisch-deutschen Grenzgebiet. Příspěvky z odborné konference, Cheb 27.-29.5. 2013. Fachtagungsvorträge, Eger 27.-29.5. 2013. Plzeň, pp. 18–31.

Honneth, Axel (1995): The struggle for recognition. The moral grammar of social conflicts. Cambridge, UK, Oxford, Cambridge, MA: Polity Press; Blackwell.

Hradil, Stefan (2008): Soziale Ungleichheit, soziale Schichtung und Mobilität. In Hermann Korte (Ed.): Einführung in Hauptbegriffe der Soziologie. 7. edition. Wiesbaden: VS, Verlag für Sozialwissenschaften, pp. 212–234.

Humphrey, Robin (Ed.) (2003): Biographical research in Eastern Europe. Altered lives and broken biographies. Aldershot: Ashgate.

Iglicka, Krystyna (1998): The Economics of Petty Trade on the Eastern Polish Border. In Krystyna Iglicka, Keith Sword (Eds.): The challenge of East-West migration for Poland. Basingstoke u.a: Macmillan u.a (Studies in Russia and East Europe), pp. 120–144.

Inowlocki, Lena (1993): Grandmothers, Mothers, and Daughters: Intergenerational Transmission in Displaced Families in Three Jewish Communities. In Daniel Bertaux, Paul Richard Thompson (Eds.): Between generations. Family models, myths, and memories. Oxford: Oxford University Press (International yearbook of oral history and life stories, 2), pp. 139–154.

Inowlocki, Lena (1995): Traditionsbildung und intergenerationale Kommunikation zwischen Müttern und Töchtern in jüdischen Familien. In Wolfram Fischer-Rosenthal (Ed.): Biographien in Deutschland. Soziologische Rekonstruktionen gelebter Gesellschaftsgeschichte. Opladen: Westdeutscher Verlag, pp. 417–431.

Inowlocki, Lena (1999): Wenn Tradition auf einmal mehr bedeutet: Einige Beobachtungen zu biographischen Prozessen der Auseinandersetzung mit Religion. In Ursula Apitzsch (Ed.): Migration und Traditionsbildung. Opladen: Westdeutcher Verlag, pp. 76–90.

Inowlocki, Lena (2000): Sich in die Geschichte hineinreden. Sich in die Geschichte hineinreden. Biographische Fallanalysen rechtsextremer Gruppenzugehörigkeit. Frankfurt am Main: Cooperative Verlag.

Inowlocki, Lena; Riemann, Gerhard (2012): Exploring European ‚Potential Space‘: A Study of the Biographies of Former Foreign Exchange Students. In Robert Miller (Ed.): The evolution of European identities. Biographical approaches. Basingstoke u.a: Palgrave Macmillan, pp. 129–149.

INSTRAW (2007): Feminization of migration: gender, remittances and development. Working Paper 1. United Nations - INSTRAW.

Iredale, Robyn (2001): The Migration of Professionals: Theories and Typologies. In International Migration 39 (5), pp. 7–26.

Iredale, Robyn (2005): Gender, immigration policies and accreditation: valuing the skills of professional women migrants. In Geoforum 36 (2), pp. 155–166.

Jelínek, Tomáš (2003): Nucená práce v nacionálním socialismu. In Kolektiv pracovníků Kanceláře pro oběti nacismu (Ed.): "Nepřichází-li práce k tobě… ". Různé podoby nucené práce ve studiích a dokumentech. Praha, pp. 16–32.

Jeřábek, Milan (1999): Shrnutí. In Milan Jeřábek (Ed.): Geografická analýza pohraničí České republiky. Praha: Sociologický ústav Akademie věd České republiky (Pracovní texty, WP 99:11), pp. 166–175.

Johnson-Hanks, Jennifer (2002): On the Limits of Life Stages in Ethnography: Toward a Theory of Vital Conjunctures. In American Anthropologist 104 (3), pp. 865–880.

Juhasz, Anne; Mey, Eva (2003): Die zweite Generation: Etablierte oder Außenseiter. Biographien von Jugendlichen ausländischer Herkunft. Wiesbaden: Westdt. Verlag.

Jungwirth, Ingrid (2011): The change of normative gender orders in the course of migration: highly qualified migrant women in Germany. In Marek Nowak, Michał Nowosielski (Eds.): (Post)transformational migration. Inequalities, welfare state, and horizontal mobility. Frankfurt am Main: Peter Lang Verlag (Dia-Logos, Bd./vol. 13), pp. 225–250.

Karakayali, Juliane (2010a): Prec(ar)ious Labor - Die Biographische Verarbeitung widersprüchlicher Klassenmobilität transnationaler ‚care workers‘ aus Osteuropa. In Ursula Apitzsch (Ed.): Care und Migration. Die Ent-Sorgung menschlicher Reproduktionsarbeit entlang von Geschlechter- und Armutsgrenzen. Opladen u.a: Budrich, pp. 163–176.

Karakayali, Juliane (2010b): Transnational Haushalten. Biografische Interviews mit care workers aus Osteuropa. Wiesbaden: VS Verlag für Sozialwissenschaften.

Kaya, Bülent; Campbell, Margaret; Reynolds, Christopher (2002): The changing face of Europe. Population flows in the 20th century. Strasbourg: Council of Europe Pub.

Kazmierska, Kaja (2009): Biographical Research in Poland. In Sektion Biographieforschung in der Deutschen Gesellschaft für Soziologie. December 2009 (Rundbrief 57), pp. 54–62.

Kaźmierska, Kaja (2012): Biography and memory. The generational experience of the Shoah survivors. Brighton, Ma.: Academic Studies Press (Jews of Poland).

Kelly, Philip; Lusis, Tom (2006): Migration and the transnational habitus: evidence from Canada and the Philippines. In Environment and Planning A 38, pp. 831–847.

Kempf, Andreas Oskar (2013): Biographien in Bewegung. Transnationale Migrationsverläufe aus dem ländlichen Raum von Ost- nach Westeuropa. Wiesbaden: Springer VS.

King, Russell (2002): Towards a New Map of European Migration. In International Journal of Population Geography (8), pp. 89–106.

King, Russell (2012): Theories and typologies of migration: an overview and a primer. In Willy Brandt Series of Working Papers in International Migration and Ethnic Relations 3, pp. 3–43.

King, Russell; Skeldon, Ronald (2010): 'Mind the Gap!' Integrating Approaches to Internal and International Migration. In Journal of Ethnic and Migration Studies 36 (10), pp. 1619–1646.

Kingma, Mireille (2006): Nurses on the move. Migration and the global health care economy. Ithaca, N.Y.: ILR Press (The culture and politics of health care work).

Klein, Kathrin (2010): Soziales Kapital als Ressource in Bildungsbiographien. Junge Erwachsene indischer Herkunft in Deutschland und Großbritannien. Berlin, Münster: Lit Verlag (Migration - Bildung - Wissen, 2).

Kleinova, Nikola (2013): Emigrace z komunistického Československa a Češi v Dánsku. Diplomová práce. Univerzita Karlova v Praze, Praha. Fakulta humanitních studií.

Knapp, Gudrun-Alexi (2009): Resonanzräume - Räsonierräume: Zur transatlantischen Reise von Race, Class und Gender. In Helma Lutz (Ed.): Gender mobil? Geschlecht und Migration in transnationalen Räumen. 1st ed. Münster: Westfälisches Dampfboot (Forum Frauen- und Geschlechterforschung, 26), pp. 215–233.

Koehler, Jobst; Laczko, Frank; Aghazarm, Christine Schad Julia (2010): Migration and the economic crisis in the European Union: Implications for policy. Edited by IOM International Organisation for Migration. Belgium. Available online at http://publications.iom.int/bookstore/free/Migration_and_the_Economic_Crisis.pdf, checked on 25/6/2015.

Kofman, Eleonore (2000): The Invisibility of Skilled Female Migrants and Gender Relations in Studies of Skilled Migration in Europe. In International Journal of Population Geography 6 (1), pp. 45–59.

Kofman, Eleonore (2008): Stratifikation und aktuelle Migrationsbewegungen. Überlegungen zu Geschlechterverhältnis und Klassenzugehörigkeit. In Peter A. Berger, Anja Weiß (Eds.): Transnationalisierung sozialer Ungleichheit. Wiesbaden: VS Verlag für Sozialwissenschaften, pp. 107–136.

Kofman, Eleonore (2009a): Arbeitsmigration qualifizierter Frauen. In Focus MIGRATION, policy Brief (13).

Kofman, Eleonore (2009b): Skilled female labour migration. In Focus MIGRATION, policy Brief (13).

Kofman, Eleonore (2012): Gender and skilled migration in Europe. In Cuadernos de Relaciones Laborales 30 (1), pp. 63–89.

Kofman, Eleonore (2014): Towards a Gendered Evaluation of (Highly) Skilled Immigration Policies in Europe. In International Migration 52 (3), pp. 116–128.

Kofman, Eleonore; Phizacklea, Annie; Raghuram, Parvati; Sales, Rosemary (2000a): 5. Chapter: Migration and women's work in Europe. In Eleonore Kofman, Annie Phizacklea, Parvati Raghuram, Rosemary Sales (Eds.): Gender and International Migration in Europe. Employment, welfare and politics. London and New York: Routledge, pp. 105–133.

Kofman, Eleonore; Phizacklea, Annie; Raghuram, Parvati; Sales, Rosemary (Eds.) (2000b): Gender and International Migration in Europe. Employment, welfare and politics. London and New York: Routledge.

Kofman, Eleonore; Raghuram, Parvati (2005): Gender and skilled migrants: into and beyond the work place. In Geoforum 36 (2), pp. 149–154.

Kogan, Irena (2011): New Immigrants — Old Disadvantage Patterns? Labour Market Integration of Recent Immigrants into Germany. In International Migration Review 49 (1), pp. 91–117.

Kohli, Martin (1981): Wie es zur „biographischen Methode" kam und was daraus geworden ist. Ein Kapitel aus der Geschichte der Sozialforschung. In Zeitschrift für Soziologie 10 (3), pp. 273–293.

Kohli, Martin (1988): Normalbiographie und Individualität: Zur institutionellen Dynamik des gegenwärtigen Lebenslaufregimes. In Hanns-Georg Brose, Bruno Hildenbrand (Eds.): Vom Ende des Individuums zur Individualität ohne Ende. Opladen: Leske + Budrich (Biographie und Gesellschaft), pp. 33–54.

Kolb, Holger (2005): The German „Green Card". In Focus MIGRATION, policy Brief November 2005 (3). Available online at http://www.bpb.de/files/UIG70N.pdf, checked on 25/6/2015.

Kontos, Maria (2009a): Executive Summary. In Maria Kontos (Ed.): Integration of Female Immigrants in Labour Market and Society. A coparative Analysis. Summary, Results and Recommendations. Frankfurt am Main: Institute of social research at the Goethe University, pp. 5–14.

Kontos, Maria (Ed.) (2009b): Integration of Female Immigrants in Labour Market and Society. A coparative Analysis. Summary, Results and Recommendations. FeMiPol. Frankfurt am Main: Institute of social research at the Goethe University.

Kontos, Maria; Voswinkel, Stephan (2010): Ungenutzte Kompetenzen. Probleme und Chancen der Beschäftigung hochqualifizierter Migrantinnen und Migranten. In Sozialwissenschaften und Berufspraxis 2 (33), pp. 212–241.

Koser, Khalid; Salt, John (1997): The Geography of Highly Skilled International Migration. In International Journal of Population Geography 3, pp. 285–303.

Kosic, Ankica; Triandafyllidou, Anna (2007): Italy. In Anna Triantaphyllidou, Ruby Gropas (Eds.): European immigration. A sourcebook. Aldershot u. a: Ashgate, pp. 185–198.

Kostlán, Antonín (2011): Útěky do emigrace a Československá akademie věd. In Soňa Štrbáňová, Antonín Kostlán (Eds.): Sto českých vědců v exilu. Encyklopedie významných vědců z řad pracovníků Československé akademie věd v emigraci. 1st ed. Praha: Academia, pp. 19–199.

Köttig, Michaela (2004): Lebensgeschichten rechtsextrem orientierter Mädchen und junger Frauen. Biographische Verläufe im Kontext der Familien- und Gruppendynamik. Gießen: Psychosozial - Verlag.

Koucký, Jan; Zelenka, Martin (2011): Postavení vysokoškoláků a uplatnění absolventů vysokých škol na pracovním trhu 2011. Univerzita Karlova v Praze. Středisko vzdělávací politiky. Praha.

Kowal, Sabine; O'Connell, Daniel C. (2000): Zur Transkription von Gesprächen. In Uwe Flick, Ernst von Kardoff, Ines Steinke (Eds.): Qualitative Forschung. Ein Handbuch. Reinbek bei Hamburg: Rowohlt Taschenbuch Verlag, pp. 437–447.

Králová, Stanislava (2010): Váš exodus? Nevěříme, vzkazují nemocnice lékařům hrozícím výpovědí. In idnes.cz, 9/30/2010. Available online at http://pardubice.idnes.cz/vas-exodus-neverime-vzkazuji-nemocnice-lekarum-hrozicim-vypovedi-1dj-/pardubice-zpravy.aspx?c=A100930_1458248_pardubice-zpravy_klu, checked on 25/6/2015.

Kreutzer, Florian (Ed.) (2006): Transnationale Karrieren. Biografien, Lebensführung und Mobilität. 1st ed. Wiesbaden: VS Verlag für Sozialwissenschaften.

Křížková, Alena; Formánková, Lenka (2011): Pracovní dráhy žen a mužů v době ekonomické krize. In Socioweb 11. Available online at http://www.socioweb.cz/index.php?disp=teorie&shw=484&lst=103, checked on 25/6/2015.

Kundera, Elzbieta; Kundera, Jaroslaw (2011): Der polnische Arbeitsmarkt im Prozess der ökonomischen Transformation. In Swen Steinberg, Daniel K. W. Trepsdorf, Christoph Wielepp (Eds.): Nach dem Umbruch. Transformationen in europäischer und globaler Perspektive. Berlin: WVB (Impulse, 2), pp. 89–99.

Kürti, László (1997): Globalisation and the Discourse of "Otherness" in the "New" Eastern and Central Europe. In Tariq Modood, Pnina Werbner (Eds.): The politics of multiculturalism in the new Europe. Racism, identity, and community. London, New York: Zed Books; Distributed by St. Martin's Press (Postcolonial encounters), pp. 29–53.

Lamnek, Siegfried (2010): Qualitative Sozialforschung. Lehrbuch; Online-Materialien. 5th ed. Edited by Claudia Krell. Weinheim u.a: Beltz.

Langer, Josef (1996): New meanings of the border in Central Europe. In György Éger, Josef Langer (Eds.): Border, region and ethnicity in Central Europe. Results of an international comparative research. Klagenfurt: Mischke.

Lavenex, Sandra (2008): The competition State and Multilateral Liberalization of Highly Skilled Migration. In Michael P. Smith, Adrian Favell (Eds.): The human face of global mobility. International highly skilled migration in Europe, North America and the Asia-Pacific. 2nd ed. New Brunswick, NJ: Transaction Press (Comparative urban and community research, 8), pp. 29–52.

Levitt, Peggy; Glick Schiller, Nina (2003): Conceptualizing Simultaneity: A Transnational Social Field Perspective on Society. In International Migration Review 38 (3), pp. 1002–1039.

Levitt, Peggy; Jaworsky, B. Nadya (2007): Transnational migration studies: Past developments and future trends. In Annual Review of Sociology 33, pp. 129–156.

Levitt, Peggy; Wind, Josh de; Vertovec, Steven (Eds.) (2003): Transnational Migration: International Perspectives. International Migration Review 37 (3).

Liapi, Maria; Vouyioukas, Anna (2009a): Language Skills, Educational Qualifications and Professional Skills. In Maria Kontos (Ed.): Integration of Female Immigrants in Labour Market and Society. A coparative Analysis. Summary, Results and Recommendations. Frankfurt am Main: Institute of social research at the Goethe University, pp. 18–33.

Liapi, Maria; Vouyioukas, Anna (2009b): Policy gaps in integration and reskilling strategies of migrant women. In Social Cohesion and Development 4 (2), pp. 159–171.

Liapi, Maria; Vouyioukas, Anna (2013): Coping with Deskilling: Strategies of Migrant Women across European Societies. In Floya Anthias, Maria Kontos, Mirjana Morokvasic-Müller (Eds.): Paradoxes of integration. Female migrants in Europe. Dordrecht, New York: Springer (International perspectives on migration, 4), pp. 79–96.

Liebold, Renate (2009): Selbtbild und Selbstinszenierung der ökonomischen Elite in autobiographischen Selbstdartellungen. In Jens Aderhold (Ed.): Beiträge zur Sozialinnovation. Eliten und Ihre Bedeutung in gesellschaftlichen Transformationsprozessen (Nr. 6), pp. 55–68. Available online at http://www.isinova.org/download/wdokumente/BzS6.pdf, checked on 25/6/2015.

Liversage, Anika (2009a): Finding a path. Investigating labour market trajectories of high-skilled immigrants. In Journal of Ethnic and Migration Studies 35 (2), pp. 203–226.

Liversage, Anika (2009b): Vital conjunctures, shifting horizons: high-skilled female immigrants looking for work. In Work, employment and society 23 (1), pp. 120–141.

Lüders, Christian (2000): Beobachten im Feld und Ethnographie. In Uwe Flick, Ernst von Kardoff, Ines Steinke (Eds.): Qualitative Forschung. Ein Handbuch. Reinbek bei Hamburg: Rowohlt Taschenbuch Verlag, pp. 384–401.

Lüthi, Barbara (2005): Transnationale Migration - Eine vielversprechende Perspektive? H-Soz-Kult. Available online at http://www.hsozkult.de/article/id/artikel-627, c checked on 25/6/2015.

Lutz, Helma (2011a): Lost in translation? The role of language in migrants' biographies: What can micro-sociologists learn from Eva Hoffman? In European Journal of Women's Studies 18 (4), pp. 347–360.

Lutz, Helma (2004a): Life in the twilight zone: migration, transnationality and gender in the private household. In Journal of Contemporary European Studies 12 (1), pp. 47–55.

Lutz, Helma (2004b): Transnationale Biographien in globalisierten Gesellschaften. In Markus Ottersbach, Erol Yildiz (Eds.): Migration in der metropolitanen Gesellschaft. Zwischen Ethnisierung und globaler Neuorientierung. Hamburg & Münster: Lit Verlag, pp. 207–217.

Lutz, Helma (2007): Vom Weltmarkt in den Privathaushalt. Die neuen Dienstmädchen im Zeitalter der Globailsierung. Leverkusen.

Lutz, Helma (2008a): Migrant Domestic Workers in Europe. In Helma Lutz (Ed.): Migration and Domestic Work. A European Perspective on a Global Theme. Aldershot: Ashgate, pp. 1–10.

Lutz, Helma (2008b): Migration and domestic work. A European perspective on a global theme. Farnham u.a.: Ashgate (Studies in migration and diaspora).

Lutz, Helma (Ed.) (2008c): Migration and Domestic Work. A European Perspective on a Global Theme. Aldershot: Ashgate.

Lutz, Helma (2008d): When Home Becomes a Workplace: Domestic Work as an Ordinary Job in Germany? In Helma Lutz (Ed.): Migration and Domestic Work. A European Perspective on a Global Theme. Aldershot: Ashgate, pp. 43–60.

Lutz, Helma (Ed.) (2009a): Gender mobil? Geschlecht und Migration in transnationalen Räumen. 1st ed. Münster: Westfälisches Dampfboot (Forum Frauen- und Geschlechterforschung, 26).

Lutz, Helma (2009b): Gender Mobil? Geschlecht und Migration in transnationalen Räumen. In Helma Lutz (Ed.): Gender mobil? Geschlecht und Migration in transnationalen Räumen. 1st ed. Münster: Westfälisches Dampfboot (Forum Frauen- und Geschlechterforschung, 26), pp. 8–26.

Lutz, Helma (2010): Gender in the Migratory Process. In Journal of Ethnic and Migration Studies 36 (10), pp. 1647–1663.

Lutz, Helma (2011b): The new maids. Transnational women and the care economy. London: Zed Books.

Lutz, Helma; Davis, Kathy (2009): Geschlechterforschung und Biographieforschung: Intersektionalität als biographische Ressource am Beispiel einer außergewöhnlichen Frau. In Bettina Völter, Bettina Dausien, Helma Lutz, Gabriele Rosenthal (Eds.): Biographieforschung im Diskurs. 2nd ed. Wiesbaden: VS Verlag für Sozialwissenschaften, pp. 228–248.

Lutz, Helma; Herrera Vivar, Maria Theresa; Supik, Linda (2011): Framing intersectionality. Debates on a multi-faceted concept in gender studies. Farnham: Ashgate (The feminist imagination - Europe and beyond).

Lutz, Helma; Koser, Khalid (1998): Introduction. The New Migration in Europe. Social Constructions and Social Realities. In Helma Lutz, Khalid Koser (Eds.): The new migration in Europe. Social constructions and social realities. Basingstoke, Hampshire: Macmillan, pp. 1–15.

Machonin, Pavel (1994): Social and political transformation in the Czech Republic. Praha: AV ČR (Working papers, 1994: 02).

Markel, Martin (2006): Vertreibung. Konstituierung des Nationalstaates, bürgerlicher Konflikt und ethnische Homogenisierung. In Tomáš Knoz (Ed.): Tschechen und Österreicher. Gemeinsame Geschichte, gemeinsame Zukunft. Brno: Matice moravská, pp. 159–172.

Mašková, Tereza; Morbacher, Lubomír (2014): Železná opona v Československu. Ústav pro studium totalitních režimů. Praha. Available online at http://www.ustrcr.cz/data/pdf/hranice/studie.pdf, checked on 25/6/2015.

Matthes, Joachim (1999): Interkulturelle Kompetenz. Ein Konzept, sein Kontext und sein Potential. In Deutsche Zeitschrift für Philosophie 47 (3), pp. 412–426.

Mau, Steffen; Büttner, Sebastian (2010): Transnationality. In Stefan Immerfall (Ed.): Handbook of European societies. Social transformations in the 21st century. New York, NY u.a: Springer, pp. 357–570.

McCall, Leslie (2005): The Complexity of Intersectionality. In Signs 30 (3), pp. 1771–1800.

Meduna, Michal (2004): Chapter 5. Employment of Foreigners in and from the Czech Republic. In OECD (Ed.): Migration for employment. Bilateral Agreements at a Crossroads. Paris: OECD Publishing, pp. 75–91.

Miethe, Ingrid (2011): Biografiearbeit. Lehr- und Handbuch für Studium und Praxis. Weinheim: Juventa Verlag.

Miller, Robert (Ed.) (2012): The evolution of European identities. Biographical approaches. Basingstoke: Palgrave Macmillan.

Mills, Charles Wright (1959): The power elite. 3. Galaxy print. New York: Oxford University Press.

Ministry of Foreign Affairs of the Czech Republic (2014): People abroad who claim Czech origin. Available online at www.mzv.cz/file/73462/statistikaANGL2007.pdf, checked on 25/6/2015.

Morokvasic, Mirjana (1984): Birds of Passage are also Women… In International Migration Review 18 (4), pp. 886–907.

Morokvasic, Mirjana (1994): Pendeln statt Auswandern. Das Beispiel der Polen. In Mirjana Morokvasic, Hedwig Rudolph (Eds.): Wanderungsraum Europa. Menschen und Grenzen in Bewegung. Berlin: Ed. Sigma, pp. 166–187.

Morokvasic, Mirjana; Rudolph, Hedwig (1994a): Einleitung. In Mirjana Morokvasic, Hedwig Rudolph (Eds.): Wanderungsraum Europa. Menschen und Grenzen in Bewegung. Berlin: Ed. Sigma, pp. 11–28.

Morokvasic, Mirjana; Rudolph, Hedwig (Eds.) (1994b): Wanderungsraum Europa. Menschen und Grenzen in Bewegung. Berlin: Ed. Sigma.

Mücke, Pavel (2009): „Před oponou, za oponou…" aneb Obraz cizinců a cizích zemí v paměti dělníků a příslušníků tzv. pracující inteligence Československa sedmdesátých a osmdesátých let 20. století. In Miroslav Vaněk (Ed.): Obyčejní lidé…?! Pohled do života tzv. mlčící většiny. Životopisná vyprávění příslušníků dělnických profesí a inteligence. Praha: Academia (Historie), pp. 162–211.

Muhirwa, Jean-Marie (2012): Funnelling Talents Back to the Source: Can distance education help to mitigate the fallouts of brain drain in sub-Saharan Africa? In Any Freitas, Antoine Pécoud (Eds.): Skilled Migration and the Brain Drain. Diversities 14 (1), pp. 45–62.

Münz, Reiner (2000): Deutschland und die Ost-West-Wanderung. In Heinz Fassmann, Reiner Münz (Eds.): Ost-West-Wanderung in Europa. Wien: Böhlau, pp. 49–82.

Murdock, Caitlin E. (2010): Changing places. Society, culture, and territory in the Saxon-Bohemian borderlands, 1870-1946. Ann Arbor: University of Michigan Press (Social history, popular culture, and politics in Germany).

Musil, Petr (2006): Tendence na českém trhu práce v období transformace. Centrum výzkumu konkurenční schopnosti české ekonomiky/Research Centre for Competitiveness of Czech Economy. Praha (Working paper 7/2006). Available online at http://is.muni.cz/do/1456/soubory/oddeleni/centrum/papers/wp2006-07.pdf, checked on 25/6/2015.

Nešpor, Zdeněk R. (2002a): Reemigranti a sociálně sdílené hodnoty. Prolegomena k sociologickému studiu českých emigračních procesů se zvláštním zřetelem k západní reemigraci 90. let. Sociologický ústav Akademie věd České republiky. Praha (Sociologické texty/Sociological Papers, 4).

Nešpor, Zdeněk R. (2002b): The Disappointed and Disgruntled: A Study of the Return in the 1990s of Czech Emigrants from the Communist Era. In Sociologický časopis/Czech Sociological Review 38 (6), pp. 789–808.

Nielsen, Chantal Pohl (2011): Immigrant over-education: evidence from Denmark. In Journal of Population Economics 24 (2), pp. 499–520.

Nohl, Arnd-Michael; Ofner, Ulrike Selma; Thomsen, Sarah (2007): Statuspassagen von gleichberechtigten hochqualifizierten Bildungsausländer(inne)n in den deutschen Arbeitsmarkt: Zur Verwertung von Wissen und Können im Kontext migrations-bezogener Orientierungen. With assistance of Yvonne Henkelmann. International VW-Study Group Cultural Capital During Migration. Available online at http://www.hsu-hh.de/download-1.5.1.php?brick_id=jvT7nufQ6x1hMq4W, checked on 25/6/2015.

Nohl, Arnd-Michael; Ofner, Ulrike Selma; Thomsen, Sarah (2010a): Hochqualifizierte BildungsausländerInnen in Deutschland: Arbeitsmarkterfahrungen unter den Bedingungen formaler Gleichberechtigung. In Arnd-Michael Nohl, Karin Schittenhelm, Oliver Schmidtke, Anja Weiß (Eds.): Kulturelles Kapital in der Migration. Hochqualifizierte Einwanderer und Einwandererinnen auf dem Arbeitsmarkt. 1st ed. Wiesbaden: VS, Verlag für Sozialwissenschaften, pp. 67–82.

Nohl, Arnd-Michael; Schittenhelm, Karin; Schmidtke, Oliver; Weiss, Anja (2006): Cultural Capital during Migration—A Multi-level Approach to the Empirical Analysis of Labor Market Integration amongst Highly Skilled Migrants. In Forum Qualitative Sozialforschung / Forum: Qualitative Social Research 7 (3). Available online at http://nbn-resolving.de/urn:nbn:de:0114-fqs0603143, checked on 25/6/2015.

Nohl, Arnd-Michael; Schittenhelm, Karin; Schmidtke, Oliver; Weiß, Anja (Eds.) (2010b): Kulturelles Kapital in der Migration. Hochqualifizierte Einwanderer und Einwandererinnen auf dem Arbeitsmarkt. 1st ed. Wiesbaden: VS, Verlag für Sozialwissenschaften.

Nohl, Arnd-Michael; Schittenhelm, Karin; Schmidtke, Oliver; Weiss, Anja (2014): Work in Transition: Cultural Capital and Highly Skilled Migrants' Pasages into the Labour Market. Toronto Buffalo London: University of Toronto Press.

Novák, Jakub; Čermák, Zdeněk; Ouředníček, Martin (2011): Migrace/ Migration. In Martin Ouředníček, Jana Temelová, Lucie Pospíšilová (Eds.): Atlas sociálně prostorové diferenciace České republiky/Atlas of Socio-spatial Differentiation of the Czech Republic. Praha: Karolinum, pp. 87–102.

Nowicka, Magdalena (2014): Migrating skills, skilled migrants and migration skills: The influence of contexts on the validation of migrants' skills. In Migration Letters 11 (2), pp. 171–186.

Nygård, Ann-Charlotte; Stacher, Irene (2001): Towards a Harmonised Migration and Asylum Regime in Europe. In Claire Wallace, Dariusz Stola (Eds.): Patterns of Migration in Central Europe. New York: Palgrave, pp. 129–150.

OECD (2008): The global competition for talent. Mobility of the highly skilled. Paris: OECD.

OECD (2012a): Free Movement of Workers and Labour Market Adjustment: Recent Experiences from OECD Countries and the European Union: OECD Publishing. Available online at http://dx.doi.org/10.1787/9789264177185-en, checked on 25/6/2015.

OECD (2012b): International Migration Outlook. Country note: Germany. OECD. Available online at http://www.oecd.org/migration/mig/IMO%202012_Country%20note%20Germany.pdf, checked on 25/6/2015.

OECD (2013): World Migration in Figures. A joint contribution by UN-DESA and the OECD to. OECD-UNDESA. Paris.

Okólski, Marek (1994): Alte und neue Muster: Aktuelle Wanderungsbewegungen in Mittel- und Osteuropa. In Mirjana Morokvasic, Hedwig Rudolph (Eds.): Wanderungsraum Europa. Menschen und Grenzen in Bewegung. Berlin: Ed. Sigma, pp. 133–148.

Okólski, Marek (2000): Polen - Wachsende Vielfalt von Migration. In Heinz Fassmann, Reiner Münz (Eds.): Ost-West-Wanderung in Europa. Wien u.a: Böhlau, pp. 141–162.

Okólski, Marek (2001): Incomplete Migration: A New Form of Mobility in Central and Eastern Europe. The Case of Polish and Ukrainian Migrants. In Claire Wallace, Dariusz Stola (Eds.): Patterns of Migration in Central Europe. New York: Palgrave, pp. 105–128.

Ouředníček, Martin; Temelová, Jana; Pospíšilová, Lucie (Eds.) (2011): Atlas sociálně prostorové diferenciace České republiky/Atlas of Socio-spatial Differentiation of the Czech Republic. Praha: Karolinum.

Palenga-Möllenbeck, Ewa (2009): Die unsichtbaren ÜbersetzerInnen in der transnationalen Forschung. Übersetzung als Methode. In Helma Lutz (Ed.): Gender mobil? Geschlecht und Migration in transnationalen Räumen. 1st ed. Münster: Westfälisches Dampfboot (Forum Frauen- und Geschlechterforschung, 26), pp. 158–174.

Palenga-Möllenbeck, Ewa (2014): Pendelmigration aus Oberschlesien. Lebensgeschichten in einer transnationalen Region Europas. Bielefeld: Transcript.

Pape, Elise (2010): Der biographische Ansatz in Frankreich - Entstehung und aktuelle Entwicklungen. In Sektion Biographieforschung in der Deutschen Gesellschaft für Soziologie. Juli 2010 (Rundbrief 58), pp. 40–49.

Pape, Elise; Takeda, Ayumi; Guhlich, Anna (2014): Three women in a city: Crossing borders and negotiating national belonging. In ZQF 15 (1-2), pp. 39-56.

Pařízková, Alena (2011a): Pracovní migrace do Velké Británie v kontextu životních drah lidí z České republiky. Dizertační práce. Západočeská univerzita v Plzni, Plzeň. Filozofická fakulta.

Pařízková, Alena (2011b): Vztah mezinárodní migrace a de-standardizace životních drah. In Sociológia 43 (1), pp. 5–27.

Park, Robert E. (1928): Human Migration and the Marginal Man. In The American Journal of Sociology 33 (6), pp. 881–893.

Parreñas, Rhacel Salazar (2001): Servants of globalization. Women, migration, and domestic work. Stanford: Stanford University Press.

Passerini, Luisa (1992): Memory and Totalitarism. International Yearbook of Oral History and Life Stories, Vol.1. Oxford: Oxford University Press.

Paukertová, Libuše (2000): Několik základních údajů o odchodech z Československa. 1948-1991. In Karel Hrubý, Stanislav Brouček (Eds.): Češi za hranicemi na přelomu 20. a 21. století. Sympozium o českém vystěhovalectví, exulantství a vztazích zahraničních Čechu k domovu, 29.-30. června 1998. 1st ed. Praha: Karolinum ve spolupráci s Etnologickým ústavem AV ČR, pp. 25–31.

Pécoud, Antoine; Guchteneire, Paul de (2006): International Migration, Border Controls and Human Rights: Assessing the Relevance of a Right to Mobility. In Journal of Borderlands Studies 21 (1), pp. 69–86.

Pessar, Patricia R.; Mahner, Sarah J. (2003): Transnational Migration: Bringing Gender in. In International Migration Review 37 (3), pp. 812–846.

Portes, Alejandro (1976): Determinants of the Brain Drain. In International Migration Review 10 (4), pp. 489–508.

Pries, Ludger (Ed.) (1997): Transnationale Migration. 1st ed. Baden-Baden: Nomos-Verl.-Ges. (Soziale Welt, 12).

Pries, Ludger (2001a): Internationale Migration. Bielefeld: Transcript.

Pries, Ludger (2001b): The Disruption of Social and Geographic Space: Mexican-US Migration and the Emergence of Transnational Social Spaces. In International Sociology 16 (1), pp. 55–74.

Pries, Ludger (2004): Integration als Raumentwicklung - Soziale Räume als Identifikationsräume. In Johannes Müller, Mattias Kiefer (Eds.): Grenzenloses ‚Recht auf Freizügigkeit'? Weltweite Mobilität zwischen Freiheit und Zwang. Stuttgart: Kohlhammer, pp. 1–27. Available online at http://134.147.141.194/pdf/publ-2004_lp_integrationalsraumentwicklung.pdf, checked on 25/6/2015.

Pries, Ludger (2008a): Die Transnationalisierung der sozialen Welt. Sozialräume jenseits von Nationalgesellschaften. 1st ed. Frankfurt am Main: Suhrkamp (Edition Suhrkamp, 2521).

Pries, Ludger (2008b): Transnationalisierung und soziale Ungleichheit Konzeptionelle Überlegungen und empirische Befunde aus der Migrationsforschung. In Peter A. Berger, Anja Weiß (Eds.): Transnationalisierung sozialer Ungleichheit. Wiesbaden: VS Verlag für Sozialwissenschaften, pp. 41–64.

Průcha, Jan (1999): Vzdělávání a školství ve světě. Základy mezinárodní komparace vzdělávácích systémů. Praha: Portál.

Pusch, Barbara (2010): Familiäre Orientierungen und Arbeitsmarktintegration von hochqualifizierten MigrantInnen in Deutschland, Kanada und der Türkei. In Arnd-Michael Nohl, Karin Schittenhelm, Oliver Schmidtke, Anja Weiß (Eds.): Kulturelles Kapital in der Migration. Hochqualifizierte Einwanderer und Einwandererinnen auf dem Arbeitsmarkt. 1st ed. Wiesbaden: VS, Verlag für Sozialwissenschaften, pp. 285–300.

Quack, Sigrid (1994): „Da muß man sich durch einen langen, dunklen Tunnel tasten …" Zur beruflichen Eingliederung von Aussiedlerinnen und Aussiedlern in Deutschland. In Mirjana Morokvasic, Hedwig Rudolph (Eds.): Wanderungsraum Europa. Menschen und Grenzen in Bewegung. Berlin: Ed. Sigma, pp. 250–269.

Raghuram, Parvati (2008): Migrant Women in Male-Dominated Sectors of the Labour Market: A Research Agenda. In Population, Space and Place 14 (1), pp. 43–57.

Raghuram, Parvati; Montiel, Dawn (2003): Skilled Migratory Regimes: the Case of Female Medical Migrants in the UK. In Yoshitaka Ishikawa, Armando Montanari (Eds.): The New geography of human mobility inequality trends? Roma: Societa Geografica Italiana (IGU-Home of geography publications series), pp. 67–84.

Ranguelov, Stanislav; Pejnovic, Svetlana (2010): Teachers' and School Heads' Salaries and Allowances in Europe, 2009/10. European Commision. Bruxelles. Available online at http://eshacommunity.wikispaces.com/file/view/Teachers+and+school+heads+salaries+in+Europe.pdf, checked on 25/6/2015.

Recchi, Ettore (2009): The social mobility of mobile Europeans. In Ettore Recchi, Adrian Favell (Eds.): Pioneers of European integration. Citizenship and mobility in the EU. Cheltenham: Edward Elgar, pp. 72–97.

Recchi, Ettore (Ed.) (2014): The Europeanisation of Everyday Life: Cross-Border Practices and Transnational Identifications Among EU and Third-Country Citizens. Final Report. EUCROSS. Crossing borders and making Europe. A research project financed by the EC 7th Framework Programme. Available online at http://www.eucross.eu/cms/index.php?option=com_docman&task=doc_downloa d&gid=87&Itemid=157, checked on 25/6/2015.

Recchi, Ettore; Favell, Adrian (Eds.) (2009): Pioneers of European integration. Citizenship and mobility in the EU. Cheltenham: Edward Elgar.

Reichertz, Jo (2006): Abduktion. In Ralf Bohnsack, Winfried Marotzki, Michael Meuser (Eds.): Hauptbegriffe qualitativer Sozialforschung. 2. Aufl. Opladen: Budrich (UTB), pp. 11–14.

Reichertz, Jo (2011): Abduktion: Die Logik der Entdeckung der Grounded Theory. In Günter Mey, Katja Mruck (Eds.): Grounded theory reader. 2. edition. Wiesbaden: VS, Verlag für Sozialwissenschaften, pp. 279–297.

Řezník, Miloš (2013): Migrace raného novověku a 19. století v česko-saském prostoru. Metody, koncepty a výzkumy v současné historiografii. In Stanislav Brouček (Ed.): Navzdory hranici. Migrační procesy na česko-německém pomezí. Trotz der Grenze. Migrationsprozesse im tschechisch-deutschen Grenzgebiet. Příspěvky z odborné konference, Cheb 27.-29.5. 2013. Fachtagungsvorträge, Eger 27.-29.5. 2013. Plzeň, pp. 7–17.

Riaño, Yvonne (2012): The Invisibility of Family in Studies of Skilled Migration and Brain Drain. In Any Freitas, Antoine Pécoud (Eds.): Skilled Migration and the Brain Drain. Diversities 14 (1), pp. 25–44.

Riemann, Gerhard (2003): A Joint Project Against the Backdrop of a Research Tradition: An Introduction to "Doing Biographical Research". In Forum Qualitative Sozialforschung / Forum: Qualitative Social Research 4 (3). Available online at http://nbn-resolving.de/urn:nbn:de:0114-fqs0303185, checked on 25/6/2015.

Riemann, Gerhard (2004): Die Befremdung der eigenen Praxis. In Andreas Hanses (Ed.): Biographie und Soziale Arbeit. Institutionelle und biographische Konstruktionen von Wirklichkeit. Baltmannsweiler: Schneider Verlag Hohengehren, pp. 190–208.

Riemann, Gerhard (2006a): Erzählanalyse. In Ralf Bohnsack, Winfried Marotzki, Michael Meuser (Eds.): Hauptbegriffe qualitativer Sozialforschung. 2. Aufl. Opladen: Budrich (UTB), pp. 45–47.

Riemann, Gerhard (2006b): Narratives Interview. In Ralf Bohnsack, Winfried Marotzki, Michael Meuser (Eds.): Hauptbegriffe qualitativer Sozialforschung. 2. Aufl. Opladen: Budrich (UTB), pp. 120–122.

Riemann, Gerhard (2009): Zur Bedeutung ethnographischer und erzahlanalytischer Arbeitsweisen fur die (Selbst-)Reflexion professioneller Arbeit. Ein Erfahrungsbericht. In Bettina Völter, Bettina Dausien, Helma Lutz, Gabriele Rosenthal (Eds.): Biographieforschung im Diskurs. 2nd ed. Wiesbaden: VS Verlag für Sozialwissenschaften, pp. 248–270.

Riemann, Gerhard (2010): Ein Forschungsansatz zur Analyse narrativer Interviews. In Karin Bock, Ingrid Miethe (Eds.): Handbuch Qualitative Methoden in der Sozialen Arbeit. Opladen and Farmington Hills: Barbara Budrich, pp. 223–231.

Riemann, Gerhard (2011): „Grounded theorizing" als Gespräch - Anmerkungen zu Alselm Strauss, der frühen Chicagoer Sozologie und der Arbeit in Forschungswerkstätten. In Günter Mey, Katja Mruck (Eds.): Grounded theory reader. 2. edition. Wiesbaden: VS, Verlag für Sozialwissenschaften, pp. 405–426.

Roberts, Brian (2010): Biographical Research in the UK. In Sektion Biographiefor-schung in der Deutschen Gesellschaft für Soziologie December 2010 (Rundbrief 59), pp. 23–45.

Rogall, Joachim (2001): Die Přemysliden und die deutsche Kolonisierung. In Walter Koschmal, Marek Nekula, Joachim Rogall (Eds.): Deutsche und Tschechen. Geschichte, Kultur, Politik. Originalausg. München: C.H. Beck (Beck'sche Reihe, 1414), pp. 33–41.

Rosenthal, Gabriele (2005): Interpretative Sozialforschung. Eine Einführung. Weinheim: Juventa-Verlag.

Rosenthal, Gabriele; Bogner, Artur (Eds.) (2009): Ethnicity, belonging and biography. Ethnographical and biographical perspectives. Berlin: Lit.

Rothland, Martin (2007): Sind „faule Säcke" passé? Anmerkungen zur Ambivalenz der öffentlichen Beurteilung von Lehrerberuf, Lehrerhandeln und Lehrpersonen. In Die Deutsche Schule 99, pp. 175–191.

Rubin, Jennifer Rendall Michael S. Rabinovich Lila; Tsang, Flavia; van Oranje-Nassau, Constantijn; Janta, Barbara (2008): Migrant women in the European labour force. Current situation and future prospects. Prepared for the European Commission, Directorate General for Employment. RAND Europe. Available online at http://www.rand.org/pubs/technical_reports/TR591.html, checked on 25/6/2015.

Ruokonen-Engler, Minna-Kristiina (2005): Grenzüberschreitungen und biographische Verortungen: Überlegungen zur Konstitution von Transnationalen Sozialen Räumen und Öffentlichkeiten. In Susanne Lettow, Ulrike Manz, Katja Sarkowsky (Eds.): Öffentlichkeiten und Geschlechterverhältnisse. Erfahrungen, Politiken, Subjekte. Königstein/Taunus: Helmer (Frankfurter feministische Texte: Sozialwissenschaften), pp. 57–72.

Ruokonen-Engler, Minna-Kristiina (2009): De/Constructing Difference: A Biographical Perspective on Constructions of Ethnicity as Transnational Positionality. In Gabriele Rosenthal, Artur Bogner (Eds.): Ethnicity, belonging and biography. Ethnographical and biographical perspectives. Berlin: Lit, pp. 251–266.

Ruokonen-Engler, Minna-Kristiina (2012): »Unsichtbare« Migration? Transnationale Positionierungen finnischer Migrantinnen. Eine biographieanalytische Studie. 1st ed. Bielefeld: Transcript.

Ruokonen-Engler, Minna-Kristiina; Siouti, Irini (2013): 'Doing Biographical Reflexivity' as a Methodological Tool in Transnational Research Settings. In Transnational Social Review: A Social Work Journal 3 (2), pp. 247–261.

Rychlík, Jan (2012): Devizové přísliby a cestování do zahraničí v období normalizace. Foreign exchange permits and other travel restrictions in Czechoslovakia, 1969-1989. Praha: ÚSD AV ČR (Česká společnost po roce 1945, 8).

Salt, John (1988): Highly-skilled International Migrants, Careers and Internal Labour Markets. In Geoforum 19 (4), pp. 387–399.

Salt, John (1997): International Movements of the Highly Skilled Labour. Paris: OECD.

Sassen, Saskia (1988): The mobility of labor and capital. A study in international investment and labor flow. Cambridge [England], New York: Cambridge University Press.

Sassen, Saskia (2000): The Global City: Strategic Site/New Frontier. In American Studies 41 (2), pp. 79–95.

Sassen, Saskia (2001): The global city: New York, London, Tokyo: Princeton University Press.

Sassen, Saskia (2007): A sociology of globalisation. New York, London: W. W. Norton & Company (Contemporary Societies).

Sassen, Saskia (2008): Two Stops in Today's New Global Geographies. Shaping Novel Labor Supplies and Employment Regimes. In American Behavioral Scientist 52 (3), pp. 457–496.

Satola, Agnieszka (2010): Ausbeutungsverhältnisse und Aushandlungsprozesse in der Pflege- und Haushaltsarbeit von polnischen Frauen in deutschen Haushalten. In Ursula Apitzsch (Ed.): Care und Migration. Die Ent-Sorgung menschlicher Reproduktionsarbeit entlang von Geschlechter- und Armutsgrenzen. Opladen u.a: Budrich, pp. 177–194.

Schittenhelm, Karin (2005): Soziale Lagen im Übergang. Junge Migrantinnen und Einheimische zwischen Schule und Berufsausbildung. 1st ed. Wiesbaden: VS Verlag für Sozialwissenschaften.

Schmitter Heisler, Barbara (2008): The Sociology of Immigration. From Assimilation to Segmented Assimilation, from the American Experience to the Global Arena. In Caroline Brettell (Ed.): Migration theory. Talking across disciplines. 2nd ed. New York u.a: Routledge, pp. 83–112.

Schmiz, Antonie (2011): Transnationalität als Ressource? Netzwerke vietnamesischer Migrantinnen und Migranten zwischen Berlin und Vietnam. Bielefeld: Transcript. (Kultur und soziale Praxis).

Schunka, Alexander (2006): Forgotten memories- Contested representations: Early Modern Bohemian Migrants in Saxony. In Mareike König, Rainer Ohliger (Eds.): Enlarging European memory. Migration movements in historical perspective. Ostfildern: Thorbecke, pp. 35–46.

Schütz, Alfred (1972): The phenomenology of the social world. London: Heinemann.

Schütze, Fritz (1976): Zur Hervorlockung und Analyse von Erzählungen thematisch relevanter Geschichten im Rahmen soziologischer Feldforschung. In Arbeitsgruppe Bielefelder Soziologen (Ed.): Kommunikative Sozialforschung. Alltagswissen und Alltagshandeln, Gemeindemachtforschung, Polizei, politische Erwachsenenbildung. München: Fink (Kritische Information, 48), pp. 159–260.

Schütze, Fritz (1980): Prozeßstrukturen des Lebensablaufs. Biographietagung Nürnberg, Februar 1980. Bielefeld: Universität.

Schütze, Fritz (1983): Biographieforschung und narratives Interview. In Neue Praxis 3, pp. 283–293. Available online at http://www.ssoar.info/ssoar/bitstream/handle/document/5314/ssoar-np-1983-3-schutze-biographieforschung_und_narratives_interview.pdf?sequence=1, checked on 25/6/2015.

Schütze, Fritz (1984): Kognitive Figuren des autobiographischen Stegreiferzählens. In Martin Kohli, Günther Robert (Eds.): Biographie und soziale Wirklichkeit. Neue Beiträge und Forschungsperspectiven. Stuttgart: Metzler, pp. 78–117.

Schütze, Fritz (1987): Das narrative Interview in Interaktionsfeldstudien I. Studienbrief der Fernuniversität Hagen. Hagen: Fernuniversität-Gesamthochschule.

Schütze, Fritz (2001): Ein biographieanalytischer Beitrag zum Verständnis von kreativen Veränderungsprozessen. Die Kategorie der Wandlung. In Roland Burkholz, Christel Gärtner, Ferdinand Zehentreiter (Eds.): Materialität des Geistes. Zur Sache Kultur - im Diskurs mit Ulrich Oevermann. 1st ed. Weilerswist: Velbrück Wiss., pp. 137–163.

Schütze, Fritz (2012a): Biography Analysis on the Empirical Base of Autobiographical Narratives: How to Analyse Autobiographical Narrative Interviews - Part II. Available online at http://www.uni-magdeburg.de/zsm/projekt/biographical/1/B2.2.pdf, checked on 25/6/2015.

Schütze, Fritz (2012b): Biography Analysis on the Empirical Base of Autobiographical Narratives: How to Analyse Autobiographical Narrative Interviews - Part I. Available online at http://www.uni-magdeburg.de/zsm/projekt/biographical/1/B2.1.pdf, checked on 25/6/2015.

Schütze, Fritz; Kallmeyer, Werner (1977): Zur Konstitution von Kommunikationsschemata. Dargestellt am Beispiel von Erzählungen und Beschreibungen. In Dirk Wegner (Ed.): Gesprächsanalysen. Hamburg: Buske, pp. 159–274.

Schütze, Fritz; Schröder-Wildhagen, Anja (2012): European Mental Space and its Biographical Relevance. In Robert Miller (Ed.): The evolution of European identities. Biographical approaches. Basingstoke u.a: Palgrave Macmillan, pp. 255–278.

Scott, Sam (2006): The Social Morphology of Skilled Migration: The Case of the British Middle Class in Paris. In Journal of Ethnic and Migration Studies 32 (7), pp. 1105–1129.

Seibt, Ferdinand (1993): Deutschland und die Tschechen. Geschichte einer Nachbarschaft in der Mitte Europas. München & Zürich: Piper.

Sen, Amartya Kumar (1985): Commodities and capabilities. Amsterdam: North-Holland (Professor Dr. P. Hennipman lectures in economics).

Shaw, Clifford R. (1966): The Jack-Roller. A delinquent boy's own story. Chicago: University of Chicago Press.

Shinozaki, Kyoko (2012): Transnational dynamics in researching migrants: selfreflexivity and boundarydrawing in fieldwork. In Ethnic and Racial Studies 35 (10), pp. 1810–1827.

Sígl, Miroslav (2014): Odchod okupačních vojsk SSSR z Československa po roce 1989. Available online at http://www.totalita.cz/1968/1968_armada_sssr_07_03.php, checked on 9/3/2014.

Simmel, Georg (1967): The sociology of Georg Simmel. [Nachdr.]. Edited by Kurt H. Wolff. New York, NY: The Free Press.

Sinke, Suzanne M. (2006): Gender and Migration: Historical Perspectives. In International Migration Review 40 (1), pp. 82–103.

Siouti, Irini (2013): Transnationale Biographien. Eine biographieanalytische Studie über Transmigrationsprozesse bei der Nachfolgegeneration griechischer Arbeitsmigranten. 1st ed. Bielefeld: Transcript.

Sládek, Milan (2002): Němci v Čechách. Německá menšina v českých zemích a Československu 1848-1946. 1st ed. Praha: Pragma.

Smith, Michael P.; Favell, Adrian (Eds.) (2008): The human face of global mobility. International highly skilled migration in Europe, North America and the Asia-Pacific. 2nd ed. New Brunswick, NJ: Transaction Press (Comparative urban and community research, 8).

Smith, Michael P.; Guarnizo, Luis (1999): Transnationalism from below. 2.th ed. New Brunswick: Transaction Books (Comparative urban and community research).

Sopemi (2005): Trends in international migration 2004. Annual Report. 2004 Edition.

Sorokin, Pitirim Aleksandrovich (1959): Social and cultural mobility. New York: Free Press of Glencoe.

Statistisches Bundesamt (2013): Weiter hohe Zuwan-derung nach Deutsch-land im Jahr 2012. Wiebaden. Available online at https://www.destatis.de/DE/PresseService/Presse/Pressemitteilungen/2013/05/PD 13_156_12711.html;jsessionid=B074A689DC06982E2CCC64FA6FE2176C.cae 3, checked on 25/6/2015.

Statistisches Bundesamt (2014a): Ausländische Bevölkerung nach Zensus und Aus-länderzentralregister (AZR). Edited by Statistisches Bundesamt. Statistisches Bundesamt. Wiebaden.

Statistisches Bundesamt (2014b): Bevölkerung nach detailliertem Migrationsstatus, höchstem schulischen Abschluss und Geschlecht 2012 in 1000. Statistisches Bundesamt. Wiesbaden.

Statistisches Bundesamt (2014c): Bevölkerungen und Erwerbstätigkeit. Wanderun-gen. 2012. Edited by Statistisches Bundesamt. Wiebaden (Fachserie 1 Reihe 1.2). Available online at https://www.destatis.de/DE/Publikationen/Thematisch/Bevoelkerung/Wanderung en/Wanderungen2010120127004.pdf?__blob=publicationFile, checked on 25/6/2015.

Statistisches Bundesamt (2014d): Lange Reihe: Ausländer nach Staatsangehörigkeiten. 1967-2012. Wiebaden: Statistisches Bundesamt.

Stölting, Erhard (2000): The East of Europe: A Historical Construction. In Roswitha Breckner, Devorah Kalekin-Fishman, Ingrid Miethe (Eds.): Biographies and the division of Europe. Experience, action, and change on the "Eastern side". Opladen: Leske und Budrich, pp. 23–38.

Strübing, Jörg (2006): Theoretisches Sampling. In Ralf Bohnsack, Winfried Marotzki, Michael Meuser (Eds.): Hauptbegriffe qualitativer Sozialforschung. 2. Aufl. Op-laden: Budrich (UTB), pp. 154–156.

Tarrius, Alain (1994): Zirkulationsterritorien von Migranten und städtische Räume. In Mirjana Morokvasic, Hedwig Rudolph (Eds.): Wanderungsraum Europa. Men-schen und Grenzen in Bewegung. Berlin: Ed. Sigma, pp. 113–132.

Tepecik, Ebru (2009): Bildungserfolge mit Migrationshintergrund. Biographien bil-dungserfolgreicher MigrantInnen türkischer Herkunft. Wiesbaden: VS Verlag für Sozialwissenschaften / Springer Fachmedien Wiesbaden GmbH.

The Ministry of Education (2011): The Education System in the Czech Republic. Edited by The Section for International Relations and EU Affairs in close coop-eration with Leona Gergelová Šteigrová. The Ministry of Education, Youth and Sport of the Czech Republic. Praha. Available online at www.msmt.cz/file/21631/download/, checked on 25/6/2015.

Thomas, William Isaac; Znaniecki, Florian (1958): The Polish peasant in Europe and America. Edited by Florian Znaniecki. New York: Dover Publications.

Thomsen, Sarah (2009): Akademiker aus dem Ausland. Biographische Rekonstrukti-onen zur Statuspassage in den Arbeitsmarkt. Berlin: Logos Verl (Berliner Arbei-ten zur Erziehungs- und Kulturwissenschaft, 45).

Thomsen, Sarah (2010): Mehr als „weak ties" – Zur Entstehung und Bedeutung von sozialem Kapital bei hochqualifizierten BildungsausländerInnen. In Arnd-Michael Nohl, Karin Schittenhelm, Oliver Schmidtke, Anja Weiß (Eds.): Kultu-relles Kapital in der Migration. Hochqualifizierte Einwanderer und Einwandererinnen auf dem Arbeitsmarkt. 1st ed. Wiesbaden: VS, Verlag für Sozialwissenschaften, pp. 260–271.

Tinguy, Anne de (1994): Die Abwanderung der Akademiker aus der „GUS" nach Frankreich: Flucht oder Mobilität? In Mirjana Morokvasic, Hedwig Rudolph (Eds.): Wanderungsraum Europa. Menschen und Grenzen in Bewegung. Berlin: Ed. Sigma, pp. 270–286.

Titzl, Boris (2006): Vztah totalitního režimu ke zdravotně postiženým. In Jiří Kocián (Ed.): Slovníková příručka k československým dějinám 1948-1989. Praha: Ústav pro soudobé dějiny AV ČR, pp. 47–53.

Trapl, Miloš (2000): Česká politická emigrace ve 20. století. (1914-1989). In Karel Hrubý, Stanislav Brouček (Eds.): Češi za hranicemi na přelomu 20. a 21. století. Sympozium o českém vystěhovalectví, exulantství a vztazích zahraničních Čechu k domovu, 29.-30. června 1998. 1st ed. Praha: Karolinum ve spolupráci s Etnologickým ústavem AV ČR, pp. 36–44.

Trevena, Paulina (2011): A question of class? Polish graduates working in low-skilled jobs in London. In Studia Migracyjne: Przeglad Polonijny 37 (1), pp. 71–96.

Trevena, Paulina (2013): Why do highly educated migrants go for low-skilled jobs? A case study of Polish graduates working in London. In Birgit Glorius, Izabela Grabowska-Lusinska, Aimee Kuvik (Eds.): Mobility in transition. Migration patterns after EU enlargement. Amsterdam: Amsterdam University Press, pp. 169–190.

Tuček, Milan (2012): Prestiž povolání – červen 2012. Centrum pro výzkum veřejného mínění, Sociologický ústav AVČR. Praha. Available online at http://cvvm.soc.cas.cz/media/com_form2content/documents/c1/a6869/f3/eu1207 20.pdf, checked on 25/6/2015.

Tuider, Elisabeth (2009): Transnationales Erzählen. Zum Umgang mit Über-Setzungen in der Biographieforschung. In Helma Lutz (Ed.): Gender mobil? Geschlecht und Migration in transnationalen Räumen. 1st ed. Münster: Westfälisches Dampfboot (Forum Frauen- und Geschlechterforschung, 26), pp. 174–192.

Ugba, Abel (2007): Ireland. In Anna Triantaphyllidou, Ruby Gropas (Eds.): European immigration. A sourcebook. Aldershot u. a: Ashgate, pp. 269-183.

Uherek, Zdeněk (2003): Cizinecké komunity a městský prostor v České republice. In Sociologický časopis 39 (2), pp. 193–216.

Ulč, Otto (2000): Exil a literatura. Pár poznámek navazujících na referát Antonína Měšťana. In Karel Hrubý, Stanislav Brouček (Eds.): Češi za hranicemi na přelomu 20. a 21. století. Sympozium o českém vystěhovalectví, exulantství a vztazích zahraničních Čechu k domovu, 29.-30. června 1998. 1st ed. Praha: Karolinum ve spolupráci s Etnologickým ústavem AV ČR, pp. 61–64.

Vargas-Silva, Carlos (2014): Migration Flows of A8 and other EU Migrants to and from the UK. Briefing. The Migration Observatory at the University of Oxford. Oxford. Available online at http://www.migrationobservatory.ox.ac.uk/sites/files/migobs/Migration%20Flow s%20of%20A8%20and%20other%20EU%20Migrants%20to%20and%20from% 20the%20UK_0.pdf, checked on 25/6/2015.

Vavrečková, Jana; Musil, Jakub; Baštýř, Ivo (2007): Počty a struktury českých migrantů v zahraničí a ekonomická motivace k zahraniční pracovní migraci. (se specifickým zaměřením na migranty ve Velké Británii). VÚPSV. Praha.

Vavrečková, Jana et al. (2005): Riziko možného odchodu kvalifikovaných odborníků z ČR do zahraničí. Migrace odborníků do zahraničí. (shrnující poznatky 1. etapy řešení projektu). VÚPSV. Praha.

Verwiebe, Roland (2006): Transnationale Migration innerhalb Europas. In Florian Kreutzer (Ed.): Transnationale Karrieren. Biografien, Lebensführung und Mobilität. 1st ed. Wiesbaden: VS Verlag für Sozialwissenschaften, pp. 301–325.

Verwiebe, Roland (2008a): Migration to Germany: Is a middle class emerging among intra-European migrants? In Migration Letters 5 (1), pp. 1–19.

Verwiebe, Roland (2008b): Statusveränderungen und innereuropäische Wanderungen. Ergebnisse einer Verknüpfung qualitativer und quantitativer Befunde. In Peter A. Berger, Anja Weiß (Eds.): Transnationalisierung sozialer Ungleichheit. Wiesbaden: VS Verlag für Sozialwissenschaften / GWV Fachverlage GmbH, Wiesbaden, pp. 185–211.

Vianello, Francesca Alice (2014): Ukrainian Migrant Workers in Italy: Coping with and Reacting to Downward Mobility. In CEEMR. Central and Eastern European Migration Review 3 (1), pp. 85–98. Available online at http://www.ceemr.uw.edu.pl/vol-3-no-1-june-2014/articles/ukrainian-migrant-workers-italy-coping-and-reacting-downward-mobility, checked on 25/6/2015.

Villares-Varela, Maria (2014): The feminisation of migration: Are more women migrating? Oxford University (Debating development. A conversational blog from researchers at the Oxford Department of International Development). Available online at http://blog.qeh.ox.ac.uk/?p=363, checked on 25/6/2015.

Vincent-Lancrin, Stéphan (2008): The Reversal of Gender Inequalities in Higher Education: An On-going Trend. Chapter 10. In OECD (Ed.): Higher Education to 2030. Washington: OECD (Vol. 1: Demography), pp. 265–298. Available online at http://www.oecd.org/edu/ceri/41939699.pdf, checked on 25/6/2015.

Vítková, Kateřina (2010): Tři stovky lékařů hrozí odchodem. Vadí jim nízké platy a špatné podmínky. In idnes.cz 2010, 9/23/2010. Available online at http://hradec.idnes.cz/tri-stovky-lekaru-hrozi-odchodem-vadi-jim-nizke-platy-a-spatne-podminky-1ap-/hradec-zpravy.aspx?c=A100923_1454913_hradec-zpravy_meb, checked on 25/6/2015.

Vogel, Lutz (2014): Mobiler Alltag. Bůhmische Einwanderer in Sachsen im 19. Jahrhundert. In Frank-Lothar Kroll, Miloš Řezník, Martin Munke (Eds.): Sachsen und Böhmen. Perspektiven ihrer historischen Verflechtung. Berlin: Duncker & Humblot (Chemnitzer Europastudien, 16), pp. 70–87.

Wadensjo, Eskil (2007): Migration to Sweden from the New EU Member States. In IZA Discussion Paper Series (Discussion Paper No. 3190). Available online at http://ssrn.com/abstract=1049101, checked on 6/26/2014.

Waldinger, Roger; Fitzgerald, David (2004): Transnationalism in Question. In American Journal of Sociology 109 (5), pp. 1177–1195.

Wallace, Claire (2002): Opening and closing borders: Migration and mobility in East-Central Europe. In Journal of Ethnic and Migration Studies 28 (4), pp. 603–625.

Wallace, Claire; Stola, Dariusz (2001): Introduction: Patterns of Migration in Central Europe. In Claire Wallace, Dariusz Stola (Eds.): Patterns of Migration in Central Europe. New York: Palgrave.

Weber, Max (1970): The Interpretation of social reality. London: Joseph.

Weber, Max (1978a): Economy and society. Berkeley: University of California Press.

Weber, Max (1978b): Selections in translation. Cambridge: Cambridge University Press.

Weiss, Anja (2005): The Transnationalization of Social Inequality: Conceptualizing Social Positions on a World Scale. In Current Sociology 53 (4), pp. 707–728.

Weiß, Anja (2006): Hoch qualifizierte MigrantInnen. Der Kern einer transnationalen Mittelklasse? In Florian Kreutzer (Ed.): Transnationale Karrieren. Biografien, Lebensführung und Mobilität. 1st ed. Wiesbaden: VS Verlag für Sozialwissenschaften.

Weiß, Anja; Berger, Peter A. (2008): Logik der Differenzen – Logik des Austausches Beiträge zur Transnationalisierung sozialer Ungleichheiten. In Peter A. Berger, Anja Weiß (Eds.): Transnationalisierung sozialer Ungleichheit. Wiesbaden: VS Verlag für Sozialwissenschaften, pp. 7–17.

Weiß, Anja; Nohl, Arnd-Michael (2012a): Fälle und Kontexte im Mehrebenenvergleich: ein Vorschlag zur Überwindung des methodologischen Nationalismus in der Migrationsforschung. In Zeitschrift für Qualitative Forschung 12 (1/2), pp. 55–75.

Weiß, Anja; Nohl, Arnd-Michael (2012b): Overcoming Methodological Nationalism in Migration Research: Cases and Contexts in Multi-Level Comparisons. In Anna Amelina, Devrimsel D. Nergiz, Thomas Faist, Nina Glick Schiller (Eds.): Beyond methodological nationalism. Research methodologies for cross-border studies. New York: Routledge (Routledge research in transnationalism, 24), pp. 65–87.

Williams, Allan M.; Baláž, Vladimir (2005): What Human Capital, Which Migrants? Returned Skilled Migration to Slovakia From the UK. In International Migration Review 39 (2), pp. 439–468.

Williams, Fiona; Gavanas, Anna (2008): The Intersection of Child Care Regimes and Migration Regimes: a Three-Country Study. In Helma Lutz (Ed.): Migration and Domestic Work. A European Perspective on a Global Theme. Aldershot: Ashgate, pp. 13–28.

Willis, Katie; Yeoh, Brenda (2002): Introduction. Transnational Elites. In Geoforum 33, pp. 505–507.

Wimmer, Andreas; Glick Schiller, Nina (2002): Methodological nationalism and beyond: nation-state building, migration and the social sciences. In Global Networks 4 (2), pp. 301–334.

Winker, Gabriele; Delege, Nina (2009): Intersektionalität. Zur Analyse sozialer Ungleichheiten. Bielefeld: Transkript Verlag.

Wismar, Matthias; Maier, Claudia B.; Glinos, Irene A.; Dussault, Gilles; Figueras, Josep (Eds.) (2011): Health professional mobility and health systems. Evidence from 17 European countries. Copenhagen: World Health Organization, on behalf of the European Observatory on Health Systems and Policies (Observatory studies series, 23).

Wohlrab-Sahr, Monika, Przyborski, Aglaja (Ed.) (2008): Qualitative Sozialforschung. Ein Arbeitsbuch. München: Oldenbourg.

WTO (2014): The General Agreement on Trade in Services (GATS): objectives, coverage and disciplines. Available online at http://www.wto.org/english/tratop_e/serv_e/gatsqa_e.htm, checked on 25/6/2015.

Zákon č. 40/1993 Sb.: Zákon České národní rady ze dne 29. prosince 1992 o nabývání a pozbývání státního občanství České republiky Změna: 272/1993 Sb. Změna:

337/1993 Sb. Změna: 140/1995 Sb. Změna: 139/1996 Sb. Změna: 194/1999 Sb. Změna: 320/2002 Sb.

Zákon č. 561/2004 Sb.: Zákon č. 561/2004 Sb. O předškolním, základním, středním, vyšším odborném a jiném vzdělávání. školský zákon. Available online at http://www.msmt.cz/dokumenty/uplne-zneni-zakona-c-561-2004-sb, checked on 25/6/2015.

Zaretsky, Eli (1996): Introduction. In William Isaac Thomas, Florian Znaniecki (Eds.): The Polish peasant in Europe and America. A classic work in immigration history. Urbana u.a.: Univ. of Illinois Press.

Zeitlhofer, Hermann (2008): Zwei Zentren temporärer kontinentaler Arbeitsmigration im Vergleich. Der Böhmerwald und das Friaul um 1900. In Annemarie Steidel, Thomas Buchner, Werner Lausecker, Alexander Pinwinkler, Sigrid Wadauer, Hermann Zeitlhofer (Eds.): Übergänge und Schnittmengen. Arbeit, Migration, Bevölkerung und Wissenschaftsgeschichte in Diskussion. Wien u.a: Böhlau.

Zich, František (2002): Občanské přeshraniční vztahy a některé otázky vytvoření přeshraničního společenství na česko-německé hranici. In Zdenka Mansfeldová, Milan Tuček (Eds.): Současná česká společnost. Sociologické studie. 1st ed. Praha: Sociologický ústav AV ČR, pp. 322–338.

Zlotnik, Hania (2003): The Global Dimensions of Female Migration. Migration Policy Institute. Available online at http://www.migrationpolicy.org/article/global-dimensions-female-migration/, checked on 25/6/2015.

Znaniecki Lopata, Helena (1965): Introduction. In Florian Znaniecki: Social relations and social roles;. The unfinished systematic sociology. San Francisco: Chandler Pub. Co.

Zwengel, Almut (Ed.) (2011): Die „Gastarbeiter" der DDR. Politischer Kontext und Lebenswelt. Berlin: Lit (Studien zur DDR-Gesellschaft).